CISSP®

Practice Exams

Second Edition

Shon Harris

New York • Chicago • San Francisco • Lisbon
London • Madrid • Mexico City • Milan • New Delhi
San Juan • Seoul • Singapore • Sydney • Toronto

The McGraw·Hill Companies

Cataloging-in-Publication Data is on file with the Library of Congress

CISSP® Practice Exams, Second Edition

1234567890 DOC DOC 1098765432

ISBN   978-0-07-179234-9
MHID   0-07-179234-1

Sponsoring Editor	**Developmental Editor**	**Indexer**
Meghan Riley Manfre	*Crystal Bedell*	*Jack Lewis*
Editorial Supervisor	**Technical Editor**	**Production Supervisor**
Jody McKenzie	*Kumar Polisetty*	*George Anderson*
Project Manager	**Copy Editor**	**Composition**
Howie Severson, Fortuitous Publishing Services	*Lisa McCoy*	*Fortuitous Publishing Services*
Acquisitions Coordinator	**Proofreader**	**Art Director, Cover**
Stephanie Evans	*Paul Tyler*	*Jeff Weeks*

I would like to dedicate this book to Greg Andelora.
We lost you too soon, Greg. I wish we had more
time to tell you how wonderful you are and how
much we truly appreciated you and all that you have
done for us. Please go in peace and know that we
will always remember you—always…

ABOUT THE AUTHOR

Shon Harris, CISSP, is the founder and CEO of Logical Security, an information security consultant, a former engineer in the Air Force's Information Warfare unit, an instructor, and an author. She has authored three bestselling CISSP books and was a contributing author to *Hacker's Challenge* (McGraw-Hill, 2001), *Gray Hat Hacking, 3rd edition* (McGraw-Hill, 2011), and *Security Information and Event Management (SIEM) Implementation* (McGraw-Hill, 2011). Ms. Harris has developed a full digital information security product series for Pearson Education.

Ms. Harris has consulted for many corporations, organizations, and government agencies over the last 15 years. Her competencies range from setting up risk management programs and developing enterprise network security architectures to constructing enterprise-wide security programs that connect computer security and business needs in a synergistic manner.

Ms. Harris has extensive knowledge and practical experience pertaining to legal and regulatory compliance. She has worked with the largest corporations within the United States to become compliant with OCC regulations, SOX, GLBA, HIPAA, PCI, and more. Ms. Harris specializes in risk management, governance, and the development of and implementation of security metrics.

Ms. Harris has taught information security to a wide range of clients, including Microsoft, the Department of Defense, the Department of Energy, National Security Agency, Defense Information Systems Agency, RSA, U.S. Military Academy at West Point, Bank of America, Cisco, Symantec, American Express, Booz Allen Hamilton, Price Waterhouse Cooper, Oracle, NASA, Boeing, Citibank, AOL, Warner Bros, and many more.

Ms. Harris was recognized as one of the top 25 women in the information security field by *Information Security* magazine.

About the Developmental Editor

Crystal Bedell is the principal of Bedell Communications, a full-service copywriting and editing firm specializing in technology and B2B communications. She has more than 15 years of combined editing, writing, and marketing experience, including eight years at TechTarget, where she developed Web content for IT professionals. Having worked as both a member of the press and in marketing, Crystal has unique insights into the information needs of IT professionals as well as an understanding of their work environment and the constraints of the typical IT decision maker. She knows how to speak their language and distill marketing language into plain English.

As a professional copywriter, Crystal writes case studies, white papers, Web copy, and more for technology companies. She is also the author of the Tech Marcom Blog, which can be found at http://bedellcommunications.com/. She also blogs at http://bedellcommunications.com.

About the Technical Editor

Polisetty Veera Subrahmanya Kumar, CISSP, CISA, PMP, PMI-RMP, MCPM, ITIL, has more than 20 years' experience in the field of information technology. His areas of specialization include information security, business continuity, project management, and risk management. Currently he is serving his term as chairperson for the Project Management Institute's PMI-RMP (PMI–Risk Management Professional) Credentialing Committee. In the past he has worked as content development team leader on a variety of PMI standards development projects. He was a lead instructor for the PMI PMBOK review seminars. He is also serving his term as a member of ISACA's India Growth Task Force team.

ACKNOWLEDGMENTS

I would like to thank my husband, David Harris. Without his steadfast confidence in me, I would not have been able to accomplish half the things I have taken on in my life.

CONTENTS

PREFACE

The objective of this book, in combination with the questions available to you online, is to prepare you for the CISSP exam by familiarizing you with the more difficult and tricky types of questions that may come up on the multiple-choice portion of the CISSP exam. The questions in this book delve into the more complex topics of the Common Body of Knowledge (CBK) you may be faced with when you take the CISSP exam.

We've developed this book to be used with the online questions at www.mhprofessional.com/CISSPExams and the *CISSP All-In-One Exam Guide, Sixth Edition* (McGraw-Hill, 2013). The best approach to prepare for the exam using all of the materials available to you is outlined here:

1. Review the questions and answers in this book.

2. If further explanation of the material is required, review the corresponding material in the *CISSP All-In-One Exam Guide, Sixth Edition.*

3. Review all of the questions available online at www.mhprofessional.com/CISSPExams.

4. As part of your self-study process, listen to the audio lectures, also available at www.mhprofessional.com/CISSPExams.

Because the primary focus of this book is to help you pass the test, we cover all aspects of the CISSP exam in the combination of this book, the online questions and audio lectures, and the *CISSP All-In-One Exam Guide, Sixth Edition.* It is critical that you use all of these available tools to be successful in achieving your certification.

Because each question in this book features a detailed explanation of why one answer choice was the correct answer and why each of the other answer choices was incorrect, we believe this book will also serve as a valuable professional resource after your exam.

In This Book

We've organized this book so that each chapter consists of a battery of practice exam questions representing a single CISSP exam domain, appropriate for experienced information security professionals as well as newcomers to security-related concepts. Each chapter covers a major domain of the exam, with the answer explanations providing the emphasis on the "why" as well as the "how-to" of working with and supporting the technology and concepts.

On the Web

More than 500 practice questions and 24 hours of audio lectures are available to you for free with the purchase of this book. You should use these tools along with the material in the book to best prepare you for the CISSP exam. You'll find the online questions and MP3 audio lecture files atwww.mhprofessional.com/CISSPExams.

For more information on the free online practice questions, please refer to the Appendix "About the Free Online Practice Questions and Audio Lectures" at the back of this book.

In Every Chapter

We've created a set of chapter components that call your attention to the key steps of the testing and review process, and provide helpful exam-taking hints. Take a look at what you'll find in every chapter:

- Every chapter includes practice exam questions from one **Certification Objective Domain**. Drill down on the types of questions from each domain that you will need to know how to answer in order to pass the exam.

- The **Practice Exam Questions** are similar to those found on the actual certification exam, and are meant to present you with some of the most common and confusing problems that you may encounter when taking the live exam. The questions are designed to help you anticipate what the exam will emphasize, and getting inside the exam with good practice questions will help ensure you know what you need to know to pass the exam.

- Each chapter includes a **Quick Answer Key**, which provides the question number and the corresponding letter for the correct answer. This allows you to score your answers quickly before you begin your review of the explanations.

- Each question is accompanied by an **In-Depth Answer Explanation**—explanations are provided for both the correct and incorrect answers, and can be found at the end of each chapter. By reading the answer explanations, you'll reinforce what you've learned from answering the questions in that chapter, while also becoming familiar with the structure of the exam questions.

- Once you've completed the chapter questions, you're ready to move on to the **Online Practice Questions**. The online practice questions are provided in a live quiz format and are meant to mimic the types of questions, by domain, that you will find on the actual exam.

INTRODUCTION

Computer, information, and physical security are becoming more important at an exponential rate. Over the last few years, the necessity for computer and information security has grown rapidly as Web sites have been defaced, denial-of-service attacks have increased, credit card information has been stolen, publicly available hacking tools have become more sophisticated, and today's viruses and worms have continued to cause more damage than ever before.

Companies have had to spend millions of dollars to clean up the effects of these issues and millions of dollars more to secure their perimeter and internal networks with equipment, software, consultants, and education. But after September 11, 2001, the necessity and urgency for this type of security has led to a new paradigm emerging. It is slowly becoming apparent that governments, nations, and societies are vulnerable to many different types of attacks that can happen over the network wire and airwaves. Societies depend heavily on all types of computing power and functionality, mostly provided by the public and private sectors. This means that although governments are responsible for protecting their citizens, it is becoming apparent that the citizens and their businesses must become more secure to protect the nation as a whole.

This type of protection can really only *begin* through proper education and understanding, and must continue with the dedicated execution of this knowledge. This book is written to provide a foundation in the many different areas that make up effective security. We need to understand *all* of the threats and dangers we are vulnerable to and the steps that must be taken to mitigate these vulnerabilities.

Information Security Governance and Risk Management

This domain includes questions from the following topics:

- Security terminology and principles
- Protection control types
- Security frameworks, models, standards, and best practices
- Security enterprise architecture
- Risk management
- Security documentation
- Information classification and protection
- Security awareness training
- Security governance

A security professional's responsibilities extend well beyond reacting to the virus and hacker news that make headlines. Their day-to-day responsibilities are far less exciting on the surface but are vital to keeping organizations protected against intrusions so that their companies don't become the next headline. The role of security within an organization is a complex one, as it touches every employee and must be managed companywide. It is important that you have an understanding of security beyond the technical details to include management and business issues, both for the CISSP exam and for your role in the field.

1. Which of the following best describes the relationship between CobiT and ITIL?

   A. CobiT is a model for IT governance, whereas ITIL is a model for corporate governance.

   B. CobiT provides a corporate governance roadmap, whereas ITIL is a customizable framework for IT service management.

   C. CobiT defines IT goals, whereas ITIL provides the process-level steps on how to achieve them.

   D. CobiT provides a framework for achieving business goals, whereas ITIL defines a framework for achieving IT service-level goals.

2. Jane has been charged with ensuring that clients' personal health information is adequately protected before it is exchanged with a new European partner. What data security requirements must she adhere to?

   A. HIPAA

   B. NIST SP 800-66

   C. Safe Harbor

   D. European Union Principles on Privacy

3. Global organizations that transfer data across international boundaries must abide by guidelines and transborder information flow rules developed by an international organization that helps different governments come together and tackle the economic, social, and governance challenges of a globalized economy. What organization is this?

   A. Committee of Sponsoring Organizations of the Treadway Commission

   B. The Organisation for Economic Co-operation and Development

   C. CobiT

   D. International Organization for Standardization

4. Steve, a department manager, has been asked to join a committee that is responsible for defining an acceptable level of risk for the organization, reviewing risk assessment and audit reports, and approving significant changes to security policies and programs. What committee is he joining?

   A. Security policy committee

   B. Audit committee

   C. Risk management committee

   D. Security steering committee

5. As head of sales, Jim is the information owner for the sales department. Which of the following is not Jim's responsibility as information owner?

A. Assigning information classifications

B. Dictating how data should be protected

C. Verifying the availability of data

D. Determining how long to retain data

6. Assigning data classification levels can help with all of the following except:

A. The grouping of classified information with hierarchical and restrictive security

B. Ensuring that nonsensitive data is not being protected by unnecessary controls

C. Extracting data from a database

D. Lowering the costs of protecting data

7. Which of the following is not included in a risk assessment?

A. Discontinuing activities that introduce risk

B. Identifying assets

C. Identifying threats

D. Analyzing risk in order of cost or criticality

8. Sue has been tasked with implementing a number of security controls, including antivirus and antispam software, to protect the company's e-mail system. What type of approach is her company taking to handle the risk posed by the system?

A. Risk mitigation

B. Risk acceptance

C. Risk avoidance

D. Risk transference

9. The integrity of data is not related to which of the following?

A. Unauthorized manipulation or changes to data

B. The modification of data without authorization

C. The intentional or accidental substitution of data

D. The extraction of data to share with unauthorized entities

10. There are several methods an intruder can use to gain access to company assets. Which of the following best describes masquerading?

A. Changing an IP packet's source address

B. Elevating privileges to gain access

C. An attempt to gain unauthorized access as another user

D. Creating a new authorized user with hacking tools

11. A number of factors should be considered when assigning values to assets. Which of the following is not used to determine the value of an asset?

    A. The asset's value in the external marketplace

    B. The level of insurance required to cover the asset

    C. The initial and outgoing costs of purchasing, licensing, and supporting the asset

    D. The asset's value to the organization's production operations

12. Jill is establishing a companywide sales program that will require different user groups with different privileges to access information on a centralized database. How should the security manager secure the database?

    A. Increase the database's security controls and provide more granularity.

    B. Implement access controls that display each user's permissions each time they access the database.

    C. Change the database's classification label to a higher security status.

    D. Decrease the security so that all users can access the information as needed.

13. As his company's CISO, George needs to demonstrate to the Board of Directors the necessity of a strong risk management program. Which of the following should George use to calculate the company's residual risk?

    A. threats × vulnerability × asset value = residual risk

    B. SLE × frequency = ALE, which is equal to residual risk

    C. (threats × vulnerability × asset value) × control gap = residual risk

    D. (total risk – asset value) × countermeasures = residual risk

14. Authorization creep is to access controls what scope creep is to software development. Which of the following is not true of authorization creep?

    A. Users have a tendency to request additional permissions without asking for others to be taken away.

    B. It is a violation of "least privilege."

    C. It enforces the "need-to-know" concept.

    D. It commonly occurs when users transfer to other departments or change positions.

15. For what purpose was the COSO framework developed?

    A. To address fraudulent financial activities and reporting

    B. To help organizations install, implement, and maintain CobiT controls

C. To serve as a guideline for IT security auditors to use when verifying compliance

D. To address regulatory requirements related to protecting private health information

16. Susan, an attorney, has been hired to fill a new position at Widgets Inc. The position is Chief Privacy Officer (CPO). What is the primary function of her new role?

A. Ensuring the protection of partner data

B. Ensuring the accuracy and protection of company financial information

C. Ensuring that security policies are defined and enforced

D. Ensuring the protection of customer, company, and employee data

17. Jared plays a role in his company's data classification system. In this role, he must practice due care when accessing data and ensure that the data is used only in accordance with allowed policy while abiding by the rules set for the classification of the data. He does not determine, maintain, or evaluate controls, so what is Jared's role?

A. Data owner

B. Data custodian

C. Data user

D. Information systems auditor

18. Risk assessment has several different methodologies. Which of the following official risk methodologies was not created for the purpose of analyzing security risks?

A. FAP

B. OCTAVE

C. ANZ 4360

D. NIST SP 800-30

19. Which of the following is not a characteristic of a company with a security governance program in place?

A. Board members are updated quarterly on the company's state of security.

B. All security activity takes place within the security department.

C. Security products, services, and consultants are deployed in an informed manner.

D. The organization has established metrics and goals for improving security.

20. Michael is charged with developing a classification program for his company. Which of the following should he do first?

   A. Understand the different levels of protection that must be provided.

   B. Specify data classification criteria.

   C. Identify the data custodians.

   D. Determine protection mechanisms for each classification level.

21. There are four ways of dealing with risk. In the graphic that follows, which method is missing and what is the purpose of this method?

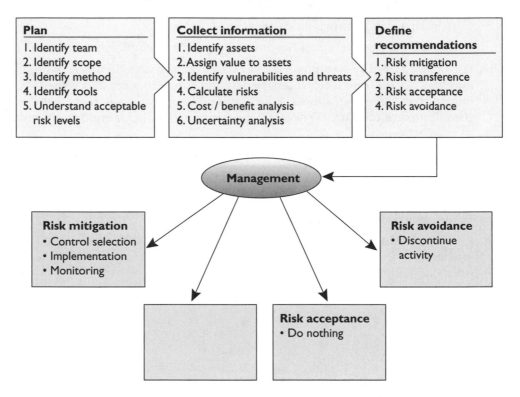

   A. Risk transference. Share the risk with other entities.

   B. Risk reduction. Reduce the risk to an acceptable level.

   C. Risk rejection. Accept the current risk.

   D. Risk assignment. Assign risk to a specific owner.

22. The following graphic contains a commonly used risk management scorecard. Identify the proper quadrant and its description.

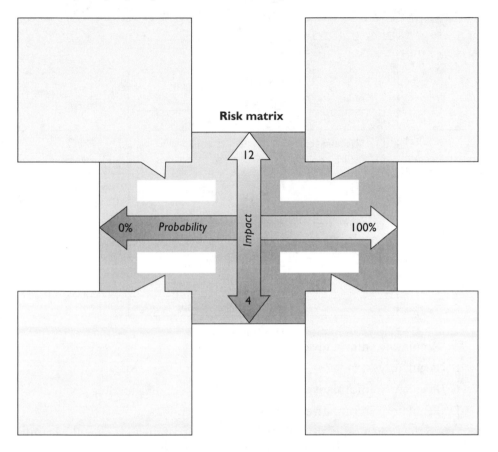

A. Top-right quadrant is high impact, low probability.

B. Top-left quadrant is high impact, medium probability.

C. Bottom-left quadrant is low impact, high probability.

D. Bottom-right quadrant is low impact, high probability.

23. What are the three types of policies that are missing from the following graphic?

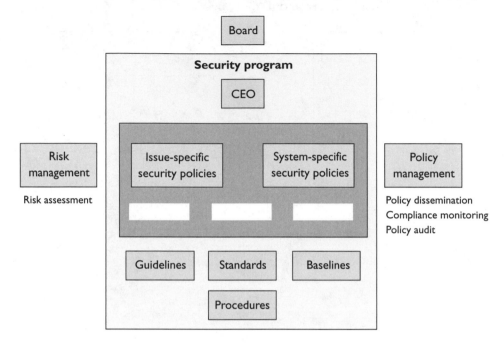

A. Regulatory, Informative, Advisory

B. Regulatory, Mandatory, Advisory

C. Regulatory, Informative, Public

D. Regulatory, Informative, Internal Use

24. List in the proper order from the table on the top of the next page the learning objectives that are missing and their proper definitions.

A. Understanding, recognition and retention, skill

B. Skill, recognition and retention, skill

C. Recognition and retention, skill, understanding

D. Skill, recognition and retention, understanding

	Awareness	Training	Education
Attribute:	"What"	"How"	"Why"
Level:	Information	Knowledge	Insight
Learning objective:			
Example teaching method:	**Media** • Videos • Newsletters • Posters	**Practical instruction** • Lecture and/or demo • Case study • Hands-on practice	**Theoretical instruction** • Seminar and discussion • Reading and study • Research
Test measure:	True/False Mutiple choice (Identify learning)	Problem solving, i.e., recognition and resolution (Apply learning)	Essay (Interpret learning)
Impact timeframe:	Short-term	Intermediate	Long-term

25. What type of risk analysis approach does the following graphic provide?

High	7–10	7–10
Medium	4–6	4–6
Low	0–3	0–3

0	10	20	30	40	50	60	70	80	90	100
0	9	18	27	36	45	54	63	72	81	90
0	8	16	24	32	40	48	56	64	72	80
0	7	14	21	28	35	42	49	56	63	70
0	6	12	18	24	30	36	42	48	54	60
0	5	10	15	20	25	30	35	40	45	50
0	4	8	12	16	20	24	28	32	36	40
0	3	6	9	12	15	18	21	24	27	30
0	2	4	6	8	10	12	14	16	18	20
0	1	2	3	4	5	6	7	8	9	10

41–100	High
20–40	Medium
0–19	Low

A. Quantitative

B. Qualitative

C. Operationally Correct

D. Operationally Critical

26. ISO/IEC 27000 is part of a growing family of ISO/IEC information security management systems (ISMS) standards. It comprises information security standards published jointly by the International Organization for Standardization (ISO) and the International Electrotechnical Commission (IEC). Which of the following provides an incorrect mapping of the individual standards that make up this family of standards?

   A. ISO/IEC 27002   Code of practice for information security management

   B. ISO/IEC 27003   Guideline for ISMS implementation

   C. ISO/IEC 27004   Guideline for information security management measurement and metrics framework

   D. ISO/IEC 27005   Guideline for bodies providing audit and certification of information security management systems

The following scenario applies to questions 27 and 28.

Sam is the security manager of a company that makes most of its revenue from its intellectual property. Sam has implemented a process improvement program that has been certified by an outside entity. His company received a Level 2 during an appraisal process, and he is putting in steps to increase this to a Level 3. A year ago when Sam carried out a risk analysis, he determined that the company was at too much of a risk when it came to potentially losing trade secrets. The countermeasure his team implemented reduced this risk, and Sam determined that the annualized loss expectancy of the risk of a trade secret being stolen once in a hundred-year period is now $400.

27. Which of the following is the criteria Sam's company was most likely certified under?

   A. SABSA

   B. Capability Maturity Model Integration

   C. Information Technology Infrastructure Library

   D. Prince2

28. What is the associated single loss expectancy value in this scenario?

   A. $65,000

   B. $400,000

   C. $40,000

   D. $4,000

The following scenario applies to questions 29, 30, and 31.

Barry has just been hired as the company security officer at an international financial institution. He has reviewed the company's data protection policies and procedures. He sees that the company stores its sensitive data within a secured database. The database is located in a network segment all by itself, which is monitored by a network-based intrusion detection system. The database is hosted on a server kept within a server room, which can only be accessed by personnel with the correct PIN value and smart card. Barry finds that the sensitive data backups are not being properly secured and requests that the company implement a secure courier service that moves backup tapes to a secured location. His management states that this option is too expensive, so Barry implements a local hierarchy storage management system that properly protects the sensitive data.

29. Which of the following best describes the control types the company originally had in place?

    A. Administrative preventive controls are the policies and procedures. Technical preventive controls are securing the system, network segmentation, and intrusion detection system. Physical detective controls are the physical location of the database and PIN and smart card access controls.

    B. Administrative preventive controls are the policies. Technical preventive controls are securing the system and intrusion detection system. Physical preventive controls are the physical location of the database and PIN and smart card access controls.

    C. Administrative corrective controls are the policies and procedures. Technical preventive controls are securing the system, network segmentation, and intrusion detection system. Physical preventive controls are the physical location of the database and PIN and smart card access controls.

    D. Administrative preventive controls are the policies and procedures. Technical preventive controls are securing the system and network segmentation. The technical detective control is the intrusion detection system. Physical preventive controls are the physical location of the database and PIN and smart card access controls.

30. The storage management system that Barry put into place is referred to as which of the following?

    A. Administrative control

    B. Compensating control

    C. Physical control

    D. Confidentiality control

31. Which are the two most common situations that require the type of control covered in the scenario to be implemented?

    A. Defense-in-depth is required, and the current controls only provide one protection layer.

    B. Primary control costs too much or negatively affects business operations.

    C. Confidentiality is the highest concern in a situation where defense-in-depth is required.

    D. Availability is the highest concern in a situation where defense-in-depth is required.

1. C	12. A	23. A
2. C	13. C	24. C
3. B	14. C	25. B
4. D	15. A	26. B
5. C	16. D	27. C
6. C	17. C	28. D
7. A	18. C	29. D
8. A	19. B	30. B
9. D	20. A	31. B
10. C	21. A	
11. B	22. D	

1. Which of the following best describes the relationship between CobiT and ITIL?

    A. CobiT is a model for IT governance, whereas ITIL is a model for corporate governance.

    B. CobiT provides a corporate governance roadmap, whereas ITIL is a customizable framework for IT service management.

    C. CobiT defines IT goals, whereas ITIL provides the process-level steps on how to achieve them.

    D. CobiT provides a framework for achieving security goals, whereas ITIL defines a framework for achieving IT service-level goals.

    ☑ **C.** The Control Objectives for Information and related Technology (CobiT) is a framework developed by the Information Systems Audit and Control Association (ISACA) and the IT Governance Institute (ITGI). It defines goals for the controls that should be used to properly manage IT and ensure IT maps to business needs, not specifically just security needs. The Information Technology Infrastructure Library (ITIL) is the de facto standard of best practices for IT service management. A customizable framework, ITIL provides the goals, the general activities necessary to achieve these goals, and the input and output values for each process required to meet these determined goals. In essence, CobiT addresses "what is to be achieved," while ITIL addresses "how to achieve it."

    ☒ **A** is incorrect because, while CobiT can be used as a model for IT governance, ITIL is not a model for corporate governance. Actually, Committee of Sponsoring Organizations of the Treadway Commission (COSO) is a model for corporate governance. CobiT is derived from the COSO framework. You can think of CobiT as a way to meet many of the COSO objectives, but only from the IT perspective. In order to achieve many of the objectives addressed in CobiT, an organization can use ITIL, which provides process-level steps for achieving IT service management objectives.

    ☒ **B** is incorrect because, as previously stated, CobiT can be used as a model for IT governance, not corporate governance. COSO is a model for corporate governance. The second half of the answer is correct. ITIL is a customizable framework that is available as a series of books or online, for IT service management.

    ☒ **D** is incorrect because CobiT defines goals for the controls that should be used to properly manage IT and ensure IT maps to business needs, not just IT security needs. ITIL provides steps for achieving IT service management goals as they relate to business needs. ITIL was created because of the increased dependence on information technology to meet business needs.

2. Jane has been charged with ensuring that clients' personal health information is adequately protected before it is exchanged with a new European partner. What data security requirements must she adhere to?

   A. HIPAA

   B. NIST SP 800-66

   C. Safe Harbor

   D. European Union Principles on Privacy

   ☑ **C.** The Safe Harbor requirements were created to harmonize the data privacy practices of the U.S. with the European Union's stricter privacy controls, and to prevent accidental information disclosure and loss. The framework outlines how any entity that is going to move private data to and from Europe must go about protecting it. By certifying against this rule base, U.S. companies that work with European entities can more quickly and easily transfer data.

   ☒ **A** is incorrect because the Health Insurance Portability and Accountability Act (HIPAA) does not specifically address data protection for the purposes of sharing it with European entities. HIPAA provides a framework and guidelines to ensure security, integrity, and privacy when handling confidential medical information within the U.S. The U.S. federal regulation also outlines how security should be managed for any facility that creates, accesses, shares, or destroys medical information.

   ☒ **B** is incorrect because NIST SP 800-66 is a risk assessment methodology. It does not point out specific data privacy requirements. NIST SP 800-66 does apply to health care. It was originally designed to be implemented in the health care field and can be used by HIPAA clients to help achieve compliance.

   ☒ **D** is incorrect because the European Union Principles on Privacy are the foundation for the European Union's strict laws pertaining to data that is considered private. The purpose of the principles is not to prepare data specifically for its exchange with U.S. companies, nor are the requirements mandated for U.S. companies. This set of principles has six areas that address using and transmitting sensitive information, and all European states must abide by these principles to be in compliance.

3. Global organizations that transfer data across international boundaries must abide by guidelines and transborder information flow rules developed by an international organization that helps different governments come together and tackle the economic, social, and governance challenges of a globalized economy. What organization is this?

A. Committee of Sponsoring Organizations of the Treadway Commission

B. The Organisation for Economic Co-operation and Development

C. CobiT

D. International Organization for Standardization

☑ **B.** Almost every country has its own rules pertaining to what constitutes private data and how it should be protected. As the digital and information age came upon us, these different laws started to negatively affect business and international trade. Thus, the Organisation for Economic Co-operation and Development (OECD) developed guidelines for various countries so that data is properly protected and everyone follows the same rules.

☒ **A** is incorrect because the Committee of Sponsoring Organizations of the Treadway Commission (COSO) was formed in 1985 to provide sponsorship for the National Commission on Fraudulent Financial Reporting, an organization that studies deceptive financial reports and what elements lead to them. The acronym COSO refers to a model for corporate governance that addresses IT at a strategic level, company culture, financial accounting principles, and more.

☒ **C** is incorrect because the Control Objectives for Information and related Technology (CobiT) is a framework that defines goals for the controls that should be used to properly manage IT and ensure that IT maps to business needs. It is an international open standard that provides requirements for the control and security of sensitive data and a reference framework.

☒ **D** is incorrect because the International Organization for Standardization (ISO) is an international standard-setting body consisting of representatives from national standards organizations. Its objective is to establish global standardizations. However, its standardizations go beyond the privacy of data as it travels across international borders. For example, some standards address quality control, while others address assurance and security.

4. Steve, a department manager, has been asked to join a committee that is responsible for defining an acceptable level of risk for the organization, reviewing risk assessment and audit reports, and approving significant changes to security policies and programs. What committee is he joining?

A. Security policy committee

B. Audit committee

C. Risk management committee

D. Security steering committee

☑ **D.** Steve is joining a security steering committee, which is responsible for making decisions on tactical and strategic security issues within the enterprise. The committee should consist of individuals from throughout the organization and meet at least quarterly. In addition to the responsibilities listed in the question, the security steering committee is responsible for establishing a clearly defined vision statement that works with and supports the organizational intent of the business. It should provide support for the goals of confidentiality, integrity, and availability as they pertain to the organization's business objectives. This vision statement should, in turn, be supported by a mission statement that provides support and definition to the processes that will apply to the organization and allow it to reach its business goals.

☒ **A** is incorrect because a security policy committee is a committee chosen by senior management to produce security policies. Usually senior management has this responsibility unless they delegate it to a board or committee. Security policies dictate the role that security plays within the organization. They can be organizational, issue-specific, or system-specific. The steering committee does not directly create policies but reviews and approves them if acceptable.

☒ **B** is incorrect because the audit committee's goal is to provide independent and open communications among the board of directors, management, internal auditors, and external auditors. Its responsibilities include the company's system of internal controls, the engagement and performance of independent auditors, and the performance of the internal audit function. The audit committee would report its findings to the steering committee, but not be responsible for overseeing and approving any part of a security program.

☒ **C** is incorrect because the purpose of a risk management committee is to understand the risks that the organization faces as a whole and work with senior management to reduce these risks to acceptable levels. This committee does not oversee the security program. The security steering committee usually reports its findings to the risk management committee as it relates to information security. A risk management committee must look at overall business risks, not just IT security risks.

5. As head of sales, Jim is the information owner for the sales department. Which of the following is not Jim's responsibility as information owner?

   A. Assigning information classifications

   B. Dictating how data should be protected

   C. Verifying the availability of data

   D. Determining how long to retain data

☑ **C.** The responsibility of verifying the availability of data is the only responsibility listed that does not belong to the information owner. Rather, it is the responsibility of the information custodian. The information custodian is also responsible for maintaining and protecting data as dictated by the information owner. This includes performing regular backups of data, restoring data from backup media, retaining records of activity, and fulfilling information security and data protection requirements in the company's policies, guidelines, and standards. Information owners work at a higher level than the custodians. The owners basically state, "This is the level of integrity, availability, and confidentiality that needs to be provided—now go do it." The custodian must then carry out these mandates and follow up with the installed controls to make sure they are working properly.

☒ **A** is incorrect because as information owner Jim is responsible for assigning information classifications. (The question asked which of the following Jim is not responsible for.)

☒ **B** is incorrect because information owners such as Jim are responsible for dictating how information should be protected. The information owner has the organizational responsibility for data protection and is liable for any negligence when it comes to protecting the organization's information assets. This means that Jim must make decisions regarding how information is protected and ensure that the information custodian (a role usually filled by IT or security) is carrying out these decisions.

☒ **D** is incorrect because determining how long to retain data is the responsibility of the information owner. The information owner is also responsible for determining who can access the information and ensuring that proper access rights are being used. He can approve access requests himself or delegate the function to business unit managers, who will approve requests based on user access criteria defined by the information owner.

6. Assigning data classification levels can help with all of the following except:

    A. The grouping of classified information with hierarchical and restrictive security

    B. Ensuring that nonsensitive data is not being protected by unnecessary controls

    C. Extracting data from a database

    D. Lowering the costs of protecting data

    ☑ **C.** Data classification does not involve the extraction of data from a database. However, data classification can be used to dictate who has access to read and write data that is stored in a database. Each classification should have separate handling requirements and procedures pertaining to how that data is accessed, used, and destroyed. For example, in a corporation, confidential information may only be accessed by senior management. Auditing could be very detailed and its results monitored daily, and degaussing or zeroization procedures may be required to erase the data. On the other hand, information classified as public may be accessed by all employees, and no special auditing or destruction methods required.

☒ **A** is incorrect because assigning data classification levels can help with the grouping of classified information with hierarchical and restrictive security. Data that shares the same classification, for example, can be grouped together and assigned the same handling requirements and procedures pertaining to how it is accessed, used, and destroyed.

☒ **B** is incorrect because assigning data classification levels can help ensure that nonsensitive data is being protected by the necessary controls. Data classification directly deals with ensuring that the different levels of sensitive data are being protected by the necessary controls. This answer is very tricky because of all the negatives, so make sure to read questions and answers slowly.

☒ **D** is incorrect because data classification helps ensure data is protected in the most cost-effective manner. Protecting and maintaining data costs money, but it is important to spend this money for the information that actually requires protection. For example, data that is classified confidential may require additional access controls as compared to public data to restrict access. It may also require additional auditing and monitoring. This may be appropriate for a soda company's proprietary recipe, but it would be a waste of resources if those same measures were implemented for the soda company's employee directory.

7. Which of the following is not included in a risk assessment?

   A. Discontinuing activities that introduce risk
   B. Identifying assets
   C. Identifying threats
   D. Analyzing risk in order of cost or criticality

   ☑ **A.** Discontinuing activities that introduce risk is a way of responding to risk through avoidance. For example, there are many risks surrounding the use of instant messaging (IM) in the enterprise. If a company decides not to allow IM activity because there is not enough business need for its use, then prohibiting this service is an example of risk avoidance. Risk assessment does not include the implementation of countermeasures such as this.

☒ **B** is incorrect because identifying assets is part of a risk assessment, and the question asks to identify what is not included in a risk assessment. In order to determine the value of assets, those assets must first be identified. Asset identification and valuation are also important tasks of risk management.

☒ **C** is incorrect because identifying threats is part of a risk assessment, and the question asks to identify what is not included in a risk assessment. Risk is present because of the possibility of a threat exploiting a vulnerability. If there were no threats, there would be no risk. Risk ties the vulnerability, threat, and likelihood of exploitation to the resulting business impact.

☒ **D** is incorrect because analyzing risk in order of cost or criticality is part of the risk assessment process, and the question asks to identify what is not included in a risk assessment. A risk assessment researches and quantifies the risk a company faces. Dealing with risk must be done in a cost-effective manner. Knowing the severity of the risk allows the organization to determine how to address it effectively.

8. Sue has been tasked with implementing a number of security controls, including antivirus and antispam software, to protect the company's e-mail system. What type of approach is her company taking to handle the risk posed by the system?

    A. Risk mitigation

    B. Risk acceptance

    C. Risk avoidance

    D. Risk transference

    ☑ **A.** Risk can be dealt with in four basic ways: transfer it, avoid it, reduce it, or accept it. By implementing security controls such as antivirus and antispam software, Sue is reducing the risk posed by her company's e-mail system. This is also referred to as risk mitigation, where the risk is decreased to a level considered acceptable. In addition to the use of IT security controls and countermeasures, risk can be mitigated by improving procedures, altering the environment, erecting barriers to the threat, and implementing early detection methods to stop threats as they occur, thereby reducing their possible damage.

    ☒ **B** is incorrect because risk acceptance does not involve spending money on protection or countermeasures, such as antivirus software. When accepting risk, the company understands the level of risk it is faced with, as well as the potential cost of damage, and decides to live with it without implementing countermeasures. Many companies accept risk when the cost/benefit ratio indicates that the cost of the countermeasure outweighs the potential loss value.

☒ **C** is incorrect because risk avoidance involves discontinuing the activity that is causing the risk, and in this case Sue's company has chosen to continue to use e-mail. A company may choose to terminate an activity that introduces risk if that risk outweighs the activity's business need. For example, a company may choose to block social media Web sites for some departments because of the risk they pose to employee productivity.

☒ **D** is incorrect because risk transference involves sharing the risks with another entity as in purchasing of insurance to transfer some of the risk to the insurance company. Many types of insurance are available to companies to protect their assets. If a company decides the total or residual risk is too high to gamble with, it can purchase insurance.

9. The integrity of data is not related to which of the following?

   A. Unauthorized manipulation or changes to data

   B. The modification of data without authorization

   C. The intentional or accidental substitution of data

   D. The extraction of data to share with unauthorized entities

   ☑ **D.** The extraction of data to share with unauthorized entities is a confidentiality issue, not an integrity issue. Confidentiality ensures that the necessary level of secrecy is enforced at each junction of data processing and prevents unauthorized disclosure. This level of confidentiality should prevail while data resides on systems and devices within the network, as it is transmitted, and once it reaches its destination. Integrity, on the other hand, is the principle that signifies the data has not been changed or manipulated in an unauthorized manner.

   ☒ **A** is incorrect because integrity is related to the unauthorized manipulation or changes to data. Integrity is upheld when any unauthorized modification is prevented. Hardware, software, and communication mechanisms must work in concert to maintain and process data correctly and move data to intended destinations without unexpected alteration. The systems and network should be protected from outside interference and contamination.

   ☒ **B** is incorrect because the modification of data without authorization is related to integrity. Integrity is about protecting data so that it cannot be changed either by users or other systems that do not have the rights to do so.

☒ **C** is incorrect because the intentional or accidental substitution of data is related to integrity. Along with the assurance that data is not modified by unauthorized entities, integrity is upheld when the assurance of the accuracy and reliability of the information and systems is provided. An environment that enforces integrity prevents attackers, for example, from inserting a virus, logic bomb, or backdoor into a system that could corrupt or replace data. Users usually affect a system or its data's integrity by mistake (although internal users may also commit malicious deeds). For example, a user may insert incorrect values into a data processing application that ends up charging a customer $3,000 instead of $300.

10. There are several methods an intruder can use to gain access to company assets. Which of the following best describes masquerading?

    A. Changing an IP packet's source address

    B. Elevating privileges to gain access

    C. An attempt to gain unauthorized access as another user

    D. Creating a new authorized user with hacking tools

    ☑ **C.** Masquerading is an attempt to gain unauthorized access by impersonating an authorized user. Masquerading is commonly used by attackers carrying out phishing attacks and has been around for a long time. For example, in 1996 hackers posed as AOL staff members and sent messages to victims asking for their passwords in order to verify correct billing information or verify information about the AOL accounts. Today, phishers often masquerade as large banking companies and well-known Internet entities like Amazon.com and eBay. Masquerading is a type of active attack because the attacker is actually doing something instead of sitting back and gathering data.

    ☒ **A** is incorrect because changing an IP packet's source address is an example of masquerading and not a definition of masquerading. IP spoofing is the act of presenting false information within packets, to trick other systems and hide the origin of the message. This is usually done by hackers so that their identity cannot be successfully uncovered.

    ☒ **B** is incorrect because elevating privileges is not part of masquerading. Elevating privileges is often the next step after being able to penetrate a system successfully, but it does not have anything to do directly with fooling a user or system about the attacker's true identity.

☒ **D** is incorrect because masquerading involves commonly posing as an authorized user that already exists in the system the attacker is attempting to access. It is common for the attacker then to attempt to create a new authorized user account on a compromised system, but successful masquerading has to happen first.

11. A number of factors should be considered when assigning values to assets. Which of the following is not used to determine the value of an asset?

    A. The asset's value in the external marketplace

    B. The level of insurance required to cover the asset

    C. The initial and outgoing costs of purchasing, licensing, and supporting the asset

    D. The asset's value to the organization's production operations

    ☑ **B.** The level of insurance required to cover the asset is not a consideration when assigning values to assets. It is actually the other way around: By knowing the value of an asset, an organization can more easily determine the level of insurance coverage to purchase for that asset. In fact, understanding the value of an asset is the first step to understanding what security mechanisms should be put in place and what funds should go toward protecting it. This knowledge can also help companies perform effective cost/benefit analyses, understand exactly what is at risk, and comply with legal and regulatory requirements.

    ☒ **A** is incorrect because the asset's value in the external marketplace is a factor that should be considered when determining the value of an asset. It should also include the value the asset might have to competitors or what others are willing to pay for a given asset.

    ☒ **C** is incorrect because the initial and outgoing costs of purchasing, licensing, and supporting the asset are considerations when determining the cost and value of an asset. The asset must be cost-effective to the business directly. If the supporting requirements of maintaining the asset outweighs the business need for the asset, its value will decrease.

    ☒ **D** is incorrect because it is a factor to be considered when determining an asset's value. The asset's value to the organization's production operations is the determination of cost to an organization if the asset is not available for a certain period of time. Along these same lines, the asset's usefulness and role in the organization should be considered as well as the operational and production activities affected if the asset is unavailable. If the asset helps operations it is valuable; the trick is to figure out how valuable.

12. Jill is establishing a companywide sales program that will require different user groups with different privileges to access information on a centralized database. How should the security manager secure the database?

A. Increase the database's security controls and provide more granularity.

B. Implement access controls that display each user's permissions each time they access the database.

C. Change the database's classification label to a higher security status.

D. Decrease the security so that all users can access the information as needed.

☑ A. The best approach to securing the database in this situation would be to increase the controls and assign very granular permissions. These measures would ensure that users cannot abuse their privileges and the confidentiality of the information would be maintained. Granularity of permissions gives network administrators and security professionals additional control over the resources they are charged with protecting, and a fine level of detail enables them to give individuals just the precise level of access they need.

☒ B is incorrect because implementing access controls that display each user's permissions each time they access the database is an example of one control. It is not the overall way of dealing with user access to a full database of information. This may be an example of increasing database security controls, but it is only one example and more would need to be put into place.

☒ C is incorrect because the classification level of the information in the database was previously determined based on its confidentiality, integrity, and availability levels. These levels do not change simply because more users need access to the data. Thus, you would never increase or decrease the classification level of information when more users or groups need to access that information. Increasing the classification level would only mean a smaller subset of users could access the database.

☒ D is incorrect because it puts data at risk. If security is decreased so that all users can access it as needed, then users with lower privileges will be able to access data of higher classification levels. Lower security also makes it easier for intruders to break into the database. As stated in answer C, a classification level is not changed just because the number of users who need to access the data increases or decreases.

13. As his company's CISO, George needs to demonstrate to the Board of Directors the necessity of a strong risk management program. Which of the following should George use to calculate the company's residual risk?

    A. threats × vulnerability × asset value = residual risk

    B. SLE × frequency = ALE, which is equal to residual risk

    C. (threats × vulnerability × asset value) × control gap = residual risk

    D. (total risk – asset value) × countermeasures = residual risk

    ☑ C. Countermeasures are implemented to reduce overall risk to an acceptable level. However, no system or environment is 100 percent secure, and with every countermeasure some risk remains. The leftover risk after countermeasures are implemented is called residual risk. Residual risk differs from total risk, which is the risk companies face when they choose not to implement any countermeasures. While the total risk can be determined by calculating threats × vulnerability × asset value = total risk, residual risk can be determined by calculating (threats × vulnerability × asset value) × control gap = residual risk. Control gap is the amount of protection the control cannot provide.

    ☒ A is incorrect because threats × vulnerability × asset value does not equal residual risk. It is the equation to calculate total risk. Total risk is the risk a company faces in the absence of any security safeguards or actions to reduce the overall risk exposure. The total risk is reduced by implementing safeguards and countermeasures, leaving the company with residual risk—or the risk left over after safeguards are implemented.

    ☒ B is incorrect because SLE × frequency is the equation to calculate the annualized loss expectancy (ALE) as a result of a threat exploiting a vulnerability and the business impact. The frequency is the threat's annual rate of occurrence (ARO). The ALE is not equal to residual risk. ALE indicates how much money a specific type of threat is likely to cost the company over the course of a year. Knowing the real possibility of a threat and how much damage, in monetary terms, the threat can cause is important in determining how much should be spent to try and protect against that threat in the first place.

    ☒ D is incorrect and is a distracter answer. There is no such formula like this used in risk assessments. The actual equations are threats × vulnerability × asset value = total risk; and (threats × vulnerability × asset value) × control gap = residual risk.

14. Authorization creep is to access controls what scope creep is to software development. Which of the following is not true of authorization creep?

    A. Users have a tendency to request additional permissions without asking for others to be taken away.

    B. It is a violation of "least privilege."

C. It enforces the "need-to-know" concept.

D. It commonly occurs when users transfer to other departments or change positions.

☑ **C.** The "need-to-know" concept is based on the idea that users are only given access rights to resources that they need in order to fulfill their job responsibilities. If access is not explicitly allowed, it should be implicitly denied. Instead of giving access to everything, and then taking privileges away based on "need-to-know," the better approach is to start with nothing and add privileges based on need to know. Authorization creep is contrary to this concept. It is about the accumulation of access rights over time, particularly those that the user does not have a need to know.

☒ **A** is incorrect because it correctly describes a cause of authorization creep and the question asks which statement is not true. Authorization creep often occurs due to users' tendency to request additional permissions without asking for others to be taken away. As a result, users have far more access rights and permissions than they require. This can pose a significant risk because too many users have too much privileged access to company assets.

☒ **B** is incorrect because authorization creep is a violation of "least privilege" and the question asks which statement is not true. Least privilege is a principle that states users should be given the least amount of privileges necessary to be productive when carrying out tasks. Enforcing least privilege on user accounts should be an ongoing job, which means each user's permissions should be reviewed to ensure the company is not putting itself at risk.

☒ **D** is incorrect because it correctly describes a cause of authorization creep, and the question asks which statement is not true. When users transfer to other departments or change positions, they are often assigned more access rights and permissions—far more than they need to get their jobs done. These rights and permissions are commonly added to their original ones, and their access to resources can be too vast and dangerous.

15. For what purpose was the COSO framework developed?

A. To address fraudulent financial activities and reporting

B. To help organizations install, implement, and maintain CobiT controls

C. To serve as a guideline for IT security auditors to use when verifying compliance

D. To address regulatory requirements related to protecting private health information

☑ **A.** COSO is an acronym for the Committee of Sponsoring Organizations of the Treadway Commission, which was formed in 1985 to provide sponsorship for the National Commission on Fraudulent Financial Reporting, an organization that studies deceptive financial reports and the elements that lead to them. Thus, the COSO framework was essentially developed to deal with fraudulent financial activities and reporting. Basically, COSO helps ensure that public companies who report their financial information to the Security Exchange Commission (SEC) are telling the truth and not "cooking the books."

☒ **B** is incorrect because COSO preceded CobiT; therefore, COSO was not developed to help organizations install, implement, and maintain CobiT controls. CobiT was derived from the COSO framework and offers a way to meet many of the COSO objectives from an IT perspective. COSO is a model for corporate governance on a strategic level, while CobiT is a model for IT governance on an operational level.

☒ **C** is incorrect because COSO was not developed to serve as a guideline to help IT security auditors. However, CobiT, which was derived from the COSO framework and defines goals for the controls that should be used to properly manage IT and ensure IT maps to business needs, is often used by auditors. CobiT lays out executive summaries, management guidelines, frameworks, control objectives, an implementation toolset, and audit guidelines. A majority of regulation compliance and audits are built on the CobiT framework.

☒ **D** is incorrect because COSO was not developed to address regulatory requirements related to private health information. However, NIST SP 800-66 is a risk assessment methodology that is designed to be implemented in the healthcare field or other regulated industries.

16. Susan, an attorney, has been hired to fill a new position at Widgets Inc. The position is Chief Privacy Officer (CPO). What is the primary function of her new role?

A. Ensuring the protection of partner data

B. Ensuring the accuracy and protection of company financial information

C. Ensuring that security policies are defined and enforced

D. Ensuring the protection of customer, company, and employee data

☑ **D.** The Chief Privacy Officer (CPO) position is being created by companies in response to the increasing demands on organizations to protect myriad types of data. The CPO is responsible for ensuring the security of customer, company, and employee data, which keeps the company free from legal prosecution and—hopefully—out of the headlines. Thus, the CPO is directly involved with setting policies on how data is collected, protected, and distributed to third parties. The CPO is usually an attorney and reports to the Chief Security Officer.

⊠ **A** is incorrect because protecting partner data is just a small subset of all the data the CPO is responsible for protecting. CPOs are responsible for ensuring the protection of customer, company, and employee data. Partner data is among the various types of data that the CPO is responsible for protecting. In addition, the CPO is responsible for knowing how its company's suppliers, partners, and other third parties are protecting its sensitive information. Many times, companies will need to review these other parties (which have copies of data needing protection).

⊠ **B** is incorrect because the accuracy of financial information is the responsibility of its data owner—the Chief Financial Officer (CFO). The CFO is responsible for the corporation's account and financial activities, and the overall financial structure of the organization. The CPO is responsible for helping to ensure the secrecy of this data, but not the accuracy of the data. The financial information is also a small subset of all the data types the CPO is responsible for protecting.

⊠ **C** is incorrect because the definition and enforcement of security policies is the responsibility of senior management, commonly delegated to the CISO or CSO—not the CPO. A security policy is an overall general statement that dictates what role security plays within the organization. The CPO's responsibilities as they relate to policies are to contribute to the setting of data protection policies, including how data is collected, protected, and distributed to third parties.

17. Jared plays a role in his company's data classification system. In this role, he must practice due care when accessing data and ensure that the data is used only in accordance with allowed policy while abiding by the rules set for the classification of the data. He does not determine, maintain, or evaluate controls, so what is Jared's role?

A. Data owner

B. Data custodian

C. Data user

D. Information systems auditor

☑ **C.** Any individual who routinely uses data for work-related tasks is a data user. Users must have the necessary level of access to the data to perform the duties within their position and are responsible for following operational security procedures to ensure the data's confidentiality, integrity, and availability to others. This means that users must practice due care and act in accordance with both security policy and data classification rules.

☒ **A** is incorrect because the data owner has a greater level of responsibility in the protection of the data. Data owners are responsible for classifying the data, regularly reviewing classification levels, and delegating the responsibility of the data protection duties to the data custodian. The data owner is typically a manager or executive in the organization and is held responsible when it comes to protecting the company's information assets.

☒ **B** is incorrect because the data custodian is responsible for the implementation and maintenance of security controls as dictated by the data owner. In other words, the data custodian is the technical caretaker of the controls that protects the data. Her duties include making backups, restoring data, implementing and maintaining countermeasures, and administering controls.

☒ **D** is incorrect because an information systems auditor is responsible for evaluating controls. After evaluating the controls, the auditor provides reports to management, illustrating the mapping between the set acceptable risk level of the organization and her findings. This does not have to do with using the data or practicing due care with the use of data.

18. Risk assessment has several different methodologies. Which of the following official risk methodologies was not created for the purpose of analyzing security risks?

A. FAP

B. OCTAVE

C. ANZ 4360

D. NIST SP 800-30

☑ **C.** While ANZ 4360 can be used to analyze security risks, it was not created for that purpose. It takes a much broader approach to risk management than other risk assessment methodologies, such as NIST and OCTAVE, which focus on IT threats and information security risks. ANZ 4360 can be used to understand a company's financial, capital, human safety, and business decisions risks.

☒ **A** is incorrect because there is no formal FAP risk analysis approach. It is a distracter answer.

☒ **B** is incorrect because OCTAVE focuses on IT threats and information security risks. OCTAVE is meant to be used in situations where people manage and direct the risk evaluation for information security within their organization. The organization's employees are given the power to determine the best approach for evaluating security.

   ☒ **D** is incorrect because NIST SP 800-30 is specific to IT threats and how they relate to information security risks. It focuses mainly on systems. Data is collected from network and security practice assessments, and from people within the organization. The data is then used as input values for the risk analysis steps outlined in the 800-30 document.

19. Which of the following is not a characteristic of a company with a security governance program in place?

   A. Board members are updated quarterly on the company's state of security.

   B. All security activity takes place within the security department.

   C. Security products, services, and consultants are deployed in an informed manner.

   D. The organization has established metrics and goals for improving security.

   ☑ **B.** If all security activity takes place within the security department, then security is working within a silo and is not integrated throughout the organization. In a company with a security governance program, security responsibilities permeate the entire organization, from executive management down the chain of command. A common scenario would be executive management holding business unit managements responsible for carrying out risk management activities for their specific business units. In addition, employees are held accountable for any security breaches they participate in, either maliciously or accidentally.

   ☒ **A** is incorrect because security governance is a set of responsibilities and practices exercised by the board and executive management of an organization with the goal of providing strategic direction, ensuring that objectives are achieved, ascertaining that risks are managed appropriately, and verifying that the organization's resources are used responsibly. An organization with a security governance program in place has a board of directors that understands the importance of security and is aware of the organization's security performance and breaches.

   ☒ **C** is incorrect because security governance is a coherent system of integrated security components that includes products, personnel, training, processes, etc. Thus, an organization with a security governance program in place is likely to purchase and deploy security products, managed services, and consultants in an informed manner. They are also constantly reviewed to ensure they are cost-effective.

☒ **D** is incorrect because security governance requires performance measurement and oversight mechanisms. An organization with a security governance program in place continually reviews its processes, including security, with the goal of continued improvement. On the other hand, an organization that lacks a security governance program is likely to march forward without analyzing its performance and therefore repeatedly makes similar mistakes.

20. Michael is charged with developing a classification program for his company. Which of the following should he do first?

    A. Understand the different levels of protection that must be provided.

    B. Specify data classification criteria.

    C. Identify the data custodians.

    D. Determine protection mechanisms for each classification level.

☑ **A.** Before Michael begins developing his company's classification program, he must understand the different levels of protection that must be provided. Only then can he develop the necessary classification levels and their criteria. One company may choose to use only two layers of classification, while another may choose to use more. Regardless, when developing classification levels, he should keep in mind that too many or too few classification levels will render the classification ineffective; there should be no overlap in the criteria definitions between classification levels; and classification levels should be developed for both data and software.

☒ **B** is incorrect because data classification criteria cannot be established until the classification levels themselves have been defined. The classification criteria are used by data owners to know what classification should be assigned to specific data. Basically, the classifications are defined buckets and the criteria help data owners determine what bucket each data set should be put into.

☒ **C** is incorrect because there is no need to identify the data custodians until classification levels are defined, criteria are determined for how data are classified, and the data owner has indicated the classification of the data she is responsible for. Remember, the data custodian is responsible for implementing and maintaining the controls specified by the data owner.

☒ **D** is incorrect because protection mechanisms for each classification level cannot be determined until the classification levels themselves are defined based on the different levels of protection that are required. The types of controls implemented per classification will depend upon the level of protection that management and the security team have determined is needed.

21. There are four ways of dealing with risk. In the graphic that follows, which method is missing and what is the purpose of this method?

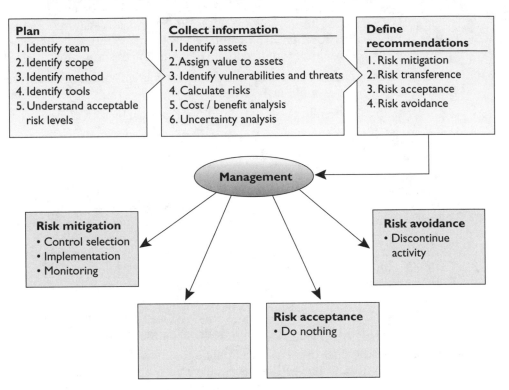

Plan	Collect information	Define recommendations
1. Identify team 2. Identify scope 3. Identify method 4. Identify tools 5. Understand acceptable risk levels	1. Identify assets 2. Assign value to assets 3. Identify vulnerabilities and threats 4. Calculate risks 5. Cost / benefit analysis 6. Uncertainty analysis	1. Risk mitigation 2. Risk transference 3. Risk acceptance 4. Risk avoidance

Management

Risk mitigation
• Control selection
• Implementation
• Monitoring

Risk avoidance
• Discontinue activity

Risk acceptance
• Do nothing

A. Risk transference. Share the risk with other entities.

B. Risk reduction. Reduce the risk to an acceptable level.

C. Risk rejection. Accept the current risk.

D. Risk assignment. Assign risk to a specific owner.

☑ **A.** Once a company knows the amount of total and residual risk it is faced with, it must decide how to handle it. Risk can be dealt with in four basic ways: transfer it, avoid it, reduce it, or accept it. Many types of insurance are available to companies to protect their assets. If a company decides the total or residual risk is too high to gamble with, it can purchase insurance, which would transfer the risk to the insurance company.

☒ **B** is incorrect because another approach is risk mitigation, where the risk is reduced to a level considered acceptable enough to continue conducting business. The implementation of firewalls, training, and intrusion/detection protection systems represent types of risk mitigation. Risk reduction is the same as risk mitigation, which is already listed in the graphic.

☒ **C** is incorrect because companies should never reject risk, which basically means that they refuse to deal with it. Risk commonly has a negative business impact and if not dealt with properly the company could have to deal with things such as the loss of production resources, legal liability issues, or a negative effect on its reputation. It is important that identified risk be dealt with properly through transferring it, avoiding it, reducing it, or accepting it.

☒ **D** is incorrect because while someone could be delegated to deal with a specific risk, this is not one of the methods that is used to deal with risk. Even if risk was assigned to a specific entity to deal with it, she would still need to either transfer, avoid, reduce, or accept the risk.

22. The following graphic contains a commonly used risk management scorecard. Identify the proper quadrant and its description.

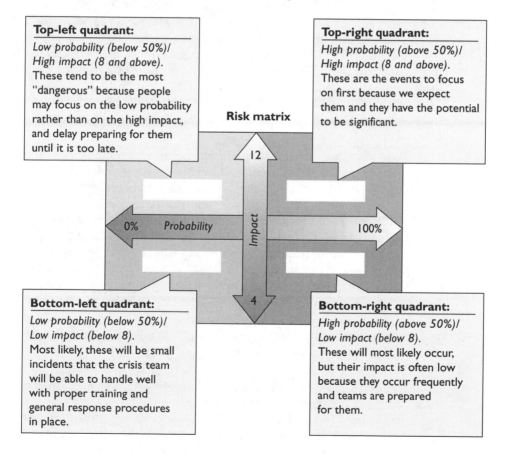

Top-left quadrant:
Low probability (below 50%)/ High impact (8 and above). These tend to be the most "dangerous" because people may focus on the low probability rather than on the high impact, and delay preparing for them until it is too late.

Top-right quadrant:
High probability (above 50%)/ High impact (8 and above). These are the events to focus on first because we expect them and they have the potential to be significant.

Risk matrix

12

4

0% *Probability* 100%

Impact

Bottom-left quadrant:
Low probability (below 50%)/ Low impact (below 8). Most likely, these will be small incidents that the crisis team will be able to handle well with proper training and general response procedures in place.

Bottom-right quadrant:
High probability (above 50%)/ Low impact (below 8). These will most likely occur, but their impact is often low because they occur frequently and teams are prepared for them.

A. Top-right quadrant is high impact, low probability.

B. Top-left quadrant is high impact, medium probability.

C. Bottom-left quadrant is low impact, high probability.

D. Bottom-right quadrant is low impact, high probability.

☑ **D.** The bottom-right quadrant contains low impact, high probability risks. This means that there is a high chance that specific threats will exploit specific vulnerabilities. Although these risks are commonly frequent, their business impact is low. Out of the four quadrants, the risks that reside in this quadrant should be dealt with after the first two higher quadrants. An example of a risk that could reside in this quadrant is a virus that infects a user workstation. Since viruses are so common this would mean that this risk has a high probability of taking place. This is only a user workstation and not a production system, so the impact would be low.

☒ **A** is incorrect because the top-right quadrant contains high impact, high probability risks. This means that there is a high chance that specific threats will exploit specific vulnerabilities. These risks are commonly frequent and their business impact is high. Out of the four quadrants, the risks that reside in this quadrant should be dealt with first. An example of a risk that would reside in this quadrant is an attacker compromising an internal mail server. If the proper countermeasures are not in place, there is a high probability that this would occur. Since this is a resource that the whole company depends upon, it would have a high business impact.

☒ **B** is incorrect because the top-left quadrant contains high impact, low probability risks. This means that there is a low chance that specific threats will exploit specific vulnerabilities. These risks are commonly infrequent and their business impact is low. Out of the four quadrants, the risks that reside in this quadrant should be dealt with after the risks that reside in the top-right quadrant. An example of this type of risk is an attacker compromising an internal DNS server. If there is an external-facing DNS server and a DMZ is in place, an attacker being able to access an internal DNS server is low. But if this does happen, this would have a high business impact since all systems depend upon this resource.

☒ **C** is incorrect because the bottom-left quadrant contains low impact, low probability risks. This means that there is a low chance that specific threats will exploit specific vulnerabilities. These risks are commonly infrequent and their business impact is low. Out of the four quadrants, the risks that reside in this quadrant should be dealt with after the risks in all of the other three quadrants. An example of this type of risk would be a legacy file server that is hardly used failing and going offline. Since it is not commonly used by users, it would have a low business impact, and if the correct countermeasures are in place, there would be a low probability of this occurring.

23. What are the three types of policies that are missing from the following graphic?

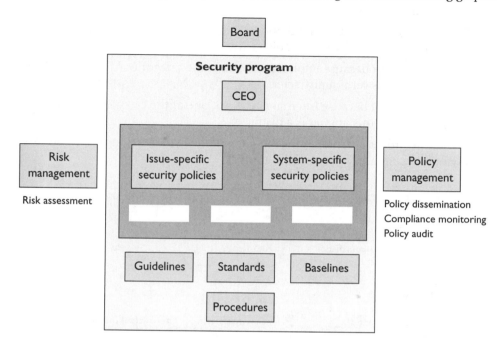

A. Regulatory, Informative, Advisory

B. Regulatory, Mandatory, Advisory

C. Regulatory, Informative, Public

D. Regulatory, Informative, Internal Use

☑ **A.** A **Regulatory** type of policy ensures that the organization is following standards set by specific industry regulations. It is very detailed and specific to a type of industry. It is used in financial institutions, healthcare facilities, public utilities, and other government-regulated industries. An **Informative** type of policy informs employees of certain topics. It is not an enforceable policy, but rather one that teaches individuals about specific issues relevant to the company. It could explain how the company interacts with partners, indicate the company's goals and mission, and provide a general reporting structure in different situations. An **Advisory** type of policy strongly advises employees as to which types of behaviors and activities should and should not take place within the organization. It also outlines possible ramifications if employees do not comply with the established behaviors and activities. This policy type can be used, for example, to describe how to handle medical information, financial transactions, or how to process confidential information.

☒ **B** is incorrect because Mandatory is not one of the categories of a type of policy; thus, this answer is a distracter.

☒ **C** is incorrect because Public is not one of the categories of a type of policy; thus, this answer is a distracter.

☒ **D** is incorrect because Internal Use is not one of the categories of a type of policy; thus, this answer is a distracter.

24. List in the proper order from the table that follows the learning objectives that are missing and their proper definitions.

	Awareness	**Training**	**Education**
Attribute:	"What"	"How"	"Why"
Level:	Information	Knowledge	Insight
Learning objective:			
Example teaching method:	**Media** • Videos • Newsletters • Posters	**Practical instruction** • Lecture and/or demo • Case study • Hands-on practice	**Theoretical instruction** • Seminar and discussion • Reading and study • Research
Test measure:	True/False Mutiple choice (Identify learning)	Problem solving, i.e., recognition and resolution (Apply learning)	Essay (Interpret learning)
Impact timeframe:	Short-term	Intermediate	Long-term

A. Understanding, recognition and retention, skill

B. Skill, recognition and retention, skill

C. Recognition and retention, skill, understanding

D. Skill, recognition and retention, understanding

☑ **C.** Awareness training and materials remind employees of their responsibilities pertaining to protecting company assets. Training provides skills needed to carry out specific tasks and functions. Education provides management skills and decision-making capabilities.

☒ **A** is incorrect because the different types of training and education do not map to the listed results. Companies today spend a lot of money on security devices and technologies, but they commonly overlook the fact that individuals must be trained to use these devices and technologies. Without such training, the money invested toward reducing threats can be wasted, and the company is still insecure.

☒ **B** is incorrect because the different types of training and education do not map to the listed results. Different roles require different types of training or education. A skilled staff is one of the most critical components to the security of a company.

☒ **D** is incorrect because the different types of training and education do not map to the listed results. A security-awareness program is typically created for at least three types of audiences: management, staff, and technical employees. Each type of awareness training must be geared toward the individual audience to ensure each group understands its particular responsibilities, liabilities, and expectations.

25. What type of risk analysis approach does the following graphic provide?

High	7–10	7–10
Medium	4–6	4–6
Low	0–3	0–3

0	10	20	30	40	50	60	70	80	90	100
0	9	18	27	36	45	54	63	72	81	90
0	8	16	24	32	40	48	56	64	72	80
0	7	14	21	28	35	42	49	56	63	70
0	6	12	18	24	30	36	42	48	54	60
0	5	10	15	20	25	30	35	40	45	50
0	4	8	12	16	20	24	28	32	36	40
0	3	6	9	12	15	18	21	24	27	30
0	2	4	6	8	10	12	14	16	18	20
0	1	2	3	4	5	6	7	8	9	10

41–100	High
20–40	Medium
0–19	Low

A. Quantitative

B. Qualitative

C. Operationally Correct

D. Operationally Critical

☑ **B.** A qualitative risk analysis approach does not assign monetary values to components and losses. Instead, qualitative methods walk through different scenarios of risk possibilities and rank the seriousness of the threats and the validity of the different possible countermeasures based on opinions. Qualitative analysis techniques include judgment, best practices, intuition, and experience. This graphic shows a rating system, which qualitative risk analysis uses instead of percentages and monetary numbers.

☒ **A** is incorrect because a quantitative risk analysis attempts to assign percentages and monetary values to all elements of the risk analysis process. These elements may include safeguard costs, asset value, business impact, threat frequency, safeguard effectiveness, exploit probabilities, and so on. When all of these are quantified, the process is said to be quantitative. Each element within the analysis (asset value, threat frequency, severity of vulnerability, impact damage, safeguard costs, safeguard effectiveness, uncertainty, and probability items) is quantified and entered into equations to determine total and residual risks.

☒ **C** is incorrect because there is no Operationally Correct formal risk analysis approach. This is a distracter answer.

☒ **D** is incorrect because there is no formal Operationally Critical risk analysis approach. This is a distracter answer.

26. ISO/IEC 27000 is part of a growing family of ISO/IEC information security management systems (ISMS) standards. It comprises information security standards published jointly by the International Organization for Standardization (ISO) and the International Electrotechnical Commission (IEC). Which of the following provides an incorrect mapping of the individual standards that make up this family of standards?

    A. ISO/IEC 27002   Code of practice for information security management

    B. ISO/IEC 27003   Guideline for ISMS implementation

    C. ISO/IEC 27004   Guideline for information security management measurement and metrics framework

    D. ISO/IEC 27005   Guideline for bodies providing audit and certification of information security management systems

    ☑ **D.** The ISO/IEC 27005 standard is the guideline for information security risk management. ISO/IEC 27005 is an international standard for how risk management should be carried out in the framework of an information security management system (ISMS).

    ☒ **A** is incorrect because ISO/IEC 27002 is the code of practice for information security management; thus, it has a correct mapping. ISO/IEC 27002 provides best practice recommendations and guidelines as they pertain to initiating, implementing, or maintaining information security management systems (ISMS).

☒ **B** is incorrect because ISO/IEC 27003 is the guideline for ISMS implementation; thus, it has a correct mapping. It focuses on the critical aspects needed for successful design and implementation of an information security management system (ISMS) in accordance with ISO/IEC 27001:2005. It describes the process of ISMS specification and design from inception to the production of implementation plans.

☒ **C** is incorrect because ISO/IEC 27004 is the guideline for information security management measurement and metrics framework; thus, it has a correct mapping. It provides guidance on the development and use of measures and measurement in order to assess the effectiveness of an implemented information security management system (ISMS) and controls or groups of controls, as specified in ISO/IEC 27001.

The following scenario applies to questions 27 and 28.

Sam is the security manager of a company that makes most of its revenue from its intellectual property. Sam has implemented a process improvement program that has been certified by an outside entity. His company received a Level 2 during an appraisal process, and he is putting in steps to increase this to a Level 3. A year ago when Sam carried out a risk analysis, he determined that the company was at too much of a risk when it came to potentially losing trade secrets. The countermeasure his team implemented reduced this risk, and Sam determined that the annualized loss expectancy of the risk of a trade secret being stolen once in a hundred-year period is now $400.

27. Which of the following is the criteria Sam's company was most likely certified under?

   A. SABSA

   B. Capability Maturity Model Integration

   C. Information Technology Infrastructure Library

   D. PRINCE2

   ☑ **B.** Capability Maturity Model Integration (CMMI) is a process improvement approach that is used to help organizations improve their performance. The CMMI model may also be used as a framework for appraising the process maturity of the organization. The levels used in CMMI are Level 1–Initial, Level 2–Managed, Level 3–Defined, Level 4–Quantitatively Managed, and Level 5–Optimizing.

   ☒ **A** is incorrect because Sherwood Applied Business Security Architecture (SABSA) is a model and methodology for the development of information security enterprise architectures. Since it is a framework, this means it provides a structure for individual architectures to be built from. Since it is a methodology also, this means it provides the processes to follow to build and maintain this architecture.

☒ **C** is incorrect because the Information Technology Infrastructure Library (ITIL) is the de facto standard of best practices for IT service management. ITIL was created because of the increased dependence on information technology to meet business needs. Although ITIL has a component that deals with security, its focus is more toward internal service level agreements between the IT department and the "customers" it serves. The customers are usually internal departments. ITIL does not use the levels described in the scenario.

☒ **D** is incorrect because PRINCE2 (PRojects IN Controlled Environments) is a process-based method for effective project management. It is commonly used by the UK government and is not a topic covered by the CISSP exam.

28. What is the associated single loss expectancy value in this scenario?

   A. $65,000

   B. $400,000

   C. $40,000

   D. $4,000

☑ **C.** The formula to calculate the Annualized Loss Expectancy value (ALE) is Single Loss Expectancy (SLE) × Annualized Rate of Occurrence (ARO) = ALE. In this scenario, if the ALE is $400 and the ARO is 0.01, then the SLE is $40,000.

☒ **A** is incorrect because the formula to obtain the SLE is Asset Value × Exposure Factor = SLE, and ALE is Single Loss Expectancy (SLE) × Annualized Rate of Occurrence (ARO) = ALE. If the ALE of the risk of a trade secret being stolen once in a hundred-year period is $400, then you have to work backwards to obtain the SLE value. If the ALE is $400 and the ARO is 0.01, then the resulting SLE value is $40,000.

☒ **B** is incorrect because the formula to obtain the SLE is Asset Value × Exposure Factor = SLE, and ALE is Single Loss Expectancy (SLE) × Annualized Rate of Occurrence (ARO) = ALE. In this scenario, the risk of an asset being stolen once in a hundred-year period is calculated at the ALE being $400. If the ALE is $400 and the ARO is 0.01, then the resulting SLE value is $40,000.

☒ **D** is incorrect because the formula to obtain the SLE is Asset Value × Exposure Factor = SLE, and ALE is Single Loss Expectancy (SLE) × Annualized Rate of Occurrence (ARO) = ALE. The goal of carrying out these calculations is to fully understand the criticality of specific risks and to know how much can be spent on implementing a countermeasure in a cost-effective manner.

The following scenario applies to questions 29, 30, and 31.

Barry has just been hired as the company security officer at an international financial institution. He has reviewed the company's data protection policies and procedures. He sees that the company stores its sensitive data within a secured database. The database is located in a network segment all by itself, which is monitored by a network-based intrusion detection system. The database is hosted on a server kept within a server room, which can only be accessed by personnel with the correct PIN value and smart card. Barry finds that the sensitive data backups are not being properly secured and requests that the company implement a secure courier service that moves backup tapes to a secured location. His management states that this option is too expensive, so Barry implements a local hierarchy storage management system that properly protects the sensitive data.

29. Which of the following best describes the control types the company originally had in place?

    A. Administrative preventive controls are the policies and procedures. Technical preventive controls are securing the system, network segmentation, and intrusion detection system. Physical detective controls are the physical location of the database and PIN and smart card access controls.

    B. Administrative preventive controls are the policies. Technical preventive controls are securing the system and intrusion detection system. Physical preventive controls are the physical location of the database and PIN and smart card access controls.

    C. Administrative corrective controls are the policies and procedures. Technical preventive controls are securing the system, network segmentation, and intrusion detection system. Physical preventive controls are the physical location of the database and PIN and smart card access controls.

    D. Administrative preventive controls are the policies and procedures. Technical preventive controls are securing the system and network segmentation. The technical detective control is the intrusion detection system. Physical preventive controls are the physical location of the database and PIN and smart card access controls.

    ☑ **D.** The administrative preventive controls are the policies and procedures. Technical preventive controls are securing the system and network segmentation. The technical detective control is the intrusion detection system. Physical preventive controls are the physical location of the database and PIN and smart card access controls.

    ☒ **A** is incorrect because an intrusion detection system is not a preventive control; this is an example of a detective control. It is important to have both prevention and detection controls in place.

☒ **B** is incorrect because this answer does not mention procedures, which is an administrative protective control. The answer also incorrectly states that an intrusion detection system is a preventive control, but it is a detective control.

☒ **C** is incorrect because the answer incorrectly states that an intrusion detection system is a preventive control, but it is a detective control. The answer also states that policies and procedures are corrective controls, but they are preventive controls.

30. The storage management system that Barry put into place is referred to as which of the following?

   A. Administrative control

   B. Compensating control

   C. Physical control

   D. Confidentiality control

   ☑ **B.** A compensating control is an alternate control. Instead of a courier service, the company implemented an internal storage management system. A compensating control can be administrative, physical, or technical in nature.

   ☒ **A** is incorrect because the storage management system is not an administrative control; it is a technical compensating control.

   ☒ **C** is incorrect because the storage management system is not a physical control; it is a technical compensating control.

   ☒ **D** is incorrect and a distracter. The main categories of controls are administrative, technical and physical. The controls can provide many different types of services and protection, confidentiality being one type of protection.

31. Which are the two most common situations that require the type of control covered in the scenario to be implemented?

   A. Defense-in-depth is required and the current controls only provide one protection layer.

   B. Primary control costs too much or negatively affects business operations.

   C. Confidentiality is the highest concern in a situation where defense-in-depth is required.

   D. Availability is the highest concern in a situation where defense-in-depth is required.

   ☑ **B.** A compensating control is implemented because the primary control that was suggested is too expensive, but this type of protection is still required. A less expensive control that provides this same type of protection is identified and implemented. Another situation where a compensating control might be implemented is if the primary control negatively affects business operations.

☒ **A** is incorrect because while a compensating control can help in providing defense-in-depth, this is not the reason this category of control would be put into place.

☒ **C** is incorrect because a compensating control may or may not provide confidentiality. But the service that a control provides, as in confidentiality, is not the reason a compensating control is put into place. A compensating control is an alternate control type.

☒ **D** is incorrect because a compensating control may or may not provide availability. But the service that a control provides, as in availability, is not the reason a compensating control is put into place. A compensating control is an alternate control type.

Access Control

This domain includes questions from the following topics:

- Identification methods and technologies
- Authentication methods, models, and technologies
- Discretionary, mandatory, and nondiscretionary models
- Accountability, monitoring, and auditing practices
- Emanation security and technologies
- Intrusion detection systems
- Threats to access control practices and technologies

Controlling access to resources is a vital element of any information security program. Controlling who can access what and when helps protect information assets and company resources from unauthorized modification and disclosure. Thus, access controls address all three services in the AIC triad—availability, integrity, and confidentiality—be they technical, physical, or administrative in nature. Security professionals should understand the principles behind access controls to ensure their adequacy and proper implementation.

1. Which of the following does not correctly describe a directory service?

   A. It manages objects within a directory by using namespaces.

   B. It enforces security policy by carrying out access control and identity management functions.

   C. It assigns namespaces to each object in databases that are based on the X.509 standard and are accessed by LDAP.

   D. It allows an administrator to configure and manage how identification takes place within the network.

2. Hannah has been assigned the task of installing Web access management (WAM) software. What is the best description for what WAM is commonly used for?

   A. Control external entities requesting access through X.500 databases

   B. Control external entities requesting access to internal objects

   C. Control internal entities requesting access through X.500 databases

   D. Control internal entities requesting access to external objects

3. There are several types of password management approaches used by identity management systems. Which of the following reduces help-desk call volume, but is also criticized for the ease with which a hacker could gain access to multiple resources if a password is compromised?

   A. Management password reset

   B. Self-service password reset

   C. Password synchronization

   D. Assisted password reset

4. A number of attacks can be performed against smart cards. Side-channel is a class of attacks that doesn't try to compromise a flaw or weakness. Which of the following is not a side-channel attack?

   A. Differential power analysis

   B. Microprobing analysis

   C. Timing analysis

   D. Electromagnetic analysis

5. Which of the following does not describe privacy-aware role-based access control?

   A. It is an example of a discretionary access control model.

   B. Detailed access controls indicate the type of data that users can access based on the data's level of privacy sensitivity.

   C. It is an extension of role-based access control.

   D. It should be used to integrate privacy policies and access control policies.

6. What was the direct predecessor to Standard Generalized Markup Language (SGML)?

   A. Hypertext Markup Language (HTML)

   B. Extensible Markup Language (XML)

   C. LaTeX

   D. Generalized Markup Language (GML)

7. Brian has been asked to work on the virtual directory of his company's new identity management system. Which of the following best describes a virtual directory?

   A. Meta-directory

   B. User attribute information stored in an HR database

   C. Virtual container for data from multiple sources

   D. A service that allows an administrator to configure and manage how identification takes place

8. Emily is listening to network traffic and capturing passwords as they are sent to the authentication server. She plans to use the passwords as part of a future attack. What type of attack is this?

   A. Brute-force attack

   B. Dictionary attack

   C. Social engineering attack

   D. Replay attack

9. Which of the following correctly describes a federated identity and its role within identity management processes?

   A. A nonportable identity that can be used across business boundaries

   B. A portable identity that can be used across business boundaries

   C. An identity that can be used within intranet virtual directories and identity stores

   D. An identity specified by domain names that can be used across business boundaries

10. Phishing and pharming are similar. Which of the following correctly describes the difference between phishing and pharming?

    A. Personal information is collected from victims through legitimate-looking Web sites in phishing attacks, while personal information is collected from victims via e-mail in pharming attacks.

    B. Phishing attacks point e-mail recipients to a form where victims input personal information, while pharming attacks use pop-up forms at legitimate Web sites to collect personal information from victims.

    C. Victims are pointed to a fake Web site with a domain name that looks similar to a legitimate site's in a phishing attack, while victims are directed to a fake Web site as a result of a legitimate domain name being incorrectly translated by the DNS server in a pharming attack.

    D. Phishing is a technical attack, while pharming is a type of social engineering.

11. Security countermeasures should be transparent to users and attackers. Which of the following does not describe transparency?

    A. User activities are monitored and tracked without negatively affecting system performance.

    B. User activities are monitored and tracked without the user knowing about the mechanism that is carrying this out.

    C. Users are allowed access in a manner that does not negatively affect business processes.

    D. Unauthorized access attempts are denied and logged without the intruder knowing about the mechanism that is carrying this out.

12. What markup language allows for the sharing of application security policies to ensure that all applications are following the same security rules?

    A. XML

    B. SPML

    C. XACML

    D. GML

13. The importance of protecting audit logs generated by computers and network devices is highlighted by the fact that it is required by many of today's regulations. Which of the following does not explain why audit logs should be protected?

    A. If not properly protected, these logs may not be admissible during a prosecution.

    B. Audit logs contain sensitive data and should only be accessible to a certain subset of people.

C. Intruders may attempt to scrub the logs to hide their activities.

D. The format of the logs should be unknown and unavailable to the intruder.

14. Harrison is evaluating access control products for his company. Which of the following is not a factor he needs to consider when choosing the products?

A. Classification level of data

B. Level of training that employees have received

C. Logical access controls provided by products

D. Legal and regulation issues

15. There are several types of intrusion detection systems (IDSs). What type of IDS builds a profile of an environment's normal activities and assigns an anomaly score to packets based on the profile?

A. State-based

B. Statistical anomaly–based

C. Misuse-detection system

D. Protocol signature–based

16. A rule-based IDS takes a different approach than a signature-based or anomaly-based system. Which of the following is characteristic of a rule-based IDS?

A. Uses IF/THEN programming within expert systems

B. Identifies protocols used outside of their common bounds

C. Compares patterns to several activities at once

D. Can detect new attacks

17. Sam plans to establish mobile phone service using the personal information he has stolen from his former boss. What type of identity theft is this?

A. Phishing

B. True name

C. Pharming

D. Account takeover

18. Of the following, what is the primary item that a capability listing is based upon?

A. A subject

B. An object

C. A product

D. An application

19. Alex works for a chemical distributor that assigns employees tasks that separate their duties and routinely rotates job assignments. Which of the following best describes the differences between these countermeasures?

    A. They are the same thing with different titles.

    B. They are administrative controls that enforce access control and protect the company's resources.

    C. Separation of duties ensures that one person cannot perform a high-risk task alone, and job rotation can uncover fraud because more than one person knows the tasks of a position.

    D. Job rotation ensures that one person cannot perform a high-risk task alone, and separation of duties can uncover fraud because more than one person knows the tasks of a position.

20. What type of markup language allows company interfaces to pass service requests and the receiving company provision access to these services?

    A. XML

    B. SPML

    C. SGML

    D. HTML

21. There are several different types of centralized access control protocols. Which of the following is illustrated in the graphic that follows?

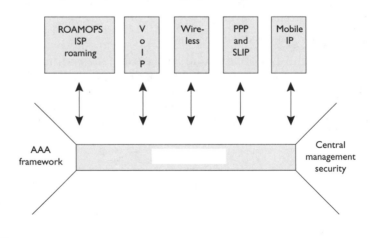

    A. Diameter

    B. Watchdog

    C. RADIUS

    D. TACACS+

22. An access control matrix is used in many operating systems and applications to control access between subjects and objects. What is the column in this type of matrix referred to as?

Access Control Matrix

Subject	File1	File2	File3	File4
Larry	Read	Read, Write	Read	Read, Write
Curly	Full Control	No Access	Full Control	Read
Mo	Read, Write	Full Control	Read	Full Control
Bob	Full Control	Full Control	No Access	No Access

   A. Capability table

   B. Constrained interface

   C. Role-based value

   D. ACL

23. What technology within identity management is illustrated in the graphic that follows?

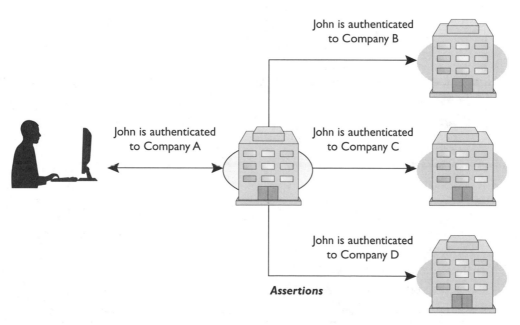

A. User provisioning

B. Federated identity

C. Directories

D. Web access management

24. There are several different types of single sign-on protocols and technologies in use today. What type of technology is illustrated in the graphic that follows?

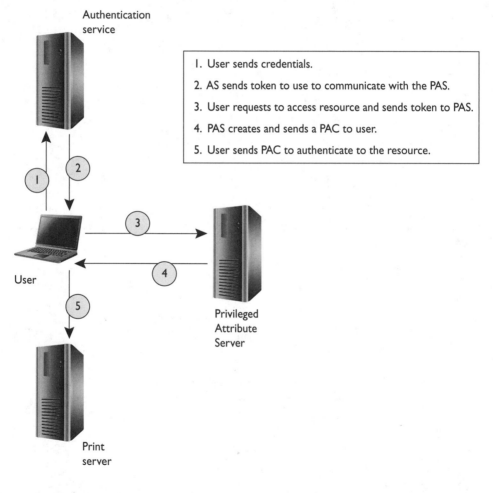

1. User sends credentials.

2. AS sends token to use to communicate with the PAS.

3. User requests to access resource and sends token to PAS.

4. PAS creates and sends a PAC to user.

5. User sends PAC to authenticate to the resource.

A. Kerberos

B. Discretionary access control

C. SESAME

D. Mandatory access control

25. There are different ways that specific technologies can create one-time passwords for authentication purposes. What type of technology is illustrated in the graphic that follows?

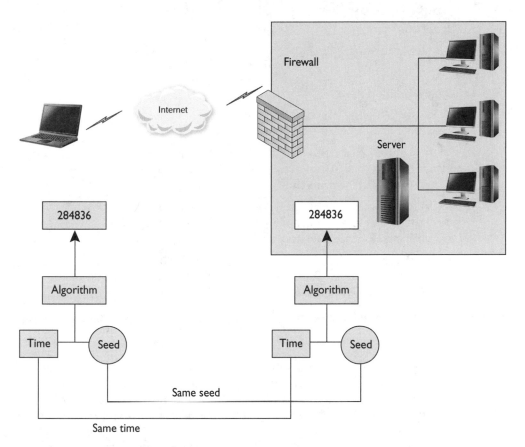

    A. Counter synchronous token

    B. Asynchronous token

    C. Mandatory token

    D. Synchronous token

26. Sally is carrying out a software analysis on her company's proprietary application. She has found out that it is possible for an attacker to force an authorization step to take place before the authentication step is completed successfully. What type of issue would allow for this type of compromise to take place?

   A. Backdoor

   B. Maintenance hook

   C. Race condition

   D. Data validation error

27. Which of the following best describes how SAML, SOAP, and HTTP commonly work together in an environment that provides Web services?

   A. Security attributes are put into SAML format. Web service request and authentication data are encrypted in a SOAP message. Message is transmitted in an HTTP connection.

   B. Security attributes are put into SAML format. Web service request and authentication data are encapsulated in a SOAP message. Message is transmitted in an HTTP connection over TLS.

   C. Authentication data are put into SAML format. Web service request and authentication data are encapsulated in a SOAP message. Message is transmitted in an HTTP connection.

   D. Authentication data are put into SAML format. HTTP request and authentication data are encapsulated in a SOAP message. Message is transmitted in an HTTP connection.

28. Tom works at a large retail company that recently deployed radio-frequency identification (RFID) to better manage its inventory processes. Employees use scanners to gather product-related information instead of manually looking up product data. Tom has found out that malicious customers have carried out attacks on the RFID technology to reduce the amount they pay on store items. Which of the following is the most likely reason for the existence of this type of vulnerability?

   A. The company's security team does not understand how to secure this type of technology.

   B. The cost of integrating security within RFID is cost prohibitive.

   C. The technology has low processing capabilities and encryption is very processor-intensive.

   D. RFID is a new and emerging technology, and the industry does not currently have ways to secure it.

29. Tanya is the security administrator for a large distributed retail company. The company's network has many different network devices and software appliances that generate logs and audit data. Tanya and her staff have become overwhelmed with trying to review all of the log files when attempting to identify if anything suspicious is taking place within the network. Which of the following is the best solution for this company to implement?

   A. Security information and event management

   B. Event correlation tools

   C. Intrusion detection systems

   D. Security event correlation management tools

30. Sarah and her security team have carried out many vulnerability tests over the years to locate the weaknesses and vulnerabilities within the systems on the network. The CISO has asked her to oversee the development of a threat model for the network. Which of the following best describes what this model is and what it would be used for?

   A. A threat model can help to assess the probability, the potential harm, and the priority of attacks, and thus help to minimize or eradicate the threats.

   B. A threat model combines the output of the various vulnerability tests and the penetration tests carried out to understand the security posture of the network as a whole.

   C. A threat model is a risk-based model that is used to calculate the probabilities of the various risks identified during the vulnerability tests.

   D. A threat model is used in software development practices to uncover programming errors.

1. C	11. A	21. A
2. B	12. C	22. D
3. C	13. D	23. B
4. B	14. B	24. C
5. A	15. B	25. D
6. D	16. A	26. C
7. C	17. B	27. C
8. D	18. A	28. C
9. B	19. C	29. A
10. C	20. B	30. A

1. Which of the following does not correctly describe a directory service?

   A. It manages objects within a directory by using namespaces.

   B. It enforces security policy by carrying out access control and identity management functions.

   C. It assigns namespaces to each object in databases that are based on the X.509 standard and are accessed by LDAP.

   D. It allows an administrator to configure and manage how identification takes place within the network.

   ☑ **C.** Most enterprises have some type of directory that contains information pertaining to the company's network resources and users. Most directories follow a hierarchical database format, based on the X.500 standard (not X.509), and a type of protocol, as in Lightweight Directory Access Protocol (LDAP), that allows subjects and applications to interact with the directory. Applications can request information about a particular user by making an LDAP request to the directory, and users can request information about a specific resource by using a similar request. A directory service assigns distinguished names (DNs) to each object in databases based on the X.500 standard that are accessed by LDAP. Each distinguished name represents a collection of attributes about a specific object and is stored in the directory as an entry.

   ☒ **A** is incorrect because objects within hierarchical databases are managed by a directory service. The directory service allows an administrator to configure and manage how identification, authentication, authorization, and access control take place within the network. The objects within the directory are labeled and identified with namespaces, which is how the directory service keeps the objects organized.

   ☒ **B** is incorrect because directory services do enforce the configured security policy by carrying out access control and identity management functions. For example, when a user logs into a domain controller in a Windows environment, the directory service (Active Directory) determines what network resources she can and cannot access.

   ☒ **D** is incorrect because directory services do allow an administrator to configure and manage how identification takes place within the network. It also allows for the configuration and management of authentication, authorization, and access control.

2. Hannah has been assigned the task of installing Web access management (WAM) software. What is the best description for what WAM is commonly used for?

   A. Control external entities requesting access through X.500 databases

   B. Control external entities requesting access to internal objects

C. Control internal entities requesting access through X.500 databases

D. Control internal entities requesting access to external objects

☑ **B.** Web access management (WAM) software controls what users can access when using a Web browser to interact with Web-based enterprise assets. This type of technology is continually becoming more robust and experiencing increased deployment. This is because of the increased use of e-commerce, online banking, content providing, Web services, and more. The basic components and activities in a Web access control management process are as follows:

1. User sends in credentials to Web server.
2. Web server validates user's credentials.
3. User requests to access a resource (object).
4. Web server verifies with the security policy to determine if the user is allowed to carry out this operation.
5. Web server allows/denies access to the requested resource.

☒ **A** is incorrect because a directory service should be carrying out access control in the directory of an X.500 database—not Web access management software. The directory service manages the entries and data, and enforces the configured security policy by carrying out access control and identity management functions. Examples of directory services include Active Directory and Novell NetWare Directory Service (NDS). While Web-based access requests may be to objects held within a database, WAM mainly controls communication between Web browsers and servers. The Web servers should communicate to a backend database, commonly through a directory service.

☒ **C** is incorrect because a directory service should be carrying out access control for internal entities requesting access to a X.500 databases using the LDAP. This type of database provides a hierarchical structure for the organization of objects (subjects and resources). The directory service develops unique distinguished names for each object and appends the corresponding attribute to each object as needed. The directory service enforces a security policy (configured by the administrator) to control how subjects and objects interact. While Web-based access requests may be to objects held within a database, WAM mainly controls communication between Web browsers and servers. WAM was developed mainly for external to internal communication, although it can be used for internal-to-internal communication also. Answer B is the best answer out of the four provided.

☒ **D** is incorrect because WAM software is most commonly used to control external entities requesting access to internal objects; not the other way around, as stated by the answer option. For example, WAM may be used by a bank to control its customers' access to backend account data.

3. There are several types of password management approaches used by identity management systems. Which of the following reduces help-desk call volume, but is also criticized for the ease with which a hacker could gain access to multiple resources if a password is compromised?

   A. Management password reset

   B. Self-service password reset

   C. Password synchronization

   D. Assisted password reset

   ☑ C. Password synchronization is designed to reduce the complexity of keeping up with different passwords for different systems. Password synchronization technology can allow users to maintain a single password across multiple systems by transparently synchronizing the password to other systems and applications. This reduces help-desk call volume. One criticism of this approach is that since only one password is used to access different resources, now the hacker only has to figure out one credential set to gain unauthorized access to all resources.

   ☒ A is incorrect because there is no such thing as a management password reset. This answer is a distracter. The most common password management approaches are password synchronization, self-service password reset, and assisted password reset.

   ☒ B is incorrect because self-service password reset does not necessarily deal with multiple passwords. However, it does help reduce the overall volume of password-related help desk calls. In the case of self-service password reset, users are allowed to reset their own passwords. For example, when a user forgets his password, he may be prompted to answer questions that he identified during the registration process. If the answer he gives matches the information he provided during registration, then he is granted the ability to change his password.

   ☒ D is incorrect because assisted password reset does not necessarily deal with multiple passwords. It reduces the resolution process for password issues by allowing the help desk to authenticate a user before resetting her password. The caller must be identified and authenticated through the password management tool before the password can be changed. Once the password is updated, the system that the user is authenticating to should require the user to change her password again. This would ensure that only she (and not she and the help-desk person) knows her password. The goal of an assisted password reset product is to reduce the cost of support calls and ensure that all calls are processed in a uniform, consistent, and secure fashion.

4. A number of attacks can be performed against smart cards. Side-channel is a class of attacks that doesn't try to compromise a flaw or weakness. Which of the following is not a side-channel attack?

A. Differential power analysis

B. Microprobing analysis

C. Timing analysis

D. Electromagnetic analysis

☑ **B.** A noninvasive attack is one in which the attacker watches how something works and how it reacts in different situations instead of trying to "invade" it with more intrusive measures. Examples of side-channel attacks are fault generation, differential power analysis, electromagnetic analysis, timing, and software attacks. These types of attacks are used to uncover sensitive information about how a component works without trying to compromise any type of flaw or weakness. A more intrusive smart card attack is microprobing. Microprobing uses needles and ultrasonic vibration to remove the outer protective material on the card's circuits. Once this is complete, data can be accessed and manipulated by directly tapping into the card's ROM chips.

☒ **A** is incorrect because differential power analysis (DPA) is a noninvasive attack. DPA involves examining the power emissions released during processing. By statistically analyzing data from multiple cryptographic operations, for example, an attacker can determine the intermediate values within cryptographic computations. This can be done without any knowledge of how the target device is designed. Thus, an attacker can extract cryptographic keys or other sensitive information from the card.

☒ **C** is incorrect because a timing analysis is a noninvasive attack. It involves calculating the time a specific function takes to complete its task. They are attacks based on measuring how much time various computations take to perform. For example, by observing how long it takes a smart card to transfer key information, it is sometimes possible to determine how long the key is in this instance.

☒ **D** is incorrect because electromagnetic analysis is a noninvasive attack that involves examining the frequencies emitted. All electric currents emit electromagnetic emanations. In smart cards, the power consumption—and, therefore, the electromagnetic emanation field—varies as data is processed. An electromagnetic analysis attempts to make correlations between the data and the electromagnetic emanations in an effort to uncover cryptographic keys or other sensitive information on the smart card.

5. Which of the following does not describe privacy-aware role-based access control?

    A. It is an example of a discretionary access control model.

    B. Detailed access controls indicate the type of data that users can access based on the data's level of privacy sensitivity.

    C. It is an extension of role-based access control.

    D. It should be used to integrate privacy policies and access control policies.

☑ **A.** A system that uses discretionary access control (DAC) enables the owner of the resource to specify which subjects can access specific resources. This model is called discretionary because the control of access is based on the discretion of the owner. Many times department managers, or business unit managers, are the owners of the data within their specific department. Being the owner, they can specify who should have access and who should not. Privacy-aware role-based access control is an extension of role-based access control (RBAC). There are three main access control models: DAC, mandatory access control (MAC), and RBAC. Privacy-aware role-based access control is a type of RBAC, not DAC.

☒ **B** is incorrect because privacy-aware role-based access control is based on detailed access controls that indicate the type of data that users can access based on the data's level of privacy sensitivity. Other access control models, such as MAC, DAC, and RBAC, do not lend themselves to protect the level of privacy of data, but the functions that users can carry out. For example, managers may be able to access a privacy folder, but there needs to be more detailed access control that indicates, for example, that they can access customers' home addresses but not Social Security numbers. The industry has advanced to needing much more detail-oriented access control when it comes to sensitive privacy information as in Social Security numbers and credit card data, which is why privacy-aware role-based access control was developed.

☒ **C** is incorrect because privacy-aware role-based access control is an extension of role-based access control. Access rights are determined based on the user's role and responsibilities within the company, and the level of privacy of the data they need access to.

☒ **D** is incorrect because the languages used for privacy policies and access control policies should be either the same or integrated when using privacy-aware role-based access control. The goal of the use of privacy-aware role-based access control is to make access control much more detailed and focused on privacy-related data, thus it should be using the same type of terms and language as the organization's original access control policy and standards.

6. What was the direct predecessor to Standard Generalized Markup Language (SGML)?

   A. Hypertext Markup Language (HTML)

   B. Extensible Markup Language (XML)

   C. LaTeX

   D. Generalized Markup Language (GML)

   ☑ **D.** A markup language is a way to structure text and also how it will be viewed. When you adjust margins and other formatting capabilities in a word processor, you are marking up the text in the word processor's markup language. If you develop a Web page, you are using some type of markup language. You can control how it looks and some of the actual functionality the page provides. Hypertext Markup Language (HTML) came out in the early 1990s. It came from Standard Generalized Markup Language (SGML), which came from the Generalized Markup Language (GML). GML is a macrolanguage developed in the 1960s for the IBM text formatter, SCRIPT/VS. GML markup simplifies the description of how a document appears (font, structure, etc.). Once the document is marked up, it can be formatted for different devices (a printer, for example) without changing the document. GML was used as the foundation for the industry-developed SGML. While GML is a structured document description language, SGML is a set of rules for the creation of such languages. SGML was developed for the purpose of enabling the sharing of machine-readable documents. It is used in a number of industries, including the government, military, and law.

   ☒ **A** is incorrect because HTML came from SGML. HTML came out in the early 1990s and was developed as a system for annotating text for Web pages. SGML is an ISO standard that defines generalized markup languages for documents. Hypertext Markup Language (HTML) was created by physicist Tim Berners-Lee for the use and sharing of documents while he was at CERN. Based on an in-house version of SGML called SGMLguid, HTML was initially defined as an application of SGML. Today the text and image formatting language is used by Web browsers to dynamically format Web pages.

   ☒ **B** is incorrect because Extensible Markup Language (XML) was developed after SGML. XML was developed as a specification to create various markup languages. From this specification more specific XML standards were created to be able to provide individual industries the functions they required. Individual industries have different needs in how they use markup languages. SGML was not a specification that was designed to allow the creation of individual and different markup languages.

   ☒ **C** is incorrect because LaTeX was written in the early 1980s as the successor to TeX. LaTeX is the markup language and document preparation system used with the TeX typesetting program. Academic scholars are the most common users of LaTeX. Together with TeX, LaTeX provides a high quality of typesetting.

7. Brian has been asked to work on the virtual directory of his company's new identity management system. Which of the following best describes a virtual directory?

   A. Meta-directory

   B. User attribute information stored in an HR database

   C. Virtual container for data from multiple sources

   D. A service that allows an administrator to configure and manage how identification takes place

☑ **C.** A network directory is a container for users and network resources. One directory does not contain (or know about) all of the users and resources within the enterprise, so a collection of directories must be used. A virtual directory gathers the necessary information used from sources scattered throughout the network and stores them in a central virtual directory (virtual container). This provides a unified view of all users' digital identity information throughout the enterprise. The virtual directory periodically synchronizes itself with all of the identity stores (individual network directories) to ensure the most up-to-date information is being used by all applications and identity management components within the enterprise.

☒ **A** is incorrect because whereas a virtual directory is similar to a meta-directory, the meta-directory works with one directory while a virtual directory works with multiple data sources. When an identity management component makes a call to a virtual directory, it has the capability to scan different directories throughout the enterprise, whereas a meta-directory only has the capability to scan the one directory it is associated with.

☒ **B** is incorrect because it best describes an identity store. A lot of information stored in an identity management directory is scattered throughout the enterprise. User attribute information (employee status, job description, department, and so on) is usually stored in the HR database; authentication information could be in a Kerberos server; role and group identification information might be in a SQL database; and resource-oriented authentication information can be stored in Active Directory on a domain controller. These are commonly referred to as identity stores and are located in different places on the network. Many identity management products use virtual directories to call upon the data in these identity stores.

☒ **D** is incorrect because it describes the directory service. The directory service allows an administrator to configure and manage how identification, authentication, authorization, and access control occur within the network.

It manages the objects within a directory by using namespaces and enforces the configured security policy by carrying out access control and identity management functions.

8. Emily is listening to network traffic and capturing passwords as they are sent to the authentication server. She plans to use the passwords as part of a future attack. What type of attack is this?

   A. Brute-force attack

   B. Dictionary attack

   C. Social engineering attack

   D. Replay attack

   ☑ **D.** A replay attack occurs when an intruder obtains and stores information, and later uses it to gain unauthorized access. In this case, Emily is using a technique called electronic monitoring (sniffing) to obtain passwords being sent over the wire to an authentication server. She can later use the passwords to gain access to network resources. Even if the passwords are encrypted, the retransmission of valid credentials can be sufficient to obtain access.

   ☒ **A** is incorrect because a brute-force attack is performed with tools that cycle through many possible character, number, and symbol combinations to uncover a password. One way to prevent a successful brute-force attack is to restrict the number of login attempts that can be performed on a system. An administrator can set operating parameters that allow a certain number of failed logon attempts to be accepted before a user is locked out; this is a type of clipping level.

   ☒ **B** is incorrect because a dictionary attack involves the automated comparison of the user's password to files of thousands of words until a match is found. Dictionary attacks are successful because users tend to choose passwords that are short, are single words, or are predictable variations of dictionary words.

   ☒ **C** is incorrect because in a social engineering attack the attacker falsely convinces an individual that she has the necessary authorization to access specific resources. Social engineering is carried out against people directly and is not considered a technical attack necessarily. The best defense against social engineering is user education. Password requirements, protection, and generation should be addressed in security-awareness programs so that users understand why they should protect their passwords, and how passwords can be stolen.

9. Which of the following correctly describes a federated identity and its role within identity management processes?

   A. A nonportable identity that can be used across business boundaries

B. A portable identity that can be used across business boundaries

C. An identity that can be used within intranet virtual directories and identity stores

D. An identity specified by domain names that can be used across business boundaries

☑ **B.** A federated identity is a portable identity, and its associated entitlements, that can be used across business boundaries. It allows a user to be authenticated across multiple IT systems and enterprises. Identity federation is based upon linking a user's otherwise distinct identities at two or more locations without the need to synchronize or consolidate directory information. Federated identity offers businesses and consumers a more convenient way of accessing distributed resources and is a key component of e-commerce.

☒ **A** is incorrect because a federated identity is portable. It could not be used across business boundaries if it was not portable—and that's the whole point of a federated identity. The world continually gets smaller as technology brings people and companies closer together. Many times, when we are interacting with just one Web site, we are actually interacting with several different companies—we just don't know it. The reason we don't know it is because these companies are sharing our identity and authentication information behind the scenes. This is done to improve ease of use for the user.

☒ **C** is incorrect because a federated identity is meant to be used across business boundaries—not within the organization. In other words, its use extends beyond the organization that owns the user data. Using federated identities, organizations with different technologies for directory services, security, and authentication can share applications, thereby allowing users to sign in to multiple applications with the same user ID, password, etc.

☒ **D** is incorrect because a federated identity is not specified by a domain name. A federated identity is a portable identity and its associated entitlements. It includes the username, password and other personal identification information used to sign in to an application.

10. Phishing and pharming are similar. Which of the following correctly describes the difference between phishing and pharming?

A. Personal information is collected from victims through legitimate-looking Web sites in phishing attacks, while personal information is collected from victims via e-mail in pharming attacks.

B. Phishing attacks point e-mail recipients to a form where victims input personal information, while pharming attacks use pop-up forms at legitimate Web sites to collect personal information from victims.

C. Victims are pointed to a fake Web site with a domain name that looks similar to a legitimate site's in a phishing attack, while victims are directed to a fake Web site as a result of a legitimate domain name being incorrectly translated by the DNS server in a pharming attack.

D. Phishing is a technical attack, while pharming is a type of social engineering.

☑ **C.** In both phishing and pharming, attackers can create Web sites that look very similar to legitimate sites in an effort to collect personal information from victims. In a phishing attack, attackers can provide URLs with domain names that look very similar to the legitimate site's address. For example, www.amazon.com might become www.amzaon.com. Or use a specially placed @ symbol. For example, www.msn.com@notmsn.com would actually take the victim to the Web site notmsn.com and provide the username of www.msn.com to this Web site. The username www.msn.com would not be a valid username for notmsn.com, so the victim would just be shown the home page of notmsn.com. Now, notmsn.com is a nefarious site created to look and feel just like www.msn.com. The victim feels he is at the legitimate site and logs in with his credentials. In a pharming attack, the victim is given a legitimate domain name, but that domain name is redirected to the attacker's Web site as a result of DNS poisoning. When the DNS server is poisoned to carry out a pharming attack, the records have been changed so that instead of sending the correct IP address for www.logicalsecurity.com, it sends the IP address of a legitimate looking, but fake Web site created by the attacker.

☒ **A** is incorrect because a pharming attack does commonly not involve the collection of information via e-mail. In fact, the benefit of a pharming attack to the attacker is that it can affect a large amount of victims without the need to send out e-mails. Like a phishing attack, a pharming attack involves a seemingly legitimate, yet fake, Web site. Victims are directed to the fake Web site because the host name is incorrectly resolved as a result of DNS poisoning.

☒ **B** is incorrect because both descriptions are true of phishing attacks. Pharming attacks do not use pop-up forms. However, some phishing attacks use pop-up forms when a victim is at a legitimate site. So if you were at your bank's actual Web site and a pop-up window appeared asking you for some sensitive information, this probably wouldn't worry you, since you were communicating with your actual bank's Web site. You may believe the window came from your bank's Web server, so you fill it out as instructed. Unfortunately, this pop-up window could be from another source entirely, and your data could be placed right in the attacker's hands, not your bank's.

☒ **D** is incorrect because both attacks are technical ways of carrying out social engineering. Phishing is a type of social engineering with the goal of obtaining personal information, credentials, credit card numbers, or financial data. The attackers lure, or fish, for sensitive data through various different methods, such as e-mail and pop-up forms. Pharming involves DNS poisoning. The attacker modifies the records in a DNS server so that it resolves a host name into an incorrect IP address. The victim's system sends a request to a poisoned DNS server, which points the victim to a different Web site. This different Web site looks and feels just like the requested Web site, so the user enters his username and password and may even be presented with Web pages that look legitimate.

11. Security countermeasures should be transparent to users and attackers. Which of the following does not describe transparency?

   A. User activities are monitored and tracked without negatively affecting system performance.

   B. User activities are monitored and tracked without the user knowing about the mechanism that is carrying this out.

   C. Users are allowed access in a manner that does not negatively affect business processes.

   D. Unauthorized access attempts are denied and logged without the intruder knowing about the mechanism that is carrying this out.

   ☑ A. Unfortunately, security components usually affect system performance in one fashion or another, although many times it is unnoticeable to the user. There is a possibility that if a system's performance is noticeably slow, this could be an indication that security countermeasures are in place. The reason that controls should be transparent is so that users and intruders do not know enough to be able to disable or bypass them. The controls should also not stand in the way of the company being able to carry out its necessary functions.

   ☒ B is incorrect because transparency is about activities being monitored and tracked without the user's knowledge of the mechanism that is doing the monitoring and the tracking. While it is a best practice to tell users if their computer use is being monitored, it is not necessary to tell them how they are being monitored. If users are aware of the mechanisms that monitor their activities, then they may attempt to disable or bypass them.

   ☒ C is incorrect because there must be a balance between security and usability. This means that users should be allowed access—where appropriate—without affecting business processes. They should have the means to get their job done.

   ☒ D is incorrect because you do not want intruders to know about the mechanisms in place to deny and log unauthorized access attempts. An intruder could use this knowledge to disable or bypass the mechanism and successfully gain unauthorized access to network resources.

12. What markup language allows for the sharing of application security policies to ensure that all applications are following the same security rules?

    A. XML

    B. SPML

    C. XACML

    D. GML

    ☑ **C.** Two or more companies can have a trust model set up to share identity, authorization, and authentication methods. This means that if Bill authenticates to his company's software, this software can pass the authentication parameters to its partner's software. This allows Bill to interact with the partner's software without having to authenticate twice. This can happen through eXtensible Access Control Markup Language (XACML), which allows two or more organizations to share application security policies based upon their trust model. XACML is a markup language and processing model that is implemented in XML. It declares access control policies and describes how to interpret them.

    ☒ **A** is incorrect because XML (Extensible Markup Language) is a method for electronically coding documents and representing data structures such as those in Web services. XML is not used to share security information. XML is an open standard that is more robust than its predecessor, HTML. In addition to serving as a markup language in and of itself, XML serves as the foundation for other more industry-specific XML standards. XML allows companies to use a markup language that meets their different needs while still being able to communicate with each other.

    ☒ **B** is incorrect because Service Provisioning Markup Language (SPML) is used by companies to exchange user, resource, and service provisioning information, not application security information. SPML is an XML-based framework developed by OASIS with the goal of allowing enterprise platforms (such as Web portals and application servers) to generate provisioning requests across multiple companies for the purpose of the secure and quick setup of Web services and applications.

    ☒ **D** is incorrect because Generalized Markup Language (GML) is a method created by IBM for formatting documents. It describes a document in terms of its parts (chapters, paragraphs, lists, etc.) and their relationship (heading levels). GML was a predecessor to Standard Generalized Markup Language (SGML) and Hypertext Markup Language (HTML).

13. The importance of protecting audit logs generated by computers and network devices is highlighted by the fact that it is required by many of today's regulations. Which of the following does not explain why audit logs should be protected?

    A. If not properly protected, these logs may not be admissible during a prosecution.

B. Audit logs contain sensitive data and should only be accessible to a certain subset of people.

C. Intruders may attempt to scrub the logs to hide their activities.

D. The format of the logs should be unknown and unavailable to the intruder.

☑ **D.** Auditing tools are technical controls that track activity within a network, on a network device, or on a specific computer. Even though auditing is not an activity that will deny an entity access to a network or computer, it will track activities so that a security administrator can understand the types of access that took place, identify a security breach, or warn the administrator of suspicious activity. This information can be used to point out weaknesses of other technical controls and help the administrator understand where changes must be made to preserve the necessary security level within the environment. Intruders can also use this information to exploit those weaknesses, so audit logs should be protected through permissions, rights, and integrity controls, as in hashing algorithms. However, the format of systems logs is commonly standardized with all like systems. Hiding log formats is not a usual countermeasure and is not a reason to protect audit log files.

☒ **A** is incorrect because due care must be taken to protect audit logs in order for them to be admissible in court. Audit trails can be used to provide alerts about any suspicious activities that can be investigated at a later time. In addition, they can be valuable in determining exactly how far an attack has gone and the extent of the damage that may have been caused. It is important to make sure a proper chain of custody is maintained to ensure any data collected can be properly and accurately represented in case it needs to be used for later events such as criminal proceedings or investigations.

☒ **B** is incorrect because only the administrator and security personnel should be able to view, modify, and delete audit trail information. No other individuals should be able to view this data, much less modify or delete it. The integrity of the data can be ensured with the use of digital signatures, message digest tools, and strong access controls. Its confidentiality can be protected with encryption and access controls, if necessary, and it can be stored on write-once media to prevent loss or modification of the data. Unauthorized access attempts to audit logs should be captured and reported.

☒ **C** is incorrect because the statement is true. If an intruder breaks into your house, he will do his best to cover his tracks by not leaving fingerprints or any other clues that can be used to tie him to the criminal activity. The same is true in computer fraud and illegal activity. The intruder will work to cover his tracks. Attackers often delete audit logs that hold this discriminating information. (Deleting specific incriminating data within audit logs is called scrubbing.) Deleting this information can cause the administrator to not be alerted or aware of the security breach, and can destroy valuable data. Therefore, audit logs should be protected by strict access control.

14. Harrison is evaluating access control products for his company. Which of the following is not a factor he needs to consider when choosing the products?

A. Classification level of data

B. Level of training that employees have received

C. Logical access controls provided by products

D. Legal and regulation issues

☑ **B.** When a company needs to decide upon the type of access control products they need, they should understand the company's legal requirements, the sensitivity of the data on their systems that need to be protected, and the types of technical controls used by the access control system. However, an access control system choice should not be based on the previous training the staff has received. Employees will need to be trained after the access control system's rollout, but training is the least important issue listed in this question.

☒ **A** is incorrect because it is important for a company to consider the classification level of data when choosing an access control product. Different security mechanisms can supply different degrees of availability, integrity, and confidentiality. The environment, the classification of data that is to be protected, and the security goals must be evaluated to ensure the proper security mechanisms are bought and put into place. Many corporations have wasted a lot of time and money not following these steps but instead buying the new "gee whiz" product that recently hit the market.

☒ **C** is incorrect because the company should consider the logical access controls that are necessary for its identification, authentication, authorization, and accountability requirements. Logical access controls are software components that enforce access control measures for systems, programs, processes, and information. The logical access controls can be embedded within operating systems, applications, add-on security packages, or database and telecommunication management systems.

☒ **D** is incorrect because legal and regulation issues should be considered when choosing and setting up an access control product. The company must ensure that due care is being taken to control access to data that may be sensitive and is protected under different laws and regulations. Such measures may protect the company from fines and other penalties should they experience a data breach.

15. There are several types of intrusion detection systems (IDSs). What type of IDS builds a profile of an environment's normal activities and assigns an anomaly score to packets based on the profile?

    A. State-based

    B. Statistical anomaly–based

    C. Misuse-detection system

    D. Protocol signature–based

    ☑ **B.** A statistical anomaly–based IDS is a behavioral-based system. Behavioral-based IDS products do not use predefined signatures but rather are put in a learning mode to build a profile of an environment's "normal" activities. This profile is built by continually sampling the environment's activities. The longer the IDS is put in a learning mode, in most instances, the more accurate a profile it will build and the better protection it will provide. After this profile is built, all future traffic and activities are compared to it. With the use of complex statistical algorithms, the IDS looks for anomalies in the network traffic or user activity. Each packet is given an anomaly score, which indicates its degree of irregularity. If the score is higher than the established threshold of "normal" behavior, then the preconfigured action will take place.

    ☒ **A** is incorrect because a state-based IDS has rules that outline which state transition sequences should sound an alarm. The initial state is the state prior to the execution of an attack, and the compromised state is the state after successful penetration. The activity that takes place between the initial and compromised state is what the state-based IDS looks for, and it sends an alert if any of the state-transition sequences match its preconfigured rules.

    ☒ **C** is incorrect because a misuse-detection system is simply another name for a signature-based IDS, which compares network or system activity to signatures or models of how attacks are carried out. Any action that is not recognized as an attack is considered acceptable. Signature-based IDS are the most popular IDS products today, and their effectiveness depends upon regularly updating the software with new signatures, as with antivirus software. This type of IDS is weak against new types of attacks because it can only recognize those that have been previously identified and have had signatures written for them.

    ☒ **D** is incorrect because a protocol signature–based IDS is not a formal IDS. This is a distracter answer.

16. A rule-based IDS takes a different approach than a signature-based or anomaly-based system. Which of the following is characteristic of a rule-based IDS?

    A. Uses IF/THEN programming within expert systems

    B. Identifies protocols used outside of their common bounds

    C. Compares patterns to several activities at once

    D. Can detect new attacks

    ☑ **A.** Rule-based intrusion detection is commonly associated with the use of an expert system. An expert system is made up of a knowledge base, an inference engine, and rule-based programming. Knowledge is represented as rules, and the data to be analyzed is referred to as facts. The knowledge of the system is written in rule-based programming (IF situation THEN action). These rules are applied to the facts, the data that comes in from a sensor, or a system that is being monitored. For example, an IDS pulls data from a system's audit log and stores it temporarily in its fact database. Then, the preconfigured rules are applied to this data to indicate whether anything suspicious is taking place. In our scenario, the rule states "IF a root user creates File1 AND creates File2 SUCH THAT they are in the same directory THEN there is a call to Administrative Tool TRIGGER send alert." This rule has been defined such that if a root user creates two files in the same directory and then makes a call to a specific administrative tool, an alert should be sent.

    ☒ **B** is incorrect because a protocol anomaly–based IDS identifies protocols used outside of their common bounds. The IDS has specific knowledge of each protocol that it will monitor. A protocol anomaly pertains to the format and behavior of a protocol. If a protocol is formatted differently or is demonstrating abnormal behavior, then the IDS triggers an alarm.

    ☒ **C** is incorrect because a stateful matching IDS compares patterns to several activities at once. It is a type of signature-based IDS, meaning that it does pattern matching, similar to antivirus software. State is a snapshot of an operating system's values in volatile, semipermanent, and permanent memory locations. In a state-based IDS, the initial state is the state prior to the execution of an attack, and the compromised state is the state after successful penetration. The IDS has rules that outline which state transition sequences should sound an alarm.

    ☒ **D** is incorrect because a rule-based IDS cannot detect new attacks. An anomaly-based IDS can detect new attacks because it doesn't rely on predetermined rules or signatures, which are only available after security researchers have had time to study an attack. Instead, an anomaly-based IDS learns the "normal" activities of an environment and triggers an alarm when it detects activity that differs from the norm. The three types of anomaly-based IDS are statistical, protocol, and traffic. They are also called behavior- or heuristic-based.

17. Sam plans to establish mobile phone service using the personal information he has stolen from his former boss. What type of identity theft is this?

   A. Phishing

   B. True name

   C. Pharming

   D. Account takeover

   ☑ **B.** Identity theft refers to a situation where someone obtains key pieces of personal information such as a driver's license number, bank account number, credentials, or Social Security number, and then uses that information to impersonate someone else. Typically, identity thieves will use the personal information to obtain credit, merchandise, or services in the name of the victim. This can result in such things as ruining the victim's credit rating, generating false criminal records, and issuing arrest warrants for the wrong individuals. Identity theft is categorized in two ways: true name and account takeover. True name identity theft means the thief uses personal information to open new accounts. The thief might open a new credit card account, establish mobile phone service like Sam, or open a new checking account in order to obtain blank checks.

   ☒ **A** is incorrect because phishing is a type of social engineering attack with the goal of obtaining personal information, credentials, credit card number, or financial data. The attackers lure, or fish, for sensitive data through various methods. While the goal of phishing is to dupe a victim into handing over his personal information, the goal of identity theft is to use that personal information for personal or financial gain. An attacker can employ a phishing attack as a means to carry out identity theft.

   ☒ **C** is incorrect because pharming is a technical attack that is carried out to trick victims into sending their personal information to an attacker via an illegitimate Web site. The victim types in a Web address, such as www .nicebank.com, into his browser. The victim's system sends a request to a poisoned DNS server, which points the victim to a Web site that is under the attacker's control. Because the site looks and feels like the requested Web site, the user enters his personal information, which the attacker can then use to commit identity theft.

   ☒ **D** is incorrect because account takeover identity theft means the imposter uses personal information to gain access to the person's existing accounts, rather than opening a new account. Typically, the thief will change the mailing address on an account and run up a huge bill before the person, whose identity has been stolen, realizes there is a problem. The Internet has made it easier for an identity thief to use the information they've stolen because transactions can be made without any personal interaction.

18. Of the following, what is the primary item that a capability list is based upon?

    A. A subject

    B. An object

    C. A product

    D. An application

☑ **A.** A capability table specifies the access rights a certain subject possesses pertaining to specific objects. A capability list (also referred to as a capability table) is different from an access control list (ACL) because the subject is bound to the capability table, whereas the object is bound to the ACL. A capability can be in the form of a token, ticket, or key. When a subject presents a capability component, the operating system (or application) will review the access rights and operations outlined in the capability component and allow the subject to carry out just those functions. A capability component is a data structure that contains a unique object identifier and the access rights the subject has to that object. The object may be a file, array, memory segment, or port.

☒ **B** is incorrect because an object is bound to an access control list (ACL), not a capability component. ACLs are used in several operating systems, applications, and router configurations. They are lists of subjects that are authorized to access a specific object, and they define what level of authorization is granted. Authorization can be specified to an individual or group. ACLs map values from the access control matrix to the object. Whereas a capability corresponds to a row in the access control matrix, the ACL corresponds to a column of the matrix.

☒ **C** is incorrect because a product can be an object or subject. If a user attempts to access a product (such as a program), the user is the subject and the product is the object. If a product attempts to access a database, the product is the subject and the database is the object. While a product could be a subject in a capability list for example, the best answer is A. A capability list indicates what objects a subject can access and the operations that can be carried out on those objects.

☒ **D** is incorrect because this is similar to answer C. If a user attempts to access an application, the user is the subject and the application is the object. If an application attempts to access a database, the application is the subject and the database is the object. While an application could be a subject in a capability list for example, the best answer is A. A capability list indicates what objects a subject can access and the operations that can be carried out on those objects.

19. Alex works for a chemical distributor that assigns employees tasks that separate their duties and routinely rotates job assignments. Which of the following best describes the differences between these countermeasures?

A. They are the same thing with different titles.

B. They are administrative controls that enforce access control and protect the company's resources.

C. Separation of duties ensures that one person cannot perform a high-risk task alone, and job rotation can uncover fraud because more than one person knows the tasks of a position.

D. Job rotation ensures that one person cannot perform a high-risk task alone, and separation of duties can uncover fraud because more than one person knows the tasks of a position.

☑ **C.** Separation of duties and job rotation are two security controls commonly used within companies to prevent and detect fraud. Separation of duties is put into place to ensure that one entity cannot carry out a task that could be damaging or risky to the company. It requires two or more people to come together to do their individual tasks to accomplish the overall task. Rotation of duties helps ensure that one person does not stay in one position for a long period of time because he may end up having too much control over a segment of the business. Such total control could result in fraud, data modification, and misuse of resources.

☒ **A** is incorrect because separation of duties and job rotation are two different concepts. They are, however, both put into place to reduce the possibilities of fraud, sabotage, misuse of information, theft, and other security compromises. Separation of duties makes sure that one individual cannot complete a critical task by herself. When a submarine captain needs to launch a nuclear torpedo, the launch usually requires three codes to be entered into the launching mechanism by three different senior crewmembers. This is an example of separation of duties. Job rotation ensures that no single person ends up having too much control over a segment of the business as a result of staying in one position for a long period of time.

☒ **B** is incorrect because answer C is a more detailed and definitive answer. Answer C describes both of these controls properly and their differences. Both of these controls are administrative in nature and are put into place to control access to company assets, but the CISSP exam requires the best answer out of four.

☒ **D** is incorrect because the description is backward. Separation of duties, not job rotation, ensures that one person cannot perform a high-risk task alone. Job rotation moves individuals in and out of an specific role to ensure that fraudulent activities are not taking place.

20. What type of markup language allows company interfaces to pass service requests and the receiving company provision access to these services?

A. XML

B. SPML

C. SGML

D. HTML

☑ **B.** Service Provisioning Markup Language (SPML) is a markup language built on the XML framework that exchanges information on which users should get access to what resources and services. So let's say that an automobile company and tire company only allow Inventory Managers within the automobile company to order tires. If Bob logs in to the automobile company's inventory software and orders 40 tires, how does the tire company know that this request is coming from an authorized vendor and user with the Inventory Managers group? The automobile company's software can pass user and group identity information to the tire company's software. The tire company uses this identity information to make an authorization decision that then allows Bob's request for 40 tires to be filled. Since both the sending and receiving companies are following one standard (XML), this type of interoperability can take place.

☒ **A** is incorrect because it is not the best answer to the question. Service Provisioning Markup Language (SPML)—which is based on XML—allows company interfaces to pass service requests and the receiving company to provision access to these services. This interoperability is made possible because the companies are both using Extensible Markup Language (XML). XML is a set of rules for electronically encoding documents and Web-based communication. It is also used to encode arbitrary data structures as in Web services. It allows groups or companies to create information formats, like SPML, that enable a consistent means of sharing data.

☒ **C** is incorrect because Standard Generalized Markup Language (SGML) was one of the first markup languages developed. It does not provide user access or provisioning functionality. SGML was a standard that defines generalized markup tags for documents. It is a successor to Generalized Markup Language and came long before XML or SPML.

☒ **D** is incorrect because Hypertext Markup Language (HTML) was developed to annotate Web pages. HTML is a precursor to XML and SGML. HTML provides a means of denoting structural semantics for text and other elements found on a Web page. It can be used to embed images and objects, and create interactive forms. However, it cannot allow company interfaces to pass service requests and the receiving company to provision access to these services.

21. There are several different types of centralized access control protocols. Which of the following is illustrated in the graphic that follows?

   A. Diameter

   B. Watchdog

   C. RADIUS

   D. TACACS+

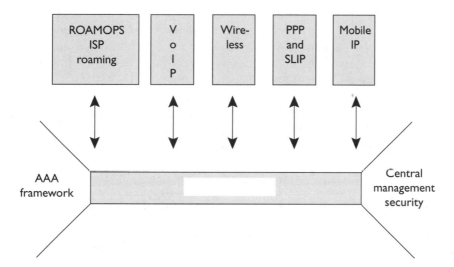

☑ **A.** Diameter is an authentication, authorization, and auditing (AAA) protocol that provides the same type of functionality as RADIUS and TACACS+ but also provides more flexibility and capabilities to meet the new demands of today's complex and diverse networks. At one time, all remote communication took place over PPP and SLIP connections and users authenticated themselves through PAP or CHAP. Technology has become much more complicated and there are more devices and protocols to choose from than ever before. The Diameter protocol allows wireless devices, smart phones, and other devices to be able to authenticate themselves to networks using roaming protocols, Mobile IP, Ethernet over PPP, Voice over IP (VoIP), and others.

☒ **B** is incorrect because Watchdog timers are commonly used to detect software faults, such as a process ending abnormally or hanging. The Watchdog functionality sends out a type of "heartbeat" packet to determine whether a service is responding. If it is not, the process can be terminated or reset. These packets help prevent against software deadlocks, infinite loops, and process prioritization problems. This functionality can be used in AAA protocols to determine whether packets need to be re-sent and whether connections experiencing problems should be closed and reopened, but it is not an access control protocol itself.

☒ C is incorrect because Remote Authentication Dial-In User Service (RADIUS) is a network protocol and provides client/server authentication, authorization, and audit for remote users. A network may have access servers, DSL, ISDN, or a T1 line dedicated for remote users to communicate through. The access server requests the remote user's logon credentials and passes them back to a RADIUS server, which houses the usernames and password values. The remote user is a client to the access server, and the access server is a client to the RADIUS server.

☒ D is incorrect because TACACS+ provides basically the same functionality as RADIUS. The RADIUS protocol combines the authentication and authorization functionality. TACACS+ uses a true authentication, authorization, accounting, and audit (AAA) architecture, which separates each function out. This gives a network administrator more flexibility in how remote users are authenticated. Neither TACACS+ or RADIUS can carry out these services for devices that need to communicate over VoIP, mobile IP, or other types of the similar types of protocols.

22. An access control matrix is used in many operating systems and applications to control access between subjects and objects. What is the column in this type of matrix referred to?

Access Control Matrix

Subject	File1	File2	File3	File4
Larry	Read	Read, Write	Read	Read, Write
Curly	Full Control	No Access	Full Control	Read
Mo	Read, Write	Full Control	Read	Full Control
Bob	Full Control	Full Control	No Access	No Access

A. Capability table

B. Constrained interface

C. Role-based value

D. ACL

☑ **D.** Access control lists (ACLs) map values from the access control matrix to the object. Whereas a capability corresponds to a row in the access control matrix, the ACL corresponds to a column of the matrix. ACLs are used in several operating systems, applications, and router configurations. They are lists of subjects that are authorized to access specific objects, and they define what level of authorization is granted. Authorization can be specified to an individual or group. So the ACL is bound to an object and indicates what subjects can access it and a capability table is bound to a subject and indicates what objects that subject can access.

☒ **A** is incorrect because a capability can be in the form of a token, ticket, or key and is a row within an access control matrix. When a subject presents a capability component, the operating system (or application) will review the access rights and operations outlined in the capability component and allow the subject to carry out just those functions. A capability component is a data structure that contains a unique object identifier and the access rights the subject has to that object. The object may be a file, array, memory segment, or port. Each user, process, and application in a capability system has a list of capabilities it can carry out.

☒ **B** is incorrect because constrained user interfaces restrict users' access abilities by not allowing them to request certain functions or information, or to have access to specific system resources. Three major types of restricted interfaces exist: menus and shells, database views, and physically constrained interfaces. When menu and shell restrictions are used, the options users are given are the commands they can execute. For example, if an administrator wants users to be able to execute only one program, that program would be the only choice available on the menu. If restricted shells were used, the shell would contain only the commands the administrator wants the users to be able to execute.

☒ **C** is incorrect because a role-based access control (RBAC) model, also called nondiscretionary access control, uses a centrally administered set of controls to determine how subjects and objects interact. This type of model lets access to resources be based on the role the user holds within the company. It is referred to as nondiscretionary because assigning a user to a role is unavoidably imposed. This means that if you are assigned only to the Contractor role in a company, there is nothing you can do about it. You don't have the discretion to determine what role you will be assigned.

23. What technology within identity management is illustrated in the graphic that follows?

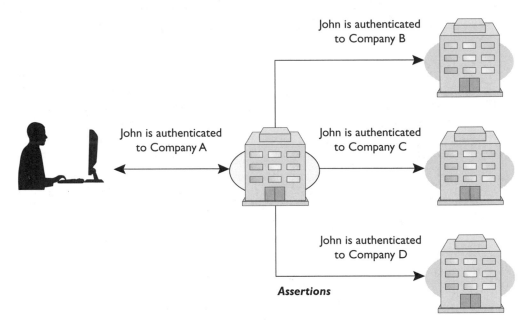

John is authenticated to Company B

John is authenticated to Company A

John is authenticated to Company C

John is authenticated to Company D

Assertions

A. User provisioning

B. Federated identity

C. Directories

D. Web access management

☑ **B.** A federated identity is a portable identity, and its associated entitlements, that can be used across business boundaries. It allows a user to be authenticated across multiple IT systems and enterprises. Identity federation is based upon linking a user's otherwise distinct identities at two or more locations without the need to synchronize or consolidate directory information. Federated identity offers businesses and consumers a more convenient way of accessing distributed resources and is a key component of e-commerce.

☒ **A** is incorrect because user provisioning refers to the creation, maintenance, and deactivation of user objects and attributes as they exist in one or more systems, directories, or applications, in response to business processes. User provisioning software may include one or more of the following components: change propagation, self-service workflow, consolidated user administration, delegated user administration, and federated change control. User objects may represent employees, contractors, vendors, partners, customers, or other recipients of a service. Services may include electronic mail, access to a database, access to a file server or mainframe, and so on. User provisioning can be a function with federation identification, but this is not what the graphic illustrates.

☒ **C** is incorrect because while most enterprises have some type of directory that contains information pertaining to the company's network resources and users, they do not commonly spread across different businesses. Most directories follow a hierarchical database format, based on the X.500 standard, and a type of protocol, as in Lightweight Directory Access Protocol (LDAP), that allows subjects and applications to interact with the directory. Applications can request information about a particular user by making an LDAP request to the directory, and users can request information about a specific resource by using a similar request. While directories can work within a federated framework, this is not what the graphic shows.

☒ **D** is incorrect because Web access management (WAM) software controls what users can access when using a Web browser to interact with Web-based enterprise assets. This type of technology is continually becoming more robust and experiencing increased deployment. This is because of the increased use of e-commerce, online banking, content providing, Web services, and more. More complexity comes in with all the different ways a user can authenticate (password, digital certificate, token, and others), the resources and services that may be available to the user (transfer funds, purchase product, update profile, and so forth), and the necessary infrastructure components. The infrastructure is usually made up of a Web server farm (many servers), a directory that contains the users' accounts and attributes, a database, a couple of firewalls, and some routers, all laid out in a tiered architecture.

24. There are several different types of single sign-on protocols and technologies in use today. What type of technology is illustrated in the graphic that follows?

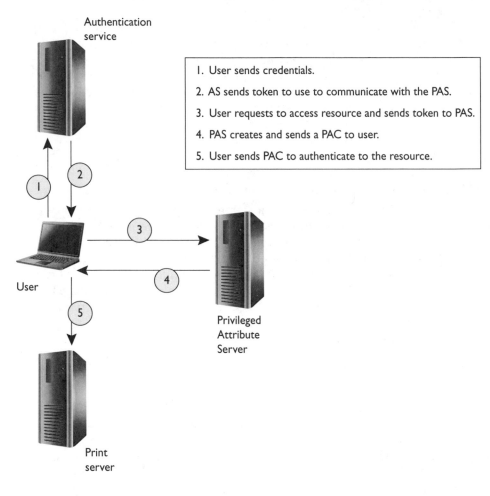

Authentication service

1. User sends credentials.
2. AS sends token to use to communicate with the PAS.
3. User requests to access resource and sends token to PAS.
4. PAS creates and sends a PAC to user.
5. User sends PAC to authenticate to the resource.

User

Privileged Attribute Server

Print server

A. Kerberos

B. Discretionary access control

C. SESAME

D. Mandatory access control

☑ C. The Secure European System for Applications in a Multivendor Environment (SESAME) project has been a single sign-on technology developed to extend Kerberos functionality and improve upon its weaknesses. SESAME uses symmetric and asymmetric cryptographic techniques to authenticate subjects to network resources. Kerberos uses tickets to authenticate subjects to objects, whereas SESAME uses Privileged Attribute Certificates (PACs), which contain the subject's identity, access capabilities for the object, access time period, and lifetime of the PAC. The PAC is digitally signed so that the object can validate it came from the trusted authentication server, which is referred to as the Privileged Attribute Server (PAS). The PAS holds a similar role to that of the Key Distribution Center (KDC) within Kerberos. After a user successfully authenticates to the authentication service (AS), he is presented with a token to give to the PAS. The PAS then creates a PAC for the user to present to the resource he is trying to access.

☒ **A** is incorrect because Kerberos is an authentication protocol and is based on symmetric key cryptography. Kerberos is an example of a single sign-on system for distributed environments (as is SESAME) but is the de facto standard for heterogeneous networks today. Kerberos incorporates a wide range of security capabilities, which gives companies much more flexibility and scalability when they need to provide an encompassing security architecture. It has four elements necessary for enterprise access control: scalability, transparency, reliability, and security. The differences between these technologies are described more in the previous answer. While SESAME and Kerberos are close in the functionality they present, SESAME is the technology shown in the graphic.

☒ **B** is incorrect because discretionary access control (DAC) is an access control model that is built right into an operating system or application, not something that works as a single sign-on technology. A system that uses DAC enables the owner of the resource to specify which subjects can access specific resources. This model is called discretionary because the control of access is based on the discretion of the owner. Many times department managers, or business unit managers, are the owners of the data within their specific department. Being the owner, they can specify who should have access and who should not. In a DAC model, access is restricted based on the authorization granted to the users. This means users are allowed to specify what type of access can occur to the objects they own. The most common implementation of DAC is through ACLs, which are dictated and set by the owners and enforced by the operating system. This can make a user's ability to access information dynamic versus the more static role of mandatory access control (MAC).

☒ **D** is incorrect because mandatory access control (MAC) is an access control model that is built right into an operating system or application, not something that works as a single sign-on technology. In a MAC model, users and data owners do not have as much freedom to determine who can access files. The operating system makes the final decision and can override the users' wishes. This model is much more structured and strict and is based on a security label system. Users are given a security clearance (secret, top secret, confidential, and so on), and data is classified in the same way. The clearance and classification data are stored in the security labels, which are bound to the specific subjects and objects. When the system makes a decision about fulfilling a request to access an object, it is based on the clearance of the subject, the classification of the object, and the security policy of the system. The rules for how subjects access objects are made by the security officer, configured by the administrator, enforced by the operating system, and supported by security technologies.

25. There are different ways that specific technologies can create one-time passwords for authentication purposes. What type of technology is illustrated in the graphic that follows?

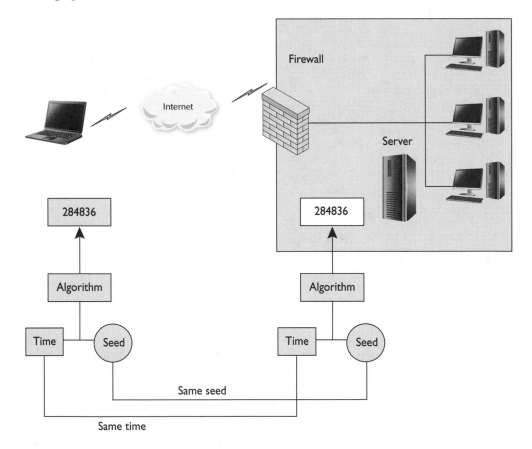

A. Counter synchronous token

B. Asynchronous token

C. Mandatory token

D. Synchronous token

☑ **D.** A synchronous token device synchronizes with the authentication service by using time or a counter as the core piece of the authentication process. If the synchronization is time-based, as shown in this graphic, the token device and the authentication service must hold the same time within their internal clocks. The time value on the token device and a secret key are used to create the one-time password, which is displayed to the user. The user enters this value and a user ID into the computer, which then passes them to the server running the authentication service. The authentication service decrypts this value and compares it to the value it expected. If the two match, the user is authenticated and allowed to use the computer and resources.

☒ **A** is incorrect because if the token device and authentication service use counter-synchronization, it is not based on time as shown in the graphic. When using a counter-synchronization token device, the user will need to initiate the creation of the one-time password by pushing a button on the token device. This causes the token device and the authentication service to advance to the next authentication value. This value and a base secret are hashed and displayed to the user. The user enters this resulting value along with a user ID to be authenticated. In either time- or counter-based synchronization, the token device and authentication service must share the same secret base key used for encryption and decryption.

☒ **B** is incorrect because a token device using an asynchronous token–generating method employs a challenge/response scheme to authenticate the user. This technology does not use synchronization but instead uses discrete steps in its authentication process. In this situation, the authentication server sends the user a challenge, a random value also called a nonce. The user enters this random value into the token device, which encrypts it and returns a value the user uses as a one-time password. The user sends this value, along with a username, to the authentication server. If the authentication server can decrypt the value and it is the same challenge value sent earlier, the user is authenticated.

☒ **C** is incorrect because there is no such thing as a mandatory token. This is a distracter answer.

26. Sally is carrying out a software analysis on her company's proprietary application. She has found out that it is possible for an attacker to force an authorization step to take place before the authentication step is completed successfully. What type of issue would allow for this type of compromise to take place?

A. Backdoor

B. Maintenance hook

C. Race condition

D. Data validation error

☑ **C.** A race condition is when processes carry out their tasks on a shared resource and there is a potential that the sequence is carried out in the wrong order. A race condition is possible when two or more processes use a shared resource, as in data within a variable. It is important that the processes carry out their functionality in the correct sequence. If process 2 carried out its task on the data before process 1, the result will be much different than if process 1 carried out its tasks on the data before process 2. If authentication and authorization steps are split into two functions, there is a possibility an attacker could use a race condition to force the authorization step to be completed before the authentication step.

☒ **A** is incorrect because a backdoor is a service that is available and "listening" on a specific port. Backdoors are implemented by attackers so that they can gain easy access to compromised systems without having to authenticate as a regular system user.

☒ **B** is incorrect because a maintenance hook is specific software code that allows easy and unauthorized access to sensitive components of a software product. Software programmers commonly use maintenance hooks to allow them to get quick access to a product's code so that fixes can be carried out, but this is dangerous. If an attacker uncovered this type of access, compromises could take place that would most likely not require authentication and would probably not be logged.

☒ **D** is incorrect because data validation errors do not commonly allow an attacker to manipulate process execution sequences. An attacker would enter invalid data through a specific interface, with the goals of having their code execute on the victim machine or carry out a buffer overflow.

27. Which of the following best describes how SAML, SOAP, and HTTP commonly work together in an environment that provides Web services?

A. Security attributes are put into SAML format. Web service request and authentication data are encrypted in a SOAP message. Message is transmitted in an HTTP connection.

B. Security attributes are put into SAML format. Web service request and authentication data are encapsulated in a SOAP message. Message is transmitted in an HTTP connection over TLS.

C. Authentication data are put into SAML format. Web service request and authentication data are encapsulated in a SOAP message. Message is transmitted in an HTTP connection.

D. Authentication data are put into SAML format. HTTP request and authentication data are encapsulated in a SOAP message. Message is transmitted in an HTTP connection.

☑ **C.** As an example, when you log in to your company's portal and double-click a link (e.g., Salesforce), your company's portal will take this request and your authentication data and package them up in an SAML format and encapsulate that data into a SOAP message. This message would be transmitted over an HTTP connection to the Salesforce vendor site, and once you are authenticated you can interact with the vendor software. SAML packages up authentication data, SOAP packages up Web service requests and SAML data, and the request is transmitted over an HTTP connection.

☒ **A** is incorrect because Security Assertion Markup Language (SAML) is an XML-based open standard for exchanging authentication and authorization data between security domains, that is, between an identity provider (a producer of assertions) and a service provider (a consumer of assertions). So authentication data are used with SAML, not security attributes. Also, SOAP encapsulates messages, it does not encrypt them.

☒ **B** is incorrect because authentication data are used with SAML and the transmission does not take place over a TLS connection by default. The transmission can take place over SSL or TLS, but this was not what was outlined in the question.

☒ **D** is incorrect because SOAP encapsulates Web service requests and data, not HTTP. After SOAP encapsulates Web service data, they are then encapsulated with HTTP for transmission purposes.

28. Tom works at a large retail company that recently deployed radio-frequency identification (RFID) to better manage its inventory processes. Employees use scanners to gather product-related information instead of manually looking up product data. Tom has found out that malicious customers have carried out attacks on the RFID technology to reduce the amount they pay on store items. Which of the following is the most likely reason for the existence of this type of vulnerability?

    A. The company's security team does not understand how to secure this type of technology.

B. The cost of integrating security within RFID is cost prohibitive.

C. The technology has low processing capabilities, and encryption is very processor-intensive.

D. RFID is a new and emerging technology, and the industry does not currently have ways to secure it.

☑ **C.** A common security issue with RFID is that the data can be captured as it moves from the tag to the reader and modified. While encryption can be integrated as a countermeasure, it is not common because RFID is a technology that has low processing capabilities and encryption is very processor-intensive.

☒ **A** is incorrect because it is not necessarily the best answer here. The company in the question may understand RFID and its common security issues, but security usually has to be integrated within the RFID technology. This means the vendor of the RFID product would have to integrate security into the product, and the available security solutions are commonly limited because RFID tags and readers do not usually have the necessary processing power to carry out the necessary cryptographic functions.

☒ **B** is incorrect because the cost of integrating security into RFID products may or may not be a factor. It usually comes down to the limitation of the technology itself, not necessarily the costs involved.

☒ **D** is incorrect because it is not the best answer here. RFID has been around for many years and many in the industry understand how it works and its security issues. Integrating security into a technology with so many limitations demands real needs and motivation. In most situations the data that are being transferred through RFID are not overly sensitive, so there has not been a true perceived need to integrate security into it. As RFID evolves it will most likely be more equipped to handle security countermeasures, but the industry has not fully gotten to this place yet.

29. Tanya is the security administrator for a large distributed retail company. The company's network has many different network devices and software appliances that generate logs and audit data. Tanya and her staff have become overwhelmed with trying to review all of the log files when attempting to identify if anything suspicious is taking place within the network. Which of the following is the best solution for this company to implement?

A. Security information and event management

B. Event correlation tools

C. Intrusion detection systems

D. Security event correlation management tools

☑ **A.** Today, many organizations are implementing security event management (SEM) systems, also called security information and event management (SIEM) systems. These products gather logs from various devices (servers, firewalls, routers, etc.) and attempt to correlate the log data and provide analysis capabilities. Companies also have different types of solutions on a network (IDS, IPS, antimalware, proxies, etc.) collecting logs in various proprietary formats, which require centralization, standardization, and normalization. Log formats are different per product type and vendor; thus, SIEM puts them into a standardized format for useful reporting.

☒ **B** is incorrect because answer A provides a more accurate portrayal of the needed solution. Security event management and security information and event management tools zero in on malicious events and provide a centralized management capability. The logs are commonly aggregated onto one system, and the SIEM software "translates" the logs into a standardized format. The standardization allows for the log data to be analyzed and reports generated.

☒ **C** is incorrect because an intrusion detection system is a product that identifies malicious activities and carries out notification activities. While these types of products may aggregate logs for analysis, they do not have the capability of standardizing log formats from different product types.

☒ **D** is incorrect because it is not the best answer here. An argument can be made that security event correlation management tools is what the correct answer "Security information and event management" is carrying out, but on the exam you will be required to pick the *best* answer. Security information and event management (SIEM) is the actual term the industry uses for products that provide this type of functionality.

30. Sarah and her security team have carried out many vulnerability tests over the years to locate the weaknesses and vulnerabilities within the systems on the network. The CISO has asked her to oversee the development of a threat model for the network. Which of the following best describes what this model is and what it would be used for?

    A. A threat model can help to assess the probability, the potential harm, and the priority of attacks, and thus help to minimize or eradicate the threats.

    B. A threat model combines the output of the various vulnerability tests and the penetration tests carried out to understand the security posture of the network as a whole.

    C. A threat model is a risk-based model that is used to calculate the probabilities of the various risks identified during the vulnerability tests.

    D. A threat model is used in software development practices to uncover programming errors.

☑ **A.** Threat modeling is a structured approach to identifying potential threats that could exploit vulnerabilities. A threat modeling approach looks at who would most likely want to attack an organization and how could they successfully do this. A threat model can help to assess the probability, the potential harm, and the priority of attacks, and thus help to minimize or eradicate the threats. Threat modeling is a process of identifying the threats that could negatively affect an asset and the attack vectors they would use to achieve their goals.

☒ **B** is incorrect because a threat model is very different from vulnerability and penetration tests. These types of tests are carried out to look for and at specific items in a very focused manner. A threat model is a conceptual construct that is developed to understand a system or network at an abstraction level. A threat model is used as a tool to think through all possible attack vectors, while these tests are carried out to detect if specific vulnerabilities exist to allow certain attacks to take place.

☒ **C** is incorrect because a threat model is not used for calculations. Quantitative risk analysis procedures are commonly carried out to calculate the probability of identified vulnerabilities turning into true risks. These procedures can be carried out after a threat model is developed, but they are not one and the same.

☒ **D** is incorrect because while a threat model can be used in software development, it is not restricted to just this portion of the industry. It is important to be able to understand all types of threats—software, physical, personnel, etc. A threat model is a high-level construct that can be used to understand different types of threats for different assets. A threat model would not necessarily be used to identify programming errors. The model is used to understand potential threats against an asset.

Security Architecture and Design

This domain includes questions from the following topics:

- System architecture
- Computer hardware architecture
- Operating system architecture
- System security architecture
- Trusted computing base and security mechanisms
- Information security software models
- Assurance evaluation criteria and ratings
- Certification and accreditation processes

As the complexity of computer systems increases, so, too, does security. Architectures, frameworks, and models have been developed to incorporate security and protection mechanisms in systems and hardware. In addition, system and hardware manufacturers seek evaluation, certification, and accreditation to assure buyers that their products are secure. As a CISSP, you need to understand these architectures and models as a foundation for the attacks that are committed against them and also how to protect them. Knowledge of assurance evaluation criteria and ratings, and certification and accreditation processes will help you be an educated buyer of enterprise systems and hardware.

1. Lacy's manager has tasked her with researching an intrusion detection system for a new dispatching center. Lacy identifies the top five products and compares their ratings. Which of the following are the evaluation criteria most in use today for these types of purposes?

   A. ITSEC

   B. Common Criteria

   C. Red Book

   D. Orange Book

2. Certain types of attacks have been made more potent by which of the following advances to microprocessor technology?

   A. Increased circuits, cache memory, and multiprogramming

   B. Dual mode computation

   C. Direct memory access I/O

   D. Increases in processing power

3. CPUs and operating systems can work in two main types of multitasking modes. What controls access and the use of system resources in preemptive multitasking mode?

   A. The user and application

   B. The program that is loaded into memory

   C. The operating system

   D. The CPU and user

4. Virtual storage combines RAM and secondary storage for system memory. Which of the following is a security concern pertaining to virtual storage?

   A. More than one process uses the same resource.

   B. It allows cookies to remain persistent in memory.

   C. It allows for side-channel attacks to take place.

   D. Two processes can carry out a denial-of-service.

5. Which of the following is a common association of the Clark-Wilson access model?

   A. Chinese Wall

   B. Access tuple

   C. Read up and write down rule

   D. Subject and application binding

6. Which of the following correctly describes the relationship between the reference monitor and the security kernel?

   A. The security kernel implements and enforces the reference monitor.

   B. The reference monitor is the core of the trusted computing base, which is made up of the security kernel.

   C. The reference monitor implements and enforces the security kernel.

   D. The security kernel, aka abstract machine, implements the reference monitor concept.

7. The trusted computing base (TCB) ensures security within a system when a process in one domain must access another domain in order to retrieve sensitive information. What function does the TCB initiate to ensure that this is done in a secure manner?

   A. I/O operational execution

   B. Process deactivation

   C. Execution domain switching

   D. Virtual memory to real memory mapping

8. The Zachman Architecture Framework is often used to set up an enterprise security architecture. Which of the following does not correctly describe the Zachman Framework?

   A. A two-dimensional model that uses communication interrogatives intersecting with different levels

   B. A security-oriented model that gives instructions in a modular fashion

   C. Used to build a robust enterprise architecture versus a technical security architecture

   D. Uses six perspectives to describe a holistic information infrastructure

9. John has been told to report to the board of directors with a vendor-neutral enterprise architecture framework that will help the company reduce fragmentation that results from the misalignment of IT and business processes. Which of the following frameworks should he suggest?

   A. DoDAF

   B. CMMI

   C. ISO/IEC 42010

   D. TOGAF

10. Protection profiles used in the Common Criteria evaluation process contain five elements. Which of the following establishes the type and intensity of the evaluation?

    A. Descriptive elements

    B. Evaluation assurance requirements

C. Evaluation assurance level

D. Security target

11. Which of the following best defines a virtual machine?

   A. A virtual instance of an operating system

   B. A piece of hardware that runs multiple operating system environments simultaneously

   C. A physical environment for multiple guests

   D. An environment that can be fully utilized while running legacy applications

12. Bethany is working on a mandatory access control (MAC) system. She has been working on a file that was classified as Secret. She can no longer access this file because it has been reclassified as Top Secret. She deduces that the project she was working on has just increased in confidentiality and she now knows more about this project than her clearance and need-to-know allows. Which of the following refers to a concept that attempts to prevent this type of scenario from occurring?

   A. Covert storage channel

   B. Inference attack

   C. Noninterference

   D. Aggregation

13. Virtualization offers many benefits. Which of the following incorrectly describes virtualization?

   A. Virtualization simplifies operating system patching.

   B. Virtualization can be used to build a secure computing platform.

   C. Virtualization can provide fault and error containment.

   D. Virtual machines offer powerful debugging capabilities.

14. Which security architecture model defines how to securely develop access rights between subjects and objects?

   A. Brewer-Nash

   B. Clark-Wilson

   C. Graham-Denning

   D. Bell-LaPadula

15. Operating systems can be programmed to carry out different methods for process isolation. Which of the following refers to a method in which an interface defines how communication can take place between two processes and no process can interact with the other's internal programming code?

   A. Virtual mapping

   B. Encapsulation of objects

C. Time multiplexing

D. Naming distinctions

16. Which of the following is not a responsibility of the memory manager?

    A. Use complex controls to ensure integrity and confidentiality when processes need to use the same shared memory segments.

    B. Limit processes to interact only with the memory segments assigned to them.

    C. Swap contents from RAM to the hard drive as needed.

    D. Run an algorithm to identify unused committed memory and inform the operating system that the memory is available.

17. Several types of read-only memory devices can be modified after they are manufactured. Which of the following statements correctly describes the differences between two types of ROM?

    A. PROM can only be programmed once, while EEPROM can be programmed multiple times.

    B. A UV light is used to erase data on EEPROM, while onboard programming circuitry and signals erase data on EPROM.

    C. The process used to delete data on PROM erases one byte at a time, while to erase data on an EPROM chip, you must remove it from the hardware.

    D. The voltage used to write bits into the memory cells of EPROM burns out the fuses that connect individual memory cells, while UV light is used to write to the memory cells of PROM.

18. There are different ways that operating systems can carry out software I/O procedures. Which of the following is used when the CPU sends data to an I/O device and then works on another process's request until the I/O device is ready for more data?

    A. I/O using DMA

    B. Interrupt-driven I/O

    C. Programmable I/O

    D. Premapped I/O

19. The Information Technology Infrastructure Library (ITIL) consists of five sets of instructional books. Which of the following is considered the core set and focuses on the overall planning of the intended IT services?

    A. Service Operation

    B. Service Design

    C. Service Transition

    D. Service Strategy

20. Widgets Inc.'s software development processes are documented and the organization is capable of producing its own standard of software processes. Which
of the following Capability Maturity Model Integration levels best describes
Widgets Inc.?

   A. Initial

   B. Repeatable

   C. Defined

   D. Managed

21. There are several different important pieces to the Common Criteria. Which of
the following best describes the first of the missing components?

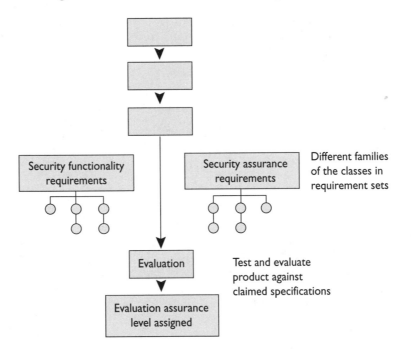

   A. Target of evaluation

   B. Protection profile

   C. Security target

   D. EALs

22. Different access control models provide specific types of security measures
and functionality in applications and operating systems. What model is being
expressed in the graphic that follows?

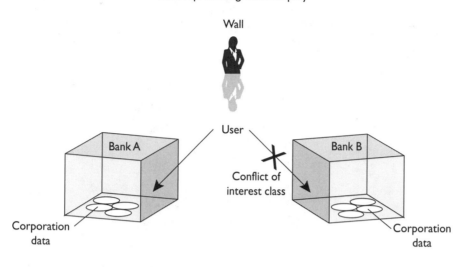

Data representing each company

Wall

User

Bank A

Bank B

Conflict of
interest class

Corporation
data

Corporation
data

A. Noninterference

B. Biba

C. Bell-LaPadula

D. Chinese Wall

23. There are many different types of access control mechanisms that are commonly embedded into all operating systems. Which of the following is the mechanism that is missing in this graphic?

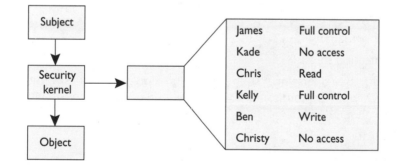

Subject		James	Full control
Security kernel		Kade	No access
		Chris	Read
Object		Kelly	Full control
		Ben	Write
		Christy	No access

A. Trusted computing base

B. Security perimeter

C. Reference monitor

D. Domain

24. There are several security enforcement components that are commonly built into operating systems. Which component is illustrated in the graphic that follows?

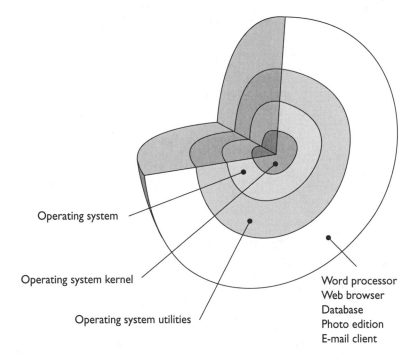

Operating system

Operating system kernel

Operating system utilities

Word processor
Web browser
Database
Photo edition
E-mail client

  A. Virtual machines

  B. Interrupt

  C. Cache memory

  D. Protection rings

25. A multitasking operating system can have several processes running at the same time. What are the components within the processes that are shown in the graphic that follows?

  A. Threads

  B. Registers

  C. Address buses

  D. Process tables

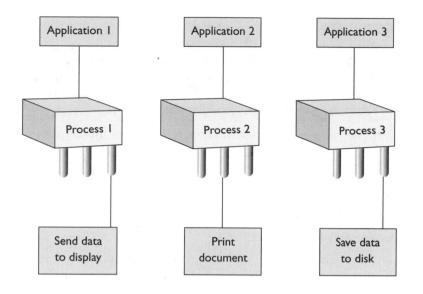

The following scenario applies to questions 26 and 27.

Charlie is a new security manager at a textile company that develops its own proprietary software for internal business processes. Charlie has been told that the new application his team needs to develop must comply with the ISO/IEC 42010 standard. He has found out that many of the critical applications have been developed in the C programming language and has asked for these applications to be reviewed for a specific class of security vulnerabilities.

26. Which of the following best describes the standard Charlie's team needs to comply with?

   A. International standard on system design to allow for better quality, interoperability, extensibility, portability, and security

   B. International standard on system security to allow for better threat modeling

   C. International standard on system architecture to allow for better quality, interoperability, extensibility, portability, and security

   D. International standard on system architecture to allow for better quality, extensibility, portability, and security

27. Which of the following is Charlie most likely concerned with in this situation?

   A. Injection attacks

   B. Memory block

   C. Buffer overflows

   D. Browsing attacks

The following scenario applies to questions 28 and 29.

Tim's development team is designing a new operating system. One of the requirements of the new product is that critical memory segments need to be categorized as nonexecutable, with the goal of reducing malicious code from being able to execute instructions in privileged mode. The team also wants to make sure that attackers will have a difficult time predicting execution target addresses.

28. Which of the following best describes the type of protection that needs to be provided by this product?

    A. Hardware isolation

    B. Memory induction application

    C. Data execution prevention

    D. Domain isolation protection

29. Which of the following best describes the type of technology the team should implement to increase the work effort of buffer overflow attacks?

    A. Address space layout randomization

    B. Memory induction application

    C. Input memory isolation

    D. Read-only memory integrity checks

The following scenario applies to questions 30, 31, and 32.

Operating systems have evolved and changed over the years. The earlier operating systems were monolithic and did not segregate critical processes from noncritical processes. As time went on operating system vendors started to reduce the amount of programming code that ran in kernel mode. Only the absolutely necessary code ran in kernel mode, and the remaining operating system code ran in user mode. This architecture introduced performance issues, which required the operating system vendors to reduce the critical operating system functionality to microkernels and allow the remaining operating system functionality to run in client/server models within kernel mode.

30. Which of the following best describes the second operating system architecture described in the scenario?

    A. Layered

    B. Microkernel

    C. Monolithic

    D. Kernel based

31. Which of the following best describes why there was a performance issue in the context of the scenario?

    A. Bloated programming code

    B. I/O and memory location procedures

    C. Mode transitions

    D. Data and address bus architecture

32. Which of the following best describes the last architecture described in this scenario?

    A. Hybrid microkernel

    B. Layered

    C. Monolithic

    D. Hardened and embedded

1. B	12. C	23. C
2. D	13. A	24. D
3. C	14. C	25. A
4. A	15. B	26. C
5. D	16. D	27. C
6. A	17. A	28. C
7. C	18. B	29. A
8. B	19. D	30. B
9. D	20. C	31. C
10. B	21. B	32. A
11. A	22. D	

1. Lacy's manager has tasked her with researching an intrusion detection system for a new dispatching center. Lacy identifies the top five products and compares their ratings. Which of the following are the evaluation criteria most in use today for these types of purposes?

   A. ITSEC

   B. Common Criteria

   C. Red Book

   D. Orange Book

   ☑ **B.** The Common Criteria were created in the early 1990s as a way of combining the strengths of both the Trusted Computer System Evaluation Criteria (TCSEC) and Information Technology Security Evaluation Criteria (ITSEC) while eliminating their weaknesses. These evaluation criteria are more flexible than TCSEC and more straightforward than ITSEC. Because it is recognized globally, the Common Criteria help consumers by reducing the complexity of the ratings and eliminating the need to understand the definition and meaning of different ratings within various evaluation schemes. This also helps manufacturers because now they can build to one specific set of requirements if they want to sell their products internationally, instead of having to meet several different ratings with varying rules and requirements.

   ☒ **A** is incorrect because ITSEC, or the Information Technology Security Evaluation Criteria, is not the most widely used. ITSEC was the first attempt at establishing a single standard for evaluating security attributes of computer systems and products by many European countries. Furthermore, ITSEC separates functionality and assurance in its evaluation, giving each a separate rating. It was developed to provide more flexibility than TCSEC, and addresses integrity, availability, and confidentiality in networked systems. While the goal of the ITSEC was to become the worldwide criteria for product evaluation, it did not meet that goal and has been replaced with the Common Criteria.

   ☒ **C** is incorrect because the Red Book is a U.S. government publication that addresses security evaluation topics for networks and network components. Officially titled the Trusted Network Interpretation, the book provides a framework for securing different types of networks. Subjects accessing objects on the network need to be controlled, monitored, and audited.

   ☒ **D** is incorrect because the Orange Book is a U.S. government publication that primarily addresses government and military requirements and expectations for operating systems. The Orange Book is used to evaluate whether a product contains the security properties the vendor claims it does and whether the product is appropriate for a specific application or function. The Orange Book is used to review the functionality, effectiveness, and assurance of a product during its evaluation, and it uses classes that were devised to address typical patterns of security requirements. It provides a broad framework for building and evaluating trusted systems with great emphasis on controlling which users can access a system. The other name for the Orange Book is the Trusted Computer System Evaluation Criteria (TCSEC).

2. Certain types of attacks have been made more potent by which of the following advances to microprocessor technology?

   A. Increased circuits, cache memory, and multiprogramming

   B. Dual-mode computation

   C. Direct memory access I/O

   D. Increases in processing power

   ☑ **D.** Due to the increase of personal computer and server processing power, it is now possible to be more successful in brute-force and cracking attacks against security mechanisms that would not have been possible a few years ago. Today's processors can execute an amazing number of instructions per second. These instructions can be used to attempt to crack passwords or encryption keys or instructions to send nefarious packets to victim systems.

   ☒ **A** is incorrect because increased circuits, cache memory, and multiprogramming do not make certain types of attacks more potent. Multiprogramming means that more than one program or process can be loaded into memory at the same time. This is what allows you to run your antivirus software, word processor, firewall, and e-mail client simultaneously. Cache memory is a type of memory used for high-speed writing and reading activities. When the system assumes (through its programmatic logic) that it will need to access specific information many times throughout its processing activities, it will store the information in cache memory so that it is easily and quickly accessible.

   ☒ **B** is incorrect because the answer is a distracter. There is no real dual-mode computation when examining the advances in microprocessors.

   ☒ **C** is incorrect because direct memory access (DMA) is a way of transferring instructions and data between I/O (input/output) devices and the system's memory without using the CPU. This speeds up data transfer rates significantly. DMA basically offloads work from the CPU by ensuring that more simple instructions are interpreted and executed through other processing capabilities within the computer system. This is not an advancement to microprocessor technology.

3. CPUs and operating systems can work in two main types of multitasking modes. What controls access and the use of system resources in preemptive multitasking mode?

   A. The user and application

   B. The program that is loaded into memory

   C. The operating system

   D. The CPU and user

   ☑ **C.** Operating systems started out as cooperative and then evolved into preemptive multitasking. With preemptive multitasking, used in Windows 9*x*, NT, 2000, and XP, as well as in Unix systems, the operating system controls how long a process can use a resource. The system can suspend a process that is using the CPU (or other system resources) and allow another process access to it through the use of time sharing. Thus, operating systems that use preemptive multitasking run the show, and one application does not negatively affect another application if it behaves badly. In operating systems that used cooperative multitasking, the processes had too much control over resource release, and when an application hung, it usually affected all the other applications and sometimes the operating system itself. Operating systems that use preemptive multitasking run the show, and one application does not negatively affect another application as easily.

   ☒ **A** is incorrect because the user and application do not control access and the use of system resources in preemptive multitasking mode. The application, however, has more control over the use of system resources in cooperative multitasking mode. The operating system itself works in either preemptive or cooperative multitasking modes, not the applications or users.

   ☒ **B** is incorrect because as described in answer A, a program does not run in a specific multitasking mode—the operating system does. Cooperative multitasking, used in Windows 3.1 and early Macintosh systems, required the processes to voluntarily release resources that they were using. This was not necessarily a stable environment because if a programmer did not write his code properly to release a resource when his application was done using it, the resource would be committed indefinitely to his application and thus unavailable to other processes.

   ☒ **D** is incorrect because the user and CPU do not control access and the use of system resources. Instead, the operating system controls the processor time slices that different processes can be allocated. Multitasking is the way that the operating system uses access to the CPU, which can be either cooperative or preemptive.

4. Virtual storage combines RAM and secondary storage for system memory. Which of the following is a security concern pertaining to virtual storage?

A. More than one process uses the same resource.

B. It allows cookies to remain persistent in memory.

C. It allows for side-channel attacks to take place.

D. Two processes can carry out a denial-of-service.

☑ **A.** When RAM and secondary storage are combined, the result is virtual memory. The system uses hard drive space—called swap space—that is reserved for the purpose of extending its RAM memory space. When a system fills up its volatile memory space, it writes data from memory onto the hard drive. When a program requests access to this data, it is brought from the hard drive back into memory in specific units, called page frames. Accessing data that is kept in pages on the hard drive takes more time than accessing data kept in memory because physical disk read/write access has to take place. There are internal control blocks, maintained by the operating system, to keep track of what page frames are residing in RAM, and what is available "offline," ready to be called into RAM for execution or processing, if needed. The payoff is that it seems as though the system can hold an incredible amount of information and program instructions in memory. A security issue with using virtual swap space is that two or more processes use the same resource and the data could be corrupted or compromised.

☒ **B** is incorrect because virtual storage is not related to cookies. Virtual storage uses hard drive space to extend its RAM memory space. Cookies are small text files used mainly by Web browsers. The cookies can contain credentials for Web sites, site preference settings, or shopping histories. Cookies are also commonly used to maintain Web server-based sessions.

☒ **C** is incorrect because a side-channel attack is a nonintrusive attack. In this type of attack, the attacker gathers information about how a mechanism (such as a smart card or encryption processor) works from the radiation that is given off, time taken to carry out processing, power consumed to carry out tasks, etc. This information is used to reverse-engineer the mechanism to uncover how it carries out its security tasks. This is not related to virtual storage.

☒ **D** is incorrect because the biggest threat within a system that has shared resources between processes, as operating systems have to share memory between all resources, is that one process will negatively interfere with the other process's resource. This is especially true with memory, since all data and instructions are stored there, whether they are sensitive or not. While it is possible for two processes to work together to carry out a denial-of-service attack, this is only one type of attack that can be carried out with or without the use of virtual storage.

5. Which of the following is a common association of the Clark-Wilson access model?

   A. Chinese Wall

   B. Access tuple

   C. Read up and write down rule

   D. Subject and application binding

   ☑ **D.** In the Clark-Wilson model, a subject cannot access an object without going through some type of application or program that controls how this access can take place. The subject (usually a user) is bound to the application and then is allowed access to the necessary objects based on the access rules within the application software. For example, when Kathy needs to update information held within her company's database, she will not be allowed to do so without a piece of software controlling these activities. First, Kathy must authenticate to the software, which is acting as a front end for the database, and then the program will control what Kathy can and cannot do to the information in the database. This is referred to as access triple: subject (user), program, and object. This is triple, not tuple. Tuple is a row within a database.

   ☒ **A** is incorrect because the Chinese Wall model is another name for the Brewer and Nash model, which was created to provide access controls that can change dynamically, depending upon a user's previous actions, in an effort to protect against conflicts of interest by users' access attempts. No information can flow between subjects and objects in a way that would result in a conflict of interest. The model states that a subject can write to an object if, and only if, the subject cannot read another object that is in a different dataset.

   ☒ **B** is incorrect because the Clark-Wilson model uses access triple, not access tuple. The access triple is subject-program-object. It ensures that subjects can only access objects through authorized programs.

   ☒ **C** is incorrect because the Clark-Wilson model does not have read up and write down rules. These rules are associated with the Bell LaPadula and Biba models. The Bell-LaPadula model includes the simple security rule, which is no read up, and the star property rule, which is no write down. The Biba model includes the simple integrity axiom, which is no read down, and the star-integrity axiom, which is no write up.

6. Which of the following correctly describes the relationship between the reference monitor and the security kernel?

   A. The security kernel implements and enforces the reference monitor.

   B. The reference monitor is the core of the trusted computing base, which is made up of the security kernel.

C. The reference monitor implements and enforces the security kernel.

D. The security kernel, aka abstract machine, implements the reference monitor concept.

☑ **A.** The trusted computing base (TCB) is the total combination of a system's protection mechanisms. These are in the form of hardware, software, and firmware. These same components also comprise the security kernel. The reference monitor is an access control concept that is implemented and enforced by the security kernel via the hardware, software, and firmware. In doing so, the security kernel ensures that subjects have the appropriate authorization to access the objects they are requesting. The subject, be it a program, user, or process, should not be able to access a file, program, or resource it is requesting until it has proven that it has the appropriate access rights.

☒ **B** is incorrect because the reference monitor is not the core of the trusted computing base (TCB). The core of the TCB is the security kernel, and the security kernel carries out the reference monitor concept. The reference monitor is a concept pertaining to access control. Since it is not a physical component, it is often referred to as an "abstract machine." The reference monitor mediates access between subjects and objects in an effort to ensure that subjects have the necessary rights to access objects and to protect objects from unauthorized access and destructive changes.

☒ **C** is incorrect because the reference monitor does not implement and enforce the security kernel. Rather, the security kernel implements and enforces the reference monitor. The reference monitor is an abstract concept, while the security kernel is a combination of hardware, software, and firmware within the trusted computing base. The security kernel has three requirements, which are also the requirements of the reference monitor. The security kernel must tamperproof and isolate the processes executing the reference monitor concept. Likewise, the security kernel must be implemented so that it is invoked for every access attempt and cannot be circumvented. Finally, the security kernel must be small enough to enable its comprehensive testing and verification.

☒ **D** is incorrect because abstract machine is not another name for the security kernel. Abstract machine is another name for the reference monitor, which can also be referred to as the reference monitor concept. The concept states that an abstract machine serves as the mediator between subjects and objects to ensure that the subjects have the necessary rights to access the objects they are requesting and to protect the objects from unauthorized access and modification. The security kernel is responsible for carrying out these activities.

7. The trusted computing base (TCB) ensures security within a system when a process in one domain must access another domain in order to retrieve sensitive information. What function does the TCB initiate to ensure that this is done in a secure manner?

A. I/O operational execution

B. Process deactivation

C. Execution domain switching

D. Virtual memory to real memory mapping

☑ **C. Execution domain switching** takes place when a CPU needs to move between executing instructions for a highly trusted process to a less trusted process or vice versa. The trusted computing base (TCB) allows processes to switch domains in a secure manner in order to access different levels of information based on their sensitivity. Execution domain switching takes place when a process needs to call upon a process in a higher protection ring. The CPU goes from executing instructions in user mode to privileged mode and back.

☒ **A** is incorrect because input/output (I/O) operations are not initiated to ensure security when a process in one domain must access another domain in order to retrieve sensitive information. I/O operations include control of all input/output devices. I/O operations are functions within an operating system that allow input devices (such as a mouse or keyboard) and output devices (such as a monitor or printer) to interact with applications and with itself.

☒ **B** is incorrect because process deactivation takes place when a process's instructions are completely executed by the CPU or when another process with a higher priority calls upon the CPU. When a process is deactivated, the CPU's registers must be filled with new information about the new requesting process. The data that is getting switched in and out of the registers may be sensitive, so the TCB components must make sure this takes place securely.

☒ **D** is incorrect because memory mapping takes place when a process needs its instructions and data processed by the CPU. The memory manager maps the logical address to the physical address so that the CPU knows where the data is located. This is the responsibility of the operating system's memory manager.

8. The Zachman Architecture Framework is often used to set up an enterprise security architecture. Which of the following does not correctly describe the Zachman Framework?

   A. A two-dimensional model that uses communication interrogatives intersecting with different levels

   B. A security-oriented model that gives instructions in a modular fashion

   C. Used to build a robust enterprise architecture versus a technical security architecture

   D. Uses six perspectives to describe a holistic information infrastructure

   ☑ **B.** The Zachman Framework is not security oriented, but it is a good template to work with to build an enterprise security architecture because it gives direction on how to understand the enterprise in a modular fashion. This framework is structured and formal and is used as a tool to understand any type of enterprise from many different angles. The Zachman Framework was developed in the 1980s by John Zachman and is based on the principles of classical architecture that contains rules that govern an ordered set of relationships.

   ☒ A is incorrect because the Zachman Framework is a two-dimensional model that addresses the what, how, where, who, when, and why from six different perspectives: the planner or visionary, the owner, the architect, the designer, the builder, and the working system. Together, this information gives a holistic view of the enterprise.

   ☒ C is incorrect because the Zachman Framework is used to create a robust enterprise architecture, not a security architecture, technical or not. The framework is not security specific. Almost all robust enterprise security architectures work with the structure provided by the Zachman Framework in one way or another. When we talk about a robust security architecture, we are talking about one that deals with many components throughout the organization—not just a network and the systems within that network.

   ☒ D is incorrect because the Zachman Framework uses six perspectives to build a holistic view of the enterprise. Those perspectives are the planner or visionary, owner, architect, designer, builder, and the working system. Those using the framework address what, how, where, who, when, and why as they relate to each of these perspectives. This is to ensure that regardless of the order in which they are put in place, components of the enterprise are organized and relationships are clearly defined so that they create a complete system. The framework does not just specify an information infrastructure.

9. John has been told to report to the board of directors with a vendor-neutral enterprise architecture framework that will help the company reduce fragmentation that results from the misalignment of IT and business processes. Which of the following frameworks should he suggest?

A. DoDAF

B. CMMI

C. ISO/IEC 42010

D. TOGAF

☑ **D.** The Open Group Architecture Framework (TOGAF) is a vendor-neutral platform for developing and implementing enterprise architectures. It focuses on effectively managing corporate data through the use of metamodels and service-oriented architecture (SOA). A proficient implementation of TOGAF is meant to reduce fragmentation that occurs due to misalignment of traditional IT systems and actual business processes. It also adjusts to new innovations and capabilities to ensure new changes can easily be integrated into the enterprise platform.

☒ **A** is incorrect because the Department of Defense Architecture Framework (DoDAF) provides guidelines for the organization of enterprise architecture for the U.S. Department of Defense systems. All DoD weapons and IT systems are required to design and document enterprise architecture according to these guidelines. They are also suitable for large and complex integrated systems in military, private, or public sectors.

☒ **B** is incorrect because Capability Maturity Model Integration (CMMI) is used during software development to design and further enhance software. The CMMI provides a standard for software development process where the level of maturity of the development process can be measured. It was developed by the Carnegie Mellon Software Engineering Institute and is an upgraded version of Capability Maturity Model (CMM).

☒ **C** is incorrect because the ISO/IEC 42010 consists of a set of recommended practices intended to simplify the design and conception of software-intensive system architectures. This standard provides a type of language (terminology) to describe the different components of a software architecture and how to integrate it into the life cycle of development. Many times the overall vision of the architecture of a piece of software is lost as the developers get caught up in the actual development procedures. This standard provides a conceptual framework to follow for architecture development and implementation.

10. Protection profiles used in the Common Criteria evaluation process contain five elements. Which of the following establishes the type and intensity of the evaluation?

A. Descriptive elements

B. Evaluation assurance requirements

C. Evaluation assurance level

D. Security target

☑ **B.** The Common Criteria use protection profiles in their evaluation process. This is a mechanism that is used to describe a real-world need of a product that is not currently on the market. The protection profile contains the set of security requirements, their meaning and reasoning, and the corresponding evaluation assurance level (EAL) rating that the intended product will require. The protection profile describes the environmental assumptions, the objectives, and the functional and assurance level expectations. Each relevant threat is listed along with how it is to be controlled by specific objectives. The protection profile also justifies the assurance level and requirements for the strength of each protection mechanism. Evaluation assurance requirements establish the type and intensity of the evaluation. The other four sections in a protection profile are descriptive elements, rationale, functional requirements, and development assurance requirements.

☒ **A** is incorrect because the descriptive elements section of a protection profile provides the name of the profile and a description of the security problem that is to be solved. The protection profile provides a means for a consumer, or others, to identify specific security needs; this is the security problem that is to be conquered. If someone identifies a security need that is not currently being addressed by any current product, that person can write a protection profile describing the product that would be a solution for this real-world problem. The protection profile goes on to provide the necessary goals and protection mechanisms to achieve the necessary level of security and a list of the things that can go wrong during this type of system development. This list is used by the engineers who develop the system, and then by the evaluators to make sure the engineers dotted every *i* and crossed every *t*.

☒ **C** is incorrect because the evaluation assurance level (EAL) is not one of the five parts of a protection profile. An EAL is assigned to a product after it has been evaluated under the Common Criteria. The thorough and stringent testing increases in detailed-oriented tasks as the assurance levels increase. The Common Criteria have seven assurance levels: EAL 1, functionally tested; EAL 2, structurally tested; EAL 3, methodically tested and checked; EAL 4, methodically designed, tested, and reviewed; EAL 5, semiformally designed and tested; EAL 6, semiformally verified design and tested; and EAL 7, formally verified design and tested.

☒ **D** is incorrect because security target is the vendor's written explanation of the security functionality and assurance mechanisms that meet the needed security solution; in other words, "This is what our product does and how it does it." Like other evaluation criteria before it, the Common Criteria work to answer two basic questions about products being evaluated: what does its security mechanisms do (functionality), and how sure are you of that (assurance)? This system sets up a framework that enables consumers to clearly specify their security issues and problems; developers to specify their security solution to those problems; and evaluators to unequivocally determine what the product actually accomplishes.

11. Which of the following best defines a virtual machine?

    A. A virtual instance of an operating system

    B. A piece of hardware that runs multiple operating system environments simultaneously

    C. A physical environment for multiple guests

    D. An environment that can be fully utilized while running legacy applications

☑ **A.** A virtual machine is a virtual instance of an operating system. A virtual machine can also be called a guest, which runs in a host environment. The host environment—usually an operating system—can run multiple guests simultaneously. The virtual machines pool resources such as RAM, processors, and storage from the host environment. This offers many benefits, including enhanced processing power utilization. Other benefits include the ability to run legacy applications. For example, an organization may choose to run its legacy applications on an instance (virtual machine) of Windows XP long after it has rolled out Windows 7.

☒ **B** is incorrect because a virtual machine is not a piece of hardware. A virtual machine is an instance of an operating system that runs on hardware. The host can run multiple virtual machines. So, basically, you can have one computer running different operating systems at the same time. One benefit of this is consolidation. Using virtual machines, you can consolidate the workloads of several under-utilized servers on to one host, thereby saving money on hardware and administrative management tasks.

☒ **C** is incorrect because virtual machines provide and work within software emulation. The host provides the resources, such as memory, processor, buses, RAM, and storage for the virtual machines. The virtual machines share these resources but do not access them directly. The host environment, which is responsible for managing the system resources, acts as an intermediary between the resources and the virtual machines.

☒ **D** is incorrect because many legacy applications are not compatible with specific hardware and newer operating systems. Because of this, the application commonly under-utilizes the server software and components. The virtual machines emulate an environment that allows legacy, and other, applications to fully use the resources available to them. This is a reason to use a virtual machine, but the answer does not provide its definition.

12. Bethany is working on a mandatory access control (MAC) system. She has been working on a file that was classified as Secret. She can no longer access this file because it has been reclassified as Top Secret. She deduces that the project she was working on has just increased in confidentiality and she now knows more about this project than her clearance and need-to-know allows. Which of the following refers to a concept that attempts to prevent this type of scenario from occurring?

   A. Covert storage channel

   B. Inference attack

   C. Noninterference

   D. Aggregation

   ☑ C. Multilevel security properties can be expressed in many ways, one being noninterference. This concept is implemented to ensure that any actions that take place at a higher security level do not affect, or interfere with, actions that take place at a lower level. So if an entity at a higher security level performs an action, it cannot change the state for the entity at the lower level. If a lower-level entity were aware of a certain activity that took place by an entity at a higher level and the state of the system changed for this lower-level entity, the entity might be able to deduce too much information about the activities of the higher state, which in turn is a way of leaking information.

   ☒ A is incorrect because a covert channel allows for the ability to share information between processes that weren't intended to communicate. Noninterference is a model intended to prevent covert channels along with other malicious ways of communication to take place. The model looks at the shared resources that the different users of a system will use and tries to identify how information can be passed from a process working at a higher security clearance to a process working at a lower security clearance. If two users are working on the same system at the same time, they will most likely have to share some type of resources. So the model is made up of rules to ensure that User A cannot carry out any activities that can allow User B to infer information she does not have the clearance to know.

   ☒ B is incorrect because an inference attack refers to Bethany's ability to infer that the project that she was working on was now Top Secret and has now increased in importance and secrecy. The question is asking for the concept that helps to prevent an inference attack. An inference attack occurs when someone has access to some type of information and can infer (or guess) something that she does not have the clearance level or authority to know. For example, let's say that Tom is working on a file that contains information about supplies that are being sent to Russia. He closes out of that file and one hour later attempts to open the same file. During this time, the file's classification has been elevated to Top Secret, so when Tom attempts to access it, he is denied. Tom can infer that some type of Top Secret mission is getting ready to take place with Russia. He does not have clearance to know this; thus, it would be an inference attack or "leaking information."

☒ **D** is incorrect because aggregation is the act of combining information from separate sources. The combination of the data forms new information, which the subject does not have the necessary rights to access. The combined information can have a sensitivity that is greater than that of the individual parts. Aggregation happens when a user does not have the clearance or permission to access specific information but does have the permission to access components of this information. She can then figure out the rest and obtain restricted information.

13. Virtualization offers many benefits. Which of the following incorrectly describes virtualization?

A. Virtualization simplifies operating system patching.

B. Virtualization can be used to build a secure computing platform.

C. Virtualization can provide fault and error containment.

D. Virtual machines offer powerful debugging capabilities.

☑ **A.** Virtualization does not simplify operating system patching. In fact, it makes it more complex because it adds at least an operating system. Each operating system commonly varies in version and configurations—increasing the complexity of patching. The operating systems for the servers themselves run as guests within the host environment. Not only do you have to patch and maintain the traditional server operating systems, but now you also have to patch and maintain the virtualization software itself.

☒ **B** is incorrect because virtualization can be used to build a secure computing platform. Untrusted applications can be run in secure, isolated sandboxes within a virtual machine. The virtualization software "compartmentalizes" the individual guest operating systems and ensures that the processes for each guest do not interact with the other guest processes in an unauthorized manner.

☒ **C** is incorrect because virtual machines can provide fault and error containment by isolating what is run within the specific guest operating systems. Developers and security researchers can proactively inject faults into software to study its behavior without impacting other virtual machines. For this reason, virtual machines are useful tools for research and academic experiments.

☒ **D** is incorrect because virtual machines enable powerful debugging, as well as performance monitoring, by allowing you to put debugging and performance monitoring tools in the virtual machine monitor. There's no need to set up complex debugging scenarios and the operating systems can be debugged without impacting productivity.

14. Which security architecture model defines how to securely develop access rights between subjects and objects?

    A. Brewer-Nash

    B. Clark-Wilson

    C. Graham-Denning

    D. Bell-LaPadula

    ☑ **C.** The Graham-Denning model addresses how access rights between subjects and objects are defined, developed, and integrated. It defines a set of basic rights in terms of commands that a specific subject can execute on an object. This model has eight primitive protection rights, or rules, on how these types of functionalities should take place securely. They are: how to securely create an object; how to securely create a subject; how to securely delete an object; how to securely delete a subject; how to securely provide the read access right; how to securely provide the grant access right; how to securely provide the delete access right; and how to securely provide transfer access rights. These things may sound insignificant, but when we are talking about building a secure system, they are very critical.

    ☒ **A** is incorrect because the Brewer-Nash model is intended to provide access controls that can change dynamically depending upon a user's previous actions. The main goal is to protect against conflicts of interest by users' access attempts. For example, if a large marketing company provides marketing promotions and materials for two banks, an employee working on a project for Bank A should not be able to look at the information the marketing company has on its other bank customer, Bank B. Such action could create a conflict of interest because the banks are competitors. If the marketing company's project manager for the Bank A project could view information on Bank B's new marketing campaign, he may try to trump its promotion to please his more direct customer. The marketing company would get a bad reputation if it allowed its internal employees to behave so irresponsibly.

    ☒ **B** is incorrect because the Clark-Wilson model is implemented to protect the integrity of data and to ensure that properly formatted transactions take place within applications. It works on the following premises: subjects can access objects only through authorized programs; separation of duties is enforced; auditing is required. The Clark-Wilson model addresses all three integrity goals: prevent unauthorized users from making modifications, prevent authorized users from making improper modifications, and maintain internal and external consistency.

☒ **D** is incorrect because the Bell-LaPadula model was developed to address the U.S. military's concern with the security of its systems and the leakage of classified information. The model's main goal is to prevent sensitive information from being accessed in an unauthorized manner. It is a state machine model that enforces the confidentiality aspects of access control. A matrix and security levels are used to determine if subjects can access different objects. The subject's clearance is compared to the object's classification and then specific rules are applied to control how subject-to-object interactions take place.

15. Operating systems can be programmed to carry out different methods for process isolation. Which of the following refers to a method in which an interface defines how communication can take place between two processes and no process can interact with the other's internal programming code?

    A. Virtual mapping

    B. Encapsulation of objects

    C. Time multiplexing

    D. Naming distinctions

    ☑ **B.** When a process is properly encapsulated, no other process understands or interacts with its internal programming code. When process A needs to communicate with process B, process A just needs to know how to communicate with process B's interface. An interface defines how communication must take place between two processes. As an analogy, think back to how you had to communicate with your third-grade teacher. You had to call her Mrs. SoandSo, say please and thank you, and speak respectfully to get whatever it was you needed. The same thing is true for software components that need to communicate with each other. They have to know how to communicate properly with each other's interfaces. The interfaces dictate the type of requests that a process will accept and the type of output that will be provided. So, two processes can communicate with each other, even if they are written in different programming languages, as long as they know how to communicate with each other's interface. Encapsulation provides data hiding, which means that outside software components will not know how a process works and will not be able to manipulate the process's internal code. This is an integrity mechanism and enforces modularity in programming code.

    ☒ **A** is incorrect because virtual mapping refers to how virtual to physical memory mapping takes place within an operating system. When an application needs memory to work with, it tells the operating system's memory manager how much memory it needs. The operating system carves out that amount of memory and assigns it to the requesting application. The application uses its own address scheme, which usually starts at 0, but in reality, the application does not work in the physical address space that it thinks it is working in. Rather, it works in the address space that the memory manager assigns to it. The physical memory is the RAM chips in the system. The operating system chops up this memory and assigns portions of it to the requesting processes. Once the process is assigned its own memory space, then it can address this portion however it needs to, which is called virtual address mapping. Virtual address mapping allows the different processes to have their own memory space; the memory manager ensures that no processes improperly interact with another process's memory. This provides integrity and confidentiality.

☒ C is incorrect because time multiplexing is a technology that allows processes to use the same resources through an interleaved method. A CPU has to be shared among many processes. Although it seems as though all applications are executing their instructions simultaneously, the operating system is splitting up time shares between each process. Multiplexing means that there are several data sources and the individual data pieces are piped into one communication channel. In this instance, the operating system is coordinating the different requests from the different processes and piping them through the one shared CPU. An operating system has to provide proper time multiplexing (resource sharing) to ensure that a stable working environment exists for software and users.

☒ D is incorrect because naming distinctions just means that the different processes have their own name or identification value. Processes are usually assigned process identification (PID) values, which the operating system and other processes use to call upon them. If each process is isolated, that means that each process has its own unique PID value.

16. Which of the following is not a responsibility of the memory manager?

   A. Use complex controls to ensure integrity and confidentiality when processes need to use the same shared memory segments.

   B. Limit processes to interact only with the memory segments assigned to them.

   C. Swap contents from RAM to the hard drive as needed.

   D. Run an algorithm to identify unused committed memory and inform the operating system that the memory is available.

☑ **D.** This answer describes the function of a garbage collector. A garbage collector is a countermeasure against memory leaks. It is software that runs an algorithm to identify unused committed memory and then tells the operating system to mark that memory as "available." Different types of garbage collectors work with different operating systems, programming languages, and algorithms. The portion of the operating system that keeps track of how different types of memory are used is called the memory manager. Its jobs are to allocate and deallocate different memory segments, enforce access control to ensure that processes are interacting only with their own memory segments, and swap memory contents from RAM to the hard drive. The memory manager has five basic responsibilities: relocation, protection, sharing, local organization, and physical organization.

☒ **A** is incorrect because as part of its sharing responsibilities, the memory manager uses complex controls to ensure integrity and confidentiality when processes need to use the same shared memory segments. This is critical to protecting memory and the data in it, since two or more processes can share access to the same segment with potentially different access rights. The memory manager is also responsible for allowing many users with different levels of access to interact with the same application running in one memory segment.

☒ **B** is incorrect because the memory manager is responsible for limiting process interactions to only those memory segments assigned to them. This responsibility falls under protection and helps prevent processes from gaining access to unpermitted segments. Another protection responsibility of the memory manager is to provide access control to memory segments.

☒ **C** is incorrect because swapping contents from RAM to the hard drive as needed is a responsibility of the memory manager that falls under relocation. When RAM and secondary storage are combined, the result is virtual memory. The system uses hard drive space to extend its RAM memory space. Another relocation responsibility is to provide pointers for applications if their instructions and memory segment have been moved to a different location in main memory.

17. Several types of read-only memory devices can be modified after they are manufactured. Which of the following statements correctly describes the differences between two types of ROM?

   A. PROM can only be programmed once, while EEPROM can be programmed multiple times.

   B. A UV light is used to erase data on EEPROM, while onboard programming circuitry and signals erase data on EPROM.

C. The process used to delete data on PROM erases one byte at a time, while to erase data on an EPROM chip, you must remove it from the hardware.

D. The voltage used to write bits into the memory cells of EPROM burns out the fuses that connect individual memory cells, while UV light is used to write to the memory cells of PROM.

☑ **A.** Programmable read-only memory (PROM) is a form of ROM that can be modified after it has been manufactured. PROM can be programmed only one time because the voltage that is used to write bits into the memory cells actually burns out the fuses that connect the individual memory cells. The instructions are "burned into" PROM using a specialized PROM programmer device. Electrically erasable programmable read-only memory (EEPROM) can be rewritten. Its data storage can be erased and modified electrically by onboard programming circuitry and signals.

☒ **B** is incorrect because a UV light is used to erase data on erasable and programmable read-only memory (EPROM). To erase an EPROM chip, you must remove the chip from the computer. The EPROM chip has a quartz window, which is where you point the UV light, which erases all of the data on the chip—not just portions of it. Electrically erasable programmable read-only memory (EEPROM) can be erased and modified electrically by onboard programming circuitry and signals.

☒ **C** is incorrect because the process used to delete data from EEPROM—not PROM—involves erasing one byte at a time. This is a slow process, so a new form of memory was developed: flash memory. The second half of this answer is correct: To erase data on EPROM, you must remove it from the computer and wave a UV wand, which erases all of the data on the chip.

☒ **D** is incorrect because the voltage that is used to write bits into the memory cells of PROM—not EPROM—burns out the fuses that connect the individual memory cells. The instructions are "burned into" PROM using a specialized PROM programmer device. Also UV light is used to erase data from EPROM—not write data to PROM. EPROM holds data that can be electrically erased or written to. To erase the data on the memory chip, you need your handy-dandy ultraviolet (UV) light device that provides just the right level of energy. The EPROM chip has a quartz window, which is where you point the UV light. Although playing with UV light devices can be fun for the whole family, we have moved on to another type of ROM technology that does not require this type of activity.

18. There are different ways that operating systems can carry out software I/O procedures. Which of the following is used when the CPU sends data to an I/O

device and then works on another process's request until the I/O device is ready for more data?

A. I/O using DMA

B. Interrupt-driven I/O

C. Programmable I/O

D. Premapped I/O

☑ **B.** If an operating system is using interrupt-driven I/O (input/output), this means that the CPU sends data to an I/O device and then goes and works on another process's request. When the I/O device is ready for more data, it sends an interrupt to the CPU. The CPU stops what it is doing, sends more data, and moves to another job. This process (send data—go, do something else—interrupt—send data) continues until the process is complete.

☒ **A** is incorrect because direct memory access (DMA) is a way of transferring data between I/O devices and the system's memory without using the CPU. This speeds up data transfer rates significantly. When used in I/O activities, the DMA controller feeds data to the I/O device without bothering the CPU. This method is sometimes referred to as unmapped I/O.

☒ **C** is incorrect because if an operating system is using programmable I/O, this means that the CPU sends data to an I/O device and polls the device to see if it is ready to accept more data. If the device is not ready to accept more data, the CPU wastes time by waiting for the device to become ready. For example, the CPU would send a byte of data (a character) to the printer and then ask the printer if it is ready for another byte. The CPU sends the text to be printed one byte at a time. This is a very slow way of working and wastes precious CPU time.

☒ **D** is incorrect because in a premapped I/O system, the CPU sends the physical memory address of the requesting process to the I/O device, and the I/O device is trusted enough to interact with the contents of memory directly. So the CPU does not control the interactions between the I/O device and memory. The operating system trusts the device to behave properly. Thus, premapped I/O does not pertain to performance, as do other methods, but provides an approach that can directly affect security. Fully mapped I/O also affects security. However, in this case, the operating system does not fully trust the I/O device. The physical address is not given to the I/O device. Instead, the device works purely with logical addresses and works on behalf (under the security context) of the requesting process. So the operating system does not trust the device to interact with memory directly. The operating system does not trust the process or device and acts as the broker to control how they communicate with each other.

19. The Information Technology Infrastructure Library (ITIL) consists of five sets of instructional books. Which of the following is considered the core set and focuses on the overall planning of the intended IT services?

    A. Service Operation

    B. Service Design

    C. Service Transition

    D. Service Strategy

    ☑ **D.** The fundamental approach of ITIL lies in the creation of Service Strategy, which focuses on the overall planning of the intended IT services. Once the initial planning has been concluded, the Service Design provides guidelines on designing valid IT services and overall implementation policies. The Service Transition stage is then initiated, where guidelines regarding evaluation, testing, and validation of the IT services are provided. This allows the transition from business environments into technology services. The Service Operation makes sure that all the decided services have met their objectives. Finally, the Continual Service Improvement points out the areas of improvements in the entire service life cycle. The Service Strategy is considered to be the core of ITIL. It consists of a set of guidelines that include best practices regarding strategy and value planning, design, and alignment between the IT and business approaches, market analysis, service assets, setting targets toward providing quality service to the clients, and implementation of service strategies.

    ☒ **A** is incorrect because Service Operation refers to an important component of the life cycle in which the services are actually delivered. This part of the life cycle defines a set of guidelines that makes sure that the agreed levels of services are delivered to the customers. The various genres incorporated by Service Operation include Event Management, Problem Management, Access Management, Incident Management, Application Management, Technical Management, and Operations Management. Service Operation also balances between the conflicting goals, such as technology vs. business requirements, stability vs. response, cost vs. quality of service, and reactive vs. proactive activities.

    ☒ **B** is incorrect because the Service Design comprises a set of optimal practices for the designing of IT services, including their processes, architectures, policies, and documentation in order to fulfill the current and future business requirements. The target of the Service Design is to design services according to their agreed business objectives, design such processes that can support life cycle, identification and management of risks, and involvement in the improvement of IT service quality as a whole.

☒ **C** is incorrect because Service Transition focuses on delivering services proposed by business strategy into operational use. It also contains guidelines that enable the smooth transition of business model into technology services. If the requirements of a service have changed after its design, the Service Transition ensures that those requirements are delivered according to its modified design. The areas focused on by these guidelines include Transition Planning and Support, Change Management, Knowledge Management, Release and Deployment Management, Service Validation and Testing, Evaluation, along with the responsibilities of personnel involved with the Service Transition.

20. Widgets Inc.'s software development processes are documented and the organization is capable of producing its own standard of software processes. Which of the following Capability Maturity Model Integration levels best describes Widgets Inc.?

    A. Initial

    B. Repeatable

    C. Defined

    D. Managed

☑ **C.** Capability Maturity Model Integration (CMMI) is a process improvement concept that consists of a collection of techniques used in the process of software development of an organization to design and further enhance software. The CMMI provides a standard for software development process where the level of maturity of the development process can be measured. The CMMI is classified into five levels which are Initial, Repeatable, Defined, Managed, and Optimized. The categorization of these levels depends upon the maturity of the software development and its quality assurance. The basis of Defined level (CMMI Level 3) is that the organizations are capable of producing their own standard of software processes. These processes are improved with the passage of time.

☒ **A** is incorrect because the processes in the Initial level (CMM Level 1) are not organized or documented and are hence chaotic. The organizations having CMMI Level 1 are expected to thrive only due to the extraordinary performance of individuals. This makes the environment of the processes more unstable. This level has a very limited scope and is used for unique projects. Success is not likely to be repeated at this level.

☒ **B** is incorrect because at the Repeatable level (CMMI Level 2), the processes are documented in a better manner and so the success is repetitive; however, the organization is not yet capable of producing its own standard of software processes. This level ensures that the processes are maintained during the downtime, ensuring that the project is implemented according to the plan.

☒ **D** is incorrect because at the Managed level (CMMI Level 4), organizations are able to monitor and control their own processes involved in the software development. It allows management to point out ways to adjust the processes of a particular project in such a way that there is no considerable loss on its quality or diversion from the main specifications. At the final level, Optimized (CMMI Level 5), processes are managed for improvement.

21. There are several different important pieces to the Common Criteria. Which of the following best describes the first of the missing components?

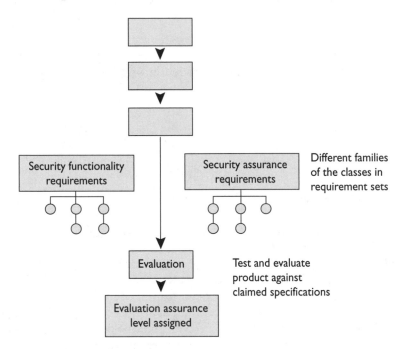

A. Target of evaluation

B. Protection profile

C. Security target

D. EALs

☑ **B.** The Common Criteria uses protection profiles in its evaluation process. This is a mechanism used to describe a real-world need of a product that is not currently on the market. The protection profile contains the set of security requirements, their meaning and reasoning, and the corresponding EAL rating that the intended product will require. The protection profile describes the environmental assumptions, the objectives, and the functional and assurance-level expectations. Each relevant threat is listed, along with how it is to be controlled by specific objectives. The protection profile also justifies the assurance level and requirements for the strength of each protection mechanism that is expected to be in the new product. The protection profile basically says, "This is what we need out of a new product."

☒ **A is incorrect** because the target of evaluation (ToE), the second of the three missing pieces in the graphic, is the actual product that is being evaluated against the Common Criteria. Where the protection profile states, "This is what we need out of a new product," the ToE is the product that a vendor creates to meet the requirements outlined in the protection profile. When there is a need in the industry for a new product that provides specific functionality and security, someone develops the protection profile to outline this need. A vendor fulfills the need by creating a new product, referred to as the ToE.

☒ **C is incorrect** because the security target, the third piece missing in the graphic, is the vendor's written explanation of the security functionality and assurance mechanisms that meet the needed solution outlined in the protection profile and fulfilled by the target of evaluation (ToE). Where the protection profile outlines, "This is what we need," the ToE is the product that fulfills this need, and the security target is the explanation on how this ToE is mapped to the protection profile. The evaluators compare the ToE with these three constructs, along with the actual requirements of the Common Criteria before assigning it an evaluation assurance level.

☒ **D is incorrect** because evaluation assurance levels (EALs) outline the assurance ratings used in the Common Criteria. It is basically the grading system used in these criteria to describe the assurance and security required by a specific product. When an evaluator evaluates a product, after all of her tests she will assign an EAL value. This value is basically the grade that the product receives after all of the tests it is put through. The Common Criteria uses a different assurance rating system than the previously used criteria. It has packages of specifications that must be met for a product to obtain the corresponding rating. These ratings and packages are collectively called the EALs. Once a product achieves any type of rating, customers can view this information on an Evaluated Products List (EPL) to understand which product provides the most security assurance. So if you are going to purchase a product and you have a certain security assurance specification that the product must meet, you can view the EPL to see what maps to your needs.

22. Different access control models provide specific types of security measures and functionality in applications and operating systems. What model is being expressed in the graphic that follows?

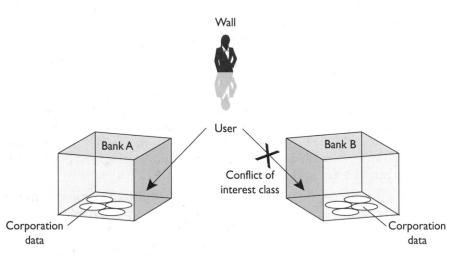

Data representing each company

Wall

User

Conflict of interest class

Bank A

Bank B

Corporation data

Corporation data

A. Noninterference

B. Biba

C. Bell-LaPadula

D. Chinese Wall

☑ **D.** The Chinese Wall model was created to provide access controls that can change dynamically, depending upon a user's previous actions. The main goal of the model is to protect against conflicts of interest by users' access attempts. For example, if a large marketing company provides marketing promotions and materials for two banks, an employee working on a project for Bank A should not look at the information the marketing company has on its other bank customer, Bank B. Such action could create a conflict of interest because the banks are competitors. If the marketing company's project manager for the Bank A project could view information on Bank B's new marketing campaign, he may try to trump its promotion to please his more direct customer.

☒ **A** is incorrect because multilevel security properties can be expressed in many ways, one being Noninterference. The Chinese Wall model does not focus on multilevel security properties and the Noninterference model does not focus on conflicts of interest. The concept of noninterference is implemented to ensure any actions that take place at a higher security level do not affect, or interfere with, actions that take place at a lower level and vice versa. This type of model does not concern itself with conflicts of interest, but rather with what a subject knows about the state of the system. So if an entity at a higher security level performs an action, it cannot change the state for the entity at the lower level. The Noninterference model is also focused on confidentiality. It works to ensure that subjects at a lower clearance level cannot access data or objects at a higher clearance level.

☒ **B** is incorrect because the Biba is a state machine model that addresses the integrity of data within applications without the use of a wall construct. Although the Biba model is very similar to the Bell-LaPadula model, the Bell-LaPadula model uses a lattice of security levels (top secret, secret, sensitive, and so on). These security levels were developed mainly to ensure that sensitive data was only available to authorized individuals. The Biba model is not concerned with security levels and confidentiality, so it does not base access decisions upon this type of lattice. The Biba model uses a lattice of integrity levels. Biba compartmentalizes data based on integrity levels. It is an information flow model that controls information flow in a way that is intended to protect the integrity of the most trusted information. The Biba model was not built to address conflicts of interest.

☒ **C** is incorrect because a system that employs the Bell-LaPadula model is called a multilevel security system, meaning users with different clearances use the system, and the system processes data at different classification levels. The level at which data is classified determines the handling procedures that should be used. The Bell-LaPadula model is a state machine model that enforces the confidentiality aspects of access control. A matrix and security levels are used to determine if subjects can access different objects. The subject's clearance is compared to the object's classification and then specific rules are applied to control how subject-to-object interactions can take place. The Bell-LaPadula model was not developed to address conflicts of interest.

23. There are many different types of access control mechanisms that are commonly embedded into all operating systems. Which of the following is the mechanism that is missing in this graphic?

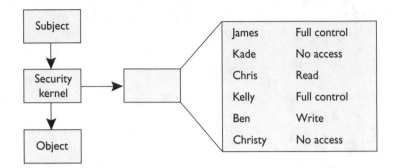

A. Trusted computing base

B. Security perimeter

C. Reference monitor

D. Domain

☑ C. The reference monitor is an abstract machine that mediates all access subjects have to objects, both to ensure that the subjects have the necessary access rights and to protect the objects from unauthorized access and destructive modification. For a system to achieve a high level of trust, it must require subjects (programs, users, or processes) to be fully authorized prior to accessing an object (file, program, or resource). A subject must not be allowed to use a requested resource until the subject has proven it has been granted access privileges to use the requested object. The reference monitor is an access control concept, not an actual physical component, which is why it is normally referred to as the "reference monitor concept" or an "abstract machine." The reference monitor is the access control concept, and the code that actually enforces this concept is the security kernel.

☒ A is incorrect because a security perimeter is a boundary that divides the trusted from the untrusted process access requests within software. The trusted processes within a system are referred to as being within the trusted computing base (TCB). The TCB is defined as the total combination of protection mechanisms within a computer system. The TCB includes hardware, software, and firmware. These are part of the TCB because the system is sure these components will enforce the security policy and not violate it. Not all components need to be trusted, and therefore not all components fall within the TCB. The security perimeter is the demarcation between what is within the TCB, the trusted processes, and what is not, the untrusted processes.

☒ **B is incorrect** because not every process and resource falls within the TCB, so some of these components fall outside of an imaginary boundary referred to as the security perimeter. A security perimeter is a boundary that divides the trusted from the untrusted. For the system to stay in a secure and trusted state, precise communication standards must be developed to ensure that when a component within the TCB needs to communicate with a component outside the TCB, the communication cannot expose the system to unexpected security compromises. This type of communication is handled and controlled through interfaces. The security perimeter is a concept that helps enforce this type of security.

☒ **D is incorrect** because a domain is defined as a set of objects that a subject is able to access. This domain can be all the resources a user can access, all the files available to a program, the memory segments available to a process, or the services and processes available to an application. A subject needs to be able to access and use objects (resources) to perform tasks, and the domain defines which objects are available to the subject and which objects are untouchable and therefore unusable by the subject. A common implementation of a domain is a networked Windows environment. Resources are logically partitioned within the network to ensure subjects can only access these resources.

24. There are several security enforcement components that are commonly built into operating systems. Which component is illustrated in the graphic that follows?

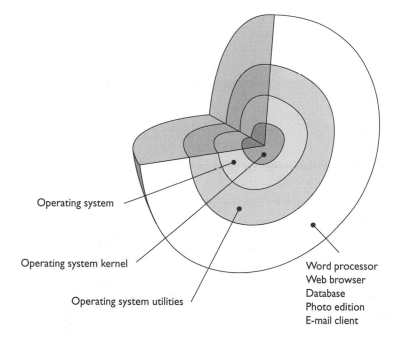

Operating system

Operating system kernel

Operating system utilities

Word processor
Web browser
Database
Photo edition
E-mail client

A. Virtual machines

B. Interrupt

C. Cache memory

D. Protection rings

☑ **D.** An operating system has several protection mechanisms to ensure processes do not negatively affect each other or the critical components. One security mechanism commonly used in operating systems is protection rings. These rings provide strict boundaries and definitions for what the processes that work within each ring can access and what operations they can successfully and securely execute. The processes that operate within the inner rings have more privileges than the processes operating in the outer rings, because the inner rings only permit the most trusted components and processes to operate within them. Protection rings support the availability, integrity, and confidentiality requirements of multitasking operating systems. The most commonly used architecture provides four protection rings:

- **Ring 0** Operating system kernel
- **Ring 1** Remaining parts of the operating system
- **Ring 2** I/O drivers and utilities
- **Ring 3** Applications and user activity

☒ **A** is incorrect because a virtual instance of an operating system is known as a virtual machine. A virtual machine is commonly referred to as a guest that is executed in the host environment. Virtualization allows a single host environment to execute multiple guests at once, with multiple virtual machines dynamically pooling resources from a common physical system. Computer resources such as RAM, processors, and storage are emulated through the host environment. The virtual machines do not directly access these resources; instead, they communicate with the host environment responsible for managing system resources. Virtual machines do not work in a circular framework as shown in the graphic.

☒ **B** is incorrect because an interrupt is a function used in operating systems that allows for slots of the CPU to be used. The most basic CPUs can do only one thing at a time. So the system has hardware and software interrupts. When a device needs to communicate with the CPU, it has to wait for its interrupt to be called upon. The same thing happens in software. Each process has an interrupt assigned to it. It is like pulling a number at a customer service department in a store. You can't go up to the counter until your number has been called out. When a process is interacting with the CPU and an interrupt takes place (another process has requested access to the CPU), the current process's information is stored in the process table, and the next process gets its time to interact with the CPU.

☒ **C** is incorrect because cache memory is a type of memory used for high-speed writing and reading activities and it is not necessarily a security mechanism. When the system assumes (through its programmatic logic) that it will need to access specific information many times throughout its processing activities, it will store the information in cache memory so it is easily and quickly accessible. Data in cache can be accessed much more quickly than data stored in real memory. Therefore, any information needed by the CPU very quickly, and very often, is usually stored in cache memory, thereby improving the overall speed of the computer system. Cache memory also does not work in a circular framework as illustrated in the graphic.

25. A multitasking operating system can have several processes running at the same time. What are the components within the processes that are shown in the graphic that follows?

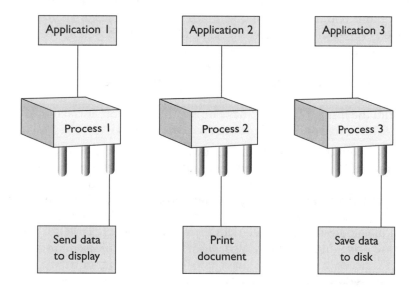

A. Threads

B. Registers

C. Address buses

D. Process tables

☑ **A.** A process is a program in memory. More precisely, a process is the program's instructions and all the resources assigned to the process by the operating system. It is just easier to group all of these instructions and resources together and control them as one entity, which is a process. When a process needs to send something to the CPU for processing, it generates a thread. A thread is made up of an individual instruction set and the data that must be worked on by the CPU. Most applications have several different functions. Word processors can open files, save files, open other programs (such as an e-mail client), and print documents. Each one of these functions requires a thread (instruction set) to be dynamically generated. So, for example, if Tom chooses to print his document, the word processor process generates a thread that contains the instructions of how this document should be printed (font, colors, text, margins, and so on). If he chooses to send a document via e-mail through this program, another thread is created that tells the e-mail client to open and what file needs to be sent. Threads are dynamically created and destroyed as needed. Once Tom is done printing his document, the thread that was generated for this functionality is destroyed.

☒ **B** is incorrect because a register is a temporary storage location. Processing chips within the CPU cover only a couple of square inches but contain millions of transistors. All operations within the CPU are performed by electrical signals at different voltages in different combinations, and each transistor holds this voltage, which represents 0s and 1s to the computer. The CPU contains registers that point to memory locations that contain the next instructions to be executed and that enable the CPU to keep status information of the data that needs to be processed. While a register can hold the instructions that make up the thread before it is fed into the CPU, it is not a component of the processes themselves.

☒ **C** is incorrect because an address bus is a hardwired connection to RAM chips and the individual input/output (I/O) devices in a computer system. In a computer, memory addresses of the instructions and data to be processed are held in registers until needed by the CPU. The CPU is connected to the address bus. Memory is cut up into sections that have individual addresses associated with them. I/O devices (CD-ROM, USB device, hard drive, and so on) are also allocated specific unique addresses. If the CPU needs to access some data, either from memory or from an I/O device, it sends down the address of where the needed data is located. The circuitry associated with the memory or I/O device recognizes the address the CPU sent down the address bus and instructs the memory or device to read the requested data and put it on the data bus. So the address bus is used by the CPU to indicate the location of the instructions to be processed, and the memory or I/O device responds by sending the data that resides at that memory location through the data bus.

☒ **D** is incorrect because a process table is a way for an operating system to keep track of processes that are running. An operating system is responsible for creating new processes, assigning them resources, synchronizing their communication, and making sure nothing insecure is taking place. The operating system keeps a process table, which has one entry per process. The table contains each individual process's state, stack pointer, memory allocation, program counter, and status of open files in use. The reason the operating system documents all of this status information is that the CPU needs all of it loaded into its registers when it needs to interact with, for example, process 1. When process 1's CPU time slice is over, all of the current status information on process 1 is stored in the process table so that when its time slice is open again, all of this status information can be put back into the CPU registers. So, when it is process 2's time with the CPU, its status information is transferred from the process table to the CPU registers; it is transferred back again when the time slice is over.

The following scenario applies to questions 26 and 27.

Charlie is a new security manager at a textile company that develops its own proprietary software for internal business processes. Charlie has been told that the new application his team needs to develop must comply with the ISO/IEC 42010 standard. He has found out that many of the critical applications have been developed in the C programming language and has asked for these applications to be reviewed for a specific class of security vulnerabilities.

26. Which of the following best describes the standard Charlie's team needs to comply with?

   A. International standard on system design to allow for better quality, interoperability, extensibility, portability, and security

   B. International standard on system security to allow for better threat modeling

   C. International standard on system architecture to allow for better quality, interoperability, extensibility, portability, and security

   D. International standard on system architecture to allow for better quality, extensibility, portability, and security

   ☑ C. ISO/IEC 42010 has the goal of internationally standardizing the use of system architecture instead of product developers coming up with their own individual approaches. A disciplined approach to system architecture allows for better quality, interoperability, extensibility, portability, and security.

   ☒ A is incorrect because the answer specifically states "design" instead of "architecture." Some people mistakenly think that these are the same things, but architecture takes place before design. Architecture works at a higher, more strategic level compared to design. Software development is becoming a more disciplined industry and it is moving toward formal architecture requirements.

☒ **B** is incorrect because the standard identified in the question does not deal with threat modeling. ISO/IEC 42010 addresses system architecture requirements and guidelines.

☒ **D** is not the best answer since it is not as complete as answer C. This standard does address interoperability issues, which is not listed in this answer.

27. Which of the following is Charlie most likely concerned with in this situation?

    A. Injection attacks

    B. Memory block

    C. Buffer overflows

    D. Browsing attacks

    ☑ **C.** The C programming language is susceptible to buffer overflow attacks because some of its commands allow for direct pointer manipulations to take place. Specific commands can provide access to low-level memory addresses without carrying out bounds checking.

    ☒ **A** is incorrect because the C programming language does not have any more vulnerabilities pertaining to injection attacks than any other languages. Injection attacks usually do not take place at the code level, but happen because an interface accepts data that are not properly filtered and validated.

    ☒ **B** is incorrect because this is a distracter answer. There is no official programming language vulnerability referred to as "memory block."

    ☒ **D** is incorrect because a browsing attack is when someone is reviewing various assets for sensitive data. This does not relate to a programming language, but how access control is implemented.

The following scenario applies to questions 28 and 29.

Tim's development team is designing a new operating system. One of the requirements of the new product is that critical memory segments need to be categorized as nonexecutable, with the goal of reducing malicious code from being able to execute instructions in privileged mode. The team also wants to make sure that attackers will have a difficult time predicting execution target addresses.

28. Which of the following best describes the type of protection that needs to be provided by this product?

    A. Hardware isolation

    B. Memory induction application

    C. Data execution prevention

    D. Domain isolation protection

☑ **C.** Data execution prevention (DEP) is a security feature included in modern operating systems. It is intended to prevent a process from executing code from a nonexecutable memory region. This helps prevent certain exploits that store code via a buffer overflow, for example. DEP can mark certain memory locations as "off limits," with the goal of reducing the "playing field" for hackers and malware.

☒ **A** is incorrect because memory hardware isolation has to be done at the hardware level, not just in an operating system. Some systems that require a high level of security can be designed to ensure that memory is not shared in any fashion. This requires hardware design, and the operating system (or other software) has to then be designed to use that specific hardware environment.

☒ **B** incorrect because this is a distracter answer. This is not an official term or security issue.

☒ **D** is incorrect because domain isolation does not deal specifically with memory protection as does data execution prevention (DEP). Domain isolation is not a specific technology, but a goal that operating systems attempt to accomplish. A domain is a set of resources that is available to an entity. Most people think of network domains in the Microsoft world, but a domain is just a set of resources. It is a general and old term. Domain isolation just means isolating one set of resources from another set of resources. This is commonly done so that one process cannot compromise another process's resources.

29. Which of the following best describes the type of technology the team should implement to increase the work effort of buffer overflow attacks?

    A. Address space layout randomization
    B. Memory induction application
    C. Input memory isolation
    D. Read-only memory integrity checks

    ☑ **A.** Address space layout randomization (ASLR) is a control that involves randomly arranging the positions of a process's address space and other memory segments. It randomly arranges the positions of key data areas, usually including the base of the executable and position of system libraries, memory heap, and memory stacks, in a process's address space. ASLR makes it more difficult for an attacker to predict target addresses for specific memory attacks.

    ☒ **B** is incorrect because this is a distracter answer. This is not an official term or security item.

    ☒ **C** is incorrect because while memory isolation may help in protecting against buffer overflows, that is not the specific reason for its existence.

Memory isolation is carried out to protect against many different memory attacks. Address space layout randomization (ASLR) has been specifically designed to try and outwit attackers and to make it more difficult for them to know a system's memory address scheme for exploitation purposes.

☒ **D** is incorrect because this is a distracter answer. This is not an official term or security item.

The following scenario applies to questions 30, 31, and 32.

Operating systems have evolved and changed over the years. The earlier operating systems were monolithic and did not segregate critical processes from noncritical processes. As time went on operating system vendors started to reduce the amount of programming code that ran in kernel mode. Only the absolutely necessary code ran in kernel mode, and the remaining operating system code ran in user mode. This architecture introduced performance issues, which required the operating system vendors to reduce the critical operating system functionality to microkernels and allow the remaining operating system functionality to run in client/server models within kernel mode.

30. Which of the following best describes the second operating system architecture described in the scenario?

   A. Layered
   B. Microkernel
   C. Monolithic
   D. Kernel based

☑ **B.** In the microkernel architecture, a reduced amount of code is running in kernel mode carrying out critical operating system functionality. Only the absolutely necessary code runs in kernel mode, and the remaining operating system code runs in user mode. Traditional operating system functions, such as device drivers, protocol stacks, and file systems, are removed from the microkernel to run in user space.

☒ **A** is incorrect because a layered operating system architecture focuses on constructing the functions of the operating system into hierarchical layers. This architecture does not focus on what is or is not running in kernel mode.

☒ **C** is incorrect because the industry started with monolithic operating systems and evolved from it. A monolithic operating system does not segregate privileged and nonprivileged processes and does not use a kernel. MS-DOS is an example of a monolithic operating system.

☒ **D** is incorrect because while there is no official architecture called "kernel-based," this answer does not actually properly address the concept of reducing the amount of code that runs in kernel mode. The microkernel architecture specifically addressed this issue. A microkernel is the near-minimum amount of software that can provide the mechanisms needed to implement an operating system.

31. Which of the following best describes why there was a performance issue in the context of the scenario?

    A. Bloated programming code

    B. I/O and memory location procedures

    C. Mode transitions

    D. Data and address bus architecture

    ☑ **C.** A mode transition is when the CPU has to change from processing code in user mode to kernel mode. This is a protection measure, but it causes a performance hit because all of the information on the new process has to be loaded into the registers for the CPU to work with. Transitions between modes are at the discretion of the executing thread when the transition is from a level of high privilege to one of low privilege (kernel to user mode), but transitions from lower to higher levels of privilege can take place only through secure, hardware-controlled "gates" that are carried out by executing special instructions or when external interrupts are received.

    ☒ **A** is incorrect. While bloated (extra) programming code can cause performance issues in many situations, that is not what this question is focusing on. When comparing operating system architectures and associated performance issues, the focus comes down to how specific functions are carried out and how efficient those procedures are—not the amount of code needed to carry out the function.

    ☒ **B** is incorrect because I/O and memory location do not have a direct correlation to operating system kernel architecture. The specific reason that many operating system vendors changed their products' architecture had to do with the performance issues of mode transitions the CPU had to continually carry out.

    ☒ **D** is incorrect because data and address bus architecture was not the specific reason that vendors moved to a microkernel architecture. This question is zeroing in on how much code ran in kernel versus user mode and how transitions took place, which has nothing to do with the bus architectures.

32. Which of the following best describes the last architecture described in this scenario?

    A. Hybrid microkernel

    B. Layered

    C. Monolithic

    D. Hardened and embedded

☑ **A.** The hybrid microkernel architecture is a combination of monolithic and microkernel architectures. The critical operating system functionality is carried out in a microkernel construct, and the remaining functionality is carried out in a client/server model running within kernel mode. This architecture allows for the critical operating system functions to run in kernel mode and not experience the performance issues with previous architectures.

☒ **B** is incorrect because a layered operating system architecture focuses on constructing the functions of the operating system into hierarchical layers. This architecture does not focus on what is or is not running in kernel mode.

☒ **C** is incorrect because the industry started with monolithic operating systems and evolved from it. A monolithic operating system does not segregate privileged and nonprivileged processes and does not use a kernel. MS-DOS is an example of a monolithic operating system.

☒ **D** is incorrect because an operating system that is hardened and embedded is not a major architecture. The term "hardened" just means secured, and "embedded" means that the operating system's functionalities are stripped down to only provide the basic and necessary functions required of the hardware the software is installed upon. Mobile phones and specialized hardware commonly have embedded operating systems.

Physical and Environmental Security

This domain includes questions from the following topics:

- Administrative, technical, and physical controls
- Facility location, construction, and management
- Physical security risks, threats, and countermeasures
- Fire prevention, detection, and suppression
- Intrusion detection systems

There's a lot more to physical security than the card keys your users carry to enter the building or show to the security guard in the parking lot. Physical security addresses a wide variety of threats that can be technical, wildly unpredictable, and catastrophic—and security professionals need to know how to plan for and deal with them. Every organization should develop, implement, and maintain a physical security program that has its foundation in risk management and mitigation. You should understand the physical security mechanisms that protect an organization's data, equipment, systems, and its greatest asset—people.

1. Robert has been given the responsibility of installing doors that provide different types of protection. He has been told to install doors that provide fail-safe, fail-secure, and fail-soft protection. Which of the following statements is true about secure door types?

   A. Fail-soft defaults to the sensitivity of the area.

   B. Fail-safe defaults to locked.

   C. Fail-secure defaults to unlocked.

   D. Fail-secure defaults to double locked.

2. Windows can have different glazing materials. What type of window may be prohibited by fire codes because of its combustibility?

   A. Tempered

   B. Polycarbonate acrylic

   C. Glass-clad polycarbonate

   D. Laminated

3. As with logical access controls, audit logs should be produced and monitored for physical access controls. Which of the following statements is correct about auditing physical access?

   A. Unsuccessful access attempts should be logged but only need to be reviewed by a security guard.

   B. Only successful access attempts should be logged and reviewed.

   C. Only unsuccessful access attempts during unauthorized hours should be logged and reviewed.

   D. All unsuccessful access attempts should be logged and reviewed.

4. Brad is installing windows on the storefront of a bank in an area known to be at risk of fires in the dry season. Which of the following is least likely to be true of the windows he is installing?

   A. The glass has embedded wires.

   B. They are made of glass-clad polycarbonate.

   C. The window material is acrylic glass.

   D. A solar window film has been added to them.

5. CCTV can use fixed focal length or varifocal lenses. Which of the following correctly describes the lenses used in CCTV?

   A. A fixed focal length lens allows you to move between various fields of view with a single lens.

   B. To cover a large area and not focus on specific items, use a large lens opening.

   C. An auto-iris lens should be used in an area with fixed lighting.

   D. A shallow depth of focus allows you to focus on smaller details.

6. Which of the following describes the type of construction materials most commonly used to build a bank's exterior walls?

   A. Dense woods fastened with metal bolts and plates

   B. Steel rods encased inside of concrete walls and support beams

   C. Untreated lumber

   D. Steel

7. Which of the following is a light-sensitive chip used in most of today's CCTV cameras?

   A. Digital Light Processing

   B. Cathode ray tube

   C. Annunciator

   D. Charged-coupled devices

8. John is installing a sprinkler system that makes use of a thermal-fusible link for a data center located in Canada. Which of the following statements is true of the system he's installing?

   A. The pipes of a dry pipe system are filled with water when pressurized air within the pipes is reduced.

   B. The pipes of a preaction system are filled with water when pressurized air within the pipes is reduced.

   C. The sprinkler heads of a deluge system are wide open to allow a larger volume of water to be released in a shorter period.

   D. The pipes in a wet pipe system always contain water.

9. What of the following allows security personnel to change the field of view of a CCTV lens to different angles and distances?

   A. Depth of field

   B. Manual iris

   C. Zoom

   D. Illumination

10. An outline for a physical security design should include program categories and the necessary countermeasures for each. What category do locks and access controls belong to?

    A. Assessment

    B. Deterrence

    C. Response

    D. Delay

11. A number of factors need to be considered when buying and implementing a CCTV system. Which of the following is the primary factor in determining whether a lens should have a manual iris or an auto-iris?

    A. If the camera must be able to move in response to commands

    B. If the environment has fixed lighting

    C. If objects to be viewed are wide angle, such as a parking lot, or narrow, such as a door

    D. The amount of light present in the environment

12. IDSs can detect intruders by employing electromechanical systems or volumetric systems. Which of the following correctly describes these systems?

    A. Because they detect changes in subtle environmental characteristics, electromechanical systems are more sensitive than volumetric.

    B. Electromechanical systems are less sensitive than volumetric systems, which detect subtle changes in environmental characteristics.

    C. Electromagnetic systems deal with environmental changes such as ultrasonic frequencies, while volumetric systems can employ pressure mats or metallic foil in windows.

    D. Electromagnetic systems are more sensitive because they detect a change or break in a circuit, while volumetric systems detect environmental changes.

13. What discipline combines the physical environment and sociology issues that surround it to reduce crime rates and the fear of crime?

    A. Layered defense model

    B. Target hardening

    C. Crime Prevention Through Environmental Design

    D. Natural access control

14. There are several types of volumetric IDSs. What type of IDS emits a measurable magnetic field that it monitors for disruptions?

    A. Capacitance detector

    B. Passive infrared system

C. Wave-pattern motion detectors

D. Photoelectric system

15. Paisley is helping her company identify potential site locations for a new facility. Which of the following is not an important factor when choosing a location?

A. Distance to police and fire stations

B. Lighting

C. Natural disaster occurrence

D. Crime rate

16. Sarah recently learned that the painting she inherited from a relative and hung in her downtown coffee shop is worth a lot of money. She is worried about its protection and wants to install an IDS. Which of the following intrusion detection systems is the most appropriate for protecting the painting?

A. Acoustical detection system

B. Proximity detector

C. Photoelectric system

D. Vibration sensor

17. David is preparing a server room at a new branch office. What locking mechanisms should he use for the primary and secondary server room entry doors?

A. The primary and secondary entrance doors should have access controlled through a swipe card or cipher lock.

B. The primary entrance door should have access controlled through a security guard. The secondary doors should be secured from the inside and allow no entry.

C. The primary entrance door should have access controlled through a swipe card or cipher lock. The secondary doors should have a security guard.

D. The primary entrance door should have access controlled through a swipe card or cipher lock. Secondary doors should be secured from the inside and allow no entry.

18. Which of the following is not true of IDSs?

A. They can be hindered by items within the room.

B. They are expensive and require human intervention to respond to the alarms.

C. They usually come with a redundant power supply and emergency backup power.

D. They should detect, and be resistant to, tampering.

19. Before an effective physical security program can be rolled out, a number of steps must be taken. Which of the following steps comes first in the process of rolling out a security program?

A. Create countermeasure performance metrics.

B. Conduct a risk analysis.

C. Design the program.

D. Implement countermeasures.

20. A number of measures should be taken to help protect devices and the environment from electric power issues. Which of the following is best to keep voltage steady and power clean?

A. Power line monitor

B. Surge protector

C. Shielded cabling

D. Regulator

21. What type of fence detects if someone attempts to climb or cut it?

A. Class IV

B. PIDAS

C. CPTED

D. PCCIP

22. Several different types of smoke and fire detectors can be used. What type of detector is shown in the following graphic?

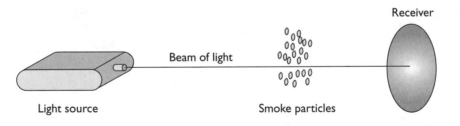

A. Photoelectric

B. Heat-activated

C. Infrared flame

D. Ionization

23. Crime Prevention Through Environmental Design (CPTED) is a discipline that outlines how the proper design of a physical environment can reduce crime by directly affecting human behavior. Of CPTED's three main components, what is illustrated in the following photo?

A. Natural surveillance

B. Target hardening

C. Natural access control

D. Territorial reinforcement

24. Different types of material are built into walls and other constructs of various types of buildings and facilities. What type of material is shown in the following photo?

A. Fire-resistant material

B. Light frame construction material

C. Heavy timber construction material

D. Rebar material

25. There are five different classes of fire. Each depends upon what is on fire. Which of the following is the proper mapping for the items missing in the provided table?

Fire class	Type of fire	Elements of fire	Suppression method
Class A			Water, soda acid
Class B			CO_2 FM-200
Class C			Gas (Halon) or CO_2 nonconductive extinguishing agent
Class D			Dry chemicals
Class K			A wet chemical

A. Class D—combustible metals

B. Class C—liquid

C. Class B—electrical

D. Class A—electrical

26. Electrical power is being provided more through smart grids, which allow for self-healing, resistance to physical and cyberattacks, increased efficiency, and better integration of renewable energy sources. Countries want their grids to be more reliable, resilient, flexible, and efficient. Why does this type of evolution in power infrastructure concern many security professionals?

A. Allows for direct attacks through Power over Ethernet

B. Increased embedded software and computing capabilities

C. Does not have proper protection against common web-based attacks

D. Power fluctuation and outages directly affect computing systems

The following scenario is to be used for questions 27, 28, and 29.

Mike is the new CSO of a large pharmaceutical company. He has been asked to revamp the company's physical security program and better align it with the company's information security practices. Mike knows that the new physical security program should be made up of controls and processes that support the following categories: deterrent, delaying, detection, assessment, and response.

27. Mike's team has decided to implement new perimeter fences and warning signs against trespassing around the company's facility. Which of the categories listed in the scenario do these countermeasures map to?

A. Deterrent

B. Delaying

C. Detection

D. Assessment

28. Mike's team has decided to implement stronger locks on the exterior doors of the new company's facility. Which of the categories listed in the scenario does this countermeasure map to?

A. Deterrent

B. Delaying

C. Detection

D. Assessment

29. Mike's team has decided to hire and deploy security guards to monitor activities within the company's facility. Which of the categories listed in the scenario does this countermeasure map to?

A. Delaying

B. Detection

C. Assessment

D. Recall

The following scenario is to be used for questions 30, 31, and 32.

Greg is the security facility officer of a financial institution. His boss has told him that visitors need a secondary screening before they are allowed into sensitive areas within the building. Greg has also been told by the network administrators that after the new HVAC system was installed throughout the facility, they have noticed that power voltage to the systems in the data center sags.

30. Which of the following is the best control that Greg should ensure is implemented to deal with his boss's concern?

A. Access and audit logs

B. Mantrap

C. Proximity readers

D. Smart card readers

31. Which of the following best describes the situation that the network administrators are experiencing?

   A. Brownouts

   B. Surges

   C. In-rush current

   D. Power line interference

32. Which of the following is a control that Greg's team could implement to address the network administrators' issue?

   A. Secondary feeder line

   B. Insulated grounded wiring

   C. Line conditioner

   D. Generator

1. A	12. B	23. A
2. B	13. C	24. D
3. D	14. A	25. A
4. C	15. B	26. B
5. D	16. B	27. A
6. B	17. D	28. B
7. D	18. C	29. C
8. B	19. B	30. B
9. C	20. D	31. C
10. D	21. B	32. C
11. B	22. A	

1. Robert has been given the responsibility of installing doors that provide different types of protection. He has been told to install doors that provide fail-safe, fail-secure, and fail-soft protection. Which of the following statements is true about secure door types?

   A. Fail-soft defaults to the sensitivity of the area.

   B. Fail-safe defaults to locked.

   C. Fail-secure defaults to unlocked.

   D. Fail-secure defaults to double locked.

   ☑ **A.** Doorways with automatic locks can be configured to be fail-secure, fail-safe, or fail-soft. Fail-soft means that locks need to default to being locked or unlocked, depending on the sensitivity of the data and systems in an area, and if people are working in specific areas of the building. The objective of a fail-soft system is to fail in a way that preserves as much data and capability as possible.

   ☒ **B** is incorrect because fail-safe does not default to locked. A fail-safe setting means that if a power disruption occurs that affects the automated locking system, the doors default to being unlocked. Fail-safe deals directly with protecting people. If people work in an area and there is a fire or the power is lost, it is not a good idea to lock them in.

   ☒ **C** is incorrect because fail-secure does not default to unlocked. A fail-secure configuration means that the doors default to being locked if there are any problems with the power. Be careful not to confuse fail-secure with fail-safe. You can think of it this way: If a fail-secure lock fails, the door is secure; i.e., the door is locked. If a fail-safe lock fails, then the people it protects are safe because they can leave through the door.

   ☒ **D** is incorrect because fail-secure does not default to double locked. The doors simply lock if there are problems with the power in a fail-secure configuration.

2. Windows can have different glazing materials. What type of window may be prohibited by fire codes because of its combustibility?

   A. Tempered

   B. Polycarbonate acrylic

   C. Glass-clad polycarbonate

   D. Laminated

   ☑ **B.** When designing and building a facility, windows are among the items that need to be addressed from a physical security point of view. In addition to their placement and accessibility to intruders, the following issues should be considered: translucent or opaque requirements, alarms, and whether they are shatterproof. Windows should be properly placed (this is where security and aesthetics can come to blows) and should have frames of the proper strengths, the necessary glazing material, and possibly a protective covering. The glazing material, which is applied to the windows as they are being made, may be standard, tempered, acrylic, wire, or laminated on glass. Polycarbonate acrylics are stronger than standard glass, tempered glass, and regular acrylic glass. Like regular acrylics, polycarbonate is made out of a type of transparent plastic. However, because of their combustibility, their use may be prohibited by fire codes. Don't confuse polycarbonate acrylics with glass-clad polycarbonate, which is the strongest window material available and is resistant to fire, chemicals, breakage, and other threats.

☒ A is incorrect because tempered glass is not combustible. Tempered glass is made by heating the glass and then suddenly cooling it. This increases its mechanical strength, which means it can handle more stress and is harder to break. It is usually five to seven times stronger than standard glass. When it does break, tempered glass usually shatters into small pieces instead of sharp shards. This way tempered glass is less likely to cause severe injury than standard glass. Because of its safety and strength, it is used for vehicle windows, glass doors and tables, and cookware.

☒ C is incorrect because glass-clad polycarbonate is resistant to a wide range of threats, including fire. Thus, they differ from polycarbonate acrylic windows, which may be prohibited by fire codes because of their combustibility and because they are made out of plastic. Glass-clad polycarbonate is the strongest window material, and as such is much more expensive than other glazing options. Glass-clad polycarbonate windows would be used in areas that are under the greatest threat.

☒ D is incorrect because laminated glass windows are not combustible. Laminated glass has two sheets of glass with a plastic film in between. This added plastic makes it much more difficult to break the window. When the glass is impacted it produces a cracking pattern that resembles a spider web. As with other types of glass, laminated glass can come in different depths. The greater the depth (more glass and plastic), the more difficult it is to break. Laminated glass windows are often used for car windshields, exterior storefronts, and skylights.

3. As with logical access controls, audit logs should be produced and monitored for physical access controls. Which of the following statements is correct about auditing physical access?

A. Unsuccessful access attempts should be logged but only need to be reviewed by a security guard.

B. Only successful access attempts should be logged and reviewed.

C. Only unsuccessful access attempts during unauthorized hours should be logged and reviewed.

D. All unsuccessful access attempts should be logged and reviewed.

☑ **D.** Physical access control systems can use software and auditing features to produce audit trails or access logs pertaining to access attempts. The following information should be logged and reviewed: the date and time of the access attempt, the entry point at which access was attempted, the user ID employed when access was attempted, and any unsuccessful access attempts, especially if they occur during unauthorized hours.

☒ **A** is incorrect because as with audit logs produced by computers, access logs are useless unless someone actually reviews them. A security guard may be required to review these logs, but a security professional or a facility manager should also review these logs periodically. Management needs to know where entry points into the facility exist and who attempts to use them. Audit and access logs are detective controls, not preventive. They are used to piece together a situation after the fact instead of attempting to prevent an access attempt in the first place.

☒ **B** is incorrect because unsuccessful access attempts should be logged and reviewed. Even though auditing is not an activity that will deny an entity access to a network, computer, or location, it will track activities so that a security professional can be warned of suspicious activity. This information can be used to point out weaknesses of other controls and help security personnel understand where changes must be made to preserve the necessary level of security in the environment.

☒ **C** is incorrect because all unauthorized access attempts should be logged and reviewed, regardless of when they occurred. Attempted break-ins can occur at any time. Operating parameters can be set up for some physical access controls to allow a certain number of failed access attempts to be accepted before a user is locked out; this is a type of clipping level. An audit trail of this information can alert security personnel to a possible intrusion.

4. Brad is installing windows on the storefront of a bank in an area known to be at risk of fires in the dry season. Which of the following is least likely to be true of the windows he is installing?

A. The glass has embedded wires.

B. They are made of glass-clad polycarbonate.

C. The window material is acrylic glass.

D. A solar window film has been added to them.

☑ **C.** It is not likely that the windows Brad is installing are made of acrylic glass. Acrylic glass is made out of polycarbonate acrylic, and while it's stronger than standard glass, it is also combustible. When it burns, acrylic glass forms carbon dioxide, water, carbon monoxide, and compounds such as formaldehyde. Because of its toxicity, it is likely that the fire codes for the bank's location prohibit the use of acrylic glass. However, acrylic glass does have its uses. It is preferred as an alternative to glass in some cases because it is easy to handle and process, and comes at a low cost. You can find acrylic glass at your local aquarium or pet shop. It is often used to build residential and commercial aquariums. It is also used for aircraft windows, motorcycle helmet visors, and as spectator protection around ice hockey rinks.

☒ **A** is incorrect because embedded wires is a safety feature that is intended to reduce the likelihood of the window being broken or shattering. Windows with embedded wires consist of two sheets of glass with the wiring in between. It is unlikely that the bank's storefront windows have embedded wires. These windows are not typically used in storefronts for aesthetic reasons. However, of the answer options available, this is not the least likely characteristic.

☒ **B** is incorrect because it is very likely that the windows Brad is installing are made of glass-clad polycarbonate. Glass-clad polycarbonate is the strongest window material available and is resistant to fire, making it a good choice for a bank at risk of going up in flames during the dry season. Be careful not to confuse glass-clad polycarbonate with polycarbonate acrylic, which not only burns but produces toxic fumes while it does so.

☒ **D** is incorrect because it is likely that a solar window film has been added to the bank's storefront windows. A lot of window types have a film on them that provides efficiency in heating and cooling. They filter out UV rays and are usually tinted, which can make it harder for the bad guy to peep in and monitor internal activities. Some window types have a different kind of film applied that makes it more difficult to break them, whether by explosive, storm, or intruder.

5. CCTV can use fixed focal length or varifocal lenses. Which of the following correctly describes the lenses used in CCTV?

   A. A fixed focal length lens allows you to move between various fields of view with a single lens.

   B. To cover a large area and not focus on specific items, use a large lens opening.

   C. An auto-iris lens should be used in an area with fixed lighting.

   D. A shallow depth of focus allows you to focus on smaller details.

☑ **D.** A shallow depth of focus allows you to focus on smaller details as opposed to a larger field. To understand depth of field, think about pictures you might take while on vacation with your family. For example, say you are on the beach on the Hawaiian island of Oahu with your family and you want to take their picture at the shoreline. Because the main object of the picture is your family, your camera will zoom in. This shallow depth of focus provides a softer backdrop, leading the viewer's eye to the foreground of the photograph. Now you want a scenic picture of Diamond Head. Your camera uses a greater depth of focus, lessening the distinction between objects in the foreground and background.

☒ **A** is incorrect because a fixed focal length lens must be changed to get a different field of view. Fixed focal length lenses are available in wide, medium, and narrow fields of view. A lens that provides a "normal" focal length creates a picture that approximates the field of view of the human eye. A wide-angle lens has a short focal length, and a telephoto lens has a long focal length. When a company selects a fixed focal length lens for a particular view of an environment, it should understand that if the field of view needs to be changed (from wide to narrow, for example), the lens must be changed.

☒ **B** is incorrect because it is best to use a wide-angle lens and a small lens opening to get the correct depth of field for a large area. It is necessary to understand the depth of field when choosing the correct lenses and configurations for your company's CCTV. The depth of field refers to the portion of the environment that is in focus when shown on the monitor. The depth of field varies depending upon the size of the lens opening, the distance of the object being focused on, and the focal length of the lens. The depth of field increases as the size of the lens opening decreases, the subject distance increases, or the focal length of the lens decreases.

☒ **C** is incorrect because an auto-iris lens should be used in environments where the light changes, as in an outdoor setting. As the environment brightens, this is sensed by the iris, which automatically adjusts itself. A manual iris lens should be used in an area with fixed lighting. Manual iris lenses have a ring around the CCTV lens that can be manually turned and controlled. A lens with a manual iris would be used in areas that have fixed lighting, since the iris cannot self-adjust to changes of light.

6. Which of the following describes the type of construction materials most commonly used to build a bank's exterior walls?

   A. Dense woods fastened with metal bolts and plates

   B. Steel rods encased inside of concrete walls and support beams

   C. Untreated lumber

   D. Steel

☑ **B.** Risk analysis results help the physical security team determine the type of construction material that should be used when constructing a new facility. Several grades of building construction are available. The team should choose its construction material based on the identified threats of the organization and the fire codes to be complied with. The construction material can be fire-retardant and have steel rods encased inside of concrete walls and support beams. This provides the most protection against fire and forced entry attempts. Facilities for government organizations, which are under threat by domestic and foreign terrorists, would be built with fire-resistant materials. A financial institution would also use fire-resistant and reinforcement material within its building. This is especially true for its exterior walls, through which thieves may attempt to drive vehicles to gain access to the vaults.

☒ **A** is incorrect because dense woods fastened with metal bolts and plates are used in heavy timber construction material, which is commonly used for office buildings. Combustible lumber is used in this type of construction, but there are requirements on the thickness and composition of the materials to provide more protection from fire. The construction materials must be at least four inches in thickness. Whereas light frame construction material has a fire survival rate of 30 minutes, the heavy timber construction material has a fire survival rate of one hour.

☒ **C** is incorrect because untreated lumber is used as light frame construction material, which provides the least amount of protection against fire and forcible entry attempts. The untreated lumber is combustible during a fire. Light frame construction is usually used to build homes, primarily because it is cheap but also because homes typically are not under the same types of fire and intrusion threats that office buildings are.

☒ **D** is incorrect because steel, an example of an incombustible material, provides a higher level of fire protection than the previously mentioned materials but loses its strength under extreme temperatures, something that may cause the building to collapse. So, although steel will not burn, it may melt and weaken.

7. Which of the following is a light-sensitive chip used in most of today's CCTV cameras?

    A. Digital Light Processing

    B. Cathode ray tube

    C. Annunciator

    D. Charged-coupled devices

☑ **D.** Most of the CCTV cameras in use today employ light-sensitive chips called charged-coupled devices (CCD). The CCD is an electrical circuit that receives input light from the lens and converts it into an electronic signal, which is then displayed on the monitor. Images are focused through a lens onto the CCD chip surface, which forms the electrical representation of the optical image. It is this technology that allows for the capture of extraordinary detail of objects and precise representation, because it has sensors that work in the infrared range, which extends beyond human perception. The CCD sensor picks up this extra "data" and integrates it into the images shown on the monitor to allow for better granularity and quality in the video. In addition to CCTV, CCDs are used in fax machines, photocopiers, bar code readers, and even telescopes.

☒ **A** is incorrect because Digital Light Processing (DLP) is a trademarked technology owned by Texas Instruments that is used in DLP front projectors and DLP rear projection television. Images are created by tiny mirrors that are organized as a matrix on a semiconductor chip. The mirrors are toggled to reflect light, thereby producing grayscales. Color is produced by a single-chip projector via a color wheel placed between the lamp and DLP chip or via individual light sources, such as LEDs or LASERs. A three-chip DLP projector splits light from the lamp with a prism. Individual primary colors of light are routed to their own DLP chip. They are then recombined and sent through the lens.

☒ **B** is incorrect because a cathode ray tube (CRT) uses electrons to display an image. The CRT is a vacuum tube that contains an electron emitter and a fluorescent screen. An electron beam is accelerated and deflected to create an image in the form of light given off by the fluorescent screen. Most of today's CCTVs use charged-coupled devices (CCDs) to allow for more granular information within an environment to be captured and shown on the monitor when compared to the older CCTV technology that relied upon CRTs. CRTs have also been replaced in other applications by technologies that are lighter and less fragile.

☒ **C** is incorrect because an annunciator system can either "listen" for noise and activate electrical devices, such as lights, sirens, or CCTV cameras, or detect movement. Instead of expecting a security guard to stare at a CCTV monitor for eight hours straight, the guard can carry out other activities and be alerted by an annunciator if movement is detected on the screen. While monitor watching is a mentally deadening activity, the CCTV monitors must be watched to be effective. An annunciator system is a solution to that.

8. John is installing a sprinkler system that makes use of a thermal-fusible link for a data center located in Canada. Which of the following statements is true of the system he's installing?

   A. The pipes of a dry pipe system are filled with water when pressurized air within the pipes is reduced.

B. The pipes of a preaction system are filled with water when pressurized air within the pipes is reduced.

C. The sprinkler heads of a deluge system are wide open to allow a larger volume of water to be released in a shorter period.

D. The pipes in a wet pipe system always contain water.

☑ **B.** Preaction systems and dry pipe systems are similar in that the water is not held in the pipes but is released when the pressurized air within the pipes is reduced. Once this happens, the pipes are filled with water, but it is not released right away. In a preaction system, a thermal-fusible link on the sprinkler head has to melt before the water is released. The purpose of combining these two techniques is to give people more time to respond to false alarms or to small fires that can be handled by other means. Putting out a small fire with a handheld extinguisher is better than losing a lot of electrical equipment to water damage. Due to their higher cost, these systems are usually used only in data processing environments rather than the whole building.

☒ **A** is incorrect because dry pipe systems do not use a thermal-fusible link. Like preaction systems, water is not held in the pipes. The water is contained in a "holding tank" until it is released. The pipes hold pressurized air, which is reduced when a fire or a smoke alarm is activated, allowing the water valve to be opened by the water pressure. Water is not allowed into the pipes that feed the sprinklers until an actual fire is detected. First, a heat or smoke sensor is activated; then, the water fills the pipes leading to the sprinkler heads, the fire alarm sounds, the electric power supply is disconnected, and finally water is allowed to flow from the sprinklers. These pipes are best used in colder climates because the pipes will not freeze.

☒ **C** is incorrect because deluge systems are not usually used in data processing environments because the water being released is in such large volumes. Instead, deluge systems are used in environments where a fire could spread quickly. The pipes of a deluge system do not have water in them until a deluge valve is tripped by a fire alarm system. However, the deluge valve is nonresetting, so once the valve is tripped, it stays open.

☒ **D** is incorrect because a wet pipe system should not be used in a colder climate or a data processing environment, nor does it use a thermal-fusible link. Wet pipe systems always contain water in the pipes and are usually discharged by temperature control level sensors. One disadvantage of wet pipe systems is that the water in the pipes may freeze in colder climates. Also, if there is a nozzle or pipe break, it can cause extensive water damage. These types of systems are also called closed-head systems.

9. Which of the following allows security personnel to change the field of view of a CCTV lens to different angles and distances?
   A. Depth of field
   B. Manual iris
   C. Zoom
   D. Illumination

   ☑ C. Zoom lenses provide flexibility by allowing the viewer to change the field of view to different angles and distances. The security personnel usually have a remote-control component integrated within the centralized CCTV monitoring area that allows them to move the cameras, and zoom in and out on objects as needed. When both wide scenes and close-up captures are needed, a zoom lens is best. This type of lens allows the focal length to change from wide angle to telephoto while maintaining the focus of the image.

   ☒ A is incorrect because depth of field refers to the portion of the environment that is in focus when shown on the CCTV monitor. The depth of field varies depending upon the size of the lens opening, the distance of the object being focused on, and the focal length of the lens. The depth of field increases as the size of the lens opening decreases, the subject distance increases, or the focal length of the lens decreases. So, if you want to cover a large area and not focus on specific items, it is best to use a wide-angle lens and a small lens opening.

   ☒ B is incorrect because an iris controls the amount of light that enters the lens. Manual iris lenses have a ring around the CCTV lens that can be manually turned and controlled. A lens with a manual iris would be used in areas that have fixed lighting, since the iris cannot self-adjust to changes of light. For example, it may be used in hospital hallways that are always lit.

   ☒ D is incorrect because illumination refers to the intensity of light present in an environment. Different CCTV camera and lens products have specific illumination requirements to ensure the best quality images possible. The illumination requirements are usually represented in the lux value, which is a metric used to represent illumination strengths. The illumination can be measured using a light meter. The intensity of light is measured and represented in measurement units of lux or footcandles. (The conversion between the two is one footcandle = 10.76 lux.) The illumination measurement is not something that can be accurately provided by the vendor of a light bulb, because the environment can directly affect the illumination. This is why illumination strengths are most effectively measured where the light source is implemented.

10. An outline for a physical security design should include program categories and the necessary countermeasures for each. What category do locks and access controls belong to?

A. Assessment

B. Deterrence

C. Response

D. Delay

☑ **D.** The physical security program design phase should begin with a structured outline that lists each category of the program: deterrence, delaying, detection, assessment, and response. The outline evolves into a framework, which is fleshed out with the necessary controls and countermeasures. The intent behind the delay category is to stall intruders to help ensure they get caught. Examples of countermeasures that belong to this category are locks, defense-in-depth measures, and access controls. Other types of delaying mechanisms include reinforced walls and rebar. The idea is that it will take a bad guy longer to get through two reinforced walls, which gives the response force sufficient time to arrive at the scene and stop the attacker. Of the categories listed in the answer options, detection is missing. Detection refers to the determination or awareness that an intrusion has occurred. Examples of detection controls include external intruder sensors and internal intruder sensors.

☒ **A** is incorrect because assessment countermeasures include security guard procedures and communication structure (calling tree). When an incident occurs, the assessment team (or security guard) is first on the scene to determine what has taken place and what needs to happen next; for example, a call to the police or fire station, management, a security service, etc. The assessment determines what type of response is needed.

☒ **B** is incorrect because deterrence refers to those controls that will discourage potential intruders from conducting criminal activity. Examples include fences, warning signs, security guards, and dogs. Another example found in residential areas is a "Neighborhood Crime Watch" sign that is erected in neighborhoods or even in home windows. The idea is that a casual intruder will be less likely to attempt an intrusion if he thinks that the neighborhood is making a concerted effort to watch for criminals and that he may be caught.

☒ **C** is incorrect because response refers to an organization's processes and the personnel it assigns to react to intrusions and disruptions. Controls in this category include a response force, emergency response procedures, and police, fire, and medical personnel.

11. A number of factors need to be considered when buying and implementing a CCTV system. Which of the following is the primary factor in determining whether a lens should have a manual iris or an auto-iris?

A. If the camera must be able to move in response to commands

B. If the environment has fixed lighting

C. If objects to be viewed are wide angle, such as a parking lot, or narrow, such as a door

D. The amount of light present in the environment

☑ B. CCTV lenses have irises, which control the amount of light that enters the lens. If the environment has fixed lighting, then a lens with a manual iris can be used. Manual iris lenses cannot self-adjust to changes in light. They have to be manually turned and controlled by moving a ring around the lens. If the environment has changing light, as in an outdoor setting, then an auto-iris lens should be used. As the environment brightens, this is sensed by the iris, which automatically adjusts itself. Security personnel will configure the CCTV to have a specific fixed exposure value, which the iris is responsible for maintaining. On a sunny day, the iris lens closes to reduce the amount of light entering the camera, while at night, the iris opens to capture more light—just like our eyes.

☒ A is incorrect because a camera's ability to move in response to security personnel commands determines its mounting requirements. Cameras can be implemented in a fixed mounting or a mounting that allows the cameras to move when necessary. A fixed camera cannot move in response to security personnel commands, whereas cameras that provide PTZ capabilities can pan, tilt, or zoom as necessary.

☒ C is incorrect because the angle of items to be viewed influences the focal length required of the lens. The focal length of a lens defines its effectiveness in viewing objects from a horizontal and vertical view. The focal length value relates to the angle of view that can be achieved. Short focal length lenses provide wider-angle views, while long focal length lenses provide a narrower view. The size of the images shown on a monitor, along with the area covered by one camera, is defined by the focal length. For example, if a company implements a CCTV camera in a warehouse, the focal length lens should be between 2.8 and 4.3 millimeters (mm) so that the whole area can be captured. If the company implements another CCTV camera that monitors an entrance, then the lens value should be around 8 mm, which allows a smaller area to be monitored.

☒ D is incorrect because the amount of light present in the environment does not determine the type of iris that should be used. The iris is determined by whether the light is fixed (the amount of light in the area is constant) or changes. The amount of light present in the environment helps determine the illumination requirements that must be met by the CCTV system. Illumination measurements must be taken within the environment itself because characteristics of the environment, such as exposure to outside light, the paint on the walls, etc., can affect illumination.

12. IDSs can detect intruders by employing electromechanical systems or volumetric systems. Which of the following correctly describes these systems?

   A. Because they detect changes in subtle environmental characteristics, electromechanical systems are more sensitive than volumetric.

   B. Electromechanical systems are less sensitive than volumetric systems, which detect subtle changes in environmental characteristics.

   C. Electromagnetic systems deal with environmental changes such as ultrasonic frequencies, while volumetric systems can employ pressure mats or metallic foil in windows.

   D. Electromagnetic systems are more sensitive because they detect a change or break in a circuit, while volumetric systems detect environmental changes.

   ☑ B. A physical IDS can employ an electromechanical or volumetric system to detect intruders. An electromechanical system is less sensitive than a volumetric system. An electromechanical system detects a change or break in a circuit. For example, electromechanical detectors can detect movement on walls, screens, ceilings, and floors when the fine wires embedded within the structure are broken. Or magnetic contact switches can be installed on windows and doors. If the contacts are separated because the window or door is opened, an alarm will sound. Volumetric systems can detect changes in vibration, microwaves, ultrasonic frequencies, infrared values, and photoelectric changes.

   ☒ A is incorrect because volumetric systems are more sensitive than electromechanical systems. Also, volumetric systems—not electromechanical systems—detect changes in subtle environmental characteristics, such as vibration and ultrasonic frequencies. Electromechanical systems work by detecting a change or break in a circuit.

   ☒ C is incorrect because the statement is backward. Electromechanical systems make use of metallic foil in windows or pressure mats to detect a change or break in a circuit. The electrical circuits can be strips of foil embedded or connected to windows. If the window breaks, the foil strip breaks, which sounds an alarm. A pressure pad is another type of electromechanical detector. It is placed underneath a rug or portion of the carpet and is activated after hours. If someone steps on the pad, an alarm activates because no one is supposed to be in the area during this time. Volumetric systems deal with environmental changes, such as ultrasonic frequencies, but also vibration, microwaves, infrared values, and photoelectric changes.

☒ D is incorrect because volumetric systems are more sensitive, the reason being that they detect subtle changes in environmental characteristics. Electromechanical systems are less sensitive and work by detecting a change or break in a circuit.

13. What discipline combines the physical environment and sociology issues that surround it to reduce crime rates and the fear of crime?

    A. Layered defense model

    B. Target hardening

    C. Crime Prevention Through Environmental Design

    D. Natural access control

    ☑ C. Crime Prevention Through Environmental Design (CPTED) is a discipline that outlines how the proper design of a physical environment can reduce crime by directly affecting human behavior. It provides guidance in loss and crime prevention through proper facility construction and environmental components and procedures. The crux of CPTED is that the physical environment can be manipulated to create behavioral effects that will reduce crime and the fear of crime. It looks at the components that make up the relationship between humans and their environment. This encompasses the physical, social, and psychological needs of the users of different types of environments and predictable behaviors of these users and offenders. For example, CCTV cameras should be mounted in full view so that criminals know their activities will be captured and other people know the environment is well monitored and thus safer.

    ☒ A is incorrect because a layered defense model is a tiered architecture of physical, logical, and administrative security controls. The concept is that if one layer fails, other layers will protect the valuable asset. Layers should be implemented moving from the perimeter toward the asset. For example, you would have a fence, then your facility walls, then an access control card device, then a guard, then an IDS, and then locked computer cases and safes. This series of layers will protect the company's most sensitive assets, which would be placed in the innermost control zone of the environment. So if the bad guy were able to climb over your fence and outsmart the security guard, he would still have to circumvent several layers of controls before getting to your precious resources and systems.

    ☒ B is incorrect because target hardening focuses on denying access through physical and artificial barriers (alarms, locks, fences, and so on). Traditional target hardening can lead to restrictions on the use, enjoyment, and aesthetics of an environment. Remember that security entails maintaining a delicate balance between ease of use and protection. A Parks and Recreation department could implement fences, intimidating signs, and barriers around its parks and green areas to discourage gangs from congregating, but who would want to play or have a picnic there? The same goes for an office building. You must provide the necessary levels of protection, but your protection mechanisms should be more subtle and unobtrusive.

☒ **D** is incorrect because natural access control is the guidance of people entering and leaving a space by the placement of doors, fences, lighting, and even landscaping. For example, an office building may have external bollards with lights in them. These bollards carry out different safety and security services. The bollards themselves protect the facility from physical destruction by preventing people from driving their cars into the building. The light emitted helps ensure that criminals do not have a dark place to hide. And the lights and bollard placement guides people along the sidewalk to the entrance, instead of using signs or railings.

14. There are several types of volumetric IDSs. What type of IDS emits a measurable magnetic field that it monitors for disruptions?

   A. Capacitance detector

   B. Passive infrared system

   C. Wave-pattern motion detectors

   D. Photoelectric system

☑ **A.** A capacitance detector, or proximity detector, emits a measurable magnetic field. The detector monitors this magnetic field, and an alarm sounds if the field is disrupted. Capacitance change in an electrostatic field can be used to catch a bad guy, but first you need to understand what capacitance change means. An electrostatic IDS creates an electrostatic magnetic field, which is just an electric field associated with static electric charges. All objects have a static electric charge. They are all made up of many subatomic particles, and when everything is stable and static, these particles constitute one holistic electric charge. This means there is a balance between the electric capacitance and inductance. Now if an intruder enters the area his subatomic particles will mess up this lovely balance in the electrostatic field, causing capacitance change, and an alarm will sound.

☒ **B** is incorrect because a passive infrared system (PIR) identifies the changes of heat waves in an area it is configured to monitor. If the particles' temperature within the air rises, it could be an indication of the presence of an intruder, so an alarm is sounded.

☒ **C** is incorrect because wave-pattern motion detectors generate a wave pattern that is one of several frequencies: microwave, ultrasonic, or low frequency. The IDS generates a wave pattern that is sent over a sensitive area and reflected back to a receiver. If the pattern is returned undisturbed, the device does nothing. If the pattern returns altered because something in the room is moving, an alarm sounds.

☒ **D** is incorrect because a photoelectric system (or photometric system) detects the change in a light beam and thus can be used only in windowless rooms. These systems work like photoelectric smoke detectors, which emit a beam that hits the receiver. If this beam of light is interrupted, an alarm sounds. The beams emitted can be cross-sectional and can be invisible or visible beams. Cross-sectional means that one area can have several different light beams extending across it, which is usually carried out by using hidden mirrors to bounce the beam from one place to another until it hits the light receiver.

15. Paisley is helping her company identify potential site locations for a new facility. Which of the following is not an important factor when choosing a location?

    A. Distance to police and fire stations

    B. Lighting

    C. Natural disaster occurrence

    D. Crime rate

    ☑ **B.** Lighting is an important issue for physical security, but not a component that is evaluated during site location. The necessary lighting can be installed while the facility is built or later. Indeed, a security professional should understand that the right illumination needs to be in place, that no dead spots (unlit areas) should exist between the lights, and that all areas where individuals may walk should be properly lit. A security professional should also understand the various types of lighting available and where they should be used. If an organization does not implement the right types of lights and ensure they provide proper coverage, it increases the probability of criminal activity, accidents, and lawsuits.

    ☒ **A** is incorrect because a location's distance from police and fire stations is an important factor to consider when evaluating potential site locations. Many times, the proximity of these entities raises the real estate value of properties, but for good reason. Each of these issues—police station, fire station, and even medical facility proximity—can also reduce insurance rates and must be looked at carefully. Remember that the ultimate goal of physical security is to ensure the safety of personnel. Always keep that in mind when implementing any sort of physical security control.

    ☒ **C** is incorrect because when evaluating a location for a facility, it is critical to take into account the risk of natural disasters. Decision makers should consider the likelihood of floods, tornadoes, earthquakes, or hurricanes, as well as hazardous terrain (mudslides, falling rock from mountains, or excessive rain or snow). The likelihood of these risks will affect the organization's business continuity and disaster recovery programs.

☒ **D** is incorrect because it is important to consider the area's crime rate when evaluating site locations for a facility. It is also wise to consider the likelihood of riots and terrorism attacks, and other possible hazards from the surrounding area.

16. Sarah recently learned that the painting she inherited from a relative and hung in her downtown coffee shop is worth a lot of money. She is worried about its protection and wants to install an IDS. Which of the following intrusion detection systems is the most appropriate for protecting the painting?

   A. Acoustical detection system

   B. Proximity detector

   C. Photoelectric system

   D. Vibration sensor

   ☑ **B.** Proximity detectors, or capacitance detectors, are usually used to protect specific objects (artwork, cabinets, or a safe) versus protecting a whole room or area. A proximity detector emits and monitors a measurable magnetic field. If the field is disrupted, the detector sounds an alarm to alert a responsible entity of a possible intrusion. All IDSs are support mechanisms that are intended to detect and announce an attempted intrusion. They will not prevent or apprehend intruders, so they should be seen as an aid to the organization's security forces. While an IDS is a very valuable control, the technology is expensive and the system requires a redundant power supply and emergency backup power.

   ☒ **A** is incorrect because an acoustical detection system, although easy to install, is very sensitive and cannot be used in areas open to sounds of storms or traffic. An acoustical detection system uses microphones installed on floors, walls, or ceilings. The goal is to detect any sound made during a forced entry.

   ☒ **C** is incorrect because a photoelectric system cannot be used in a room with windows. A photoelectric system triggers an alarm when it detects changes in a light beam that is emitted. The beams can be visible or invisible. Photoelectric systems are commonly used in museums to protect works of art. If a visitor attempts to cross a room to steal a priceless sculpture, a beam will be broken and an alarm will sound.

   ☒ **D** is incorrect because, similar to an acoustical detection system, vibration sensors are sensitive to things like traffic and storms that could cause false positives. A vibration sensor senses vibrations in walls and floors. Financial institutions may choose to implement them on exterior walls where bank robbers may attempt to drive a vehicle through. They are also commonly used around the ceiling and flooring of vaults to detect someone attempting to break in.

17. David is preparing a server room at a new branch office. What locking mechanisms should he use for the primary and secondary server room entry doors?

A. The primary and secondary entrance doors should have access controlled through a swipe card or cipher lock.

B. The primary entrance door should have access controlled through a security guard. The secondary doors should be secured from the inside and allow no entry.

C. The primary entrance door should have access controlled through a swipe card or cipher lock. The secondary doors should have a security guard.

D. The primary entrance door should have access controlled through a swipe card or cipher lock. Secondary doors should be secured from the inside and allow no entry.

☑ **D.** Data centers, server rooms, and wiring closets should be located in the core areas of a facility, near wiring distribution centers. Strict access control mechanisms and procedures should be implemented for these areas. The access control mechanisms may be smart card readers, biometric readers, or combination locks. These restricted areas should have only one access door, but fire code requirements typically dictate there must be at least two doors to most data centers and server rooms. Only one door should be used for daily entry and exit and the other door should be used only in emergency situations. This second door should not be an access door, which means people should not be able to come in through this door. It should be locked, but it should have a panic bar that will release the lock if pressed from inside and used as an exit.

☒ **A** is incorrect because entrance should not be permitted through the secondary door—even with identification, authentication, and authorization processes. There should only be one entry point into a server room. Other doors should not provide entrance but can be used for emergency exits. Thus, the secondary doors should be secured from the inside to prevent entry.

☒ **B** is incorrect because the primary entrance door to a server room needs to carry out identification, authentication, and authorization processes. A swipe card or cipher lock fulfills these functions. A server room, ideally, should not be directly accessible from public areas like stairways, corridors, loading docks, elevators, and restrooms. This helps prevent foot traffic from casual passersby. Those who are by the doors to secured areas should have a legitimate reason for being there, as opposed to being on their way to a meeting room, for example.

☒ **C** is incorrect because the secondary door should not have a security guard. The door should simply be secured from the inside so that it cannot be used as an entry. The secondary door should serve as an emergency exit.

18. Which of the following is not true of IDSs?

    A. They can be hindered by items within the room.

    B. They are expensive and require human intervention to respond to the alarms.

    C. They usually come with a redundant power supply and emergency backup power.

    D. They should detect, and be resistant to, tampering.

    ☑ C. Intrusion detection systems do not commonly come with a redundant power supply and emergency backup power. However, these things are necessary. Without them, an IDS will be inoperable if the main source of power becomes unavailable, leaving assets at risk.

    ☒ A is incorrect because IDSs can be hindered by items within a room. In fact, the items within the room, as well as the size and shape of the room, may cause barriers, in which case more detectors are needed to provide the necessary level of coverage.

    ☒ B is incorrect because IDSs are relatively expensive and they do require human intervention to respond to the alarms. IDSs are used to detect unauthorized entries and alert a responsible entity to respond. These systems can monitor entries, doors, windows, devices, or removable coverings of equipment. Many work with magnetic contacts or vibration-detection devices that are sensitive to certain types of changes in the environment. When a change is detected, the IDS device sounds an alarm either in the local area, or in both the local area and a remote police or guard station.

    ☒ D is incorrect because IDSs should detect, and be resistant to, tampering. Intruders like to cover their tracks to avoid detection. Obviously, if the IDS can be disabled or tampered with so that an alarm does not trigger or evidence of an intrusion is destroyed, then the IDS cannot do its job. So an IDS worth its salt should have its own intrusion prevention mechanisms.

19. Before an effective physical security program can be rolled out, a number of steps must be taken. Which of the following steps comes first in the process of rolling out a security program?

    A. Create countermeasure performance metrics.

    B. Conduct a risk analysis.

    C. Design the program.

    D. Implement countermeasures.

    ☑ B. Of the steps listed, the first in the process of rolling out an effective physical security program is to carry out a risk analysis to identify the vulnerabilities and threats, and calculate the business impact of each threat. But before this is done, a team of internal employees and/or external consultants needs to be identified to build the physical security program. The team presents the risk analysis findings to management and works with them to define an acceptable risk level for the physical security program. From there, the team must develop baselines and metrics in order to evaluate and determine if the baselines are being met by the implemented countermeasures. Once the team identifies and implements the countermeasures, the performance of these countermeasures should be continually evaluated and expressed in the previously created metrics. These performance values are compared to the set baselines. If the baselines are continually maintained, then the security program is successful because the company's acceptable risk level is not being exceeded.

☒ A is incorrect because of the steps listed, creating countermeasure performance metrics is not the first step in creating a physical security program. It is, however, a very important one because it is only possible to determine how beneficial and effective the program is if it is monitored through a performance-based approach. This means you should devise measurements and metrics to measure the effectiveness of the chosen countermeasures. This enables management to make informed business decisions when investing in the protection of the organization's physical security. The goal is to increase the performance of the physical security program and decrease the risk to the company in a cost-effective manner. You should establish a baseline of performance and thereafter continually evaluate performance to make sure that the company's protection objectives are being met. Examples of possible performance metrics include number of successful crimes, number of successful disruptions, and the time it took for a criminal to defeat a control.

☒ C is incorrect because designing the program should take place after the risk analysis. Once the level of risk is understood then the design phase can take place to protect from the threats identified in the risk analysis. The design will incorporate the controls required for each category of the program: deterrence, delaying, detection, assessment, and response.

☒ D is incorrect because implementing countermeasures is of one of the last steps in the process rolling out a physical security program. Before countermeasures can be identified and implemented, it is important to conduct a risk analysis and work with management to define an acceptable level of risk. From the acceptable risk level, the team should derive the required performance baselines, and then create countermeasure performance metrics. Next, the team should develop criteria from the results of the analysis, outlining the level of protection and performance required for deterrence, delaying, detection, assessment, and response. Only after these steps are completed should the team identify and implement countermeasures for each of these categories.

20. A number of measures should be taken to help protect devices and the environment from electric power issues. Which of the following is best to keep voltage steady and power clean?

A. Power line monitor

B. Surge protector

C. Shielded cabling

D. Regulator

☑ **D.** When clean power is being provided, the power supply contains no interference or voltage fluctuation. Mechanisms should be in place to detect unwanted power fluctuations and protect the integrity of your data processing environment. Voltage regulators and line conditioners can be used to ensure a clean and smooth distribution of power. The primary power runs through a regulator or conditioner. They have the capability to absorb extra current if there is a spike, and to store energy to add current to the line if there is a sag. The goal is to keep the current flowing at a nice, steady level so neither motherboard components nor employees get fried.

☒ **A** is incorrect because power line monitors are employed to detect frequency and voltage amplitude changes. Interference interrupts the flow of an electrical current, and fluctuations can actually deliver a different level of voltage than what was expected. Each fluctuation can be damaging to devices and people. In order to effectively monitor frequency and voltage amplitude changes, you should understand what they are. Power excess can be described as a spike, which is momentary high voltage, or a surge, which is prolonged high voltage. Power loss can be experienced as a fault—momentary power outage—or a blackout—prolonged, complete loss of electric power. A sag or dip is a momentary low voltage condition, from one cycle to a few seconds. A brownout, also a type of power degradation, is a prolonged power supply that is below normal voltage. Finally, an in-rush current is an initial surge of current required to start a load.

☒ **B** is incorrect because a surge protector is used to move excess voltage to ground when a surge occurs. A surge is a prolonged rise in voltage from a power source. Surges can cause a lot of damage very quickly. A surge is one of the most common power problems and is controlled with surge protectors. A surge can come from a strong lightning strike, a power plant going online or offline, a shift in the commercial utility power grid, and electrical equipment within a business starting and stopping. Most computers have a built-in surge protector in their power supplies, but these are small surge protectors and cannot provide protection against the damage that larger surges (say, from storms) can cause. So, you need to ensure all devices are properly plugged into larger surge protectors, whose only job is to absorb any extra current before it is passed to electrical devices.

☒ **C** is incorrect because shielded cabling should be used for long cable runs and cables that run in buildings with fluorescent lighting or other interference mechanisms. Fluorescent lighting gives off radio frequency interference (RFI), which is disturbance to the flow of electric power while it travels across a power line. We could rip out all the fluorescent lighting in our buildings—or we can use shielded cabling where fluorescent lighting could cause a problem. If you were to climb up into your office's dropped ceiling and look around, you would probably see wires bundled and tied up to the true ceiling. If your office is using fluorescent lighting, the power and data lines should not be running over, or on top of, the fluorescent lights. This is because the radio frequencies being given off can interfere with the data or power current as it travels through these wires.

21. What type of fence detects if someone attempts to climb or cut it?

    A. Class IV

    B. PIDAS

    C. CPTED

    D. PCCIP

☑ **B.** Perimeter Intrusion Detection and Assessment System (PIDAS) is a type of fencing that has sensors located on the wire mesh and at the base of the fence. It is used to detect if someone attempts to cut or climb the fence. It has a passive cable vibration sensor that sets off an alarm if an intrusion is detected. PIDAS is very sensitive and can cause many false alarms. PIDAS fencing serves as a detective control. It is used in high-security areas, such as around military and prison facilities, and is also useful in areas that cannot be easily observed.

☒ **A** is incorrect because fencing is not classified in this manner. Classes are used to refer to gates. A Class IV gate means that it provides restricted access. This includes a prison entrance that is monitored in person or via closed circuitry. Each gate classification has its own long list of implementation and maintenance guidelines in order to ensure the necessary level of protection. These classifications and guidelines are developed by Underwriters Laboratory (UL), a nonprofit organization that tests, inspects, and classifies electronic devices, fire protection equipment, and specific construction materials.

☒ **C** is incorrect because CPTED is not a type of fencing. CPTED stands for Crime Prevention Through Environmental Design. It is a discipline that describes how to design a physical environment to affect human behavior, thereby reducing crime. CPTED has been used to develop physical security programs, as well as neighborhoods, towns, and cities. It addresses landscaping, entrances, facility and neighborhood layouts, lighting, road placement, and traffic circulation patterns—all in an effort to discourage criminal activity.

☒ **D** is incorrect because the PCCIP is the President's Commission on Critical Infrastructure Protection. PCCIP is an executive order that requires organizations that are part of the national critical infrastructure to have adequate protection mechanisms in place. This includes the technical protection of systems and data, as well as the physical protection of the facilities themselves. It outlines that power systems, emergency services, water supply systems, gas and oil transportation, and government services must be evaluated to ensure that proper physical security is implemented.

22. Several different types of smoke and fire detectors can be used. What type of detector is shown in the following graphic?

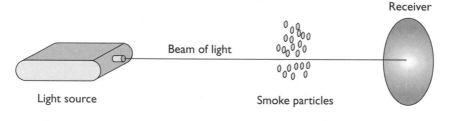

A. Photoelectric

B. Heat-activated

C. Infrared flame

D. Ionization

☑ **A.** A photoelectric device, also referred to as an optical detector, detects the variation in light intensity. The detector produces a beam of light across a protected area, and if the beam is obstructed, the alarm sounds. If the light source is obscured, the alarm will sound.

☒ **B** is incorrect because heat-activated detectors can be configured to sound an alarm either when a predefined temperature (fixed temperature) is reached or when the temperature increases over a period of time (rate-of-rise). Rate-of-rise temperature sensors usually provide a quicker warning than fixed-temperature sensors because they are more sensitive, but they can also cause more false alarms.

☒ **C** is incorrect because an infrared flame detector reacts to emissions of flames and senses pulsation of flames. This type of detector does not use a beam of light to identify smoke; thus, it is not a smoke detector. This type is a fire detector because it actually initiates when it is affected by flames.

☒ **D** is incorrect because an ionization detector reacts to charged particles of smoke. It is a smoke detector and not a fire detector because it activates when it encounters smoke particles. It does not use a beam of light to identify smoke, but has sensors that can identify the charged (ionized) components within the smoke itself.

23. Crime Prevention Through Environmental Design (CPTED) is a discipline that outlines how the proper design of a physical environment can reduce crime by directly affecting human behavior. Of CPTED's three main components, what is illustrated in the following photo?

A. Natural surveillance

B. Target hardening

C. Natural access control

D. Territorial reinforcement

☑ **A.** CPTED provides three main strategies to bring together the physical environment and social behavior to increase overall protection: natural access control, natural surveillance, and territorial reinforcement. Surveillance can take place through organized means (security guards), mechanical means (CCTV), and natural strategies (straight lines of sight, low landscaping, raised entrances). The goal of natural surveillance is to make criminals feel uncomfortable by providing many ways observers could potentially see them, and make all other people feel safe and comfortable, by providing an open and well-designed environment.

Natural surveillance is the use and placement of physical environmental features, personnel walkways, and activity areas in ways that maximize visibility. This photo shows a stairway in a building designed to be open and allow easy observation.

☒ **B** is incorrect because target hardening focuses on denying access through physical and artificial barriers (alarms, locks, fences, and so on). Target hardening is not a component of CPTED. Traditional target hardening can lead to restrictions on the use, enjoyment, and aesthetics of an environment. If your environment is a prison, this look might be just what you need. But if your environment is an office building, you're not looking for Fort Knox décor. Nevertheless, you still must provide the necessary levels of protection, but your protection mechanisms should be more subtle and unobtrusive. Let's say your organization's team needs to protect a side door at your facility. The traditional target-hardening approach would be to put locks, alarms, and cameras on the door, install an access control mechanism, such as a proximity reader, and instruct security guards to monitor this door.

☒ **C** is incorrect because natural access control is the guidance of people entering and leaving a space by the placement of doors, fences, lighting, and even landscaping. For example, an office building may have external bollards with lights in them. These bollards actually carry out different safety and security services. The bollards themselves protect the facility from physical destruction by preventing people from driving their cars into the building. The light emitted helps ensure that criminals do not have a dark place to hide. And the lights and bollard placement guides people along the sidewalk to the entrance, instead of using signs or railings. They work together to give individuals a feeling of being in a safe environment and help dissuade criminals by working as deterrents.

☒ **D** is incorrect because the third CPTED strategy is territorial reinforcement, which creates physical designs that emphasize or extend the company's physical sphere of influence so legitimate users feel a sense of ownership of that space. Territorial reinforcement can be implemented through the use of walls, fences, landscaping, light fixtures, flags, clearly marked addresses, and decorative sidewalks. The goal of territorial reinforcement is to create a sense of a dedicated community. Companies implement these elements so employees feel proud of their environment and have a sense of belonging, which they will defend if required to do so. These elements are also implemented to give potential offenders the impression that they do not belong there, that their activities are at risk of being observed, and that their illegal activities will not be tolerated or ignored.

24. Different types of material are built into walls and other constructs of various types of buildings and facilities. What type of material is shown in the following photo?

   A. Fire-resistant material

   B. Light frame construction material

   C. Heavy timber construction material

   D. Rebar material

☑ **D.** Calculations of approximate penetration times for different types of explosives and attacks are based on the thickness of the concrete walls and the gauge of rebar used. (Rebar refers to the steel rods encased within the concrete.) So even if the concrete can be damaged, it will take longer to actually cut or break through the rebar. Using thicker rebar and properly placing it within the concrete provides even more protection. Reinforced walls, rebar, and the use of double walls can be used as delaying mechanisms.

☒ **A** is incorrect because a building could be made up of incombustible material, such as steel, which provides a higher level of fire protection but loses its strength under extreme temperatures, something that may cause the building to collapse. This type of material has to do with the reduction of time and amount of fire damage instead of the difficulty of getting through a wall. The photo illustrates rebar, which is a material that reinforces the strength of walls.

☒ **B** is incorrect because light frame construction material is not illustrated in this photo. Light frame construction is composed of untreated lumber and is usually used to build homes, primarily because it is cheap but also because homes typically are not under the same types of fire and intrusion threats that office buildings are. The photo illustrates rebar, which is a material that reinforces the strength of walls.

☒ C is incorrect because heavy timber construction material is not illustrated in this photo. Heavy timber is commonly used for office buildings. The photo illustrates rebar, which is a material that reinforces the strength of walls.

25. There are five different classes of fire. Each depends upon what is on fire. Which of the following is the proper mapping for the items missing in the provided table?

Fire class	Type of fire	Elements of fire	Suppression method
Class A			Water, soda acid
Class B			CO_2 FM-200
Class C			Gas (Halon) or CO_2 nonconductive extinguishing agent
Class D			Dry chemicals
Class K			A wet chemical

A. Class D—combustible metals

B. Class C—liquid

C. Class B—electrical

D. Class A—electrical

☑ A. There are five classes (A, B, C, D, and K) of fire. You need to know the differences among the types of fire so that you know how to properly extinguish each type. Portable fire extinguishers have markings that indicate what type of fire they should be used on. A fire is a Class D if there are combustible metals on fire. These metals can be magnesium, sodium, or potassium. These types of fires should be suppressed and extinguished with dry chemicals.

☒ B is incorrect because a fire is a Class C if there is something electrical on fire. This can be computers or any other types of devices that run on electricity. These types of fires should be suppressed and extinguished with a type of gas as in Halon or CO_2.

☒ C is incorrect because a fire is a Class B if there is something liquid on fire. This can be petroleum, tars, or oils. These types of fires should be suppressed and extinguished with a type of gas as in FM-200 or CO_2.

☒ D is incorrect because a fire is a Class A if there is a type of common combustible material on fire. This can be wood, paper, or cloth. These types of fires should be suppressed and extinguished with water or soda acid.

26. Electrical power is being provided more through smart grids, which allow for self-healing, resistance to physical and cyberattacks, increased efficiency, and better integration of renewable energy sources. Countries want their grids to be more reliable, resilient, flexible, and efficient. Why does this type of evolution in power infrastructure concern many security professionals?

A. Allows for direct attacks through Power over Ethernet

B. Increased embedded software and computing capabilities

C. Does not have proper protection against common Web-based attacks

D. Power fluctuation and outages directly affect computing systems

☑ **B.** We are moving to smart grids, which mean that there is a lot more computing software and technology embedded into the grids and the items that make up the grids to optimize and automate these functions. This means that almost every component of the new power grid has to be computerized in some manner; thus, it can be vulnerable to digital-based attacks. Power grids are considered critical infrastructures to countries and can have negative consequences for a country if it is affected.

☒ **A** is incorrect because smart grids do not directly deal with providing Power over Ethernet (PoE). PoE provides both data and power connections on one cable. This means that a company does not need to have one cable for Ethernet and one for power—the power and network data can be converged onto one cable. For equipment that does not already have a power or data connection, PoE can be attractive when the power demand is low.

☒ **C** is incorrect because implementing computing capabilities in various power grid components does not have a direct correlation to Web-based attacks. Power grid components are not going to necessarily have direct access to Web servers and sites. The general term for infrastructure types of systems is SCADA (supervisory control and data acquisition) and generally refers to industrial control systems (ICSs). These systems monitor and control industrial, infrastructure, or facility-based processes. An attacker needs to know how to specifically exploit vulnerabilities in these types of systems, which would be different from common Web site vulnerabilities.

☒ **D** is incorrect because power fluctuations and outages are not necessarily security issues, and these are not the most critical topics most security professionals would be concerned with as the traditional power grid moves to a smart grid. A smart grid is made up of many embedded systems, which contain software that can have vulnerabilities for exploitation.

The following scenario is to be used for questions 27, 28, and 29.

Mike is the new CSO of a large pharmaceutical company. He has been asked to revamp the company's physical security program and better align it with the company's information security practices. Mike knows that the new physical security program should be made up of controls and processes that support the following categories: deterrent, delaying, detection, assessment, and response.

27. Mike's team has decided to implement new perimeter fences and warning signs against trespassing around the company's facility. Which of the categories listed in the scenario do these countermeasures map to?

    A. Deterrent

    B. Delaying

    C. Detection

    D. Assessment

    ☑ A. Fences, warning signs, and security guards are examples of countermeasures that can be put into place to deter unauthorized entry. A physical security program should contain controls in each of the following categories: deterrent, delaying, detection, assessment, and response.

    ☒ B is incorrect because reinforced walls, rebar, locks, and the use of double walls can be used as delaying mechanisms. The idea is that it will take the bad guy longer to get through these types of controls, which gives the response force sufficient time to arrive at the scene and stop the attacker. Deterrent controls reduce the likelihood of a vulnerability being exploited; a delaying control tries to ensure that if a bad thing happens, it will slow down the intruder.

    ☒ C is incorrect because detection tools are implemented not to deter malicious individuals but to detect their activities. Detection tools can be intrusion detection systems, sensors, and PIDAS fencing.

    ☒ D is incorrect because assessment controls pertain to how different situations will be identified and assessed. The most common control in this category is a security guard because he can connect the pieces of a situation together and determine what next steps should take place. It is important that there are controls in place that will carry out incident assessment and procedures that will be followed depending upon the outcome of the assessment.

28. Mike's team has decided to implement stronger locks on the exterior doors of the new company's facility. Which of the categories listed in the scenario does this countermeasure map to?

A. Deterrent

B. Delaying

C. Detection

D. Assessment

☑ **B.** Locks, defense-in-depth measures, and access controls are commonly used to delay potential intruders. A physical security program should contain controls in each of the following categories: deterrent, delaying, detection, assessment, and response.

☒ **A** is incorrect because fences, warning signs, and security guards are examples of countermeasures that can be put into place to deter unauthorized entry. The goal of these types of controls is for a potential attacker to not carry out his activities in the first place.

☒ **C** is incorrect because detection tools are implemented not to deter malicious individuals but to detect their activities. Detection tools can be intrusion detection systems, sensors, and PIDAS fencing.

☒ **D** is incorrect because assessment controls pertain to how different situations will be identified and assessed. The most common control in this category is a security guard because he can connect the pieces of a situation together and determine what next steps should take place. It is important that there are controls in place that will carry out incident assessment and procedures that will be followed depending upon the outcome of the assessment.

29. Mike's team has decided to hire and deploy security guards to monitor activities within the company's facility. Which of the categories listed in the scenario does this countermeasure map to?

A. Delaying

B. Detection

C. Assessment

D. Recall

☑ **C.** The assessment requirement of a physical security program pertains to how various situations will be assessed, triaged, and dealt with. The most common countermeasure to meet this need is the use of security guards.

☒ **A** is incorrect because locks, defense-in-depth measures, and access controls are commonly used to delay potential intruders. A physical security program should contain controls in each of the following categories: deterrent, delaying, detection, assessment, and response.

☒ **B** is incorrect because detection tools are implemented not to deter malicious individuals but to detect their activities. Detection tools can be intrusion detection systems, sensors, and PIDAS fencing.

☒ **D** is incorrect because it is a distracter answer.

The following scenario is to be used for questions 30, 31, and 32.

Greg is the security facility officer of a financial institution. His boss has told him that visitors need a secondary screening before they are allowed into sensitive areas within the building. Greg has also been told by the network administrators that after the new HVAC system was installed throughout the facility, they have noticed that power voltage to the systems in the data center sags.

30. Which of the following is the best control that Greg should ensure is implemented to deal with his boss's concern?

A. Access and audit logs

B. Mantrap

C. Proximity readers

D. Smart card readers

☑ **B.** Mantraps can be used so unauthorized individuals entering a facility cannot get in or out if it is activated. A mantrap is a small room with two doors. The first door is locked; a person is identified and authenticated by a security guard, biometric system, smart card reader, or swipe card reader. Once the person is authenticated and access is authorized, the first door opens and allows the person into the mantrap. The first door locks and the person is trapped. The person must be authenticated again before the second door unlocks and allows him into the facility. This requires two different authentication and authorization processes to complete successfully before someone is allowed entrance.

☒ **A** is incorrect because access and audit logs are not controls that can be used to carry out secondary screening activities. These are detective controls that are commonly reviewed after an incident has occurred.

☒ **C** is incorrect because it is not necessarily the best answer to this question. Proximity cards are most commonly used to gain physical access to a facility or location. The question specifically points out a requirement of secondary authentication to take place before someone can enter a sensitive area within a facility, and this is the reason that mantraps exist.

☒ **D** is incorrect because it is not necessarily the best answer to this question. Smart cards can be used for authentication purposes in many different situations. The question specifically points out a requirement of secondary authentication to take place before someone can enter a sensitive area within a facility, and this is the reason that mantraps exist. The mantrap might use smart cards as one of its authentication steps.

31. Which of the following best describes the situation that the network administrators are experiencing?

    A. Brownouts

    B. Surges

    C. In-rush current

    D. Power line interference

    ☑ C. When a heavy electrical device is turned on, it can draw a large amount of current, which is referred to as in-rush current. If the device sucks up enough current, it can cause a sag in the available power for surrounding devices. This could negatively affect their performance. It is a good idea to have the data processing center and devices on a different electrical wiring segment from that of the rest of the facility, if possible, so the devices will not be affected by these issues.

    ☒ A is incorrect because when power companies are experiencing high demand, they frequently reduce the voltage in an electrical grid, which is referred to as a brownout. Constant-voltage transformers can be used to regulate this fluctuation of power. They can use different ranges of voltage and only release the expected 120 volts of alternating current to devices. Brownouts are not usually associated with HVAC systems.

    ☒ B is incorrect because a surge is a quick rise in voltage from a power source. Surges can cause a lot of damage very quickly. A surge is one of the most common power problems and is controlled with surge protectors. These protectors use a device called a metal oxide varistor, which moves the excess voltage to ground when a surge occurs.

    ☒ D is incorrect because when clean power is being provided, the power supply contains no interference or voltage fluctuation. The possible types of interference (line noise) are electromagnetic interference (EMI) and radio frequency interference (RFI), which is disturbance to the flow of electric power while it travels across a power line. This question does not address interference issues like these.

32. Which of the following is a control that Greg's team could implement to address the network administrators' issue?

    A. Secondary feeder line

    B. Insulated grounded wiring

C. Line conditioner

D. Generator

☑ **C.** Because these and other occurrences are common, mechanisms should be in place to detect unwanted power fluctuations and protect the integrity of data processing environments. Voltage regulators and line conditioners can be used to ensure a clean and smooth distribution of power. The primary power runs through a regulator or conditioner. They have the capability to absorb extra current if there is a spike, and to store energy to add current to the line if there is a sag.

☑ **A** is incorrect because a secondary feeder line from a transformer does not address the issue outlined in this scenario. A secondary line would be put into place for redundancy and failover purposes.

☒ **B** is incorrect because an insulated grounded wire does not address the issue outlined in the scenario. The issue in the scenario has to do with in-rush currents, which means that the voltage of the power supply is uneven and potentially damaging. Wires are grounded to ensure that an excessive current goes to the ground and not to a piece of equipment or person. Grounding wires does not address voltage and current fluctuation.

☒ **D** is incorrect because a generator is implemented in case there is a power outage. A generator does not have any effect on power voltage changes.

Telecommunications and Network Security

This domain includes questions from the following topics:

- OSI and TCP/IP models
- Protocol types and security issues
- LAN, WAN, MAN, intranet, and extranet technologies
- Cable types and data transmission types
- Network devices and services
- Communications security management
- Telecommunications devices and technologies
- Remote connectivity technologies
- Wireless technologies
- Threat and attack types

A network forms the backbone of an organization's IT infrastructure. Without it, systems couldn't communicate and users couldn't share resources in real time. Because of the myriad protocols, technologies, and concepts involved in networking, it is one of the more complex topics you need to understand for the CISSP and in your role as a security professional. The many different types of devices, protocols, and security mechanisms within an environment provide different functionality. You must understand how the technologies work, how they interact with each other, how they're configured, and how they must be secured.

1. Layer 2 of the OSI model has two sublayers. What are those sublayers, and what are two IEEE standards that describe technologies at that layer?

    A. LCL and MAC; IEEE 802.2 and 802.3

    B. LCL and MAC; IEEE 802.1 and 802.3

    C. Network and MAC; IEEE 802.1 and 802.3

    D. LLC and MAC; IEEE 802.2 and 802.3

2. Which of the following is not an effective countermeasure against spam?

    A. Open mail relay servers

    B. Properly configured mail relay servers

    C. Filtering on an e-mail gateway

    D. Filtering on the client

3. Robert is responsible for implementing a common architecture used when customers need to access confidential information through Internet connections. Which of the following best describes this type of architecture?

    A. Two-tiered model

    B. Screened subnet

    C. Three-tiered model

    D. Public and private DNS zones

4. Two commonly used networking protocols are TCP and UPD. Which of the following correctly describes the two?

    A. TCP provides best-effort delivery, and UDP sets up a virtual connection with the destination.

    B. TCP provides more services and is more reliable in data transmission, whereas UDP takes less resources and overhead to transmit data.

    C. TCP provides more services and is more reliable, but UDP provides more security services.

    D. TCP is reliable, and UDP deals with flow control and ACKs.

5. Which of the following indicates to a packet where to go and how to communicate with the right service or protocol on the destination computer?

    A. Socket

    B. IP address

    C. Port

    D. Frame

6. Several different tunneling protocols can be used in dial-up situations. Which of the following would be best to use as a VPN tunneling solution?

   A. L2P

   B. PPTP

   C. IPSec

   D. L2TP

7. Which of the following correctly describes Bluejacking?

   A. Bluejacking is a harmful, malicious attack.

   B. It is the process of taking over another portable device via a Bluetooth-enabled device.

   C. It is commonly used to send contact information.

   D. The term was coined by the use of a Bluetooth device and the act of hijacking another device.

8. DNS is a popular target for attackers due to its strategic role on the Internet. What type of attack uses recursive queries to poison the cache of a DNS server?

   A. DNS spoofing

   B. Manipulation of the hosts file

   C. Social engineering

   D. Domain litigation

9. IP telephony networks require the same security measures as those implemented on an IP data network. Which of the following is unique to IP telephony?

   A. Limiting IP sessions going through media gateways

   B. Identification of rogue devices

   C. Implementation of authentication

   D. Encryption of packets containing sensitive information

10. Cross-site scripting (XSS) is an application security vulnerability usually found in Web applications. What type of XSS vulnerability occurs when a victim is tricked into opening a URL programmed with a rogue script to steal sensitive information?

    A. Persistent XSS vulnerability

    B. Nonpersistent XSS vulnerability

    C. Second-order vulnerability

    D. DOM-based vulnerability

11. Angela wants to group together computers by department to make it easier for them to share network resources. Which of the following will allow her to group computers logically?

    A. VLAN

    B. Open network architecture

    C. Intranet

    D. VAN

12. Which of the following incorrectly describes how routing commonly takes place on the Internet?

    A. EGP is used in the areas "between" each AS.

    B. Regions of nodes that share characteristics and behaviors are called ASs.

    C. CAs are specific nodes that are responsible for routing to nodes outside of their region.

    D. Each AS uses IGP to perform routing functionality.

13. Both de facto and proprietary interior protocols are in use today. Which of the following is a proprietary interior protocol that chooses the best path between the source and destination?

    A. IGRP

    B. RIP

    C. BGP

    D. OSPF

14. Which of the following categories of routing protocols builds a topology database of the network?

    A. Dynamic

    B. Distance-vector

    C. Link-state

    D. Static

15. Which of the following does not describe IP telephony security?

    A. VoIP networks should be protected with the same security controls used on a data network.

    B. Softphones are more secure than IP phones.

    C. As endpoints, IP phones can become the target of attacks.

    D. The current Internet architecture over which voice is transmitted is less secure than physical phone lines.

16. When an organization splits naming zones, the names of its hosts that are only accessible from an intranet are hidden from the Internet. Which of the following best describes why this is done?

    A. To prevent attackers from accessing servers

    B. To prevent the manipulation of the hosts file

    C. To avoid providing attackers with valuable information that can be used to prepare an attack

    D. To avoid providing attackers with information needed for cybersquatting

17. Which of the following best describes why e-mail spoofing is easily executed?

    A. SMTP lacks an adequate authentication mechanism.

    B. Administrators often forget to configure an SMTP server to prevent inbound SMTP connections for domains it doesn't serve.

    C. Keyword filtering is technically obsolete.

    D. Blacklists are undependable.

18. Which of the following is not a benefit of VoIP?

    A. Cost

    B. Convergence

    C. Flexibility

    D. Security

19. Today, satellites are used to provide wireless connectivity between different locations. What two prerequisites are needed for two different locations to communicate via satellite links?

    A. They must be connected via a phone line and have access to a modem.

    B. They must be within the satellite's line of site and footprint.

    C. They must have broadband and a satellite in low Earth orbit.

    D. They must have a transponder and be within the satellite's footprint.

20. Brad is a security manager at Thingamabobs Inc. He is preparing a presentation for his company's executives on the risks of using instant messaging (IM) and his reasons for wanting to prohibit its use on the company network. Which of the following should not be included in his presentation?

    A. Sensitive data and files can be transferred from system to system over IM.

    B. Users can receive information—including malware—from an attacker posing as a legitimate sender.

    C. IM use can be stopped by simply blocking specific ports on the network firewalls.

    D. A security policy is needed specifying IM usage restrictions.

21. There are several different types of authentication technologies. Which type is being shown in the graphic that follows?

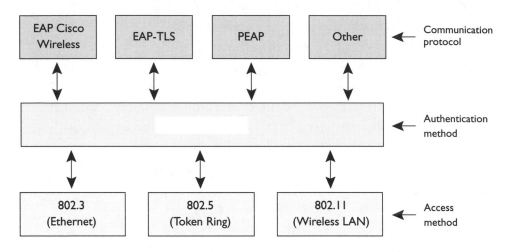

A. 802.1x

B. Extensible Authentication Protocol

C. Frequency hopping spread spectrum

D. Orthogonal frequency-division multiplexing

22. What type of security encryption component is missing from the table that follows?

	802.1x Dynamic WEP	Wi-Fi Protected Access	Robust Security Network
Access Control	802.1x	802.1x or preshared key	802.1x or preshared key
Authentication	EAP methods	EAP methods or preshared key	EAP methods or preshared key
Encryption	WEP		CCMP (AES Counter Mode)
Integrity	None	Michael MIC	CCMP (AES CBC-MAC)

A. Service Set ID

B. Temporal Key Integrity Protocol

C. Ad hoc WLAN

D. Open system authentication

23. What type of technology is represented in the graphic that follows?

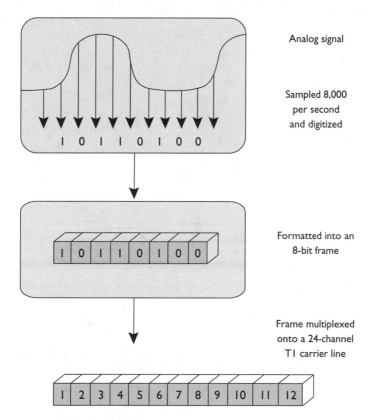

A. Asynchronous Transfer Mode

B. Synchronous Optical Networks

C. Frequency-division multiplexing

D. Multiplexing

24. What type of telecommunication technology is illustrated in the graphic that follows?

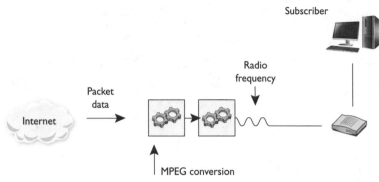

A. Digital Subscriber Line

B. Integrated Services Digital Network

C. BRI ISDN

D. Cable modem

25. Which type of WAN tunneling protocol is missing from the table that follows?

PPTP
Internetwork Must Be IP Based
No Header Compression
No Tunnel Authentication
Built-In PPP Encryption

Internetwork Can Be IP Frame Relay, x.25, or ATM Based
Header Compression
Tunnel Authentication
Uses IPSec Encryption

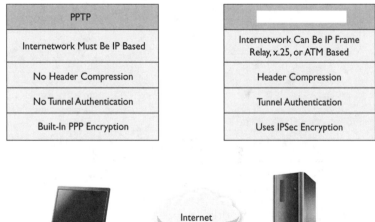

Client

Internet

Server

A. IPSec

B. FDDI

C. L2TP

D. CSMA/CD

26. IPv6 has many new and different characteristics and functionality compared to IPv4. Which of the following is an incorrect functionality or characteristic of IPv6?

   i.   IPv6 allows for nonscoped addresses, which enables an administrator to restrict specific addresses for specific servers or file and print sharing, for example.

   ii. IPv6 has IPSec integrated into the protocol stack, which provides application-based secure transmission and authentication.

   iii. IPv6 has more flexibility and routing capabilities compared to IPv4 and allows for Quality of Service (QoS) priority values to be assigned to time-sensitive transmissions.

   iv. The protocol offers autoconfiguration, which makes administration much easier compared to IPv4, and it does not require network address translation (NAT) to extend its address space.

   A. i, iii

   B. i, ii

   C. ii, iii

   D. ii, iv

27. Hanna is a new security manager for a computer consulting company. She has found out that the company has lost intellectual property in the past because malicious employees installed rogue devices on the network, which were used to capture sensitive traffic. Hanna needs to implement a solution that ensures only authorized devices are allowed access to the company network. Which of the following IEEE standards was developed for this type of protection?

   A. IEEE 802.1AR

   B. IEEE 802.1AE

   C. IEEE 802.1AF

   D. IEEE 802.1XR

28. There are common cloud computing service models. _____ usually requires companies to deploy their own operating systems, applications, and software onto the provided infrastructure. _____ is the software environment that runs on top of the infrastructure. In the _____ model the provider commonly gives the customers network-based access to a single copy of an application.

   A. Platform as a Service, Infrastructure as a Service, Software as a Service

   B. Platform as a Service, Platform as Software, Application as a Service

   C. Infrastructure as a Service, Application as a Service, Software as a Service

   D. Infrastructure as a Service, Platform as Software, Software as a Service

29. _____ is a set of extensions to DNS that provides to DNS clients (resolvers) origin authentication of DNS data to reduce the threat of DNS poisoning, spoofing, and similar attack types.

    A. Resource records

    B. Zone transfer

    C. DNSSEC

    D. Resource transfer

30. Which of the following best describes the difference between a virtual firewall that works in bridge mode versus one that is embedded into a hypervisor?

    A. Bridge-mode virtual firewall allows the firewall to monitor individual traffic links, and hypervisor integration allows the firewall to monitor all activities taking place within a host system.

    B. Bridge-mode virtual firewall allows the firewall to monitor individual network links, and hypervisor integration allows the firewall to monitor all activities taking place within a guest system.

    C. Bridge-mode virtual firewall allows the firewall to monitor individual traffic links, and hypervisor integration allows the firewall to monitor all activities taking place within a guest system.

    D. Bridge-mode virtual firewall allows the firewall to monitor individual guest systems, and hypervisor integration allows the firewall to monitor all activities taking place within a network system.

1. D	11. A	21. A
2. A	12. C	22. B
3. C	13. A	23. D
4. B	14. C	24. D
5. A	15. B	25. C
6. B	16. C	26. B
7. C	17. A	27. A
8. A	18. D	28. D
9. A	19. B	29. C
10. B	20. C	30. A

1. Layer 2 of the OSI model has two sublayers. What are those sublayers, and what are two IEEE standards that describe technologies at that layer?

   A. LCL and MAC; IEEE 802.2 and 802.3

   B. LCL and MAC; IEEE 802.1 and 802.3

   C. Network and MAC; IEEE 802.1 and 802.3

   D. LLC and MAC; IEE E 802.2 and 802.3

   ☑ **D.** The data link layer, or Layer 2, of the OSI model is responsible for adding a header and a trailer to a packet to prepare the packet for the local area network or wide area network technology binary format for proper line transmission. Layer 2 is divided into two functional sublayers. The upper sublayer is the Logical Link Control (LLC) and is defined in the IEEE 802.2 specification. It communicates with the network layer, which is immediately above the data link layer. Below the LLC is the Media Access Control (MAC) sublayer, which specifies the interface with the protocol requirements of the physical layer. Thus, the specification for this layer depends on the technology of the physical layer. The IEEE MAC specification for Ethernet is 802.3, Token Ring is 802.5, wireless LAN is 802.11, and so on. When you see a reference to an IEEE standard, such as 802.11 or 802.16, it refers to the protocol working at the MAC sublayer of the data link layer of the protocol stack.

   ☒ **A** is incorrect because LCL is a distracter. The correct acronym for the upper sublayer of the data link layer is LLC. It stands for the Logical Link Control. By providing multiplexing and flow control mechanisms, the LLC enables the coexistence of network protocols within a multipoint network and their transportation over the same network media.

   ☒ **B** is incorrect because LCL is a distracter. The sublayers of the data link layer are the Logical Link Control (LLC) and the Media Access Control (MAC). Furthermore, the LLC is defined in the IEEE 802.2 specification, not 802.1. The IEEE 802.1 specifications are concerned with protocol layers above the MAC and LLC layers. It addresses LAN/MAN architecture, network management, internetworking between LANs and WANs, and link security, etc.

   ☒ **C** is incorrect because network is not a sublayer of the data link layer. The sublayers of the data link layer are the Logical Link Control (LLC) and the Media Access Control (MAC). The LLC sits between the network layer (the layer immediately above the data link layer) and the MAC sublayer. Also, the LLC is defined in the IEEE 802.2 specification, not IEEE 802.1. As just explained, 802.1 standards address areas of LAN/MAN architecture, network management, internetworking between LANs and WANs, and link security. The IEEE 802.1 group's four active task groups are Internetworking, Security, Audio/Video Bridging, and Data Center Bridging.

2. Which of the following is not an effective countermeasure against spam?

    A. Open mail relay servers

    B. Properly configured mail relay servers

    C. Filtering on an e-mail gateway

    D. Filtering on the client

    ☑ **A.** An open mail relay server is not an effective countermeasure against spam; in fact, spammers often use them to distribute spam, as they allow an attacker to mask their identity. An open mail relay is an SMTP server that is configured to allow inbound SMTP connections from anyone and to anyone on the Internet. This is how the Internet was originally set up, but many relays are now properly configured to prevent attackers from using them to distribute spam or pornography.

    ☒ **B** is incorrect because a properly configured mail relay server only allows e-mail that is destined and originating from known users to pass through it. In this way, a closed mail relay server helps prevent the distribution of spam. In order to be considered closed, an SMTP server should be configured to accept and forward messages from local IP addresses to local mailboxes, from local IP addresses to nonlocal mailboxes, from known and trusted IP addresses to local mailboxes, and from clients that are authenticated and authorized. Servers that are left open are considered to be the result of poor systems administration.

    ☒ **C** is incorrect because implementing spam filters on an e-mail gateway is the most common countermeasure against spam. Doing so helps protect network and server capacity, reduces the risk of legitimate e-mail being discarded, and saves users time. A number of commercial spam filters based on a variety of algorithms are available. The filtering software accepts e-mail as its input and either forwards the message unchanged to the recipient, redirects the message for delivery elsewhere, or discards the message.

    ☒ **D** is incorrect because filtering on the client is a countermeasure against spam. In fact, filtering can take place at the gateway, which is the most popular method, on the e-mail server, or on the client. There are also different methods of filtering. Filtering based on keywords was once a popular method but has since become obsolete because it is prone to false positives and spammers can easily bypass them. Now more sophisticated filters are used. These are based on statistical analysis or analysis of e-mail traffic patterns.

3. Robert is responsible for implementing a common architecture used when customers need to access confidential information through Internet connections. Which of the following best describes this type of architecture?

A. Two-tiered model

B. Screened host

C. Three-tiered model

D. Public and private DNS zones

☑ **C.** Many of today's e-commerce architectures use a three-tiered architecture approach. The three-tier architecture is a client-server architecture in which the user interface, functional process logic, and data storage run as independent components that are developed and maintained, often on separate platforms. The three-tier architecture allows for any one of the tiers to be upgraded or modified as needed without affecting the other two tiers because of its modularity. In the case of e-commerce, the presentation layer is a front-end Web server that users interact with. It can serve both static and cached dynamic content. The business logic layer is where the request is reformatted and processed. This is commonly a dynamic content processing and generation-level application server. The data storage is where the sensitive data is held. It is a backend database that holds both the data and the database management system software that is used to manage and provide access to the data. The separate tiers may be connected with middleware and run on separate physical servers.

☒ **A** is incorrect because two-tiered, or client-server, describes an architecture in which a server provides services to one or more clients that request those services. Many of today's business applications and Internet protocols use the client-server model. This architecture uses two systems: a client and a server. The client is one tier and the server is another tier, hence the two-tier architecture. Each instance of the client software is connected to one or more servers. The client sends its information request to a server, which processes the request and returns the data to the client. A three-tier architecture is a better approach for protecting sensitive information when requests are coming in from the Internet. It provides one extra tier that an attacker must exploit to gain access to the sensitive data being held on the backend server.

☒ **B** is incorrect because a screened host architecture means that one firewall is in place to protect one server, which is basically a one-tier architecture. An external, public-facing firewall screens the requests coming in from an untrusted network as in the Internet. If the one tier, the only firewall, is compromised, then the attacker can gain access to the sensitive data that resides on the server relatively easily.

☒ **D** is incorrect because while separating DNS servers into public and private servers provides protection, it is not an actual architecture used for the purpose requested in the question. Organizations should implement split DNS (public and private facing), which means a DNS server in the DMZ handles external resolution requests, while an internal DNS server handles only internal requests. This helps ensure that the internal DNS has layers of protection and is not exposed to Internet connections.

4. Two commonly used networking protocols are TCP and UPD. Which of the following correctly describes the two?

    A. TCP provides best-effort delivery, and UDP sets up a virtual connection with the destination.

    B. TCP provides more services and is more reliable in data transmission, whereas UDP takes less resources and overhead to transmit data.

    C. TCP provides more services and is more reliable, but UDP provides more security services.

    D. TCP is reliable, and UDP deals with flow control and ACKs.

    ☑ **B.** Two main protocols within the TCP/IP stack work at the transport layer: TCP and UDP. TCP is a reliable and connection-oriented protocol, which means it ensures packets are delivered to the destination computer. If a packet is lost during transmission, TCP has the ability to identify this issue and resend the lost or corrupted packet. TCP is referred to as a connection-oriented protocol because, before any user data is actually sent, handshaking takes place between the two systems that want to communicate. Once the handshaking completes successfully, a virtual connection is set up between the two systems. UDP is considered a connectionless protocol because it does not go through these steps. Instead, UDP sends out messages without first contacting the destination computer and does not know whether the packets were received properly or dropped. TCP provides a full-duplex, reliable communication mechanism, and if any packets are lost or damaged, they are re-sent; however, TCP requires a lot of system overhead when compared to UDP. If a programmer knows data dropped during transmission is not detrimental to the application, he may choose to use UDP because it is faster and requires fewer resources.

    ☒ A is incorrect because the descriptions are backward. UDP is a connectionless protocol that does not send or receive acknowledgments when a datagram is received. It does not ensure that data arrives at its destination. It provides best-effort delivery. TCP is a connection-oriented protocol; thus, it performs handshaking and develops a virtual connection with the destination computer. It ensures data arrives at its destination.

    ☒ C is incorrect because UDP does not provide security services. However, TCP is more reliable and provides more services than UDP. Unlike UDP, TCP ensures that packets reach their destinations, returns ACKs when a packet is received, and is a reliable protocol. It supports flow and congestion control, and error detection and correction.

☒ **D** is incorrect because the description of UDP describes TCP. UDP does not return ACKs and does not guarantee that a packet will reach its destination. It is an unreliable protocol. Furthermore, the destination computer does not communicate back to the source computer about flow control through UDP.

5. Which of the following indicates to a packet where to go and how to communicate with the right service or protocol on the destination computer?

   A. Socket

   B. IP address

   C. Port

   D. Frame

   ☑ **A.** UDP and TCP are transport protocols that applications use to get their data across a network. They both use ports to communicate with upper OSI layers and to keep track of various conversations that take place simultaneously. The ports are also the mechanism used to identify how other computers access services. When a TCP or UDP message is formed, a source and a destination port are contained within the header information along with the source and destination IP addresses. This makes up a socket, which is how packets know where to go—by the address—and how to communicate with the right service or protocol on the other computer—by the port number. The IP address acts as the doorway to a computer, and the port acts as the doorway to the actual protocol or service. To communicate properly, the packet needs to know these doors.

   ☒ **B** is incorrect because an IP address does not tell a packet how to communicate with a service or protocol. The purpose of an IP address is host or network interface identification and location addressing. Each node in a network has a unique IP address. This information, along with the source and destination ports, makes up a socket. The IP address tells the packet where to go, and the port indicates how to communicate with the right service or protocol.

   ☒ **C** is incorrect because the port only tells the packet how to communicate with the right service or protocol. It does not tell the packet where to go. The IP address provides this information. A port is a communications endpoint used by IP protocols such as TCP and UDP. Ports are identified by a number. They are also associated with an IP address and a protocol used for communication.

   ☒ **D** is incorrect because frame is the term used to refer to a datagram after it is given a header and trailer at the data link layer. A message is formed and passed to the application layer from a program and sent down through the protocol stack. Each protocol at each layer adds its own information (headers and trailers) to the message and passes it down to the next level. As the message is passed down the stack, it goes through a sort of evolution, and each stage has a specific name that indicates what is taking place. When an application formats data to be transmitted over the network, the data is called a message. The message is sent to the transport layer, where TCP does its magic on the data. The bundle of data is now a segment. The segment is sent to the network layer. The network layer adds routing and addressing, and now the bundle is called a datagram. The network layer passes off the datagram to the data link layer, which frames the datagram with a header and a trailer, and now it is called a frame.

6. Several different tunneling protocols can be used in dial-up situations. Which of the following would be best to use as a VPN tunneling solution?

   A. L2P

   B. PPTP

   C. IPSec

   D. L2TP

   ☑ **B.** A virtual private network (VPN) is a secure, private connection through a public network or an otherwise unsecure environment. It is a private connection because the encryption and tunneling protocols are used to ensure the confidentiality and integrity of the data in transit. It is important to remember that VPN technology requires a tunnel to work, and it assumes encryption. The protocols that can be used for VPNs are Point-to-Point Tunneling Protocol (PPTP), IPSec, and L2TP. Point-to-Point Tunneling Protocol (PPTP), a Microsoft protocol, allows remote users to set up a PPP connection to a local ISP and then create a secure VPN to their destination. PPTP has been the de facto industry-standard tunneling protocol for years, but the new de facto standard for VPNs is IPSec. PPTP is designed for client/server connectivity and establishes a single point-to-point connection between two computers. It works at the data link layer and transmits only over IP networks.

   ☒ **A** is incorrect because L2P does not exist. This is a distracter answer.

   ☒ **C** is incorrect because although IPSec is one of the three primary VPN tunneling protocols, it is not used over dial-up connections. It supports only IP networks and works at the network layer, providing security on top of IP. IPSec handles multiple connections at the same time, and provides secure authentication and encryption.

   ☒ **D** is incorrect because L2TP is not a tunneling protocol that works over a dial-up connection. L2TP is a tunneling protocol that can extend a VPN over various WAN network types (IP, X.25, frame relay). A hybrid of L2F and PPTP, L2TP works at the data link layer and transmits over multiple types of networks, not just IP. However, it must be combined with IPSec for security so it is not considered a VPN solution by itself.

7. Which of the following correctly describes Bluejacking?

   A. Bluejacking is a harmful, malicious attack.

   B. It is the process of taking over another portable device via a Bluetooth-enabled device

   C. It is commonly used to send contact information.

   D. The term was coined by the use of a Bluetooth device and the act of hijacking another device.

   ☑ C. Bluetooth is vulnerable to an attack called Bluejacking, which entails an attacker sending an unsolicited message to a device that is Bluetooth-enabled. Bluejackers look for a receiving device, such as a mobile device or laptop, and then send a message to it. Often, the Bluejacker is trying to send their business card to be added to the victim's contact list in their address book. The countermeasure is to put the Bluetooth-enabled device into nondiscoverable mode so that others cannot identify this device in the first place. If you receive some type of message this way, just look around you. Bluetooth only works within a ten-meter distance, so it is coming from someone close by.

   ☒ A is incorrect because Bluejacking is actually a harmless nuisance rather than a malicious attack. It is the act of sending unsolicited messages to Bluetooth-enabled devices. The first act took place in a bank in which the attacker polled the network and found an active Nokia phone. He then sent the message "Buy Ericcson."

   ☒ B is incorrect because Bluejacking does not involve taking over another device. It does not give the attacker control of the target device. Rather, the Bluejacker simply sends an unsolicited message to the Bluetooth-enabled device. These messages are usually text only, but it is possible to also send images or sounds. Victims are often unfamiliar with Bluejacking and may think their phone is malfunctioning or that they have been attacked by a virus or hijacked by a Trojan horse.

   ☒ D is incorrect because the term Bluejacking has nothing to do with hijacking, which means to take over something. The name Bluejacking was invented by a Malaysian IT consultant who sent the message "Buy Ericsson" to another Bluetooth-enabled device.

8. DNS is a popular target for attackers due to its strategic role on the Internet. What type of attack uses recursive queries to poison the cache of a DNS server?

A. DNS spoofing

B. Manipulation of the hosts file

C. Social engineering

D. Domain litigation

☑ **A.** DNS plays a strategic role in the transmission of traffic on the Internet. The DNS directs traffic to the appropriate address by mapping domain names to their corresponding IP addresses. DNS queries can be classified as either recursive or iterative. In a recursive query the DNS server often forwards the query to another server and returns the inquirer the proper response. In an iterative query, the DNS server responds with an address for another DNS server that might be able to answer the question, and the client then proceeds to ask the new DNS server. Attackers use recursive queries to poison the cache of a DNS server. In this manner, attackers can point systems to a Web site that they control and that contains malware or some other form of attack. Here's how it works: An attacker sends a recursive query to a victim DNS server asking for the IP address of the domain www .logicalsecurity.com. The DNS server forwards the query to another DNS server. However, before the other DNS server responds, the attacker injects his own IP address. The victim server accepts the IP address and stores it in its cache for a specific period of time. The next time a system queries the server to resolve www.logicalsecurity.com to its IP address, the server will direct users to the attacker's IP address. This is called DNS spoofing or DNS poisoning.

☒ **B** is incorrect because manipulating the hosts file does not use recursive queries to poison the cache of a DNS server. A client first queries a hosts file before issuing a request to a DNS server. Some viruses add invalid IP addresses of antivirus vendors to the hosts file in order to prevent the download of virus definitions and prevent detection. This is an example of manipulating the hosts file.

☒ **C** is incorrect because social engineering does not involve querying a DNS server. Social engineering refers to the manipulation of individuals for the purpose of gaining unauthorized access or information. Social engineering takes advantage of people's desire to be helpful and/or trusting. It is a nontechnical attack that may use technology in its execution. For example, an attacker might pose as a user's manager and send him a spoofed e-mail asking for the password to an application. The user, wanting to help and keep his manager's favor, is likely to provide the password.

☒ **D** is incorrect because domain litigation does not involve poisoning a DNS server's cache. Domain names are subject to trademark risks, including the temporary unavailability or permanent loss of an established domain name. A victim company could lose its entire Internet presence as a result of domain litigation. Organizations concerned over the possibility of trademark disputes related to their domain name(s) should establish contingency plans. For example, a company may establish a second, unrelated domain that can still represent the company's name.

9. IP telephony networks require the same security measures as those implemented on an IP data network. Which of the following is unique to IP telephony?

A. Limiting IP sessions going through media gateways

B. Identification of rogue devices

C. Implementation of authentication

D. Encryption of packets containing sensitive information

☑ A. A media gateway is the translation unit between disparate telecommunications networks. VoIP Media Gateways perform the conversion between Time Division Multiplexing (TDM) voice to Voice over Internet Protocol (VoIP). As a security measure, the number of calls via media gateways should be limited. Otherwise, media gateways are vulnerable to denial-of-service attacks, hijacking, and other types of attacks.

☒ B is incorrect because it is necessary to identify rogue devices on both IP telephony and data networks. On IP telephony networks, it is necessary to look specifically for rogue IP phones and softphones. Rogue means that these devices are unauthorized. They are therefore not managed or secured by IT and can introduce additional risk to the network. A common rogue device found on data networks is wireless access points. A rogue access point can provide an entry to the network for unauthorized users.

☒ C is incorrect because authentication is recommended for both data and voice networks. In both cases, authentication allows you to register users and equipment on the network so that you can verify they are who they say they are when they try to connect to the network. Authentication also allows you to deny access to users and devices that are not authorized.

☒ D is incorrect because sensitive data can be transmitted on either a voice or data network and should be encrypted in both cases. Eavesdropping is a very real threat for VoIP networks. Consider all the sales meetings, management meetings, financial meetings, etc., that are conducted over the phone. Every word that is spoken in those meetings is vulnerable to eavesdropping. Encrypting voice data is one of the best ways to protect this sensitive data.

10. Cross-site scripting (XSS) is an application security vulnerability usually found in Web applications. What type of XSS vulnerability occurs when a victim is tricked into opening a URL programmed with a rogue script to steal sensitive information?

A. Persistent XSS vulnerability

B. Nonpersistent XSS vulnerability

C. Second-order vulnerability

D. DOM-based vulnerability

☑ **B.** XSS attacks enable an attacker to inject their malicious code into vulnerable Web pages. When an unsuspecting user visits the infected page, the malicious code executes on the victim's browser and may lead to stolen cookies, hijacked sessions, malware execution, bypassed access control, or aid in exploiting browser vulnerabilities. There are three different XSS vulnerabilities: persistent, nonpersistent, and DOM-based. A nonpersistent vulnerability (also called a reflected vulnerability) occurs when an attacker tricks the victim into opening a URL programmed with a rogue script to steal the victim's sensitive information, such as a cookie or session ID. The principle behind this attack lies in exploiting the lack of proper input or output validation on dynamic Web sites. An XSS attack such as this can potentially cause damage on a huge scale. The stolen cookies can lead to compromised Web mail systems, flooded blogs, and disclosed bank accounts. Most of the phishing attacks are caused by XSS vulnerabilities.

☒ **A** is incorrect because a persistent vulnerability is targeted at Web sites that allow users to input data that is stored in a database or similar location, such as a forum or message board. The code for this type of attack can be rendered automatically without the need of luring a user to a third party Web site. The best way to overcome the XSS vulnerability is through secure programming practices. Web application developers must ensure that every user input is filtered. Only a limited set of known and secure characters should be allowed for user input.

☒ **C** is incorrect because a second-order vulnerability is another name for a persistent XSS vulnerability, which targets Web sites that allow users to input data that is stored in a database.

☒ **D** is incorrect because in a DOM-based XSS vulnerability the attacker uses the Document Object Model (DOM) environment to modify the original client-side JavaScript. This causes the victim's browser to execute the resulting abusive JavaScript code. Thus, cross-site attacks can be used to exploit vulnerabilities in the victim's Web browser. Once the system is successfully compromised by the attacker, he may further penetrate into other systems on the network or execute scripts that may spread through the internal network. As for the client's side, the most effective way to prevent XSS attacks is to disable scripting language support in the browser. If this is not feasible, then content filtering proxy servers may be used.

11. Angela wants to group together computers by department to make it easier for them to share network resources. Which of the following will allow her to group computers logically?

A. VLAN

B. Open network architecture

C. Intranet

D. VAN

☑ **A.** Virtual LANs (VLANs) enable the logical separation and grouping of computers based on resource requirements, security, or business needs in spite of the standard physical location of the systems. This technology allows Angela to logically place all computers within the same department on the same VLAN network so that all users can receive the same broadcast messages and can access the same types of resources, regardless of their physical location. This means that computers can be grouped together even if they are not located on the same network.

☒ **B** is incorrect because open network describes technologies that can make up a network. It is one that no vendor owns, that is not proprietary, and that can easily integrate various technologies and vendor implementations of those technologies. The OSI model provides a framework for developing products that will work within an open network architecture. Vendors use the OSI model as a blueprint and develop their own protocols and interfaces to produce functionality that is different from that of other vendors. However, because these vendors use the OSI model as their starting place, integration of other vendor products is an easier task, and the interoperability issues are less burdensome than if the vendors had developed their own networking framework from scratch.

☒ **C** is incorrect because an intranet is a private network that a company uses when it wants to use the Internet and Web-based technologies for internal networks. The company has Web servers and client machines using Web browsers, and it uses the TCP/IP protocol suite. The Web pages are written in HTML or XML, and are accessed via HTTP.

☒ **D** is incorrect because a value-added network (VAN) is an electronic data interchange (EDI) infrastructure developed and maintained by a service bureau. Here's an example of how a VAN works: A retail store such as Target tracks its inventory by having employees scan bar codes on individual items. When the inventory of an item—such as garden hoses—becomes low, an employee sends a request for more garden hoses. The request goes to a mailbox at a VAN that Target pays to use, and the request is then pushed out to the garden hose supplier. Because Target deals with thousands of suppliers, using a VAN simplifies the ordering process. There is no need to manually track down the right supplier and submit a purchase order.

12. Which of the following incorrectly describes how routing commonly takes place on the Internet?

   A. EGP is used in the areas "between" each AS.

   B. Regions of nodes that share characteristics and behaviors are called ASs.

   C. CAs are specific nodes that are responsible for routing to nodes outside of their region.

   D. Each AS uses IGP to perform routing functionality.

   ☑ **C.** A CA, or Certificate Authority, is a trusted third party that provides digital certificates for use in a public key infrastructure. Certificate Authorities have nothing to do with routing. A PKI environment provides a hierarchical trust model but does not deal with routing of traffic.

   ☒ **A** is incorrect because the statement is true. The Exterior Gateway Protocol (EGP) functions between each autonomous system (AS). The architecture of the Internet that supports these various ASs is created so that no entity that needs to connect to a specific AS has to know or understand the interior protocols that can be used. Instead, for ASs to communicate, they just have to be using the same exterior routing protocols.

   ☒ **B** is incorrect because the statement is true; regions of nodes (networks) that share characteristics and behaviors are called autonomous systems (ASs). These ASs are independently controlled by different corporations and organizations. An AS is made up of computers and devices, which are administered by a single entity and use a common Interior Gateway Protocol (IGP). The boundaries of these ASs are delineated by border routers. These routers connect to the border routers of other ASs and run interior and exterior routing protocols. Internal routers connect to other routers within the same AS and run interior routing protocols. So, in reality, the Internet is just a network made up of ASs and routing protocols.

   ☒ **D** is incorrect because Interior Gateway Protocol (IGP) handles routing tasks within each AS. There are two categories of IGPs: distance-vector routing protocols and link-state routing protocols. Distance-vector routing protocols include Routing Information Protocol (RIP) and Interior Gateway Routing Protocol (IGRP). Routers using these protocols do not possess information about the entire network topology. Nodes using link-state routing protocols, on the other hand, possess information about the complete network topology. Examples of these protocols include Open Shortest Path First (OSPF) and Intermediate System to Intermediate System (IS-IS).

13. Both de facto and proprietary interior protocols are in use today. Which of the following is a proprietary interior protocol that chooses the best path between the source and destination?

A. IGRP

B. RIP

C. BGP

D. OSPF

☑ A. Interior Gateway Routing Protocol (IGRP) is a distance-vector routing protocol that was developed by, and is proprietary to, Cisco Systems. Whereas Routing Information Protocol (RIP) uses one criterion to find the best path between the source and the destination, IGRP uses five criteria to make a "best route" decision. A network administrator can set weights on these different metrics so that the protocol works best in that specific environment.

☒ B is incorrect because Routing Information Protocol (RIP) is not proprietary. RIP is a standard that outlines how routers exchange routing table data and is considered a distance-vector protocol, which means it calculates the shortest distance between the source and the destination. It is considered a legacy protocol, because of its slow performance and lack of functionality. It should only be used in small networks. RIP version 1 has no authentication, and RIP version 2 sends passwords in clear text or hashed with MD5.

☒ C is incorrect because the Border Gateway Protocol (BGP) is an Exterior Gateway Protocol (EGP). BGP enables routers on different ASs to share routing information to ensure effective and efficient routing between the different networks. BGP is commonly used by Internet service providers to route data from one location to the next on the Internet.

☒ D is incorrect because Open Shortest Path First (OSPF) is not proprietary. OSPF uses link-state algorithms to send out routing table information. The use of these algorithms allows for smaller, more frequent routing table updates to take place. This provides a more stable network than RIP but requires more memory and CPU resources to support this extra processing. OSPF allows for a hierarchical routing network that has a backbone link connecting all subnets together. OSPF is the preferred protocol and has replaced RIP in many networks today. Authentication can take place with clear text passwords or hashed passwords, or you can choose to configure no authentication on the routers using this protocol.

14. Which of the following categories of routing protocols builds a topology database of the network?

A. Dynamic

B. Distance-vector

C. Link-state

D. Static

☑ **C.** Routing protocols indicate how routers talk to each other. Routing protocols circulate information that enables routers to choose a route between two nodes on a network. Routers then choose a route with the use of a routing algorithm. Each router has knowledge of the networks it is directly attached to. This information is shared with immediate neighbors, then throughout the network, via a routing protocol. Thus, routers learn about the topology of the network. Two main types of routing protocols are used: distance-vector and link-state routing. Link-state routing protocols build a more accurate routing table than distance-vector protocols because they build a topology database of the network. Link-state routing protocols look at more variables than just the number of hops between two destinations. They use packet size, link speed, delay, loading, and reliability as the variables in their algorithms to determine the best routes for packets to take.

☒ **A** is incorrect because a dynamic routing protocol does not build a topology database of the network. However, a link-state routing table (which does build a topology database of the network) is classified as a dynamic routing protocol because it discovers routes and builds a routing table. Routers use these tables to make decisions on the best route for the packets they receive. A dynamic routing protocol can change the entries in the routing table based on changes that take place to the different routes. When a router that is using a dynamic routing protocol finds out that a route has gone down or is congested, it sends an update message to the other routers around it. The other routers use this information to update their routing table, with the goal of providing efficient routing functionality.

☒ **B** is incorrect because distance-vector routing protocols do not build a topology database of the network. Routing protocols are classified as either distance-vector or link-state. Distance-vector routing protocols make their routing decisions based on the distance (or number of hops) and a vector (a direction). The protocol takes these variables and uses them with an algorithm to determine the best route for a packet. Distance-vector routing protocols build a less accurate routing table than link-state because distance-vector routing protocols use fewer variables to determine the best route.

☒ **D** is incorrect because a static routing protocol does not build a topology database of the network. Routing protocols can be either dynamic or static. Whereas a dynamic routing protocol can discover routes and build a routing table on its own, a static routing table requires the administrator to manually configure the router's routing table.

15. Which of the following does not describe IP telephony security?

    A. VoIP networks should be protected with the same security controls used on a data network.

    B. Softphones are more secure than IP phones.

    C. As endpoints, IP phones can become the target of attacks.

    D. The current Internet architecture over which voice is transmitted is less secure than physical phone lines.

    ☑ **B.** IP softphones should be used with caution. A softphone is a software application that allows the user to make phone calls via a computer over the Internet. A softphone, which replaces dedicated hardware, behaves like a traditional telephone. It can be used with a headset connected to a PC's sound card or with a USB phone. Skype is an example of a softphone application. Compared to hardware-based IP phones, softphones make an IP network more vulnerable. However, softphones are no worse than any other interactive Internet application. In addition, data-centered malware can more easily enter a network via softphones because they do not separate voice traffic from data as do IP phones.

    ☒ **A** is incorrect because the statement correctly describes IP telephony network security. An IP telephony network uses the same technology as a traditional IP network, only it can support voice applications. Therefore, the IP telephony network is susceptible to the same vulnerabilities as a traditional IP network and should be protected accordingly. This means the IP telephony network should be engineered to have the proper security.

    ☒ **C** is incorrect because the statement is true. IP phones on an IP telephony network are the equivalent of a workstation on a data network in terms of their vulnerability to attack. Thus, IP phones should be protected with many of the same security controls that are implemented in a traditional workstation. For example, default administrator passwords should be changed. Unnecessary remote access features should be disabled. Logging should be enabled and the firmware upgrade process should be secured.

    ☒ **D** is incorrect because the statement is true. For the most part, the current Internet architecture over which voice is transmitted is less secure than physical phone lines. Physical phone lines provide point-to-point connections, which are harder to tap into than the software-based tunnels that make up most of the Internet. This is an important factor to take into consideration when securing an IP telephony network because the network is now transmitting two invaluable assets—data and voice. It is not unusual for personally identifiable information, financial information, and other sensitive data to be spoken over the phone. Intercepting this information over an IP telephony network is as easy as intercepting regular data. Now voice traffic needs to be encrypted, too.

16. When an organization splits naming zones, the names of its hosts that are only accessible from an intranet are hidden from the Internet. Which of the following best describes why this is done?

A. To prevent attackers from accessing servers

B. To prevent the manipulation of the hosts file

C. To avoid providing attackers with valuable information that can be used to prepare an attack

D. To avoid providing attackers with information needed for cybersquatting

☑ **C.** Many companies have their own internal DNS servers to resolve their internal hostnames. These companies usually also use the DNS servers at their ISPs to resolve hostnames on the Internet. An internal DNS server can be used to resolve hostnames on the entire network, but usually more than one DNS server is used so that the load can be split up and so that redundancy and fault tolerance are in place. Within DNS servers, networks are split into zones. One zone may contain all hostnames for the marketing and accounting departments, and another zone may contain hostnames for the administration, research, and legal departments. It is a good idea to split DNS zones when possible so that the names of hosts that are accessible only from an intranet are not visible from the Internet. This information is valuable to an attacker who is planning an attack because it can lead to other information, such as the network structure, organizational structure, or server operating systems.

☒ **A** is incorrect because this is not the best answer for this question. Naming zones are split up so that attackers cannot learn information about internal systems, such as names, IP addresses, functions, and so on. One of the secondary attacks after exploiting a DNS server could be accessing a server in an unauthorized manner, but ensuring unauthorized access just to servers is not the main reason to split DNS zones.

☒ **B** is incorrect because splitting naming zones has to do with how DNS servers are set up to resolve hostnames, not manipulate the hosts file. The hosts file can be manipulated for a number of reasons, both for good and bad. The hosts file always maps the hostname localhost to the IP address 127.0.0.1 (this is the loopback network interface, which is defined in RFC 3330), as well as other hosts. Some viruses add invalid IP addresses of antivirus vendors to the hosts file to avoid detection. By adding frequently visited IP addresses to the hosts file, you can increase the speed of Web browsing. You can also block spyware and ad networks by adding lists of spyware and ad network sites to the hosts file and mapping them to the loopback network interface. This way, these sites always point back to the user's machine and the sites cannot be reached.

☒ **D** is incorrect because hackers do not need information on a DNS server to carry out cybersquatting. Cybersquatting occurs when an attacker purchases a well-known brand or company name, or variation thereof, as a domain name with the goal of selling it to the rightful owner. In the meantime, the company can be misrepresented to the public. The only way an organization can avoid cybersquatting is by registering adjacent domains and variations on the domain, or by trademark litigation.

17. Which of the following best describes why e-mail spoofing is easily executed?

    A. SMTP lacks an adequate authentication mechanism.

    B. Administrators often forget to configure an SMTP server to prevent inbound SMTP connections for domains it doesn't serve.

    C. Keyword filtering is technically obsolete.

    D. Blacklists are undependable.

    ☑ **A.** E-mail spoofing is easy to execute because SMTP lacks an adequate authentication mechanism. An attacker can spoof e-mail sender addresses by sending a TELNET command to port 25 of a mail server followed by a number of SMTP commands. Spammers use e-mail spoofing to obfuscate their identity. Oftentimes, the purported sender of a spam e-mail is actually another victim of spam whose e-mail address has been sold to or harvested by a spammer.

    ☒ **B** is incorrect because the answer alludes to open mail relay servers. The failure to configure an SMTP server to prevent SMTP connections for domains it doesn't serve is not a common mistake. It is well known that an open mail relay allows spammers to hide their identity and is a principal tool in the distribution of spam. Open mail relays are, therefore, considered a sign of bad system administration. An open relay is not required for e-mail spoofing.

    ☒ **C** is incorrect because keyword filtering is a countermeasure that can be used to help suppress spam. While keyword filtering by itself was popular at one time, it is no longer an effective countermeasure when used just by itself. Keyword filtering is prone to false positives and spammers have found creative ways to work around it. For example, keywords may be intentionally misspelled or one or two letters of a common word swapped with a special character.

    ☒ **D** is incorrect because blacklists list open mail relay servers that are known for sending spam. Administrators can use blacklists to prevent the delivery of e-mail originating from those hosts in an effort to suppress spam. However, blacklists cannot be depended upon for complete protection because they are often managed by private organizations and individuals according to their own rules.

18. Which of the following is not a benefit of VoIP?

   A. Cost

   B. Convergence

   C. Flexibility

   D. Security

☑ **D.** Voice over Internet Protocol (VoIP) refers to transmission technologies that deliver voice communications over IP networks. IP telephony uses technologies that are similar to TCP/IP, so its vulnerabilities are also similar. The voice system is vulnerable to application manipulation (such as toll fraud and blocking), unauthorized administrative access, and poor implementation. In terms of the network and media, it is also vulnerable to denial-of-service attacks against the gateways and network resources. Eavesdropping is also a concern, since data traffic is sent in cleartext unless it is encrypted.

☒ **A** is incorrect because cost is a benefit of VoIP. Using VoIP means a company has to pay for and maintain only one network, instead of one network dedicated to data transmission and another network dedicated to voice transmission. Telephony features such as conference calling, call forwarding, and automatic redial are free from open-source VoIP implementations, while traditional telecommunications companies charge extra for them. And, finally, VoIP costs are lower because of the way they are billed. VoIP calls are billed per megabyte, while regular telephone calls are billed by the minute. In general, it is cheaper to send data over the Internet for a given period of time than it is to use the regular telephone for that same amount of time.

☒ **B** is incorrect because convergence is a benefit of VoIP. Convergence refers to the merging of the traditional IP network with the traditional analog phone network. This is a benefit because a company no longer has to pay for and maintain separate networks for data and voice. However, while convergence saves money and administration overhead, certain security issues must be understood and dealt with.

☒ **C** is incorrect because flexibility is a benefit of VoIP. The technology easily supports multiple telephone calls over a single Internet broadband connection without having to add extra lines. It also offers location independence. All that is needed to obtain a WAN or MAN phone connection to a VoIP provider is an adequate Internet connection. VoIP can also be integrated with other Internet services, such as video conversation, file exchange during a call, and audio conferencing.

19. Today, satellites are used to provide wireless connectivity between different locations. What two prerequisites are needed for two different locations to communicate via satellite links?

    A. They must be connected via a phone line and have access to a modem.

    B. They must be within the satellite's line of site and footprint.

    C. They must have broadband and a satellite in low Earth orbit.

    D. They must have a transponder and be within the satellite's footprint.

    ☑ **B.** For two different locations to communicate via satellite links, they must be within the satellite's line of sight and footprint (area covered by the satellite). The sender of information modulates the data onto a radio signal that is transmitted to the satellite. A transponder on the satellite receives this signal, amplifies it, and relays it to the receiver. The receiver must have a certain type of antenna, which is one of those circular, dish-like components on top of buildings. The antenna contains one or more microwave receivers, depending upon how many satellites it is accepting data from. The size of the footprint depends upon the type of satellite being used. It can be as large as a country or only a few hundred feet in circumference.

    ☒ **A** is incorrect because a phone line and a modem are not wireless. However, in most cases satellite broadband is a hybrid system that uses a regular phone line and modem-like technologies for data and requests sent from the user's machine, but employs a satellite link to send data to the user.

    ☒ **C** is incorrect because the satellite provides broadband transmission. It is commonly used for television channels and PC Internet access. While it is certainly necessary to have a satellite in orbit, and those in low Earth orbit are commonly used for two-way paging, international cellular communication, TV stations, and Internet use, it is not the best answer to this question.

    ☒ **D** is incorrect because the two locations do not require a transponder. The transponder is on the satellite itself. The transponder receives a signal, amplifies it, and sends it to the receiver. However, it is necessary for the two locations to be within the satellite's footprint.

20. Brad is a security manager at Thingamabobs Inc. He is preparing a presentation for his company's executives on the risks of using instant messaging (IM) and his reasons for wanting to prohibit its use on the company network. Which of the following should not be included in his presentation?

    A. Sensitive data and files can be transferred from system to system over IM.

    B. Users can receive information—including malware—from an attacker posing as a legitimate sender.

C. IM use can be stopped by simply blocking specific ports on the network firewalls.

D. A security policy is needed specifying IM usage restrictions.

☑ **C.** Instant messaging (IM) allows people to communicate with one another through a type of real-time and personal chat room. It alerts individuals when someone who is on their "buddy list" has accessed the intranet/Internet so that they can send text messages back and forth in real time. The technology also allows for files to be transferred from system to system. The technology is made up of clients and servers. The user installs an IM client (AOL, ICQ, Yahoo Messenger, and so on) and is assigned a unique identifier. This user gives out this unique identifier to people whom she wants to communicate with via IM. Blocking specific ports on the firewalls is not usually effective because the IM traffic may be using common ports that need to be open (HTTP port 80 and FTP port 21). Many of the IM clients autoconfigure themselves to work on another port if their default port is unavailable and blocked by the firewall.

☒ **A** is incorrect because in addition to text messages, instant messaging allows for files to be transferred from system to system. These files could contain sensitive information, putting the company at business and legal risk. And, of course, sharing files over IM can eat up network bandwidth and impact network performance as a result.

☒ **B** is incorrect because the statement is true. Because of the lack of strong authentication, accounts can be spoofed so that the receiver accepts information from a malicious user instead of the legitimate sender. There have also been numerous buffer overflow and malformed packet attacks that have been successful with different IM clients. These attacks are usually carried out with the goal of obtaining unauthorized access to the victim's system.

☒ **D** is incorrect because Brad should include in his presentation the need for a security policy specifying IM usage restrictions. This is just one of several best practices for protecting an environment from IM-related security breaches. Other best practices include implementing an integrated antivirus/firewall product on all computers, configuring firewalls to block IM traffic, upgrading IM software to more secure versions, and implementing corporate IM servers so that internal employees communicate within the organization's network only.

21. There are several different types of authentication technologies. Which type is being shown in the graphic that follows?

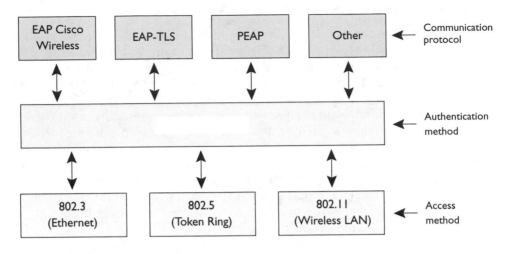

A. 802.1x

B. Extensible Authentication Protocol

C. Frequency hopping spread spectrum

D. Orthogonal frequency-division multiplexing

☑ **A.** The 802.1x standard is a port-based network access control that ensures a user cannot make a full network connection until he is properly authenticated. This means a user cannot access network resources and no traffic is allowed to pass, other than authentication traffic, from the wireless device to the network until the user is properly authenticated. An analogy is having a chain on your front door that enables you to open the door slightly to identify a person who knocks before you allow him to enter your house. User authentication provides a higher degree of confidence and protection than system authentication.

☒ **B** is incorrect because Extensible Authentication Protocol (EAP) is not a specific authentication technology; instead, it provides a framework to enable many types of authentication techniques to be used during point-to-point (PPP) connections. As the name states, it extends the authentication possibilities from the norm (PAP and CHAP) to other methods such as one-time passwords, token cards, biometrics, Kerberos, and future mechanisms. So when a user connects to an authentication server and both have EAP capabilities, they can negotiate between a longer list of possible authentication methods.

☒ **C** is incorrect because spread spectrum means that something is distributing individual signals across the allocated frequencies in some fashion. This is used in wireless communication and is not an authentication technology. Frequency hopping spread spectrum (FHSS) takes the total amount of bandwidth (spectrum) and splits it into smaller subchannels. The sender and receiver work at one of these channels for a specific amount of time and then move to another channel. The sender puts the first piece of data on one frequency, the second on a different frequency, and so on. The FHSS algorithm determines the individual frequencies that will be used and in what order, and this is referred to as the sender's and receiver's hop sequence.

☒ **D** is incorrect because orthogonal frequency-division multiplexing (OFDM) is a digital multicarrier modulation scheme that compacts multiple modulated carriers tightly together, reducing the required bandwidth. The modulated signals are orthogonal (perpendicular) and do not interfere with each other. OFDM uses a composite of narrow channel bands to enhance its performance in high-frequency bands. This is used in wireless communication and is not an authentication technology.

22. What type of security encryption component is missing from the table that follows?

	802.1x Dynamic WEP	Wi-Fi Protected Access	Robust Security Network
Access Control	802.1x	802.1x or preshared key	802.1x or preshared key
Authentication	EAP methods	EAP methods or preshared key	EAP methods or preshared key
Encryption	WEP		CCMP (AES Counter Mode)
Integrity	None	Michael MIC	CCMP (AES CBC-MAC)

A. Service Set ID

B. Temporal Key Integrity Protocol

C. Ad hoc WLAN

D. Open system authentication

☑ **B.** The Temporal Key Integrity Protocol (TKIP) generates random values used in the encryption process, which makes it much harder for an attacker to break. To allow for an even higher level of encryption protection, the standard also includes the new Advanced Encryption Standard (AES) algorithm to be used in new WLAN implementations. TKIP actually works with the wired equivalent privacy (WEP) protocol by feeding it keying material, which is data to be used for generating new dynamic keys. WEP uses the RC4 encryption algorithm, and the current implementation of the algorithm provides very little protection. More complexity is added to the key generation process with the use of TKIP, which makes it much more difficult for attackers to uncover the encryption keys. The IEEE working group developed TKIP so that customers would only need to obtain firmware or software updates instead of purchasing new equipment for this type of protection.

☒ **A** is incorrect because when wireless devices work in infrastructure mode, the access point (AP) and wireless clients form a group referred to as a Basic Service Set (BSS). This group is assigned a name, which is the Service Set ID (SSID) value. This value has nothing to do with encryption. Any hosts that wish to participate within a particular WLAN must be configured with the proper SSID. Various hosts can be segmented into different WLANs by using different SSIDs. The reasons to segment a WLAN into portions are the same reasons wired systems are segmented on a network: the users require access to different resources, have different business functions, or have different levels of trust.

☒ **C** is incorrect because an ad hoc WLAN has nothing to do with encryption, but rather with how wireless devices on a network are set up. An ad hoc WLAN has no access points; the wireless devices communicate with each other through their wireless NICs instead of going through a centralized device. To construct an ad hoc network, wireless client software is installed on contributing hosts and configured for peer-to-peer operation mode.

☒ **D** is incorrect because open system authentication (OSA) just means a wireless device does not need to prove it has a specific cryptographic key for authentication. Depending upon the product and the configuration, a network administrator can also limit access to specific MAC addresses. OSA does not require the wireless device to prove to an access point it has a specific cryptographic key to allow for authentication purposes. In many cases, the wireless device needs to provide only the correct SSID value. In OSA implementations, all transactions are in clear text because no encryption is involved. So an intruder can sniff the traffic, capture the necessary steps of authentication, and walk through the same steps to be authenticated and associated to an AP.

23. What type of technology is represented in the graphic that follows?

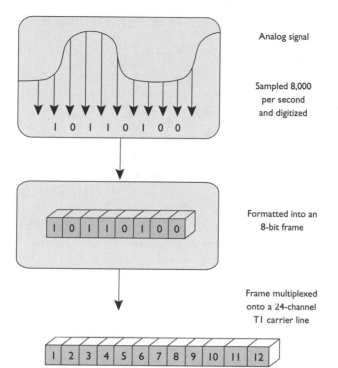

A. Asynchronous Transfer Mode

B. Synchronous Optical Networks

C. Frequency-division multiplexing

D. Multiplexing

☑ **D.** Multiplexing is a method of combining multiple channels of data over a single transmission path. The transmission is so fast and efficient that the ends do not realize they are sharing a line with many other entities. The systems "think" they have the line all to themselves. Telephone systems have been around for about 100 years, and they started as copper-based analog systems. Central switching offices connected individual telephones manually (via human operators) at first, and later by using electronic switching equipment. After two telephones were connected, they had an end-to-end connection, or an end-to-end circuit. Multiple phone calls were divided up and placed on the same wire, which is multiplexing.

☒ **A** is incorrect because Asynchronous Transfer Mode (ATM) is a high-speed network technology that is used in LAN and WAN implementations by carriers, ISPs, and telephone companies. This technology is not what is shown in the graphic. ATM encapsulates data in fixed cells and can be used to deliver data over the Synchronous Optical Networks (SONET) network. The analogy of a highway and cars is used to describe the SONET and ATM relationship. SONET is the highway that provides the foundation (or network) for the cars—the ATM packets—to travel on.

☒ **B** is incorrect because Synchronous Optical Networks (SONET) is actually a standard for telecommunications transmissions over fiber-optic cables. Carriers and telephone companies have deployed SONET networks for North America, and if they follow the SONET standards properly, these various networks can communicate with little difficulty. A metropolitan area network (MAN) is usually a backbone that connects LANs to each other and LANs to WANs, the Internet, and telecommunications and cable networks. A majority of today's MANs are SONET or FDDI rings provided by the telecommunications service providers.

☒ **C** is incorrect because frequency-division multiplexing is a form of signal multiplexing that involves assigning nonoverlapping frequency ranges to different signals or to each "user" of a medium. This is a type of multiplexing, but works over wireless signal spectrums instead of a time-based approach shown in the graphic. It can also be used to combine multiple signals before final modulation onto a carrier signal. In this case the carrier signals are referred to as subcarriers; each frequency within the spectrum is used as a channel to move data. An example is a stereo FM transmission.

24. What type of telecommunication technology is illustrated in the graphic that follows?

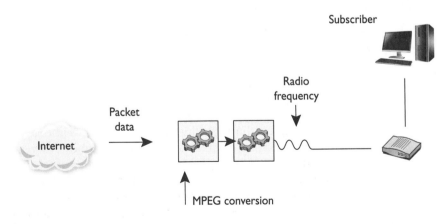

A. Digital Subscriber Line

B. Integrated Services Digital Network

C. BRI ISDN

D. Cable modem

☑ **D.** The cable television companies have been delivering television services to homes for years, and then they started delivering data transmission services for users who have cable modems and want to connect to the Internet at high speeds. Cable modems provide high-speed access, up to 50 Mbps, to the Internet through existing cable coaxial and fiber lines. The cable modem provides upstream and downstream conversions. Not all cable companies provide Internet access as a service, mainly because they have not upgraded their infrastructure to move from a one-way network to a two-way network. Once this conversion takes place, data can come down from a central point (referred to as the head) to a residential home and back up to the head and onto the Internet.

☒ **A** is incorrect because Digital Subscriber Line (DSL) is another type of high-speed connection technology used to connect a home or business to the service provider's central office. It uses existing phone lines and provides a 24-hour connection to the Internet. This does indeed sound better than sliced bread, but only certain people can get this service because you have to be within a 2.5-mile radius of the DSL service provider's equipment. As the distance between a residence and the central office increases, the transmission rates for DSL decrease. DSL does not go through the cable TV lines and does not have to go through the conversion from analog to digital and back as illustrated in the graphic. DSL is a broadband technology that can provide up to a 52 Mbps transmission speed without replacing the carrier's copper wire.

☒ **B** is incorrect because the Integrated Services Digital Network (ISDN) is a communications protocol provided by telephone companies and ISPs that does not need to go through the conversion process shown in the graphic. This protocol and the necessary equipment enable data, voice, and other types of traffic to travel over a medium in a digital manner previously used only for analog voice transmission. Telephone companies went all digital many years ago, except for the local loops, which consist of the copper wires that connect houses and businesses to their carrier provider's central offices. These central offices contain the telephone company's switching equipment, and it is here the analog-to-digital transformation takes place.

☒ **C** is incorrect because the Integrated Services Digital Network (ISDN) breaks the telephone line into different channels and transmits data in a digital form rather than the old analog form. ISDN provides two basic home and business services: Basic Rate Interface (BRI) and Primary Rate Interface (PRI). BRI has two B channels that enable data to be transferred and one D channel that provides for call setup, connection management, error control, caller ID, and more. The bandwidth available with BRI is 144 Kbps, whereas the top modems can provide only 56 Kbps. The BRI service is common for residential use, and the PRI, which has 23 B channels and one D channel, is more commonly used in corporations.

25. Which type of WAN tunneling protocol is missing from the table that follows?

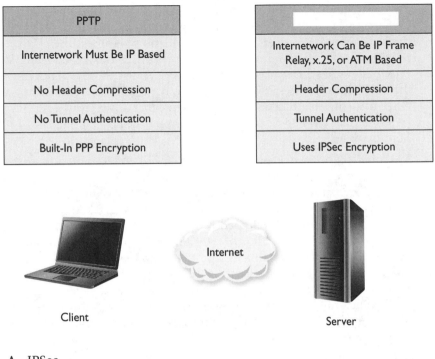

PPTP
Internetwork Must Be IP Based
No Header Compression
No Tunnel Authentication
Built-In PPP Encryption

Internetwork Can Be IP Frame Relay, x.25, or ATM Based
Header Compression
Tunnel Authentication
Uses IPSec Encryption

Client   Internet   Server

A. IPSec

B. FDDI

C. L2TP

D. CSMA/CD

☑ C. Tunneling is the main ingredient to a VPN because that is how the VPN creates its connection. Three main tunneling protocols are used in VPN connections: PPTP, L2TP, and IPSec. L2TP provides the functionality of the Point-to-Point Tunneling Protocol (PPTP), but it can work over networks other than just IP, and it provides a higher level of security when combined with IPSec. L2TP does not provide any encryption or authentication services, so it needs to be combined with IPSec if those services are required. The processes that L2TP uses for encapsulation are similar to those used by PPTP. The PPP frame is encapsulated with L2TP. One limitation of PPTP is that it can work only over IP networks, so other protocols must be used to move data over frame relay, X.25, and ATM links.

☒ A is incorrect because the Internet Protocol Security (IPSec) protocol suite provides a method of setting up a secure channel for protected data exchange between two devices. The devices that share this secure channel can be two servers, two routers, a workstation and a server, or two gateways between different networks. IPSec is a widely accepted standard for providing network layer protection. IPSec is commonly used with L2TP to provide protection for the data that travels over this type of communication path as shown in the graphic.

☒ **B** is incorrect because Fiber Distributed Data Interface (FDDI) technology is a high-speed token-passing media access technology. FDDI has a data transmission speed of up to 100 Mbps and is usually used as a backbone network using fiber-optic cabling. FDDI also provides fault tolerance by offering a second counter-rotating fiber ring. The primary ring has data traveling clockwise and is used for regular data transmission. The second ring transmits data in a counterclockwise fashion and is invoked only if the primary ring goes down. Sensors watch the primary ring and, if it goes down, invoke a ring wrap so that the data will be diverted to the second ring. Each node on the FDDI network has relays that are connected to both rings, so if a break in the ring occurs, the two rings can be joined. L2TP is used for WAN connections, while FDDI is commonly used for MAN connections.

☒ **D** is incorrect because Carrier Sense Multiple Access with Collision Detection (CSMA/CD) is a network access method in which a carrier sensing scheme is used. A transmission is called a carrier, so if a computer is transmitting frames, it is performing a carrier activity. When computers use the CSMA/CD protocol, they monitor the transmission activity, or carrier activity, on the wire so they can determine when would be the best time to transmit data. Each node monitors the wire continuously and waits until the wire is free before it transmits its data. As an analogy, consider several people gathered in a group talking here and there about this and that. If a person wants to talk, she usually listens to the current conversation and waits for a break before she proceeds to talk. If she does not wait for the first person to stop talking, she will be speaking at the same time as the other person, and the people around them may not be able to understand fully what each is trying to say.

26. IPv6 has many new and different characteristics and functionality compared to IPv4. Which of the following is an incorrect functionality or characteristic of IPv6?

    i. IPv6 allows for nonscoped addresses, which enables an administrator to restrict specific addresses for specific servers or file and print sharing, for example.

    ii. IPv6 has IPSec integrated into the protocol stack, which provides application-based secure transmission and authentication.

    iii. IPv6 has more flexibility and routing capabilities compared to IPv4 and allows for Quality of Service (QoS) priority values to be assigned to time-sensitive transmissions.

iv. The protocol offers autoconfiguration, which makes administration much easier compared to IPv4, and it does not require network address translation (NAT) to extend its address space.

A. i, iii

B. i, ii

C. ii, iii

D. ii, iv

☑ **B.** IPv6 allows for scoped addresses, which enables an administrator to restrict specific addresses for specific servers or file and print sharing, for example. IPv6 has IPSec integrated into the protocol stack, which provides end-to-end secure transmission and authentication.

☒ **A** is incorrect. IPv6 allows for scoped addresses, which enables an administrator to restrict specific addresses for specific servers or file and print sharing, for example. IPv6 has more flexibility and routing capabilities and allows for Quality of Service (QoS) priority values to be assigned to time-sensitive transmissions.

☒ **C** is incorrect. IPv6 has more flexibility and routing capabilities and allows for Quality of Service (QoS) priority values to be assigned to time-sensitive transmissions. IPv6 has IPSec integrated into the protocol stack, which provides end-to-end secure transmission and authentication.

☒ **D** is incorrect because IPv6 has IPSec integrated into the protocol stack, which provides end-to-end secure transmission and authentication. The protocol offers autoconfiguration, which makes administration much easier, and it does not require network address translation (NAT) to extend its address space.

27. Hanna is a new security manager for a computer consulting company. She has found out that the company has lost intellectual property in the past because malicious employees installed rogue devices on the network, which were used to capture sensitive traffic. Hanna needs to implement a solution that ensures only authorized devices are allowed access to the company network. Which of the following IEEE standards was developed for this type of protection?

A. IEEE 802.1AR

B. IEEE 802.1AE

C. IEEE 802.1AF

D. IEEE 802.1XR

☑ **A.** The IEEE 802.1AR standard specifies unique per-device identifiers (DevID) and the management and cryptographic binding of a device (router, switch, access point) to its identifiers. A verifiable unique device identity allows establishment of the trustworthiness of devices; thus, it facilitates secure device provisioning. A secure device identifier (DevID) is cryptographically bound to a device and supports authentication of the device's identity. Locally significant identities can be securely associated with an initial manufacturer-provisioned DevID and used in provisioning and authentication protocols to allow a network administrator to establish the trustworthiness of a device and select appropriate policies for transmission and reception of data and control protocols to and from the device.

☒ **B** is incorrect because 802.1AE is the IEEE MAC Security standard (MACSec), which defines a security infrastructure to provide data confidentiality, data integrity, and data origin authentication. Where a VPN connection provides protection at the higher networking layers, MACSec provides hop-by-hop protection at layer 2.

☒ **C** is incorrect because 802.1AR provides a unique ID for a device. 802.1AE provides data encryption, integrity, and origin authentication functionality. 802.1AF carries out key agreement functions for the session keys used for data encryption. Each of these standards provides specific parameters to work within an 802.1X EAP-TLS framework.

☒ **D** is incorrect because this is a distracter answer. This is not a valid standard.

28. There are common cloud computing service models. _____ usually requires companies to deploy their own operating systems, applications, and software onto the provided infrastructure. _____ is the software environment that runs on top of the infrastructure. In the _____ model the provider commonly gives the customers network-based access to a single copy of an application.

    A. Platform as a Service, Infrastructure as a Service, Software as a Service

    B. Platform as a Service, Platform as Software, Application as a Service

    C. Infrastructure as a Service, Application as a Service, Software as a Service

    D. Infrastructure as a Service, Platform as Software, Software as a Service

    ☑ **D.** The most common cloud service models are Infrastructure as a Service (IaaS), Platform as a Service (PaaS), and Software as a Service (SaaS).

    ☒ **A** is incorrect because these items are not in the correct order. Infrastructure as a Service (IaaS) is when cloud providers offer the infrastructure environment of a traditional data center in an on-demand delivery method. Companies deploy their own operating systems, applications, and software onto this provided infrastructure and are responsible for maintaining them.

    ☒ **B** is incorrect because the most common cloud service models are Infrastructure as a Service (IaaS), Platform as a Service (PaaS), and Software as a Service (SaaS). There are no models called Platform as Software or Application as a Service. These are distracters. Platform as a Service (PaaS) is when cloud providers deliver a computing platform, which can include an operating system, database, and Web server as a holistic execution environment. Where IaaS is the "raw IT network," PaaS is the software environment that runs on top of the IT network.

☒ C is incorrect because the most common cloud service models are Infrastructure as a Service (IaaS), Platform as a Service (PaaS), and Software as a Service (SaaS). There is no model called Platform as Software. With Software as a Service (SaaS), the provider gives users access to specific application software (CRM, e-mail, games). The provider gives the customers network-based access to a single copy of an application created specifically for SaaS distribution and use.

29. _____ is a set of extensions to DNS that provide to DNS clients (resolvers) origin authentication of DNS data to reduce the threat of DNS poisoning, spoofing, and similar attack types.

    A. Resource records

    B. Zone transfer

    C. DNSSEC

    D. Resource transfer

☑ C. DNSSEC is a set of extensions to DNS that provide to DNS clients (resolvers) origin authentication of DNS data to reduce the threat of DNS poisoning, spoofing, and similar attack types. DNSSEC is a suite of Internet Engineering Task Force (IETF) specifications for securing services provided by the DNS as used on IP networks.

☒ A is incorrect because a DNS server contains records that map hostnames to IP addresses, which are referred to as resource records. When a user's computer needs to resolve a hostname to an IP address, it looks to its networking settings to find its DNS server. The computer then sends a request containing the hostname to the DNS server for resolution. The DNS server looks at its resource records and finds the record with this particular hostname, retrieves the address, and replies to the computer with the corresponding IP address.

☒ B is incorrect because primary and secondary DNS servers synchronize their information through a zone transfer. After changes take place to the primary DNS server, those changes must be replicated to the secondary DNS server. It is important to configure the DNS server to allow zone transfers to take place only between the specific servers.

☒ D is incorrect because it is a distracter answer.

30. Which of the following best describes the difference between a virtual firewall that works in bridge mode versus one that is embedded into a hypervisor?

A. Bridge-mode virtual firewall allows the firewall to monitor individual traffic links, and hypervisor integration allows the firewall to monitor all activities taking place within a host system.

B. Bridge-mode virtual firewall allows the firewall to monitor individual network links, and hypervisor integration allows the firewall to monitor all activities taking place within a guest system.

C. Bridge-mode virtual firewall allows the firewall to monitor individual traffic links, and hypervisor integration allows the firewall to monitor all activities taking place within a guest system.

D. Bridge-mode virtual firewall allows the firewall to monitor individual guest systems, and hypervisor integration allows the firewall to monitor all activities taking place within a network system.

☑ **A.** Virtual firewalls can be bridge-mode products, which monitor individual traffic links between virtual machines, or they can be integrated within the hypervisor of a virtualized environment. The hypervisor is the software component that carries out virtual machine management and oversees guest system software execution. If the firewall is embedded within the hypervisor, then it can "see" and monitor all the activities taking place within the host system.

☒ **B** is incorrect because bridge-mode virtual firewall allows the firewall to monitor individual traffic links between hosts, not network links. Hypervisor integration allows the firewall to monitor all activities taking place within a host system, not a guest system.

☒ **C** is incorrect because bridge-mode virtual firewall allows the firewall to monitor individual traffic links, and hypervisor integration allows the firewall to monitor all activities taking place within a host system, not a guest system. The hypervisor is the software component that carries out virtual machine management and oversees guest system software execution. If the firewall is embedded within the hypervisor, then it can "see" and monitor all the activities taking place within the system.

☒ **D** is incorrect because a bridge-mode virtual firewall allows the firewall to monitor individual traffic between guest systems, and hypervisor integration allows the firewall to monitor all activities taking place within a host system, not a network system.

Cryptography

This domain includes questions from the following topics:

- Cryptography components and their relationships
- Symmetric and asymmetric key algorithms
- Public key infrastructure (PKI) concepts and mechanisms
- Hashing algorithms and uses
- Types of attacks on cryptosystems

Cryptography has been around since 2000 B.C., when the first encryption methods were considered an art form. Encryption was later used to protect sensitive information in warfare, commerce, government, and other arenas. Today, encryption is a vital tool that is used in everyday transactions. It also continues to be used to gain a competitive edge in business and warfare, reduce vulnerability, hide one's true intentions, and more. As a CISSP, you need to understand how different cryptographic algorithms work, the security services they provide, and their most appropriate use cases.

1. There are several components involved with steganography. Which of the following refers to a file that has hidden information in it?

   A. Stego-medium

   B. Concealment cipher

   C. Carrier

   D. Payload

2. Which of the following correctly describes the relationship between SSL and TLS?

   A. TLS is the open-community version of SSL.

   B. SSL can be modified by developers to expand the protocol's capabilities.

   C. TLS is a proprietary protocol, while SSL is an open-community protocol.

   D. SSL is more extensible and backward compatible with TLS.

3. Which of the following incorrectly describes steganography?

   A. It is a type of security through obscurity.

   B. Modifying the most significant bit is the most common method used.

   C. Steganography does not draw attention to itself like encryption does.

   D. Media files are ideal for steganographic transmission because of their large size.

4. Which of the following correctly describes a drawback of symmetric key systems?

   A. Computationally less intensive than asymmetric systems

   B. Work much more slowly than asymmetric systems

   C. Carry out mathematically intensive tasks

   D. Key must be delivered via secure courier

5. Which of the following occurs in a PKI environment?

   A. The RA creates the certificate, and the CA signs it.

   B. The CA signs the certificate.

   C. The RA signs the certificate.

   D. The user signs the certificate.

6. Encryption can happen at different layers of an operating system and network stack. Where does PPTP encryption take place?

    A. Data link layer

    B. Within applications

    C. Transport layer

    D. Data link and physical layers

7. Which of the following correctly describes the difference between public key cryptography and public key infrastructure?

    A. Public key cryptography is the use of an asymmetric algorithm, while public key infrastructure is the use of a symmetric algorithm.

    B. Public key cryptography is used to create public/private key pairs, and public key infrastructure is used to perform key exchange and agreement.

    C. Public key cryptography provides authentication and nonrepudiation, while public key infrastructure provides confidentiality and integrity.

    D. Public key cryptography is another name for asymmetric cryptography, while public key infrastructure consists of public key cryptographic mechanisms.

8. Which of the following best describes Key Derivation Functions (KDFs)?

    A. Keys are generated from a master key.

    B. Session keys are generated from each other.

    C. Asymmetric cryptography is used to encrypt symmetric keys.

    D. A master key is generated from a session key.

9. An elliptic curve cryptosystem is an asymmetric algorithm. What sets it apart from other asymmetric algorithms?

    A. It provides digital signatures, secure key distribution, and encryption.

    B. It computes discrete logarithms in a finite field.

    C. It uses a larger percentage of resources to carry out encryption.

    D. It is more efficient.

10. If implemented properly, a one-time pad is a perfect encryption scheme. Which of the following incorrectly describes a requirement for implementation?

    A. The pad must be securely distributed and protected at its destination.

    B. The pad must be made up of truly random values.

    C. The pad must always be the same length.

    D. The pad must be used only one time.

11. Sally is responsible for key management within her organization. Which of the following incorrectly describes a principle of secure key management?

    A. Keys should be backed up or escrowed in case of emergencies.

    B. The more a key is used, the shorter its lifetime should be.

    C. Less secure data allows for a shorter key lifetime.

    D. Keys should be stored and transmitted by secure means.

12. Mandy needs to calculate how many keys must be generated for the 260 employees using the company's PKI asymmetric algorithm. How many keys are required?

    A. 33,670

    B. 520

    C. 67,340

    D. 260

13. Which of the following works similarly to stream ciphers?

    A. One-time pad

    B. AES

    C. Block

    D. RSA

14. There are two main types of symmetric ciphers: stream and block. Which of the following is not an attribute of a good stream cipher?

    A. Statistically unbiased keystream

    B. Statistically predictable

    C. Long periods of no repeating patterns

    D. Keystream not linearly related to key

15. Which of the following best describes how a digital signature is created?

    A. The sender encrypts a message digest with his private key.

    B. The sender encrypts a message digest with his public key.

    C. The receiver encrypts a message digest with his private key.

    D. The receiver encrypts a message digest with his public key.

16. In cryptography, different steps and algorithms provide different types of security services. Which of the following provides only authentication, non-repudiation, and integrity?

    A. Encryption algorithm

    B. Hash algorithm

    C. Digital signature

    D. Encryption paired with a digital signature

17. Advanced Encryption Standard is an algorithm used for which of the following?

    A. Data integrity

    B. Bulk data encryption

    C. Key recovery

    D. Distribution of symmetric keys

18. SSL is a de facto protocol used for securing transactions that occur over untrusted networks. Which of the following best describes what takes place during an SSL connection setup process?

    A. The server creates a session key and encrypts it with a public key.

    B. The server creates a session key and encrypts it with a private key.

    C. The client creates a session key and encrypts it with a private key.

    D. The client creates a session key and encrypts it with a public key.

19. The CA is responsible for revoking certificates when necessary. Which of the following correctly describes a CRL and OSCP?

    A. The CRL was developed as a more streamlined approach to OCSP.

    B. OCSP is a protocol that submits revoked certificates to the CRL.

    C. OCSP is a protocol developed specifically to check the CRL during a certificate validation process.

    D. CRL carries out real-time validation of a certificate and reports to the OCSP.

20. End-to-end encryption is used by users, and link encryption is used by service providers. Which of the following correctly describes these technologies?

    A. Link encryption does not encrypt headers and trailers.

    B. Link encryption encrypts everything but data link messaging.

    C. End-to-end encryption requires headers to be decrypted at each hop.

    D. End-to-end encryption encrypts all headers and trailers.

21. What do the SA values in the graphic of IPSec that follows represent?

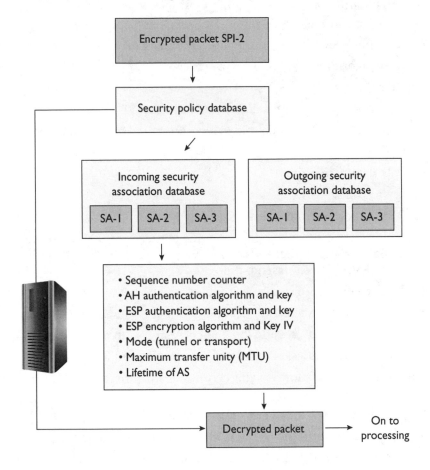

Encrypted packet SPI-2

Security policy database

Incoming security
association database

SA-1　SA-2　SA-3

Outgoing security
association database

SA-1　SA-2　SA-3

- Sequence number counter
- AH authentication algorithm and key
- ESP authentication algorithm and key
- ESP encryption algorithm and Key IV
- Mode (tunnel or transport)
- Maximum transfer unity (MTU)
- Lifetime of AS

Decrypted packet

On to
processing

A. Security parameter index

B. Security ability

C. Security association

D. Security assistant

22. There are several different types of technologies within cryptography that provide confidentiality. What is represented in the graphic that follows?

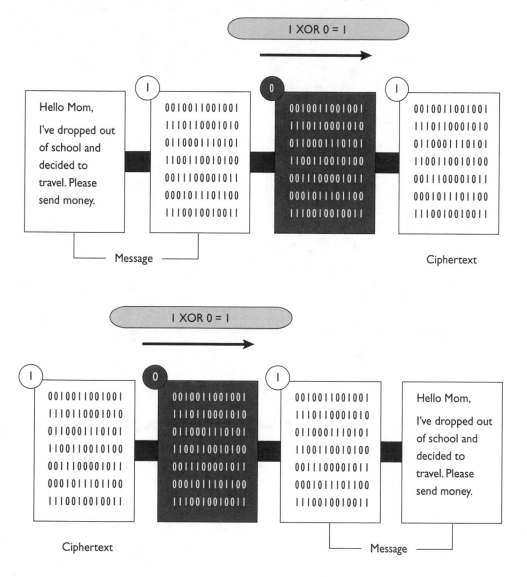

A. Running key cipher

B. Concealment cipher

C. Steganography

D. One-time pad

23. There are several different types of important architectures within public key infrastructures. Which architecture does the graphic that follows represent?

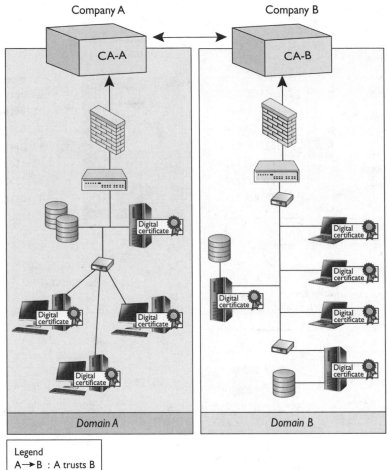

A. Cross-certification

B. Cross-revocation list

C. Online Certificate Status Protocol

D. Registration authority

24. There are different ways of providing integrity and authentication within cryptography. What type of technology is shown in the graphic that follows?

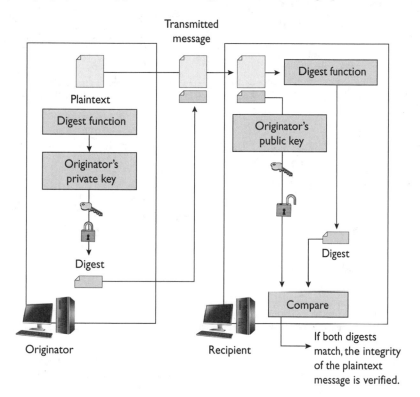

A. One-way hash

B. Digital signature

C. Birthday attack

D. Collision

25. There are several different modes that block ciphers can work in. Which mode does the graphic that follows portray?

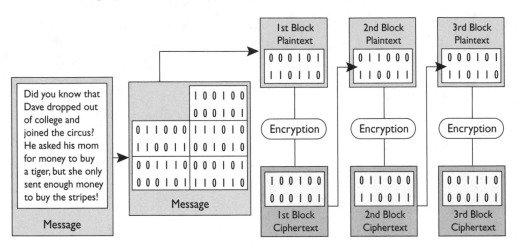

   A. Electronic Code Book Mode
   B. Cipher Block Chaining
   C. Output Feedback Mode
   D. Counter Mode

26. If Marge uses her private key to create a digital signature on a message she is sending to George, but she does not show or share her private key with George, what is it an example of?
   A. Key clustering
   B. Avoiding a birthday attack
   C. Providing data confidentiality
   D. Zero-knowledge proof

27. There are two main functions that Trusted Platform Modules (TPMs) carry out within systems today. Which of the following best describes these two functions?
   A. Sealing a hard disk drive is when the decryption key that can be used to decrypt data on the drive is stored on the TPM. Binding is when data pertaining to the system's state are hashed and stored on the TPM.
   B. Binding a hard disk drive is when whole-disk encryption is enabled through the use of the TPM. Sealing is when a digital certificate is sealed within a TPM and the system cannot boot up without this certificate being validated.

C. Sealing a hard disk drive is when whole-disk encryption is enabled through the use of the TPM. Binding is when a digital certificate is sealed within a TPM and the system cannot boot up without this certificate being validated.

D. Binding a hard disk drive is when the decryption key that can be used to decrypt data on the drive is stored on the TPM. Sealing is when data pertaining to the system's state are hashed and stored on the TPM.

The following scenario will be used for questions 28 and 29.

Jack has been told that successful attacks have been taking place and data that have been encrypted by his company's software systems have leaked to the company's competitors. Through Jack's investigation he has discovered that the lack of randomness in the seeding values used by the encryption algorithms in the company's software uncovered patterns and allowed for successful reverse engineering.

28. Which of the following is most likely the item that is the root of the problem when it comes to the necessary randomness explained in the scenario?

   A. Asymmetric algorithm

   B. Out-of-band communication compromise

   C. Number generator

   D. Symmetric algorithm

29. Which of the following best describes the role of the values that is allowing for patterns as described in the scenario?

   A. Initialization vector

   B. One-time password

   C. Master symmetric key

   D. Subkey

30. What cryptographic attack type carries out a mathematical analysis by trying to break a math problem from the beginning and the end of the mathematical formula simultaneously?

   A. Known plaintext

   B. Adaptive ciphertext

   C. Known ciphertext

   D. Meet-in-the-middle

1. C	11. C	21. C
2. A	12. B	22. D
3. B	13. A	23. A
4. D	14. B	24. B
5. B	15. A	25. B
6. A	16. C	26. D
7. D	17. B	27. D
8. A	18. D	28. C
9. D	19. C	29. A
10. C	20. B	30. D

1. There are several components involved with steganography. Which of the following refers to a file that has hidden information in it?

   A. Stego-medium

   B. Concealment cipher

   C. Carrier

   D. Payload

   ☑ **C.** Steganography is a method of hiding data in another media type so that the very existence of the data is concealed. Only the sender and receiver are supposed to be able to see the message because it is secretly hidden in a graphic, wave file, document, or other type of media. The message is not necessarily encrypted, just hidden. Encrypted messages can draw attention because it tells the bad guy, "This is something sensitive." A message hidden in a picture would not attract this type of attention, even though the exact same secret message can be embedded into this image. Steganography is a type of security through obscurity. The components involved with steganography are the carrier, stego-medium, and payload. The carrier is a signal, data stream, or file that has hidden information inside of it. In other words, it carries the payload.

   ☒ **A** is incorrect because the stego-medium is the medium in which the information is hidden in steganography. If the message were held within a graphic, the stego-medium could be JPEG or TIFF. If the message were embedded within a file, the stego-medium could be a Word document. A stego-medium can be a graphic type, wave file type, document type, or other type of media.

   ☒ **B** is incorrect because a concealment cipher is a type of steganography method that involves putting a message within a message. It is a way to hide a secret message within something familiar from the world around us. This answer does not specify a specific component of steganography but is a specific type of steganography.

   ☒ **D** is incorrect because the payload is the information that is to be concealed and transported through the use of steganography. The payload is the actual information that the sender wants to keep secret.

2. Which of the following correctly describes the relationship between SSL and TLS?

   A. TLS is the open-community version of SSL.

   B. SSL can be modified by developers to expand the protocol's capabilities.

   C. TLS is a proprietary protocol, while SSL is an open-community protocol.

   D. SSL is more extensible and backward compatible with TLS.

   ☑ **A.** Secure Sockets Layer (SSL) and Transport Layer Security (TLS) are cryptographic protocols that are used to secure communications by encrypting segments of network connections. Both protocols work at the transport layer. TLS is the open-community version of SSL. Because TLS is an open-community protocol, its specifications can be modified by vendors within the community to expand what it can do and what technologies it can work with. SSL is a proprietary protocol, and TLS was developed by a standards body, making it an open-community protocol.

   ☒ **B** is incorrect because SSL is a proprietary protocol developed by Netscape. This means the technology community cannot easily extend SSL to interoperate and expand in its functionality. If a protocol is proprietary in nature, as SSL is, the technology community cannot directly change its specifications and functionality. The reason that TLS was developed was to standardize how data can be transmitted securely through a protocol and how vendors can modify the protocol and still allow for interoperability.

   ☒ **C** is incorrect because the statement is backward. TLS is not proprietary. It is the open-community version of SSL, which is proprietary. The differences between the latest version of SSL (3.0) and TLS are slight, but TLS can be modified by developers to increase its functionality and work with other technologies. SSL, on the other hand, can only be modified by Netscape. Its code is not open to others.

   ☒ **D** is incorrect because TLS is actually more extensible than SSL and is not backward compatible with SSL. TLS and SSL provide the same type of functionality and are very similar, but not similar enough to work directly together. If two devices need to communicate securely, they need to be using either TLS or SSL—they cannot use a hybrid approach and still be able to communicate.

3. Which of the following incorrectly describes steganography?

    A. It is a type of security through obscurity.

    B. Modifying the most significant bit is the most common method used.

    C. Steganography does not draw attention to itself like encryption does.

    D. Media files are ideal for steganographic transmission because of their large size.

☑ **B.** Steganography is the method of hiding data in another media type so that the very existence of the data is concealed. One of the most common methods of embedding the message into some type of medium is using the least significant bit (LSB)—not the most significant bit. Many types of files have some bits that can be modified and not affect the file they are in, which is where secret data can be hidden without altering the file in a visible manner. In the LSB approach, graphics with a high resolution or an audio file that has many different types of sounds (high bit rate) are the most successful in hiding information within. There is commonly no noticeable distortion, and the file is usually not increased to a size that can be detected. A 24-bit bitmap file will have 8 bits representing each of the three color values, which are red, green, and blue. These 8 bits are within each pixel. If we consider just the blue, there will be 2^8 different values of blue. The difference between 11111111 and 11111110 in the value for blue intensity is likely to be undetectable by the human eye.

☒ **A** is incorrect because steganography is a type of security through obscurity. Security through obscurity means that instead of actually securing something with a countermeasure, someone uses secrecy as the way to protect the asset. An example of security through obscurity is if a network administrator changes his HTTP port from 80 to 8080 with the hopes that no one will figure this out. Security through obscurity means that you are trying to fool the potential attacker and you assume that the attacker will not be clever enough to figure out your trickery.

☒ **C** is incorrect because it is true that steganography does not draw attention to itself as does encryption. An encrypted message can draw attention because it tells the bad guy that the encrypted information is sensitive (otherwise, it wouldn't be encrypted in the first place). An attacker may then be motivated to break the encryption and uncover the information. The goal of steganography is that the attacker not even know that the sensitive information exists and thus will not attempt to capture it.

☒ **D** is incorrect because it is true that larger media files are ideal for steganographic transmission because there are more bits to manipulate with a lower chance that anyone will notice. As a simple example, a sender might start with an innocuous image file and adjust the color of every hundredth pixel to correspond to a letter in the alphabet, a change so subtle that someone not specifically looking for it is unlikely to notice it. The larger the file, the more obscurity can be accomplished because there are more bits to work with and manipulate.

4. Which of the following correctly describes a drawback of symmetric key systems?

    A. Computationally less intensive than asymmetric systems

    B. Work much more slowly than asymmetric systems

    C. Carry out mathematically intensive tasks

    D. Key must be delivered via secure courier

    ☑ **D.** In order for two users to exchange messages encrypted with a symmetric algorithm, they must first figure out how to distribute the key. If a key is compromised, then all messages encrypted with that key can be decrypted and read by an intruder. It is not safe to simply send the key in an e-mail message, because the key is not protected and can be easily intercepted and used by attackers. Thus, one user must send the key to the other using an out-of-band method. The user can save the key on a thumb drive and walk it over to the other person's desk, or have a secure courier deliver it. This is a disadvantage of symmetric cryptography because distribution is a hassle, as well as clumsy and insecure.

    ☒ **A** is incorrect because it describes an advantage of symmetric algorithms. Because they are less computationally intensive than asymmetric algorithms, symmetric algorithms tend to be much faster. They can encrypt and decrypt relatively quickly large amounts of data that would take an unacceptable amount of time to encrypt and decrypt with an asymmetric algorithm.

    ☒ **B** is incorrect because asymmetric systems work much more slowly than symmetric systems. The speed with which symmetric algorithms work is an advantage. Asymmetric algorithms are slower than symmetric algorithms because they use much more complex mathematics to carry out their functions, which requires more processing time. However, asymmetric algorithms can provide authentication and nonrepudiation, whereas symmetric algorithms cannot. Because both users employ the same key to encrypt and decrypt messages, symmetric cryptosystems can provide confidentiality but they cannot provide authentication or nonrepudiation. There is no way to prove through cryptography who actually sent a message if two people are using the same key.

    ☒ **C** is incorrect because asymmetric algorithms carry out mathematically intensive tasks. Symmetric algorithms, on the other hand, carry out relatively simplistic mathematical functions on the bits during the encryption and decryption processes. They substitute and scramble (transpose) bits, which is not overly difficult or processor-intensive. The reason it is hard to break this type of encryption is that the symmetric algorithms carry out this type of functionality over and over again. So a set of bits will go through a long series of being substituted and transposed.

5. Which of the following occurs in a PKI environment?

   A. The RA creates the certificate, and the CA signs it.

   B. The CA signs the certificate.

   C. The RA signs the certificate.

   D. The user signs the certificate.

   ☑ **B.** A certificate authority (CA) is a trusted organization (or server) that maintains and issues digital certificates. When a person requests a certificate, the registration authority (RA) verifies that individual's identity and passes the certificate request off to the CA. The CA constructs the certificate, digitally signs it, sends it to the requester, and maintains the certificate over its lifetime. The CA digitally signs it so that the receiver can verify that the certificate came from that specific CA. The CA digitally signs the certificate with its private key, and the receiver verifies this signature with the CA's public key.

   ☒ **A** is incorrect because the registration authority (RA) does not create the certificate; the certificate authority (CA) creates it and signs it. The RA performs the certification registration duties. The RA establishes and confirms the identity of the individual requesting the certificate, initiates the certification process with a CA on behalf of an end user, and can perform certificate life-cycle management functions. The RA cannot issue certificates but can act as a broker between the user and the CA. When users need new certificates, they make requests to the RA, and the RA verifies all necessary identification information before allowing a request to go to the CA.

   ☒ **C** is incorrect because the registration authority (RA) does not sign the certificate. The certificate authority (CA) signs the certificate. The RA validates the user's identity and then sends the request for a certificate to the CA.

   ☒ **D** is incorrect because the user does not sign the certificate. In a PKI environment, a user's certificate is created and signed by the certificate authority (CA). The CA is a trusted third party that generates and maintains user certificates, which hold their public keys. The certificate is digitally signed to provide confidence to others that the certificate was created by that specific CA.

6. Encryption can happen at different layers of an operating system and network stack. Where does PPTP encryption take place?

   A. Data link layer

   B. Within applications

   C. Transport layer

   D. Data link and physical layers

☑ **A.** The Point-to-Point Tunneling Protocol (PPTP) is a method for implementing virtual private networks (VPNs). It is a Microsoft-proprietary VPN protocol that works at the data link layer of the OSI model. PPTP can only provide a single connection and can only work over PPP connections.

☒ **B** is incorrect because end-to-end encryption takes place within the applications. End-to-end encryption means that only the data payload is encrypted. If encryption works at any layer of the OSI model, then headers and trailers can also be encrypted. Since PPTP works at the data link layer, headers and trailers from the upper layers can be encrypted and protected along with the data payload.

☒ **C** is incorrect because SSL is an example of an encryption technology that works at the transport layer, not PPTP. SSL uses public key encryption and provides data encryption, server authentication, message integrity, and optional client authentication to display secured portions of a Web site to a user. When HTTP runs over SSL, you have HTTP Secure (HTTPS). HTTP works at the application layer, but SSL still works at the transport layer.

☒ **D** is incorrect because PPTP works at the data link layer, but not the physical layer. The physical layer technologies convert the bits from the data link layer into some type of transmission format. If the data transmission is taking place over a UTP connection, then the data is converted into electronic voltage at the physical layer. If data transmission is taking place over fiber lines, then the data is converted into photons. Specifications for the physical layer include the timing of voltage changes, voltage levels, and the physical connectors for electrical, optical, and mechanical transmission.

7. Which of the following best describes the difference between public key cryptography and public key infrastructure?

   A. Public key cryptography is the use of an asymmetric algorithm, while public key infrastructure is the use of a symmetric algorithm.

   B. Public key cryptography is used to create public/private key pairs, and public key infrastructure is used to perform key exchange and agreement.

   C. Public key cryptography provides authentication and nonrepudiation, while public key infrastructure provides confidentiality and integrity.

   D. Public key cryptography is another name for asymmetric cryptography, while public key infrastructure consists of public key cryptographic mechanisms.

   ☑ **D.** Public key cryptography is asymmetric cryptography; the terms are used interchangeably. Public key cryptography is one piece in a public key infrastructure (PKI), which is made up of many different parts, including certificate authorities, registration authorities, certificates, keys, programs, and users. The infrastructure contains the pieces that will identify users, create and distribute certificates, maintain and revoke certificates, distribute and maintain encryption keys, and enable all technologies to communicate and work together for the purpose of encrypted communication and authentication.

☒ **A** is incorrect because PKI uses a hybrid system of symmetric and asymmetric key algorithms and methods. Public key cryptography is the use of an asymmetric algorithm. Thus, the terms asymmetric cryptography and public key cryptography are interchangeable and mean the same thing. Examples of asymmetric algorithms are RSA, elliptic curve cryptosystem (ECC), Diffie-Hellman, and El Gamal.

☒ **B** is incorrect because public key cryptography is the use of asymmetric algorithms, which are used to create public/private key pairs, perform key exchange or agreement, and generate and verify digital signatures. Public key infrastructure, on the other hand, is not an algorithm, a protocol, or an application—it is an infrastructure based on symmetric and asymmetric cryptography.

☒ **C** is incorrect because a PKI does not provide authentication, nonrepudiation, confidentiality, and integrity directly—it can use algorithms that provide these security services. A PKI uses asymmetric, symmetric, and hashing algorithms. Symmetric algorithms provide confidentiality, asymmetric algorithms provide authentication and nonrepudiation, and hashing algorithms provide integrity.

8. Which of the following best describes Key Derivation Functions (KDFs)?

A. Keys are generated from a master key.

B. Session keys are generated from each other.

C. Asymmetric cryptography is used to encrypt symmetric keys.

D. A master key is generated from a session key.

☑ **A.** For complex keys to be generated, commonly a master key is created and then symmetric keys (subkeys) are generated from it. Key Derivation Functions (KDFs) derive encryption keys from a secret value. The secret value can be a master key, passphrase, or password. KDFs are used to help ensure the randomness of the key values to make it harder for the attacker to uncover them. The KDF commonly uses a pseudorandom number generator with the secret value to make each encryption key unique.

☒ **B** is incorrect because session keys are commonly generated from the master key—not from each other. For example, if an application is responsible for creating a session key for each subject that requests one, it should not be giving out the same instance of that one key. Different systems need to have different symmetric keys to ensure that the window for the bad guy to capture and uncover that key is smaller than if the same key is used over and over again. When two or more keys are created from a master key, they are called subkeys.

☒ **C** is incorrect because the encryption of keys has nothing to do with KDFs. KDF pertains to the procedures of creating unique and strong encryption keys.

KDF helps to ensure that enough randomness is involved when generating new keys so that the attacker has a harder time uncovering them.

☒ **D** is incorrect because the statement is backward. A session key is commonly generated from a master key. When keys are generated from an original value, as in a master key, the resulting keys are referred to as subkeys or subsession keys.

9. The elliptic curve cryptosystem is an asymmetric algorithm. What sets it apart from other asymmetric algorithms?

   A. It provides digital signatures, secure key distribution, and encryption.

   B. It computes discrete logarithms in a finite field.

   C. It uses a larger percentage of resources to carry out encryption.

   D. It is more efficient.

   ☑ **D.** Elliptic curves are rich mathematical structures that have shown usefulness in many different types of applications. An elliptic curve cryptosystem (ECC) differs from other asymmetric algorithms due to its efficiency. ECC is more efficient than any other asymmetric algorithm because of less intensive mathematics. In most cases, the longer the key, the more protection that is provided, but ECC can provide the same level of protection with a key size that is shorter than what RSA requires. Because longer keys require more resources to perform mathematical tasks, the smaller keys used in ECC require fewer resources of the device. And fewer resources make for a more efficient algorithm.

   ☒ **A** is incorrect because ECC is not the only asymmetric algorithm that provides digital signatures, secure key distribution, and encryption. These services are also provided by RSA and other asymmetric algorithms. Using its one-way function, ECC provides encryption and signature verification, and the inverse direction performs decryption and signature generation. It can also be used as a key exchange protocol, meaning it is used to encrypt the symmetric key to get it securely to its destination.

   ☒ **B** is incorrect because Diffie-Hellman and El Gamal calculate discrete logarithms in a finite field. In the field of mathematics that deals with elliptic curves, points on the curves compose a structure called a group. These points are the values used in mathematical formulas for ECC's encryption and decryption processes. The algorithm computes discrete logarithms of elliptic curves, which is different from calculating discrete logarithms in a finite field.

   ☒ **C** is incorrect because ECCs use much fewer resources when compared to other asymmetric algorithms. Some devices, like wireless devices and cellular phones, have limited processing capacity, storage, power, and bandwidth. With these types of devices, efficiency of resource use is very important.

10. If implemented properly, a one-time pad is a perfect encryption scheme. Which of the following incorrectly describes a requirement for implementation?

A. The pad must be securely distributed and protected at its destination.

B. The pad must be made up of truly random values.

C. The pad must always be the same length.

D. The pad must be used only one time.

☑ **C.** A one-time pad is a perfect encryption scheme because it is considered unbreakable if implemented properly. It was invented by Gilbert Vernam in 1917, so sometimes it is referred to as the Vernam cipher. The pad must be at least as long as the message. If it is not as long as the message, the pad will need to be reused to cover the whole message. This would be the same thing as using a pad more than one time, which could introduce patterns.

☒ **A** is incorrect because it is true that the pad must be securely distributed and protected at its destination. This is a very cumbersome process to accomplish, because the pads are usually just individual pieces of paper that need to be delivered by a secure courier and properly guarded at each destination. One-time pads have been used throughout history to protect different types of sensitive data. Today, they are still in place for many types of militaries as a backup encryption option if current encryption processes (that require computers and a power source) are unavailable for reasons of war or attacks.

☒ **B** is incorrect because it is true that the pad must be made up of truly random values. This may not seem like a difficult task, but even our computer systems today do not have truly random number generators; rather, they have pseudorandom number generators. These generators are seeded by an initial value from some component within the computer system (time, CPU cycles, etc.). Although a computer system is complex, it is a predictable environment, so if the seeding value is predictable in any way, the resulting values created are not truly random—but pseudorandom.

☒ **D** is incorrect because it is true that the pad must be used only one time. If the pad is used more than one time, this might introduce patterns in the encryption process that will aid an evildoer in his goal of breaking the encryption. Although the one-time pad approach to encryption can provide a very high degree of security, it is impractical in most situations because of all of its different requirements. Each possible pair of entities that might want to communicate in this fashion must receive, in a secure fashion, a pad. This type of key management can be overwhelming and may require more overhead than it is worth. The distribution of the pad can be challenging, and the sender and receiver must be perfectly synchronized so that each is using the same pad.

11. Sally is responsible for key management within her organization. Which of the following incorrectly describes a principle of secure key management?

    A. Keys should be backed up or escrowed in case of emergencies.

    B. The more a key is used, the shorter its lifetime should be.

    C. Less secure data allows for a shorter key lifetime.

    D. Keys should be stored and transmitted by secure means.

    ☑ C. Key management is critical for proper protection. Part of key management is determining the lifespan of keys. The key's lifetime should correspond with the sensitivity of the data it is protecting. Less secure data may allow for a longer key lifetime, whereas more sensitive data might require a shorter key lifetime. Keys should be properly destroyed when their lifetime comes to an end. The processes of changing and destroying keys should be automated and hidden from the user. They should be integrated into software or the operating system. It only adds complexity and opens the doors for more errors when processes are done manually and depend upon end users to perform certain functions.

    ☒ A is incorrect because it is true that keys should be backed up or escrowed in case of emergencies. Keys are at risk of being lost, destroyed, or corrupted. Backup copies should be available and easily accessible when required. If data are encrypted and then the user accidentally loses the necessary key to decrypt it, this information would be lost forever if there were not a backup key. The application being used for cryptography may have key recovery options, or it may require copies of the keys to be kept in a secure place.

    ☒ B is incorrect because it is true that the more a key is used, the shorter its lifetime should be. The frequency of use of a cryptographic key has a direct correlation to how often the key should be changed. The more a key is used, the more likely it is to be captured and compromised. If a key is used infrequently, then this risk drops dramatically. The necessary level of security and the frequency of use can dictate the frequency of key updates. A mom-and-pop diner might only change its cryptography keys every month, whereas an information warfare military unit might change them every day or every week.

    ☒ D is incorrect because it is true that keys should be stored and transmitted by secure means. Keys are stored before and after distribution. When a key is distributed to a user, it needs a secure place within the file system to be stored and used in a controlled method. The key, the algorithm that will use the key, configurations, and parameters are stored in a module that also needs to be protected. If an attacker is able to obtain these components, she could masquerade as another user and decrypt, read, and re-encrypt messages not intended for her.

12. Mandy needs to calculate how many keys must be generated for the 260 employees using the company's PKI asymmetric algorithm. How many keys are required?

A. 33,670

B. 520

C. 67,340

D. 260

☑ **B.** With asymmetric algorithms, every user must have at least one pair of keys (private and public). In public key systems, each entity has different keys, or asymmetric keys. The two different asymmetric keys are mathematically related. If a message is encrypted by one key, the other key is required in order to decrypt the message. The formula for determining the number of keys needed in this environment is $N \times 2$, which is the number of people (N) multiplied by the number of keys each person would need (2). In a public key system, the pair of keys is made up of one public key and one private key. The public key can be known to everyone, and the private key must be known and used only by the owner.

☒ A is incorrect because 33,670 is the number of keys needed in a symmetric key cryptosystem. Each pair of users who want to exchange data using symmetric key encryption must have two instances of the same key. This means that if Dan and Bob want to communicate, both need to obtain a copy of the same key. If Dan also wants to communicate using symmetric encryption with Norm and Dave, he needs to have three separate keys, one for each friend. This might not sound like a big deal until Dan realizes that he may communicate with hundreds of people over a period of several months, and keeping track and using the correct key that corresponds to each specific receiver can become a daunting task. If ten people needed to communicate securely with each other using symmetric keys, then 45 keys would need to be kept track of. If 100 people were going to communicate, then 4,950 keys would be involved. The equation used to calculate the number of symmetric keys needed is: $N(N - 1) / 2$ = number of keys.

☒ C is incorrect because 67,340 is the total derived from $N(N - 1)$, which is part of the formula used to determine the number of keys needed in a symmetric key cryptosystem. The complete formula is $N(N - 1) / 2$. The question, however, asked for the number of keys that would be used in a public key infrastructure's asymmetric algorithms. Asymmetric—not symmetric—keys are used in a public key cryptosystem. The formula for determining the number of asymmetric keys that are needed is $N \times 2$.

☒ D is incorrect because each user in a public key infrastructure requires at least one key pair—a public key and a private key. One key cannot encrypt and decrypt the same message. So each user requires at least two keys. Thus, the formula for determining the number of asymmetric keys that are needed is $N \times 2$.

13. Which of the following works similarly to stream ciphers?

    A. One-time pad

    B. AES

    C. Block

    D. RSA

☑ **A.** Stream ciphers were developed to provide the same type of protection one-time pads do, which is why they work in such a similar manner. In reality, stream ciphers cannot provide the level of protection one-time pads do, but because stream ciphers are implemented through software and automated means, they are much more practical. A one-time pad is a perfect encryption scheme because it is considered unbreakable if implemented properly. This cipher uses a pad made up of random values. A plaintext message that needs to be encrypted is converted into bits, and a one-time pad is made up of random bits. This encryption process uses a binary mathematical function called exclusive-OR, usually abbreviated as XOR. XOR is an operation that is applied to two bits and is a function commonly used in binary mathematics and encryption methods. Stream ciphers also encrypt at the bit level, which is how they are similar to one-time pad encryption schemes.

☒ **B** is incorrect because AES is a symmetric block cipher. When a block cipher is used for encryption and decryption purposes, the message is divided into blocks of bits. These blocks are then put through mathematical functions, one block at a time. Stream ciphers encrypt data one bit at a time whereas a block cipher encrypts data one block of bits at a time. Suppose you need to encrypt a message you are sending to your friend and you are using a block cipher that uses 64 bits block size. Your message of 640 bits is chopped up into 10 individual blocks of 64 bits. Each block is put through a succession of mathematical formulas, and what you end up with is 10 blocks of encrypted text. You send this encrypted message to your friend. He has to have the same block cipher and key, and those 10 ciphertext blocks go back through the algorithm in the reverse sequence and end up in your plaintext message.

☒ **C** is incorrect because as stated in the preceding answer, when a block cipher is used for encryption and decryption purposes, the message is divided into blocks of bits. These blocks are then put through mathematical functions, one block at a time.

☒ **D** is incorrect because RSA is a public key algorithm that is the most popular when it comes to asymmetric algorithms. Asymmetric algorithms use a different type of mathematics than symmetric and are nothing similar to one-time pad encryption schemes. The security of this algorithm comes from the difficulty of factoring large numbers into their original prime numbers.

14. There are two main types of symmetric ciphers: stream and block. Which of the following is not an attribute of a good stream cipher?

    A. Statistically unbiased keystream

    B. Statistically predictable

    C. Long periods of no repeating patterns

    D. Keystream not linearly related to key

    ☑ **B.** The two main types of symmetric algorithms are block ciphers and stream ciphers. A block cipher performs mathematical functions on blocks of bits at a time. A stream cipher, on the other hand, does not divide a message into blocks. Instead, a stream cipher treats the message as a stream of bits and performs mathematical functions on each bit individually. Good stream ciphers offer the following: unpredictable statistical results, long periods of no repeating patterns, a statistically unbiased keystream, and a keystream that is not linearly related to the key. If a stream cipher is statistically predictable, then it will be possible for an attacker to uncover the key and break the cipher.

    ☒ A is incorrect because a statistically unbiased keystream is an attribute of a good stream cipher. A statistically unbiased keystream means that there are as many zeros as there are ones. There should be no dominance in the number of zeros or ones in the keystream.

    ☒ C is incorrect because long periods of no repeating patterns within keystream values is a characteristic of a good stream cipher. The ultimate goal of any encryption is to provide a high level of randomness so that an attacker cannot reverse engineer and uncover the key that was used during the encryption process.

    ☒ D is incorrect because a keystream not linearly related to a key is an attribute of a good stream cipher. This means that if someone figures out the keystream values, that does not mean he now knows the key value. This is important because the key provides the randomness of the encryption process. Most encryption algorithms are public, so people know how they work. The secret to the secret sauce is the key. The key provides randomness, so that the stream of bits that are XORed to the plaintext are as random as possible.

15. Which of the following best describes how a digital signature is created?

    A. The sender encrypts a message digest with his private key.

    B. The sender encrypts a message digest with his public key.

    C. The receiver encrypts a message digest with his private key.

    D. The receiver encrypts a message digest with his public key.

☑ **A.** A digital signature is a hash value that has been encrypted with the sender's private key. The act of digital signing means encrypting the message's hash value with a private key. If Sam wants to ensure that the message he sends to Debbie is not modified and he wants her to be sure it came only from him, he can digitally sign the message. This means that a one-way hashing function would be run on the message, and then Sam would encrypt that hash value with his private key. When Debbie receives the message, she will perform the hashing function on the message and come up with her own hash value. Then she will decrypt the sent hash value (digital signature) with Sam's public key. She then compares the two values, and if they are the same, she can be sure the message was not altered during transmission. She is also sure the message came from Sam because the value was encrypted with his private key.

☒ **B** is incorrect because if the sender encrypts the message digest with his public key, the recipient will not be able to decrypt it. The recipient would need access to the sender's private key, which should never happen. The private key should always be kept secret.

☒ **C** is incorrect because the receiver should decrypt the message digest with the sender's public key. The message digest is encrypted with the sender's private key, which can only be decrypted with the sender's public key.

☒ **D** is incorrect because the receiver should decrypt the message digest with the sender's public key. The message digest is encrypted with the sender's private key, which can only be decrypted with the sender's public key.

16. In cryptography, different steps and algorithms provide different types of security services. Which of the following provides only authentication, non-repudiation, and integrity?

    A. Encryption algorithm

    B. Hash algorithm

    C. Digital signature

    D. Encryption paired with a digital signature

    ☑ **C.** A digital signature is a hash value that has been encrypted with the sender's private key. The act of signing means encrypting the message's hash value with a private key. A message can be digitally signed, which provides authentication, nonrepudiation, and integrity. The hashing function ensures the integrity of the message, and the signing of the hash value provides authentication and nonrepudiation.

    ☒ **A** is incorrect because encryption algorithms provide confidentiality. Encryption is most commonly carried out with the use of symmetric algorithms. Symmetric algorithms can only provide confidentiality and not authentication, nonrepudiation, and integrity.

☒ **B** is incorrect because hashing algorithms provide data integrity. Hashing algorithms generate message digests (also called hash values) to detect whether modification has taken place. The sender and receiver independently generate their own digests, and the receiver compares these values. If they differ, the receiver knows the message has been altered. A hashing algorithm cannot provide authentication or nonrepudiation.

☒ **D** is incorrect because encryption and a digital signature provide confidentiality, authentication, nonrepudiation, and integrity. The encryption alone provides confidentiality. And the digital signature provides authentication, nonrepudiation, and integrity. The question asks for which can only provide authentication, nonrepudiation, and integrity.

17. Advanced Encryption Standard is an algorithm used for which of the following?

    A. Data integrity

    B. Bulk data encryption

    C. Key recovery

    D. Distribution of symmetric keys

    ☑ **B.** The Advanced Encryption Standard (AES) is a data encryption standard that was developed to improve upon the previous de facto standard—the Data Encryption Standard (DES). As a symmetric algorithm, AES is used to encrypt bulk data. Symmetric algorithms, of any kind, are used to encrypt large amounts of data (bulk), while asymmetric algorithms are used to encrypt a small amount of data as in keys and hashing values.

    ☒ **A** is incorrect because the Advanced Encryption Standard (AES) is an encryption algorithm and therefore provides confidentiality, not data integrity. Hashing algorithms, such as SHA-1, MD2, MD4, MD5, and HAVAL, provide data integrity.

    ☒ **C** is incorrect because the Advanced Encryption Standard (AES) is not used for key recovery. However, AES generates and makes use of keys, which require key recovery procedures. Keys are at risk of being lost, destroyed, or corrupted. Backup copies should be available and easily accessible when required. If data are encrypted and then the user accidentally loses the necessary key to decrypt it, this information would be lost forever if there were not a backup key to save the day. The application being used for cryptography may have key recovery options, or it may require copies of the keys to be kept in a secure place.

    ☒ **D** is incorrect because asymmetric algorithms are used to protect symmetric keys while being distributed. AES is a symmetric algorithm. In a hybrid system, the symmetric algorithm creates a secret key that will be used to encrypt the bulk, or the message, and the asymmetric key encrypts the secret key for transmission.

18. SSL is a de facto protocol used for securing transactions that occur over untrusted networks. Which of the following best describes what takes place during an SSL connection setup process?

   A. The server creates a session key and encrypts it with a public key.

   B. The server creates a session key and encrypts it with a private key.

   C. The client creates a session key and encrypts it with a private key.

   D. The client creates a session key and encrypts it with a public key.

   ☑ D. Secure Sockets Layer (SSL) uses public key encryption and provides data encryption, server authentication, message integrity, and optional client authentication. When a client accesses a Web site, that Web site may have both secured and public portions. The secured portion would require the user to be authenticated in some fashion. When the client goes from a public page on the Web site to a secured page, the Web server will start the necessary tasks to invoke SSL and protect this type of communication. The server sends a message back to the client, indicating a secure session should be established, and the client in response sends its security parameters. The server compares those security parameters to its own until it finds a match. This is the handshaking phase. The server authenticates to the client by sending it a digital certificate, and if the client decides to trust the server, the process continues. The client generates a session key and encrypts it with the server's public key. This encrypted key is sent to the Web server, and they both use this symmetric key to encrypt the data they send back and forth.

   ☒ A is incorrect because the server does not create the session key; the client creates a session key and encrypts it with the server's public key. SSL is commonly used in Web transactions and works in the following way: client creates session key, client encrypts session key with server's public key and sends it to the server, server receives session key and decrypts it with its private key.

   ☒ B is incorrect because the server does not create the session key, and it is not encrypted with the private key. The client creates a session key and encrypts it with the server's public key. The server receives the session key and decrypts it with its private key. The session key is then used to encrypt the data that is transmitted between the client and server.

   ☒ C is incorrect because the client uses the server's public key to encrypt the session key it generates. If the client encrypted the session key with the private key, then any entity that possessed the client's public key would be able to decrypt the session key. This does not provide any security. By encrypting the session key with the server's public key, only the server— which possesses the corresponding private key—can decrypt it.

19. The CA is responsible for revoking certificates when necessary. Which of the following correctly describes a CRL and OSCP?

    A. The CRL was developed as a more streamlined approach to OCSP.

    B. OCSP is a protocol that submits revoked certificates to the CRL.

    C. OCSP is a protocol developed specifically to check the CRL during a certificate validation process.

    D. CRL carries out real-time validation of a certificate and reports to the OCSP.

    ☑ **C.** The CA is responsible for creating and handing out certificates, maintaining them, and revoking them if necessary. Revocation is handled by the CA, and the revoked certificate information is stored on a certificate revocation list (CRL). This is a list of every certificate that has been revoked. This list is maintained and updated periodically. A certificate may be revoked because the key holder's private key was compromised or because the CA discovered the certificate was issued to the wrong person. If the certificate becomes invalid for some reason, the CRL is the mechanism for the CA to let others know this information. The Online Certificate Status Protocol (OCSP) is being used more and more compared to the cumbersome CRL approach. When using just a CRL, the user's browser must either check a central CRL to find out if the certification has been revoked or the CA continually pushes out CRL values to the clients to ensure they have an updated CRL. If OCSP is implemented, it does this work automatically in the background. It carries out real-time validation of a certificate and reports back to the user whether the certificate is valid, invalid, or unknown.

    ☒ **A** is incorrect because a certificate revocation list (CRL) is actually a cumbersome approach to managing and validating revoked certificates. The Online Certificate Status Protocol (OCSP) is increasingly being used to address this. OCSP does this work in the background, doing what the user's Web browser would do when just using CRL. OCSP checks a central CRL to see if a certification has been revoked.

    ☒ **B** is incorrect because the Online Certificate Status Protocol (OCSP) does not submit revoked certificates to the certificate revocation list (CRL). The certificate authority (CA) is responsible for the creation, distribution, and maintenance of certificates. This includes revoking them when necessary and storing the information on a CRL.

    ☒ **D** is incorrect because the Online Certificate Status Protocol (OCSP), not the certificate revocation list (CRL), carries out real-time validation of a certificate. In addition, the OCSP reports back to the user whether the certificate is valid, invalid, or unknown.

20. End-to-end encryption is used by users, and link encryption is used by service providers. Which of the following correctly describes these technologies?

A. Link encryption does not encrypt headers and trailers.

B. Link encryption encrypts everything but data link messaging.

C. End-to-end encryption requires headers to be decrypted at each hop.

D. End-to-end encryption encrypts all headers and trailers.

☑ **B.** Encryption can be performed at different communication levels, each with different types of protection and implications. Two general modes of encryption implementation are link encryption and end-to-end encryption. Link encryption encrypts all the data along a specific communication path, as in a satellite link, T3 line, or telephone circuit. Not only is the user information encrypted, but the header, trailers, addresses, and routing data that are part of the packets are also encrypted. The only traffic not encrypted in this technology is the data link control messaging information, which includes instructions and parameters that the different link devices use to synchronize communication methods. Link encryption provides protection against packet sniffers and eavesdroppers. In end-to-end encryption, the headers, addresses, routing, and trailer information are not encrypted, enabling attackers to learn more about a captured packet and where it is headed. With end-to-end encryption only the data payload is encrypted.

☒ **A** is incorrect because link encryption does encrypt the headers and trailers. This is a major advantage to using link encryption: the headers, trailers, and data payload are encrypted except for the data link messaging. It also works seamlessly at a lower layer in the OSI model, so users do not need to do anything to initiate it.

☒ **C** is incorrect because the headers are not encrypted with end-to-end encryption, so there is no need to decrypt them at each hop. This is an advantage of using end-to-end encryption. Other advantages include additional flexibility for the user in choosing what gets encrypted and how, and a higher granularity of functionality because each application or user can choose specific configurations.

☒ **D** is incorrect because end-to-end encryption does not encrypt any headers or trailers. As a result, they are not protected. This is the primary disadvantage to using end-to-end encryption. If the headers and trailers need to be protected, then link encryption should be used.

21. What do the SA values in the graphic of IPSec that follows represent?

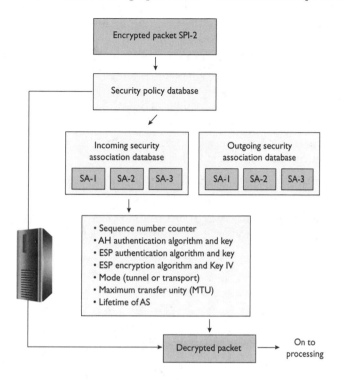

A. Security parameter index

B. Security ability

C. Security association

D. Security assistant

☑ **C.** Each IPSec VPN device will have at least one security association (SA) for each secure connection it uses. The SA, which is critical to the IPSec architecture, is a record of the configurations the device needs to support an IPSec connection over a VPN connection. When two devices complete their handshaking process, which means they have agreed upon a long list of parameters they will use to communicate, these data must be recorded and stored somewhere, which is in the SA. The SA can contain the authentication and encryption keys, the agreed-upon algorithms, the key lifetime, the source IP address, and other information. When a device receives a packet via the IPSec protocol, it is the SA that tells the device what to do with the packet. So if device B receives a packet from device C via IPSec, device B will look to the corresponding SA to tell it how to decrypt the packet, how to properly authenticate the source of the packet, which key to use, and how to reply to the message if necessary.

☒ **A** is incorrect because a security parameter index (SPI) keeps track of the different SAs. SAs are directional, so a device will have one SA for outbound traffic and a different SA for inbound traffic for each individual communication channel. If a device is connecting to three devices, it will have at least six SAs, one for each inbound or outbound connection per remote device. So how can a device keep all of these SAs organized and ensure that the right SA is invoked for the right connection? With the SPI, that's how. Each device has an SPI that keeps track of the different SAs and tells the device which one is appropriate to invoke for the different packets it receives.

☒ **B** is incorrect because there is no component within IPSec officially referred to as security ability. This is a distracter answer.

☒ **D** is incorrect because there is no component within IPSec officially referred to as security assistant. This is a distracter answer.

22. There are several different types of technologies within cryptography that provide confidentiality. What is represented in the graphic that follows?

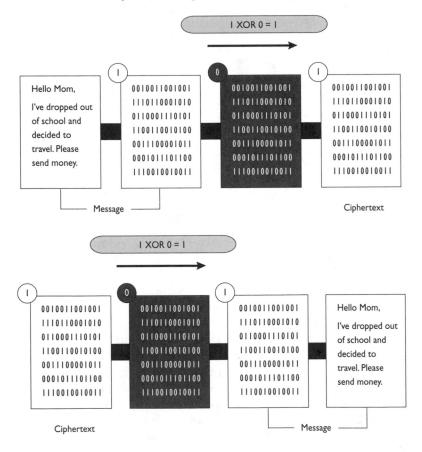

A. Running key cipher

B. Concealment cipher

C. Steganography

D. One-time pad

☑ **D.** A one-time pad is a perfect encryption scheme because it is considered unbreakable if implemented properly. A one-time pad uses a pad with random values that are XORed against the message to produce ciphertext. The plaintext message shown in the graphic that needs to be encrypted has been converted into bits, and our one-time pad is made up of random bits. This encryption process uses a binary mathematical function called exclusive-OR, usually abbreviated as XOR. The receiver must have the same one-time pad to decrypt the message, by reversing the process.

☒ **A** is incorrect because a running key cipher uses a key that does not require an electronic algorithm and bit alterations but cleverly uses components in the physical world around you. For instance, the algorithm could be a set of books agreed upon by the sender and receiver. The key in this type of cipher could be a book page, line number, and column count. If I get a message from my super-secret spy buddy and the message reads "149l6c7.299l3c7.91115c8," this could mean for me to look at the 1st book in our predetermined series of books, the 49th page, 6th line down the page, and the 7th column. So I write down the letter in that column, which is *m*. The second set of numbers starts with 2, so I go to the 2nd book, 99th page, 3rd line down, and then to the 7th column, which is *p*. The last letter I get from the 9th book, 11th page, 5th line, 8th column, which is *t*. So now I have come up with my important secret message, which is *mpt*.

☒ **B** is incorrect because a concealment cipher is a message within a message. If my spy buddy and I decide our key value is every third word, then when I get a message from him, I will pick out every third word and write it down. Suppose he sends me a message that reads, "The saying, 'The time is right' is not cow language, so is now a dead subject." Because my key is every third word, I come up with "The right cow is dead."

☒ **C** is incorrect because steganography is a method of hiding data in another media type so that the very existence of the data is concealed. Only the sender and receiver are supposed to be able to see the message because it is secretly hidden in a graphic, wave file, document, or other type of media. The message is not encrypted, just hidden. Encrypted messages can draw attention because it tells the bad guy, "This is something sensitive." A message hidden in a picture would not attract this type of attention, even though the exact same secret message can be embedded into this image. Steganography is a type of security through obscurity.

23. There are several different types of important architectures within public key infrastructures. Which architecture does the graphic that follows represent?

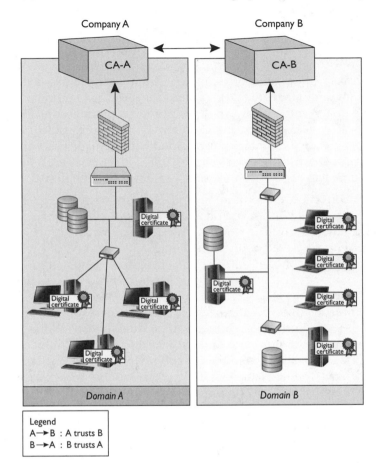

A. Cross-certification

B. Cross-revocation list

C. Online Certificate Status Protocol

D. Registration authority

☑ **A.** When independent PKIs need to interconnect to allow for secure communication to take place (either between departments or different companies), there must be a way for the two root CAs to trust each other. The two CAs do not have a CA above them they can both trust, so they must carry out cross-certification. A cross-certification is the process undertaken by CAs to establish a trust relationship in which they rely upon each other's digital certificates and public keys as if they had issued them themselves. When this is set up, a CA for one company can validate digital certificates from the other company and vice versa.

☒ **B is incorrect** because a cross-revocation list (CRL) contains all of the revoked certifications within a PKI. The CA is responsible for creating and handing out certificates, maintaining them, and revoking them if necessary. Revocation is handled by the CA, and the revoked certificate information is stored on a CRL. This is a list of every certificate that has been revoked. This list is maintained and updated periodically. A certificate may be revoked because the key holder's private key was compromised or because the CA discovered the certificate was issued to the wrong person. An analogy for the use of a CRL is how a driver's license is used by a police officer. If an officer pulls over Sean for speeding, the officer will ask to see Sean's license. The officer will then run a check on the license to find out if Sean is wanted for any other infractions of the law and to verify the license has not expired. The same thing happens when a person compares a certificate to a CRL. If the certificate became invalid for some reason, the CRL is the mechanism for the CA to let others know this information.

☒ **C is incorrect** because the Online Certificate Status Protocol (OCSP) carries out real-time validation of a certificate and reports back to the user whether the certificate is valid, invalid, or unknown. When using just a CRL, the user's browser must either check a central CRL to find out if the certification has been revoked or continually push out CRL values to the clients to ensure they have an updated CRL. If OCSP is implemented, it does this work automatically in the background. OCSP checks the CRL that is maintained by the CA. So the CRL is still being used, but now we have a protocol developed specifically to check the CRL during a certificate validation process.

☒ **D is incorrect** because the registration authority (RA) performs the certification registration duties. The RA establishes and confirms the identity of an individual and initiates the certification process with a CA on behalf of an end user. The RA cannot issue certificates but can act as a broker between the user and the CA. When users need new certificates, they make requests to the RA, and the RA verifies all necessary identification information before allowing a request to go to the CA.

24. There are different ways of providing integrity and authentication within cryptography. What type of technology is shown in the graphic that follows?

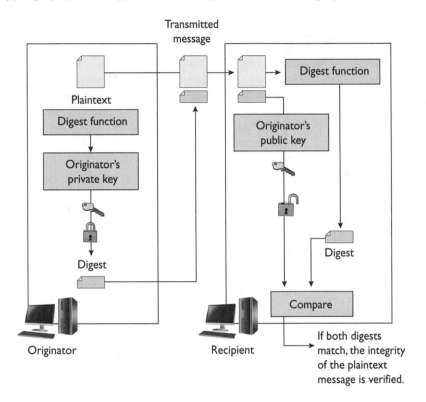

A. One-way hash

B. Digital signature

C. Birthday attack

D. Collision

☑ **B.** When a hash algorithm is applied to a message, it produces a message digest, and this value is signed with a private key to produce a digital signature. It provides authentication, data integrity, and nonrepudiation. The act of signing is the actual encryption of the value with the private key. When Maureen receives the message, she will perform the hashing function on the message and come up with her own hash value. Then she will decrypt the sent hash value (digital signature) with Kevin's public key. She then compares the two values, and if they are the same, she can be sure the message was not altered during transmission. She is also sure the message came from Kevin because the value was encrypted with his private key.

☒ **A** is incorrect because a one-way hash is a function that takes a variable-length string and a message and produces a fixed-length value called a hash value. For example, if Kevin wants to send a message to Maureen and he wants to ensure the message does not get altered in an unauthorized fashion while it is being transmitted, he would calculate a hash value for the message and append it to the message itself. When Maureen receives the message, she performs the same hashing function Kevin used and then compares her result with the hash value sent with the message. If the two values are the same, Maureen can be sure the message was not altered during transmission. If the two values are different, Maureen knows the message was altered, either intentionally or unintentionally, and she discards the message.

☒ **C** is incorrect because a birthday attack is an attack on hashing functions through brute force. The attacker tries to create two messages with the same hashing value. A good hashing algorithm should not produce the same hash value for two different messages. If the algorithm does produce the same value for two distinctly different messages, this is called a collision. An attacker can attempt to force a collision, which is referred to as a birthday attack. Hash algorithms usually use message digest sizes (the value of n) that are large enough to make collisions difficult to accomplish, but they are still possible. An algorithm that has 160-bit output, like SHA-1, may require approximately 2^{80} computations to break. This means there is a less than 1 in 2^{80} chance that someone could carry out a successful birthday attack. A hashing algorithm that has a larger bit output is less vulnerable to brute-force attacks such as a birthday attack.

☒ **D** is incorrect because a collision is when two hashed messages result in the same value. A strong one-hash function should not provide the same hash value for two or more different messages. If a hashing algorithm takes steps to ensure it does not create the same hash value for two or more messages, it is said to be collision free. If a hashing algorithm generates a message digest of 60 bits, there is a high likelihood that an adversary can find a collision using only 2^{30} inputs.

25. There are several different modes that block ciphers can work in. Which mode does the graphic that follows portray?

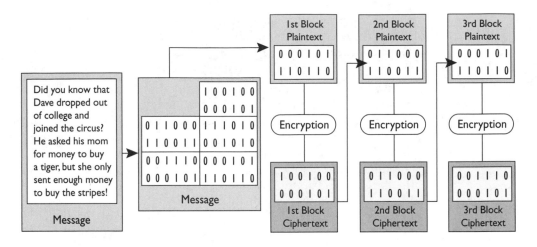

A. Electronic Code Book Mode

B. Cipher Block Chaining

C. Output Feedback Mode

D. Counter Mode

☑ **B.** Block ciphers have several modes of operation. Each mode specifies how a block cipher will operate. One mode may work better in one type of environment for specific functionality, whereas another mode may work better in another environment with totally different requirements. Cipher Block Chaining (CBC) does not reveal a pattern, because each block of text, the key, and the value based on the previous block are processed in the algorithm and applied to the next block of text. This results in more random ciphertext. Ciphertext is extracted and used from the previous block of text. This provides dependence between the blocks, in a sense chaining them together. This is where the name Cipher Block Chaining comes from, and it is this chaining effect that hides any patterns.

☒ **A** is incorrect because Electronic Code Book Mode (ECB) operates like a code book. A 64-bit data block is entered into the algorithm with a key, and a block of ciphertext is produced. For a given block of plaintext and a given key, the same block of ciphertext is always produced. Not all messages end up in neat and tidy 64-bit blocks, so ECB incorporates padding to address this problem. ECB is the easiest and fastest mode to use, but as we will see, it has its dangers. In ECB mode, a block of plaintext and a key will always give the same ciphertext. This means that if the word "balloon" were encrypted and the resulting ciphertext were "hwicssn," each time it was encrypted using the same key, the same ciphertext would always be given.

This can show evidence of a pattern, enabling an evildoer, with some effort, to discover the pattern and get a step closer to compromising the encryption process.

☒ **C** is incorrect because Output Feedback Mode (OFB) is a mode that a block cipher can work in when it needs to emulate a stream, because it encrypts small amounts of data at a time, but it has a smaller chance of creating and extending errors throughout the full encryption process.

☒ **D** is incorrect because Counter Mode (CTR) is very similar to OFB mode, but instead of using a randomly unique initialization vector (IV) value to generate the keystream values, this mode uses an IV counter that increments for each plaintext block that needs to be encrypted.

26. If Marge uses her private key to create a digital signature on a message she is sending to George, but she does not show or share her private key with George, what is it an example of?

A. Key clustering

B. Avoiding a birthday attack

C. Providing data confidentiality

D. Zero-knowledge proof

☑ **D. Zero-knowledge proof** means that someone can tell you something without telling you more information than you need to know. In cryptography, it means proving that you have a specific key without sharing that key or showing it to anyone. A zero-knowledge proof is an interactive method for one party to prove to another that a (usually mathematical) statement is true without revealing anything sensitive.

☒ **A** is incorrect because key clustering is an instance when two different keys generate the same ciphertext from the same plaintext. This is caused if there is a logical flaw in an algorithm.

☒ **B** is incorrect because if the algorithm does produce the same value for two distinctly different messages, this is called a collision. An attacker can attempt to force a collision, which is referred to as a birthday attack. This attack is based on the mathematical birthday paradox that exists in standard statistics. It is a cryptographic attack that exploits the mathematics behind the birthday problem in the probability theory. This is not what is being addressed in the question.

☒ **C** is incorrect because confidentiality provided through cryptography is usually in place when data are encrypted with a key. If the data are considered bulk data, then a symmetric key is used. Not showing others a private key keeps the private key secret, but this is not necessarily confidentiality.

27. There are two main functions that Trusted Platform Modules (TPMs) carry out within systems today. Which of the following best describes these two functions?

A. Sealing a hard disk drive is when the decryption key that can be used to decrypt data on the drive is stored on the TPM. Binding is when data pertaining to the system's state are hashed and stored on the TPM.

B. Binding a hard disk drive is when whole-disk encryption is enabled through the use of the TPM. Sealing is when a digital certificate is sealed within a TPM and the system cannot boot up without this certificate being validated.

C. Sealing a hard disk drive is when whole-disk encryption is enabled through the use of the TPM. Binding is when a digital certificate is sealed within a TPM and the system cannot boot up without this certificate being validated.

D. Binding a hard disk drive is when the decryption key that can be used to decrypt data on the drive is stored on the TPM. Sealing is when data pertaining to the system's state are hashed and stored on the TPM.

☑ **D.** The essence of the TPM lies in a protected and encapsulated microcontroller security chip that provides a safe haven for storing and processing security-intensive data such as keys, passwords, and digital certificates. "Binding" a hard disk drive is the most common usage scenario of the TPM—where the content of a given hard disk drive is affixed with a particular computing system. Another application of the TPM is "sealing" a system's state to a particular hardware and software configuration.

☒ **A** is incorrect because binding a hard disk drive is when the decryption key that can be used to decrypt data on the drive is stored on the TPM. Sealing is when data pertaining to the system's state are hashed and stored on the TPM.

☒ **B** is incorrect because binding a hard disk drive is when the decryption key that can be used to decrypt data on the drive is stored on the TPM. Sealing is when data pertaining to the system's state are hashed and stored on the TPM. The content of the hard disk drive is encrypted, and the decryption key is stored away in the TPM chip. To ensure safe storage of the decryption key, it is further "wrapped" with another encryption key. Binding a hard disk drive makes its content basically inaccessible to other systems, and any attempt to retrieve the drive's content by attaching it to another system will be very difficult.

☒ **C** is incorrect because sealing a system is fairly straightforward. The TPM generates hash values based on the system's configuration files and is stored. A sealed system will only be activated once the TPM verifies the integrity of the system's configuration by comparing it with the original "sealing" value.

The following scenario will be used for questions 28 and 29.

Jack has been told that successful attacks have been taking place and data that have been encrypted by his company's software systems have leaked to the company's competitors. Through Jack's investigation he has discovered that the lack of randomness in the seeding values used by the encryption algorithms in the company's software uncovered patterns and allowed for successful reverse engineering.

28. Which of the following is most likely the item that is the root of the problem when it comes to the necessary randomness explained in the scenario?

    A. Asymmetric algorithm

    B. Out-of-band communication compromise

    C. Number generator

    D. Symmetric algorithm

    ☑ **C.** A number generator is used to create a stream of random values and must be seeded by an initial value. This piece of software obtains its seeding value from some component within the computer system (time, CPU cycles, etc.). Although a computer system is complex, it is a predictable environment, so if the seeding value is predictable in any way, the resulting values created are not truly random, but pseudorandom. If the values from a number generated illustrate patterns and those patterns are recognizable during cryptographic processes, this weakness could allow an attacker to reverse engineer the algorithm and gain access to confidential data.

    ☒ **A** is incorrect because an asymmetric algorithm carries out cryptographic functions through the use of two different key types, public and private. This is also called public key cryptography. Components, as in number generators, can be used with asymmetric algorithms, but they are a class of algorithms and do not necessarily integrate randomness issues.

    ☒ **B** is incorrect because out-of-band communication just means that communication data are being sent through a channel that is different from the encrypted data that are traveling. It does not have any direct correlation with randomness issues.

    ☒ **D** is incorrect because a symmetric algorithm carries out cryptographic functions through the use of two instances of the same key. Components, as in number generators, can be used with symmetric algorithms, but they are a class of algorithms and do not necessarily cause randomness issues.

29. Which of the following best describes the role of the values that is allowing for patterns as described in the scenario?

    A. Initialization vector

    B. One-time password

C. Master symmetric key

D. Subkey

☑ **A.** Initialization vectors (IVs) are random values that are used with algorithms to ensure patterns are not created during the encryption process. They are used with keys and do not need to be encrypted when being sent to the destination. If IVs are not used, then two identical plaintext values that are encrypted with the same key will create the same ciphertext. Providing attackers with these types of patterns can make their job easier in breaking the encryption method and uncovering the key.

☒ **B** is incorrect because a one-time pad is an encryption method created by Gilbert Vernam that is considered impossible to crack if carried out properly. A one-time pad uses a pad with random values that are XORed against the message to produce ciphertext. The pad is at least as long as the message itself and is used once and then discarded. This technology is not addressed in this scenario.

☒ **C** is incorrect because for complex keys to be generated, commonly a master key is created, and then symmetric keys are generated from it. For example, if an application is responsible for creating a session key for each subject that requests one, it should not be giving out the same instance of that one key. Different subjects need to have different symmetric keys to ensure that the window for the attack to capture and uncover that key is smaller than if the same key were to be used over and over again. When two or more keys are created from a master key, they are called subkeys. This is not a component of the randomness issue addressed in the scenario.

☒ **D** is incorrect because when two or more keys are created from a master key, they are called subkeys. This is not a component of the randomness issue addressed in the scenario.

30. What cryptographic attack type carries out a mathematical analysis by trying to break a math problem from the beginning and the end of the mathematical formula simultaneously?

A. Known plaintext

B. Adaptive ciphertext

C. Known ciphertext

D. Meet-in-the-middle

☑ **D.** Meet-in-the-middle attack refers to a mathematical analysis used to try and break a math problem from both ends. It is a technique that works on the forward mapping of a function and the inverse of the second function at the same time. The attack works by encrypting from one end and decrypting from the other end, thus meeting in the middle.

☒ **A** is incorrect because known plaintext attacks are a type of cryptanalysis attack where the attacker is assumed to have access to sets of corresponding plaintext and ciphertext. The attacker has the plaintext and corresponding ciphertext of one or more messages. The goal is to discover the key used to encrypt the messages so other messages can be deciphered and read.

☒ **B** is incorrect because all cryptographic attacks have a derivative form, the names of which are the same except for putting the word "adaptive" in front of them, such as adaptive chosen-plaintext and adaptive chosen-ciphertext. What this means is that the attacker can carry out one of these attacks and, depending upon what she gleaned from that first attack, modify her next attack. This is the process of reverse-engineering or cryptanalysis attacks: using what you learned to improve your next attack.

☒ **C** is incorrect because this is a distracter answer. Attacks can always "know" the ciphertext. This is just the encrypted version of the text.

Business Continuity and Disaster Recovery

This domain includes questions from the following topics:

- Business continuity management
- Business continuity planning components
- Standards and best practices
- Selecting, developing, and implementing disaster and continuity solutions
- Recovery and redundant technologies
- Backup and offsite facilities
- Types of drills and tests

A single, catastrophic act of nature or terrorist attack can effectively put a company out of business. In order to survive such traumas, organizations must think ahead, plan for the worst, estimate the possible damages that could occur, and implement controls to protect themselves. This is all part of disaster recovery and business continuity planning. These are not easy tasks, and their accomplishment does not show immediate returns. But organizations that choose not to plan accordingly are accepting a significant risk. As a CISSP, you need to know how to create and carry out a business continuity and disaster recovery plan to ensure that your organization can recover from a disaster.

1. The NIST organization has defined best practices for creating continuity plans. Which of the following phases deals with identifying and prioritizing critical functions and systems?

    A. Identify preventive controls.

    B. Develop the continuity planning policy statement.

    C. Develop recovery strategies.

    D. Conduct the business impact analysis.

2. As his company's business continuity coordinator, Matthew is responsible for helping recruit members to the business continuity planning (BCP) committee. Which of the following does not correctly describe this effort?

    A. Committee members should be involved with the planning stages, as well as the testing and implementation stages.

    B. The smaller the team the better, to keep meetings under control.

    C. The business continuity coordinator should work with management to appoint committee members.

    D. The team should consist of people from different departments across the company.

3. A business impact analysis is considered a functional analysis. Which of the following is not carried out during a business impact analysis?

    A. A parallel or full-interruption test

    B. The application of a classification scheme based on criticality levels

    C. The gathering of information via interviews

    D. Documentation of business functions

4. Which of the following is the best way to ensure that the company's backup tapes can be restored and used at a warm site?

    A. Ask the offsite vendor to test them and label the ones that were properly read.

    B. Test them on the vendor's machine, which won't be used during an emergency.

    C. Retrieve the tapes from the offsite facility and verify that the equipment from the original site can read them.

    D. Inventory each tape kept at the vendor's site twice a month.

5. An approach to alternate offsite facilities is to establish a reciprocal agreement. Which of the following describes the pros and cons of a reciprocal agreement?

 A. It is fully configured and ready to operate within a few hours, but is the most expensive of the offsite choices.

 B. It is an inexpensive option, but it takes the most time and effort to get up and running after a disaster.

 C. It is a good alternative for companies that depend upon proprietary software, but annual testing is not usually available.

 D. It is the cheapest of the offsite choices, but mixing operations could introduce many security issues.

6. Which of the following steps comes first in a business impact analysis?

 A. Calculate the risk for each different business function.

 B. Identify critical business functions.

 C. Create data-gathering techniques.

 D. Identify vulnerabilities and threats to business functions.

7. The operations team is responsible for defining which data gets backed up and how often. Which type of backup process backs up files that have been modified since the last time all data was backed up?

 A. Incremental process

 B. Full backup

 C. Partial backup

 D. Differential process

8. After a disaster occurs, a damage assessment needs to take place. Which of the following steps occurs last in a damage assessment?

 A. Determine the cause of the disaster.

 B. Identify the resources that must be replaced immediately.

 C. Declare a disaster.

 D. Determine how long it will take to bring critical functions back online.

9. Of the following plans, which establishes senior management and a headquarters after a disaster?

 A. Continuity of operations plan

 B. Cyber-incident response plan

 C. Occupant emergency plan

 D. IT contingency plan

10. It is not unusual for business continuity plans to become out of date. Which of the following is not a reason why plans become outdated?

    A. Changes in hardware, software, and applications

    B. Infrastructure and environment changes

    C. Personnel turnover

    D. That the business continuity process is integrated into the change management process

11. Preplanned business continuity procedures provide organizations a number of benefits. Which of the following is not a capability enabled by business continuity planning?

    A. Resuming critical business functions

    B. Letting business partners know your company is unprepared

    C. Protecting lives and ensuring safety

    D. Ensuring survivability of the business

12. Management support is critical to the success of a business continuity plan. Which of the following is the most important to be provided to management to obtain their support?

    A. Business case

    B. Business impact analysis

    C. Risk analysis

    D. Threat report

13. Gizmos and Gadgets has restored its original facility after a disaster. What should be moved in first?

    A. Management

    B. Most critical systems

    C. Most critical functions

    D. Least critical functions

14. Which of the following is a critical first step in disaster recovery and contingency planning?

    A. Plan testing and drills.

    B. Complete a business impact analysis.

    C. Determine offsite backup facility alternatives.

    D. Organize and create relevant documentation.

15. Which of the following is not a reason to develop and implement a disaster recovery plan?

    A. Provide steps for a post-disaster recovery.

    B. Extend backup operations to include more than just backing up data.

    C. Outline business functions and systems.

    D. Provide procedures for emergency responses.

16. Business continuity plans can be assessed via a number of tests. Which type of test continues up to the point of actual relocation to an offsite facility and actual shipment of replacement equipment?

    A. Parallel test

    B. Checklist test

    C. Structured walk-through test

    D. Simulation test

17. With what phase of a business continuity plan does a company proceed when it is ready to move back into its original site or a new site?

    A. Reconstitution phase

    B. Recovery phase

    C. Project initiation phase

    D. Damage assessment phase

18. Several teams should be involved in carrying out the business continuity plan. Which team is responsible for starting the recovery of the original site?

    A. Damage assessment team

    B. BCP team

    C. Salvage team

    D. Restoration team

19. ACME Inc. paid a software vendor to develop specialized software, and that vendor has gone out of business. ACME Inc. does not have access to the code and therefore cannot keep it updated. What mechanism should the company have implemented to prevent this from happening?

    A. Reciprocal agreement

    B. Software escrow

    C. Electronic vaulting

    D. Business interruption insurance

20. Which of the following incorrectly describes the concept of executive succession planning?

    A. Predetermined steps protect the company if a senior executive leaves.

    B. Two or more senior staff cannot be exposed to a particular risk at the same time.

    C. It documents the assignment of deputy roles.

    D. It covers assigning a skeleton crew to resume operations after a disaster.

21. What is the missing second step in the graphic that follows?

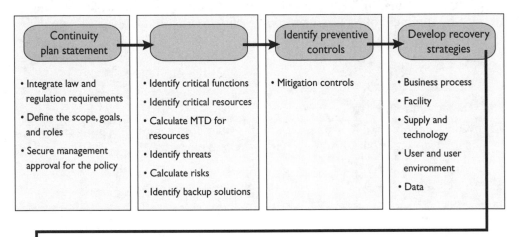

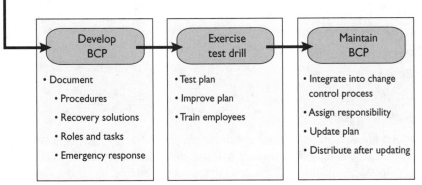

    A. Identify continuity coordinator

    B. Business impact analysis

    C. Identify BCP committee

    D. Dependency identification

22. Different threats need to be evaluated and ranked based upon their severity of business risk when developing a BCP. Which ranking approach is illustrated in the graphic that follows?

> Choose the following statement that best describes the effect on this business unit/cost center should there be an unplanned interruption of normal business operations.
>
> ○ **8 hours** of an interruption. This business unit/cost center is **Vital.**
> ○ **24 hours** of an interruption. This business unit/cost center is **Critical.**
> ○ **3 days** of an interruption. This business unit/cost center is **Essential.**
> ○ **5 days** of an interruption. This business unit/cost center is **Important.**
> ○ **10 days** of an interruption. This business unit/cost center is **Noncritical.**
> ○ **30 days** of an interruption. This business unit/cost center is **Deferrable.**

A. Mean time to repair

B. Mean time between failures

C. Maximum critical downtime

D. Maximum tolerable downtime

23. What type of infrastructural setup is illustrated in the graphic that follows?

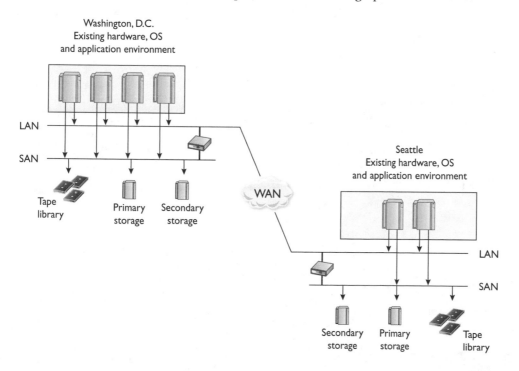

A. Hot site

B. Warm site

C. Cold site

D. Reciprocal agreement

24. There are several types of redundant technologies that can be put into place. What type of technology is shown in the graphic that follows?

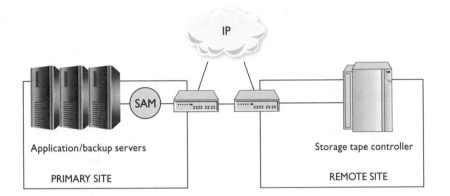

A. Tape vaulting

B. Remote journaling

C. Electronic vaulting

D. Redundant site

25. Here is a graphic of a business continuity policy. Which component is missing from this graphic?

A. Damage assessment phase

B. Reconstitution phase

C. Business resumption phase

D. Continuity of operations plan

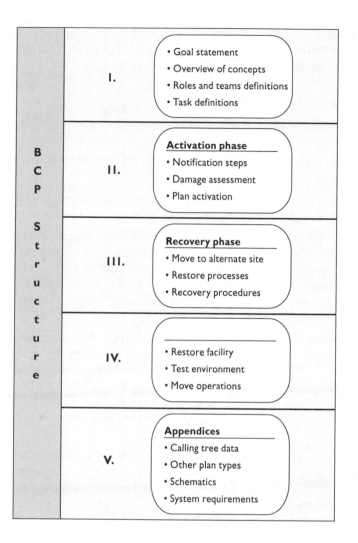

BCP Structure

I.
- Goal statement
- Overview of concepts
- Roles and teams definitions
- Task definitions

II.
Activation phase
- Notification steps
- Damage assessment
- Plan activation

III.
Recovery phase
- Move to alternate site
- Restore processes
- Recovery procedures

IV.
- Restore facility
- Test environment
- Move operations

V.
Appendices
- Calling tree data
- Other plan types
- Schematics
- System requirements

26. The Recovery Time Objective (RTO) and Maximum Tolerable Downtime (MTD) metrics have similar roles, but their values are very different. Which of the following best describes the difference between RTO and MTD metrics?

    A. The RTO is a time period that represents the inability to recover, and the MTD represents an allowable amount of downtime.

    B. The RTO is an allowable amount of downtime, and the MTD represents a time period that represents the inability to recover.

    C. The RTO is a metric used in disruptions, and the MTD is a metric used in disasters.

    D. The RTO is a metric pertaining to loss of access to data, and the MTD is a metric pertaining to loss of access to hardware and processing capabilities.

27. High availability (HA) is a combination of technologies and processes that work together to ensure that specific critical functions are always up and running at the necessary level. To provide this level of high availability, a company has to have a long list of technologies and processes that provide redundancy, fault tolerance, and failover capabilities. Which of the following best describes these characteristics?

    A. Redundancy is the duplication of noncritical components or functions of a system with the intention of decreasing reliability of the system. Fault tolerance is the capability of a technology to discontinue to operate as expected even if something unexpected takes place. If a technology has a failover capability, this means that if there is a failure that cannot be handled through normal means, then processing is "switched over" to a working system.

    B. Redundancy is the duplication of critical components or functions of a system with the intention of increasing reliability of the system. Fault tolerance is the capability of a technology to continue to operate as expected even if something unexpected takes place. If a technology has a failover capability, this means that if there is a failure that cannot be handled through normal means, then processing is "switched over" to a working system.

    C. Redundancy is the duplication of critical components or functions of a system with the intention of increasing reliability of the system. Fault tolerance is the capability of a technology to continue to operate as expected even if something unexpected takes place. If a technology has a failover capability, this means that if there is a failure that cannot be handled through normal means, then processing is "switched over" to a nonworking system.

D. Redundancy is the duplication of critical components or functions of a system with the intention of increasing reliability of the system. Fault tolerance is the capability of a technology to continue to operate as expected even if something unexpected takes place. If a technology has a failover capability, this means that if there is a failure that cannot be handled through normal means, then processing is "switched over" to a working system.

The following scenario will be used to answer questions 28 and 29.

Sean has been hired as business continuity coordinator. He has been told by his management that he needed to ensure that the company is in compliance with the ISO/IEC standard that pertained to technology readiness for business continuity. He has also been instructed to find a way to transfer the risk of being unable to carry out critical business functions for a period of time because of a disaster.

28. Which of the following is most likely the standard that Sean has been asked to comply with?

   A. ISO/IEC 27031

   B. ISO/IEC 27005

   C. ISO/IEC BS7799

   D. ISO/IEC 2899

29. Which of the following would be best for Sean to implement as it pertains to his company's needs?

   A. Infrastructure cloud computing

   B. Co-location at a multiprocessing center

   C. Business interruption insurance

   D. Shared partner extranet with integrated redundancy

The following scenario will be used to answer questions 30, 31 and 32.

Jeff is leading the business continuity group in his company. They have completed a business impact analysis and have determined that if the company's credit card processing functionality was unavailable for 48 hours the company would most likely experience such a large financial hit that it would have to go out of business. The team has calculated that this functionality needs to be up and running within 28 hours after experiencing a disaster for the company to stay in business. The team has also determined that the restoration steps must be able to restore data that are one hour old or less.

30. In this scenario, which of the following is the Recovery Time Objective (RTO) value?

    A. 48 hours

    B. 28 hours

    C. 20 hours

    D. 1 hour

31. In this scenario, which of the following is the Work Recovery Time value?

    A. 48 hours

    B. 28 hours

    C. 20 hours

    D. 1 hour

32. In this scenario, what would the 1-hour time period be referred to as?

    A. Recovery Time Period

    B. Maximum Tolerable Downtime

    C. Recovery Point Objective

    D. Recovery Point Time Period

1. D	12. A	23. A
2. B	13. D	24. A
3. A	14. B	25. B
4. C	15. C	26. B
5. D	16. D	27. D
6. C	17. A	28. A
7. D	18. C	29. C
8. C	19. B	30. B
9. A	20. D	31. C
10. D	21. B	32. C
11. B	22. D	

1. The NIST organization has defined best practices for creating continuity plans. Which of the following phases deals with identifying and prioritizing critical functions and systems?

   A. Identify preventive controls.

   B. Develop the continuity planning policy statement.

   C. Develop recovery strategies.

   D. Conduct the business impact analysis.

   ☑ **D.** Although no specific scientific equation must be followed to create continuity plans, certain best practices have proven themselves over time. The National Institute of Standards and Technology (NIST) organization is responsible for developing many of these best practices and documenting them so that they are easily available to all. NIST outlines seven steps in its Special Publication 800-34, *Continuity Planning Guide for Information Technology Systems*: develop the continuity planning statement; conduct the business impact analysis; identify preventive controls; develop recovery strategies; develop the contingency plan; test the plan and conduct training and exercises; and maintain the plan. Conducting a business impact analysis involves identifying critical functions and systems, and allowing the organization to prioritize them based on necessity. It also includes identifying vulnerabilities and threats, and calculating risks.

   ☒ **A** is incorrect because identifying preventive controls must be done after critical functions and systems have been prioritized, and their vulnerabilities, threats, and risks identified—which is all part of the business impact analysis. Conducting a business impact analysis is step two of creating a continuity plan, and identifying preventive controls is step three.

   ☒ **B** is incorrect because developing the continuity planning policy statement involves writing a policy that provides the guidance necessary to develop a business continuity plan and that assigns authority to the necessary roles to carry out these tasks. It is the first step in creating a business continuity plan and thus comes before identifying and prioritizing critical systems and functions, which is part of the business impact analysis.

   ☒ **C** is incorrect because developing recovery strategies involves formulating methods to ensure systems and critical functions can be brought online quickly. Before this can be done, a business impact analysis must be carried out to determine which systems and functions are critical and should be given priority during recovery.

2. As his company's business continuity coordinator, Matthew is responsible for helping recruit members to the business continuity planning (BCP) committee. Which of the following does not correctly describe this effort?

   A. Committee members should be involved with the planning stages, as well as the testing and implementation stages.

   B. The smaller the team the better, to keep meetings under control.

   C. The business continuity coordinator should work with management to appoint committee members.

   D. The team should consist of people from different departments across the company.

   ☑ **B.** The BCP committee should be as large as it needs to be in order to represent each department within the organization. The team must be composed of people who are familiar with the different departments within the company, because each department is unique in its functionality and has distinctive risks and threats. The best plan is when all issues and threats are brought to the table and discussed. This cannot be done effectively with a few people who are familiar with only a couple of departments. The committee should be made up of representatives from at least the following departments: business units, senior management, IT department, security department, communications department, and legal department.

   ☒ **A** is incorrect because it is true that committee members should be involved with the planning stages, as well as the testing and implementation stages. If Matthew, the BCP coordinator, is a good management leader, he will understand that it is best to make team members feel a sense of ownership pertaining to their tasks and roles. The people who develop the BCP should also be the ones who execute it. If you knew that in a time of crisis you would be expected to carry out some critical tasks, you might pay more attention during the planning and testing phases.

   ☒ **C** is incorrect because the BCP coordinator should work with management to appoint committee members. But management's involvement does not stop there. The BCP team should work with management to develop the ultimate goals of the plan, identify the critical parts of the business that must be dealt with first during a disaster, and ascertain the priorities of departments and tasks. Management also needs to help direct the team on the scope of the project and the specific objectives.

   ☒ **D** is incorrect because it is true that the team should be composed of people from different departments across the company. This is the only way the team will be able to consider the distinctive risks and threats that each department faces.

3. A business impact analysis is considered a functional analysis. Which of the following is not carried out during a business impact analysis?

A. A parallel or full-interruption test

B. The application of a classification scheme based on criticality levels

C. The gathering of information via interviews

D. Documentation of business functions

☑ A. A business impact analysis (BIA) is considered a functional analysis, in which a team collects data through interviews and documentary sources; documents business functions, activities, and transactions; develops a hierarchy of business functions; and finally applies a classification scheme to indicate each individual function's criticality level. Parallel and full-interruption tests are not part of a BIA. These tests are carried out to ensure the continued validity of a business continuity plan, since environments continually change. A parallel test is done to ensure that specific systems can actually perform adequately at the alternate offsite facility, while a full-interruption test involves shutting down the original site and resuming operations and processing at the alternate site.

☒ B is incorrect because the application of a classification scheme based on criticality levels is carried out during a business impact analysis (BIA). This is done by identifying the critical assets of the company and mapping them to the following characteristics: maximum tolerable downtime, operational disruption and productivity, financial considerations, regulatory responsibilities, and reputation.

☒ C is incorrect because the gathering of information during interviews is conducted during a business impact analysis. The BCP committee will not truly understand all business processes, the steps that must take place, or the resources and supplies those processes require. So the committee must gather this information from the people who do know, which are department managers and specific employees throughout the organization. The committee must identify the individuals who will provide information and how that information will be collected (surveys, interviews, or workshops).

☒ D is incorrect because the BCP committee does document business functions as part of a business impact analysis (BIA). Business activities and transactions must also be documented. This information is obtained from the department managers and specific employees that are interviewed or surveyed. Once the information is documented, the BCP committee can conduct an analysis to determine which processes, devices, or operational activities are the most critical.

4. Which of the following is the best way to ensure that the company's backup tapes can be restored and used at a warm site?

   A. Ask the offsite vendor to test them and label the ones that were properly read.

   B. Test them on the vendor's machine, which won't be used during an emergency.

   C. Retrieve the tapes from the offsite facility and verify that the equipment from the original site can read them.

   D. Inventory each tape kept at the vendor's site twice a month.

   ☑ **C.** A warm site is a facility that will not be fully equipped with the company's main systems. The goal of using a warm site is that, if a disaster takes place, the company will bring its systems with it to the warm site. If the company cannot bring the systems with it because they are damaged, the company must purchase new systems that are exactly like the original systems. So, to properly test backups, the company needs to test them by recovering the data on its original systems at its main site.

   ☒ **A** is incorrect because a warm site is a leased or rented facility that is usually partially configured with some equipment, but not the actual computers. Staging a facility with duplicate hardware and computers configured for immediate operation is extremely expensive, so a warm site provides an alternate facility with some peripheral devices. This is the most widely used model. It is less expensive than a hot site and can be up and running within a reasonably time period. It may be a better choice for companies that depend upon proprietary and unusual hardware and software, because they will bring their own hardware and software with them to the site after the disaster hits.

   ☒ **B** is incorrect because testing backups on machines that won't be used during an emergency does not provide assurance that the backups will work on the machines that will be used. The backups should be tested by recovering the data on the original systems at the company's main site because these systems will need to be moved to the warm site in the case of an emergency.

   ☒ **D** is incorrect because inventorying backup tapes does not provide assurance that the data on the tapes will be properly recovered. The tapes must be tested by recovering the data on them on the systems at the company's main site.

5. An approach to alternate offsite facilities is to establish a reciprocal agreement. Which of the following describes the pros and cons of a reciprocal agreement?

   A. It is fully configured and ready to operate within a few hours, but is the most expensive of the offsite choices.

   B. It is an inexpensive option, but takes the most time and effort to get up and running after a disaster.

C. It is a good alternative for companies that depend upon proprietary software, but annual testing is not usually available.

D. It is the cheapest of the offsite choices, but mixing operations could introduce many security issues.

☑ **D.** A reciprocal agreement, also referred to as mutual aid, means that company A agrees to allow company B to use its facilities if company B is hit by a disaster, and vice versa. This is a cheaper way to go than the other offsite choices, but it is not always the best choice. Most environments are maxed out pertaining to the use of facility space, resources, and computing capability. To allow another company to come in and work out of the same shop could prove to be detrimental to both companies. The stress of two companies working in the same environment could cause tremendous levels of tension. If it did work out, it would only provide a short-term solution. Configuration management could be a nightmare, and the mixing of operations could introduce many security issues. Reciprocal agreements have been known to work well in specific businesses, such as newspaper printing. These businesses require very specific technology and equipment that will not be available through any subscription service. For most other organizations, they are generally, at best, a secondary option for disaster protection.

☒ **A** is incorrect because a hot site—not a reciprocal agreement—is fully configured and ready to operate within a few hours. A hot site is also the most expensive offsite option. The only missing resources from a hot site are usually the data, which will be retrieved from a backup site, and the people who will be processing the data. The equipment and system software must be compatible with the data being restored from the main site and must not cause any negative interoperability issues. Hot sites are a good choice for a company that needs to ensure a site will be available for it as soon as possible.

☒ **B** is incorrect because a cold site is an inexpensive offsite option, but it takes the most time and effort to actually get up and functioning right after a disaster. With cold sites the vendor supplies the basic environment, electrical wiring, air conditioning, plumbing, and flooring, but none of the equipment or additional services. It may take weeks to get the site activated and ready for work.

☒ **C** is incorrect because a warm site is a good alternative for companies that depend upon proprietary software. A warm site is equipped with some equipment, but not the actual computers. It is a better choice than a reciprocal agreement or hot site for a company that depends upon proprietary and unusual hardware and software, because they will bring their own hardware and software with them to the site after a disaster hits. The disadvantage of using a warm site is that the vendors' contracts do not usually include annual testing, which helps ensure that the company can return to an operating state within hours.

6. Which of the following steps comes first in a business impact analysis?

 A. Calculate the risk for each different business function.

 B. Identify critical business functions.

 C. Create data-gathering techniques.

 D. Identify vulnerabilities and threats to business functions.

 ☑ **C.** Of the steps listed, the first step in a business impact analysis (BIA) is creating data-gathering techniques. The BCP committee can use surveys, questionnaires, and interviews to gather information from key personnel about how different tasks get accomplished within the organization, whether it's a process, transaction, or service, along with any relevant dependencies. Process flow diagrams should be built from this data, which will be used throughout the BIA and plan development stages.

 ☒ **A** is incorrect because calculating the risk of each business function occurs after business functions have been identified. And before that can happen, the BCP team must gather data from key personnel. To calculate the risk of each business function, qualitative and quantitative impact information should be gathered and properly analyzed and interpreted. Upon completion of the data analysis, it should be reviewed with the most knowledgeable people within the company to ensure that the findings are appropriate and describe the real risks and impacts the organization faces. This will help flush out any additional data points not originally obtained and will give a fuller understanding of all the possible business impacts.

 ☒ **B** is incorrect because identifying critical business functions takes place after the BCP committee has learned about the business functions that exist by interviewing and surveying key personnel. Upon completion of the data collection phase, the BCP committee conducts an analysis to establish which processes, devices, or operational activities are critical. If a system stands on its own, doesn't affect other systems, and is of low criticality, then it can be classified as a tier two or three recovery step. This means these resources will not be dealt with during the recovery stages until the most critical (tier one) resources are up and running.

 ☒ **D** is incorrect because identifying vulnerabilities and threats to business functions takes place toward the end of a business impact analysis. Of the steps listed in the answers, it is the last one. Threats can be manmade, natural, or technical. It is important to identify all possible threats and estimate the probability of them happening. Some issues may not immediately come to mind when developing these plans. These issues are often best addressed in a group with scenario-based exercises. This ensures that if a threat becomes a reality, the plan includes the ramifications on all business tasks, departments, and critical operations. The more issues that are thought of and planned for, the better prepared a company will be if and when these events occur.

7. The operations team is responsible for defining which data gets backed up and how often. Which type of backup process backs up files that have been modified since the last time all data was backed up?

A. Incremental process

B. Full backup

C. Partial backup

D. Differential process

☑ **D.** Backups can be full, differential, or incremental, and are usually used in some type of combination with each other. Most files are not altered every day, so to save time and resources, it is best to devise a backup plan that does not continually back up data that has not been modified. Backup software reviews the archive bit setting when making its determination on what gets backed up and what does not. If a file is modified or created, the file system sets the archive bit to 1, and the backup software knows to back up that file. A differential process backs up the files that have been modified since the last full backup; in other words, the last time all the data was backed up. When the data needs to be restored, the full backup is laid down first, and then the differential backup is put down on top of it.

☒ **A** is incorrect because an incremental process backs up all the files that have changed since the last full or incremental backup. If a company experienced a disaster and it used the incremental process, it would first need to restore the full backup on its hard drives and lay down every incremental backup that was carried out before the disaster took place. So, if the full backup was done six months ago and the operations department carried out an incremental backup each month, the restoration team would restore the full backup and start with the older incremental backups and restore each one of them until they are all restored.

☒ **B** is incorrect because with a full backup, all data is backed up and saved to some type of storage media. During a full backup, the archive bit is cleared, which means that it is set to 0. A company can choose to do full backups only, in which case the restoration process is just one step, but the backup and restore processes could take a long time.

☒ **C** is incorrect because it is not the best answer to this question. While a backup can be a partial backup, it does not necessarily mean that it backs up all the files that have been modified since the last time a backup process was run.

8. After a disaster occurs, a damage assessment needs to take place. Which of the following steps occurs last in a damage assessment?

A. Determine the cause of the disaster.

B. Identify the resources that must be replaced immediately.

C. Declare a disaster.

D. Determine how long it will take to bring critical functions back online.

☑ **C.** The final step in a damage assessment is to declare a disaster. After information from the damage assessment is collected and assessed, it will indicate what teams need to be called to action and whether the BCP actually needs to be activated. The BCP coordinator and team must develop activation criteria before a disaster takes place. After the damage assessment, if one or more of the situations outlined in the criteria have taken place, then the team is moved into recovery mode. Different organizations have different criteria, because the business drivers and critical functions will vary from organization to organization. The criteria may consist of danger to human life, danger to state or national security, damage to facility, damage to critical systems, and estimated value of downtime that will be experienced.

☒ **A** is incorrect because determining the cause of the disaster is the first step of the damage assessment. The issue that caused the damage may still be taking place and the team must figure out how to stop it before a full damage assessment can take place.

☒ **B** is incorrect because identifying the resources that must be replaced immediately is not the last step of a damage assessment. It does occur near the end of the assessment, however. Once the resources are identified, the team must estimate how long it will take to bring critical functions back online, and then declare a disaster, if necessary.

☒ **D** is incorrect because determining how long it will take to bring critical functions back online is the second to last step in a damage assessment. If it will take longer than the previously determined maximum tolerable downtime (MTD) values to restore operations, then a disaster should be declared and the BCP should be put into action.

9. Of the following plans, which establishes senior management and a headquarters after a disaster?

A. Continuity of operations plan

B. Cyber-incident response plan

C. Occupant emergency plan

D. IT contingency plan

☑ **A.** A continuity of operations plan (COOP) establishes senior management and a headquarters after a disaster. It also outlines roles and authorities, orders of succession, and individual role tasks. Creating a COOP begins with assessing how the organization operates to identify mission-critical staff, materials, procedures, and equipment. If one exists, review the business process flowchart. Identify suppliers, partners, contractors, and other businesses the organization interacts with on a daily basis, and create a list of these and other businesses the organization could use in an emergency. It is important for an organization to make plans for what it will do if the building becomes inaccessible.

☒ **B** is incorrect because a cyber-incident response plan focuses on malware, hackers, intrusions, attacks, and other security issues. It outlines procedures for incident response with the goal of limiting damage, minimizing recovery time, and reducing costs. A cyber-incident response plan should include a description of the different types of incidents, who to call when an incident occurs and each person's responsibilities, procedures for addressing different types of incidents, and forensic procedures. The plan should be tested, and all participants should be trained on their responsibilities.

☒ **C** is incorrect because an occupant emergency plan establishes personnel safety and evacuation procedures. The goal of an occupant emergency plan is to reduce the risk to personnel and minimize the disruption to work and operations in the case of an emergency. The plan should include procedures for ensuring the safety of employees with disabilities, including their evacuation from the facility if necessary. All employees should have access to the occupant emergency response plan, and it should be practiced so that everyone knows how to execute it.

☒ **D** is incorrect because an IT contingency plan establishes procedures for the recovery of systems, networks, and major applications after disruptions. Steps for creating IT contingency plans are addressed in the NIST 800-34 document.

10. It is not unusual for business continuity plans to become out of date. Which of the following is not a reason why plans become outdated?

    A. Changes in hardware, software, and applications

    B. Infrastructure and environment changes

    C. Personnel turnover

    D. That the business continuity process is integrated into the change management process

    ☑ **D.** Unfortunately, business continuity plans can become quickly out of date. An out-of-date BCP may provide a company with a false sense of security, which could be devastating if and when a disaster actually takes place. One of the simplest and most cost-effective and process-efficient ways to keep a plan up to date is to incorporate it within the change management process of the organization. When you think about it, it makes a lot of sense. Where do you document new applications, equipment, or services? Where do you document updates and patches? Your change management process should be updated to incorporate fields and triggers that alert the BCP team when a significant change will occur and should provide a means to update the recovery documentation. Other measures that can help ensure that the BCP remains current include the performance of regular drills that use the plan, including the plan's maintenance in personnel evaluations, and making business continuity a part of every business decision.

☒ **A** is incorrect because changes in hardware, software, and applications occur frequently, and unless the BCP is part of the change management process, then these changes are unlikely to be included in the BCP. When changes to the environment take place, the BCP needs to be updated. If it is not updated after changes, it is out of date.

☒ **B** is incorrect because infrastructure and environment changes occur frequently. Just as with software, hardware, and application changes, unless the BCP is part of the change management process, infrastructure and environment changes are unlikely to make it into the BCP.

☒ **C** is incorrect because plans often become outdated as a result of personnel turnover. It is not unusual for a BCP to become abandoned when the person or people responsible for its maintenance leave the organization. These responsibilities must be reassigned. To ensure this happens, maintenance responsibilities should be incorporated into job descriptions and properly monitored.

11. Preplanned business continuity procedures provide organizations a number of benefits. Which of the following is not a capability enabled by business continuity planning?

    A. Resuming critical business functions

    B. Letting business partners know your company is unprepared

    C. Protecting lives and ensuring safety

    D. Ensuring survivability of the business

    ☑ **B.** Preplanned business continuity procedures afford organizations a number of benefits. They allow an organization to provide an immediate and appropriate response to emergency situations, reduce business impact, and work with outside vendors during a recovery period—in addition to the other answer options listed above. The efforts in these areas should be communicated to business partners to let them know that the company is prepared in case a disaster takes place.

☒ A is incorrect because a business continuity plan allows an organization to resume critical business functions. As part of the BCP creation, the BCP team conducts a business impact analysis, which includes identifying the maximum tolerable downtime for critical resources. This effort helps the team prioritize recovery efforts so that the most critical resources can be recovered first.

☒ C is incorrect because a business continuity plan allows an organization to protect lives and ensure safety. People are a company's most valuable asset; thus, human resources are a critical component to any recovery and continuity process and need to be fully thought out and integrated into the plan. When this is done, a business continuity plan helps a company protect its employees.

☒ D is incorrect because a preplanned business continuity plan allows a company to ensure the survivability of the business. A business continuity plan provides methods and procedures for dealing with longer-term outages and disasters. It includes getting critical systems to another environment while the original facility is being repaired and conducting business operations in a different mode until regular operations are back in place. In short, the business continuity plan deals with how business is conducted during the aftermath of an emergency.

12. Management support is critical to the success of a business continuity plan. Which of the following is the most important to be provided to management to obtain their support?

    A. Business case

    B. Business impact analysis

    C. Risk analysis

    D. Threat report

    ☑ A. The most critical part of establishing and maintaining a current continuity plan is management support. Management may need to be convinced of the necessity of such a plan. Therefore, a business case must be made to obtain this support. The business case may include current vulnerabilities, regulatory and legal obligations, the current status of recovery plans, and recommendations. Management is commonly most concerned with cost/benefit issues, so preliminary numbers can be gathered and potential losses estimated. The decision of how a company should recover is a business decision and should always be treated as such.

☒ **B** is incorrect because a business impact analysis (BIA) is conducted after the BCP team has obtained management's support for their efforts. A BIA is performed to identify the areas that would suffer the greatest financial or operational loss in the event of a disaster or disruption. It identifies the company's critical systems needed for survival and estimates the outage time that can be tolerated by the company as a result of a disaster or disruption.

☒ **C** is incorrect because a risk analysis is a method of identifying risks and assessing the possible damage that could be caused in order to justify security safeguards. In the context of BCP, risk analysis methodologies are used during a business impact analysis to establish which processes, devices, or operational activities are critical and should therefore be recovered first.

☒ **D** is incorrect because threat report is a distracter. However, it is critical that management understand what the real threats are to the company, the consequences of those threats, and the potential loss values for each threat. Without this understanding, management may only give lip service to continuity planning, and in some cases that is worse than not having any plans at all because of the false sense of security that it creates.

13. Gizmos and Gadgets have restored its original facility after a disaster. What should be moved in first?

    A. Management

    B. Most critical systems

    C. Most critical functions

    D. Least critical functions

    ☑ **D.** After the primary site has been repaired, the least critical components are moved in first. This ensures that the primary site is really ready to resume processing. By doing this, you can validate that environmental controls, power, and communication links are working properly. It can also avoid putting the company into another disaster. If the less critical functions survive, then the more critical components of the company can be moved over.

    ☒ **A** is incorrect because personnel should not be moved into the facility until it is determined that the environment is safe, everything is in good working order, and all necessary equipment and supplies are present. Least critical functions should be moved back first, so if there are issues in network configurations or connectivity, or important steps were not carried out, the critical operations of the company are not negatively affected.

    ☒ **B** is incorrect because the most critical systems should not be resumed in the new environment until it has been properly tested. You do not want to go through the trouble of moving the most critical systems and operations from a safe and stable site, only to return them to a main site that is untested. When you move less critical departments over first, they act as the canary. If they survive, then move on to critical systems.

☒ C is incorrect because the most critical functions should not be moved over before less critical functions, which serve to test the stability and safety of the site. If the site proves to need further preparation, then no harm is done to the critical functions.

14. Which of the following is a critical first step in disaster recovery and contingency planning?

A. Plan testing and drills.

B. Complete a business impact analysis.

C. Determine offsite backup facility alternatives.

D. Organize and create relevant documentation.

☑ B. Of the steps listed in this question, completing a business impact analysis would take the highest priority. The BIA is essential in determining the most critical business functions and identifying the threats that correlate them. Qualitative and quantitative data needs to be gathered, analyzed, interpreted, and presented to management.

☒ A is incorrect because plan testing and drills are the last step in disaster recovery and contingency planning. It is important to test the business continuity plan regularly because environments continually change. Tests and disaster recovery drills and exercises should be performed at least once a year. Most companies cannot afford for these exercises to interrupt production or productivity, so the exercises may need to take place in sections or at specific times, which requires logistical planning.

☒ C is incorrect because determining offsite backup facility alternatives is part of the recovery strategy, which takes place in the middle of the disaster recovery and contingency planning process. Organizations must have alternative offsite backup facilities in the case of a larger disaster. Generally, contracts are established with third-party vendors to provide such services. The client pays a monthly fee to retain the right to use the facility in a time of need, and then incurs an activation fee when the facility has to be used.

☒ D is incorrect because organizing and creating relevant documentation takes place toward the end of the disaster recovery and contingency planning process. Procedures need to be documented because when they are actually needed, it will most likely be a chaotic and frantic atmosphere with a demanding time schedule. The documentation may need to include information on how to install images, configure operating systems and servers, and properly install utilities and proprietary software. Other documentation could include a calling tree, and contact information for specific vendors, emergency agencies, offsite facilities, etc.

15. Which of the following is not a reason to develop and implement a disaster recovery plan?

    A. Provide steps for a post-disaster recovery.

    B. Extend backup operations to include more than just backing up data.

    C. Outline business functions and systems.

    D. Provide procedures for emergency responses.

☑ **C.** Outlining business functions and systems is not a viable reason to create and implement a disaster recovery plan. Although these tasks will most likely be accomplished as a result of a disaster recovery plan, it is not a good reason to carry out the plan compared to the other answers in the question. You don't develop and implement a disaster recovery plan just to outline business functions and systems, although that usually takes place during the planning process.

☒ **A** is incorrect because providing steps for a post-disaster recovery is a good reason to develop and implement a disaster recovery plan. In fact, that is exactly what a disaster recovery plan provides. The goal of disaster recovery is to minimize the effects of a disaster and take the necessary steps to ensure that the resources, personnel, and business processes are able to resume operation in a timely manner. The goal of a disaster recovery plan is to handle the disaster and its ramifications right after the disaster hits.

☒ **B** is incorrect because extending backup operations to include more than just backing up data is a good reason to develop and implement a disaster recovery plan. When looking at disaster recovery plans, some companies focus mainly on backing up data and providing redundant hardware. Although these items are extremely important, they are just small pieces of the company's overall operations. Hardware and computers need people to configure and operate them, and data is usually not useful unless it is accessible by other systems and possibly outside entities. All of these things can require backups, not just data.

☒ **D** is incorrect because providing procedures for emergency responses is a good reason to develop and implement a disaster recovery plan. A disaster recovery plan is carried out when everything is still in emergency mode and everyone is scrambling to get all critical systems back online. Having well-thought-out written procedures makes this whole process much more effective.

16. Business continuity plans can be assessed via a number of tests. Which type of test continues up to the point of actual relocation to an offsite facility and actual shipment of replacement equipment?

   A. Parallel test

   B. Checklist test

   C. Structured walk-through test

   D. Simulation test

   ☑ **D.** In a simulation test, all employees who participate in operational and support functions come together to practice executing the disaster recovery plan based on a specific scenario. The scenario is used to test the reaction of each operational and support representative. This is done to ensure that specific steps were not left out and certain threats were not overlooked, as well as to act as a catalyst to raise awareness of the people involved. The drill includes only those materials available in an actual disaster to portray a more realistic environment. The simulation test continues up to the point of actual relocation to an offsite facility and actual shipment of replacement equipment.

   ☒ **A** is incorrect because a parallel test is carried out to ensure that the specific systems can actually perform adequately at the alternate offsite facility. The systems are moved to the alternate site and processing takes place. The results are compared with the regular processing that is done at the original site. This activity points out any necessary tweaking, reconfiguring, or steps that need to take place to ensure that proper processing can take place at the alternate site.

   ☒ **B** is incorrect because in a checklist test copies of the disaster recovery and business continuity plans are distributed to the different departments and functional areas for review. This is done so that each functional manager or team can review the plan and indicate if anything has been left out or if some approaches should be modified or deleted. This is a method that ensures that some things have not been taken for granted or omitted. Once the departments have reviewed their copy and made suggestions, the planning team then integrates those changes into the master plan.

   ☒ **C** is incorrect because in a structured walk-through test representatives from each department or functional area come together to go over the plan to ensure its accuracy. The group goes over the objectives of the plan; discusses the scope and assumptions of the plan; reviews the organization and reporting structure; and evaluates the testing, maintenance, and training requirements described. This gives the people who will be responsible for making sure that a disaster recovery happens effectively and efficiently a chance to review what has been decided upon and what is expected of them. The group walks through different scenarios of the plan from beginning to end to make sure nothing was left out and to raise the awareness of the recovery team members.

17. With what phase of a business continuity plan does a company proceed when it is ready to move back into its original site or a new site?

    A. Reconstitution phase

    B. Recovery phase

    C. Project initiation phase

    D. Damage assessment phase

    ☑ **A.** When it is time for the company to move back into its original site or a new site, the company is ready to enter into the reconstitution phase. A company is not out of an emergency state until it is back in operation at the original primary site or a new site that was constructed to replace the primary site, because the company is always vulnerable while operating in a backup facility. Many logistical issues need to be considered as to when a company must return from the alternate site to the original site. Some of these issues include ensuring the safety of the employees, ensuring proper communications and connectivity methods are working, and properly testing the new environment. Once the coordinator, management, and salvage team sign off on the readiness of the facility, the salvage team should back up data from the alternate site and restore it within the new facility, carefully terminate contingency operations, and securely transport equipment and personnel to the new facility.

    ☒ **B** is incorrect because the recovery phase includes the preparation of the offsite facility (if needed), the rebuilding of the network and systems, and the organization of staff to move into a new facility. The recovery process needs to be as organized as possible to get the company up and running as soon as possible. Templates should be developed during the plan development stage that can be used by the different teams during the recovery phase to step them through the necessary phases and to document their findings. The templates keep the teams on task and also quickly tell the team leaders about the progress, obstacles, and potential recovery time.

    ☒ **C** is incorrect because the project initiation phase is how the actual planning of the business continuity plan begins. It does not occur during the execution of the plan. The project initiation phase involves getting management support, developing the scope of the plan, and securing funding and resources.

    ☒ **D** is incorrect because the damage assessment takes place at the start of actually carrying out the business continuity procedures. A damage assessment helps determine whether the business continuity plan should be put into action based on activation criteria predefined by the BCP coordinator and team. After the damage assessment, if one or more of the situations outlined in the criteria have taken place, then the team is moved into recovery mode.

18. Several teams should be involved in carrying out the business continuity plan. Which team is responsible for starting the recovery of the original site?

   A. Damage assessment team

   B. BCP team

   C. Salvage team

   D. Restoration team

   ☑ **C.** The BCP coordinator should have an understanding of the needs of the company and the types of teams that need to be developed and trained. Employees should be assigned to the specific teams based on their knowledge and skill set. Each team needs to have a designated leader, who will direct the members and their activities. These team leaders will be responsible not only for ensuring that their team's objectives are met, but also for communicating with each other to make sure each team is working in parallel phases. The salvage team is responsible for starting the recovery of the original site. It is also responsible for backing up data from the alternate site and restoring it within the new facility, carefully terminating contingency operations, and securely transporting equipment and personnel to the new facility.

   ☒ **A** is incorrect because the damage assessment team is responsible for determining the scope and severity of the damage caused. Whether or not a disaster is declared and the BCP put into action is based on this information collected and assessed by the damage assessment team.

   ☒ **B** is incorrect because the BCP team is responsible for creating and maintaining the business continuity plan. As such, its responsibilities also include identifying regulatory and legal requirements that must be met, identifying all possible vulnerabilities and threats, performing a business impact analysis, and developing procedures and steps in resuming business after a disaster. The BCP team is made up of representatives from a variety of business units and departments, including senior management, the security department, the communications department, and the legal department. This is not the team that starts the physical recovery of the original site.

   ☒ **D** is incorrect because the restoration team is responsible for getting the alternate site into a working and functioning environment. Both the restoration team and the salvage team must know how to do many tasks, such as install operating systems, configure workstations and servers, string wire and cabling, set up the network and configure networking services, and install equipment and applications. Both teams must also know how to restore data from backup facilities, and how to do so in a secure manner that ensures that the systems' and data's confidentiality, integrity, and availability are not compromised.

19. ACME Inc. paid a software vendor to develop specialized software, and that vendor has gone out of business. ACME Inc. does not have access to the code and therefore cannot keep it updated. What mechanism should the company have implemented to prevent this from happening?

A. Reciprocal agreement

B. Software escrow

C. Electronic vaulting

D. Business interruption insurance

☑ **B.** The protection mechanism that ACME Inc. should have implemented is called software escrow. Software escrow means that a third party holds the source code, and backups of the compiled code, manuals, and other supporting materials. A contract between the software vendor, customer, and third party outlines who can do what and when with the source code. This contract usually states that the customer can have access to the source code only if and when the vendor goes out of business, is unable to carry out stated responsibilities, or is in breach of the original contract. If any of these activities takes place, then the customer is protected because it can still gain access to the source code and other materials through the third-party escrow agent.

☒ **A** is incorrect because a reciprocal agreement is an offsite facility option that involves two companies agreeing to share their facility in case a disaster renders one of the facilities unusable. Reciprocal agreements deal with disaster recovery and not software protection when dealing with the developing vendor.

☒ **C** is incorrect because electronic vaulting is a type of electronic backup solution. Electronic vaulting makes copies of files as they are modified and periodically transmits them to an offsite backup site. The transmission does not happen in real time but is carried out in batches. So, a company can choose to have all files that have been changed sent to the backup facility every hour, day, week, or month. The information can be stored in an offsite facility and retrieved from that facility in a short period of time. Electronic vaulting has to do with backing up data so that it is available if there is a disruption or disaster.

☒ **D** is incorrect because a business interruption insurance policy covers specified expenses and lost earnings if a company is out of business for a certain length of time. This insurance is commonly purchased to protect a company in case a disaster takes place and they have to shut down their services for a specific period of time. It does not have anything to do with protection or accessibility of source code.

20. Which of the following incorrectly describes the concept of executive succession planning?

   A. Predetermined steps protect the company if a senior executive leaves.

   B. Two or more senior staff cannot be exposed to a particular risk at the same time.

   C. It documents the assignment of deputy roles.

   D. It covers assigning a skeleton crew to resume operations after a disaster.

   ☑ D. A skeleton crew consists of the employees who carry out the most critical functions following a disaster. They are put to work first during the recovery process. A skeleton crew is not related to the concept of executive succession planning, which addresses the steps that will be taken to fill a senior executive role should that person retire, leave the company, or die. The objective of a skeleton crew is to maintain critical operations, while the objective of executive succession planning is to protect the company by maintaining leadership roles.

   ☒ A is incorrect because executive succession planning includes predetermined steps that protect the company if someone in a senior executive position retires, leaves the company, or is killed. The loss of a senior executive could tear a hole in the company's fabric, creating a leadership vacuum that must be filled quickly with the right individual. The line of succession plan defines who would step in and assume responsibility for this role.

   ☒ B is incorrect because the concept of two or more senior staff not being exposed to a particular risk at the same time is a policy that some larger organizations establish as part of their executive succession planning efforts. The idea is to protect senior personnel and the organization if a disaster were to strike. For example, an organization may decide that the CEO and president cannot travel on the same plane. If the plane went down and both individuals were killed, then the company could be in danger.

   ☒ C is incorrect because executive succession planning can include the assignment of deputy roles. An organization may have a deputy CIO, deputy CFO, and deputy CEO ready to take over the necessary tasks if the CIO, CFO, or CEO becomes unavailable. Executive succession planning is the decision to have these deputies step into the CIO, CFO, or CEO roles.

21. What is the missing second step in the graphic that follows?

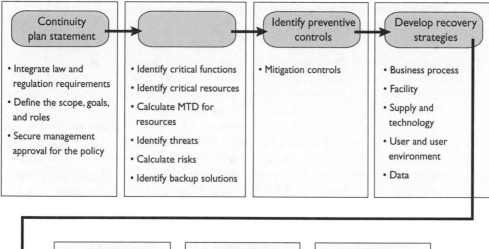

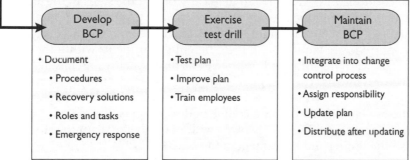

- **A.** Identify continuity coordinator
- **B.** Business impact analysis
- **C.** Identify BCP committee
- **D.** Dependency identification

☑ **B.** A business impact analysis (BIA) is considered a functional analysis, in which a team collects data through interviews and documentary sources; documents business functions, activities, and transactions; develops a hierarchy of business functions; and finally applies a classification scheme to indicate each individual function's criticality level. It is one of the most important first steps in the planning development of a business continuity plan (BCP). Qualitative and quantitative data needs to be gathered, analyzed, interpreted, and presented to management. Identifying critical functions and systems allow the organization to prioritize them based on necessity.

☒ **A** is incorrect because the business continuity coordinator needs to be put into position before this whole process starts. He will be the leader for the BCP team and will oversee the development, implementation, and testing of the continuity and disaster recovery plans. The coordinator should be identified in the project initiation and oversee all the steps shown in the graphic. It is best if this person has good social skills and is somewhat of a politician because he will need to coordinate a lot of different departments and busy individuals who have their own agendas. This person needs to have direct access to management and have the credibility and authority to carry out leadership tasks.

☒ **C** is incorrect because a BCP committee needs to be put together after the coordinator is identified to help carry out all the steps in the graphic. Management and the coordinator should work together to appoint specific, qualified people to be on this committee. The team must be composed of people who are familiar with the different departments within the company, because each department is unique in its functionality and has distinctive risks and threats. The best plan is when all issues and threats are brought to the table and discussed. This cannot be done effectively with a few people who are familiar with only a couple of departments. Representatives from each department must be involved with not only the planning stages but also the testing and implementation stages.

☒ **D** is incorrect because dependencies between company critical functions and resources are carried out during the BIA. This is only one of the components in the overall BIA process. Identifying these types of dependencies is critical because it is important to look at a company as a complex animal instead of a static two-dimensional entity. It comprises many types of equipment, people, tasks, departments, communications mechanisms, and interfaces to the outer world. The biggest challenge of true continuity planning is understanding all of these intricacies and their interrelationships. A team may develop plans to back up and restore data, implement redundant data processing equipment, educate employees on how to carry out automated tasks manually, and obtain redundant power supplies. But if all of these components don't know how to work together in a different environment to get the products out the door, it might all be a waste of time.

22. Different threats need to be evaluated and ranked based upon their severity of business risk when developing a BCP. Which ranking approach is illustrated in the graphic that follows?

> Choose the following statement that best describes the effect on this business unit/cost center should there be an unplanned interruption of normal business operations.
>
> ○ **8 hours** of an interruption. This business unit/cost center is **Vital.**
> ○ **24 hours** of an interruption. This business unit/cost center is **Critical.**
> ○ **3 days** of an interruption. This business unit/cost center is **Essential.**
> ○ **5 days** of an interruption. This business unit/cost center is **Important.**
> ○ **10 days** of an interruption. This business unit/cost center is **Noncritical.**
> ○ **30 days** of an interruption. This business unit/cost center is **Deferrable.**

- **A.** Mean time to repair
- **B.** Mean time between failures
- **C.** Maximum critical downtime
- **D.** Maximum tolerable downtime

☑ **D.** The BIA identifies which of the company's critical systems are needed for survival and estimates the outage time that can be tolerated by the company as a result of various unfortunate events. The outage time that can be endured by a company is referred to as the maximum tolerable downtime (MTD). This is the time frame between an unplanned interruption of business operations and the resumption of business at a reduced level of service. During the BIA, the BCP team identifies the maximum tolerable downtime for the critical resources. This was done to understand the business impact that would be caused if the assets were unavailable for one reason or another.

☒ **A** is incorrect because the mean time to repair (MTTR) is the amount of time it will be expected to take to get a device fixed and back into production. For a hard drive in a redundant array, the MTTR is the amount of time between the actual failure and the time when, after noticing the failure, someone has replaced the failed drive and the redundant array has completed rewriting the information on the new drive. This is likely to be measured in hours. For an unplanned reboot, the MTTR is the amount of time between the failure of the system and the point in time when it has rebooted its operating system, checked the state of its disks (hopefully finding nothing that its file systems cannot handle), restarted its applications, allowed its applications to check the consistency of their data (hopefully finding nothing that their journals cannot handle), and once again begun processing transactions. For well-built hardware running high-quality, well-managed operating systems and software, this may be only minutes. For commodity equipment without high-performance journaling file systems and databases, this may be hours, or, worse, days if automated recovery/rollback does not work and a restore of data from tape is required.

☒ **B** is incorrect because the mean time between failures (MTBF) is the estimated lifespan of a piece of equipment. MTBF is calculated by the vendor of the equipment or a third party. The reason for using this value is to know approximately when a particular device will need to be replaced. Either based on historical data or scientifically estimated by vendors, it is used as a benchmark for reliability by predicting the average time that will pass in the operation of a component or a system until its final death. Organizations trending MTBF over time for the device they use may be able to identify types of devices that are failing above the averages promised by manufacturers and take action such as proactively contacting manufacturers under warranty, or deciding that old devices are reaching the end of their useful life and choosing to replace them en masse before larger-scale failures and operational disruptions occur.

☒ **C** is incorrect because maximum critical downtime is not an official term used in BCP and is a distracter answer.

23. What type of infrastructural setup is illustrated in the graphic that follows?

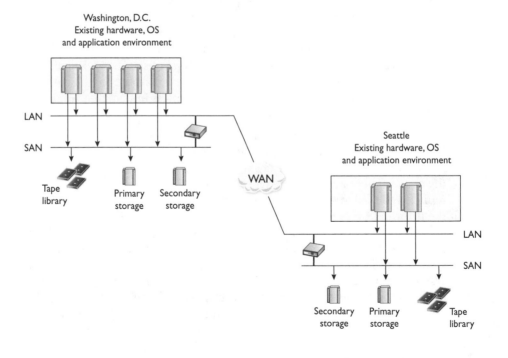

A. Hot site

B. Warm site

C. Cold site

D. Reciprocal agreement

☑ **A.** A hot site is a facility that is leased or rented and is fully configured and ready to operate within a few hours. The only missing resources from a hot site are usually the data, which will be retrieved from a backup site, and the people who will be processing the data. The equipment and system software must absolutely be compatible with the data being restored from the main site and must not cause any negative interoperability issues. These sites are a good choice for a company that needs to ensure a site will be available for it as soon as possible.

☒ **B** is incorrect because a warm site is a leased or rented facility that is usually partially configured with some equipment, but not the actual computers. In other words, a warm site is usually a hot site without the expensive equipment. Staging a facility with duplicate hardware and computers configured for immediate operation is extremely expensive, so a warm site provides an alternate facility with some peripheral devices. This is the most widely used model. It may be a better choice for companies that depend upon proprietary and unusual hardware and software, because they will bring their own hardware and software with them to the site after the disaster hits.

☒ **C** is incorrect because a cold site is a leased or rented facility that supplies the basic environment, electrical wiring, air conditioning, plumbing, and flooring, but none of the equipment or additional services. It may take weeks to get the site activated and ready for work. The cold site could have equipment racks and dark fiber (fiber that does not have the circuit engaged) and maybe even desks, but it would require the receipt of equipment from the client, since it does not provide any. The cold site is the least expensive option but takes the most time and effort to actually get up and functioning right after a disaster.

☒ **D** is incorrect because a reciprocal agreement is one in which a company promises another company it can move into its facility and share space if it experiences a disaster and vice versa. Reciprocal agreements are very tricky to implement and are unenforceable. This is a cheaper way to go than the other offsite choices, but it is not always the best choice. Most environments are maxed out pertaining to the use of facility space, resources, and computing capability.

24. There are several types of redundant technologies that can be put into place. What type of technology is shown in the graphic that follows?

A. Tape vaulting

B. Remote journaling

C. Electronic vaulting

D. Redundant site

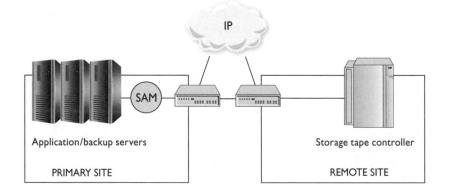

☑ **A.** Each site should have a full set of the most current and updated information and files, and a commonly used software backup technology is referred to as tape vaulting. Many businesses back up their data to tapes that are then manually transferred to an offsite facility by a courier or an employee. With automatic tape vaulting, the data is sent over a serial line to a backup tape system at the offsite facility. The company that maintains the offsite facility maintains the systems and changes out tapes when necessary. Data can be quickly backed up and retrieved when necessary. This technology reduces the manual steps in the traditional tape backup procedures. Basic vaulting of tape data is sending backup tapes to an offsite location, but a manual process can be error prone. Electronic tape vaulting transmits data over a network to tape devices located at an alternate data center. Electronic tape vaulting improves recovery speed and reduces errors, and backups can be run more frequently.

☒ **B** is incorrect because remote journaling is a technology used to transmit data to an offsite facility, but this usually only includes moving the journal or transaction logs to the offsite facility, not the actual files. This graphic specifically shows a tape controller and remote journaling mainly takes place between databases. Remote journaling involves transmitting the journal or transaction log offsite to a backup facility. These logs contain the deltas (changes) that have taken place to the individual files. If and when data are corrupted and need to be restored, the company can retrieve these logs, which are used to rebuild the lost data. Journaling is efficient for database recovery, where only the reapplication of a series of changes to individual records is required to resynchronize the database.

☒ **C is incorrect** because electronic vaulting most commonly takes place between databases and makes copies of files as they are modified and periodically transmits them to an offsite backup site. The transmission does not happen in real time but is carried out in batches. So, a company can choose to have all files that have been changed sent to the backup facility every hour, day, week, or month. The information can be stored in an offsite facility and retrieved from that facility in a short period of time. This form of backup takes place in many financial institutions, so when a bank teller accepts a deposit or withdrawal, the change to the customer's account is made locally to that branch's database and to the remote site that maintains the backup copies of all customer records.

☒ **D is incorrect** because while the graphic could be illustrating that the tape controller is located at a redundant site, a redundant site is not actually a technology. Some companies choose to have redundant sites, meaning one site is equipped and configured exactly like the primary site, which serves as a redundant environment. These sites are owned by the company and are mirrors of the original production environment. This is one of the most expensive backup facility options, because a full environment must be maintained even though it usually is not used for regular production activities until after a disaster takes place that triggers the relocation of services to the redundant site.

25. The following is a graphic of a business continuity policy. Which component is missing from this graphic?

    A. Damage assessment phase

    B. Reconstitution phase

    C. Business resumption phase

    D. Continuity of operations plan

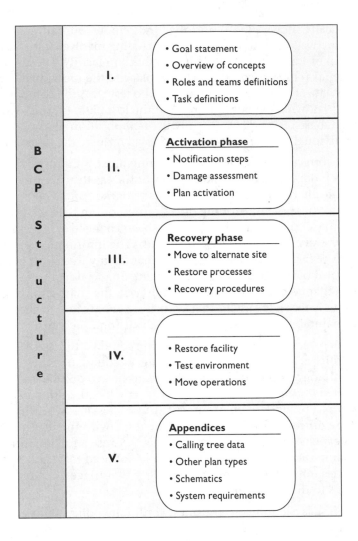

I.
- Goal statement
- Overview of concepts
- Roles and teams definitions
- Task definitions

II.
Activation phase
- Notification steps
- Damage assessment
- Plan activation

III.
Recovery phase
- Move to alternate site
- Restore processes
- Recovery procedures

IV.
- Restore facility
- Test environment
- Move operations

V.
Appendices
- Calling tree data
- Other plan types
- Schematics
- System requirements

B C P S t r u c t u r e

☑ **B.** After a disaster takes place and a company moves out of its facility, it must move back in after the facility is reconstructed. When it is time for the company to move back into its original site or a new site, the company is ready to enter into the reconstitution phase. A company is not out of an emergency state until it is back in operation at the original primary site or a new site that was constructed to replace the primary site, because the company is always vulnerable while operating in a backup facility. Many logistical issues need to be considered as to when a company must return from the alternate site to the original site. The following lists a few of these issues:

- Ensuring the safety of employees
- Ensuring an adequate environment is provided (power, facility infrastructure, water, HVAC)
- Ensuring that the necessary equipment and supplies are present and in working order
- Ensuring proper communications and connectivity methods are working
- Properly testing the new environment

☒ **A** is incorrect because a role, or a team, needs to be created to carry out a damage assessment once a disaster has taken place. The assessment procedures should be properly documented and include the following steps:

- Determine the cause of the disaster.
- Determine the potential for further damage.
- Identify the affected business functions and areas.
- Identify the level of functionality for the critical resources.
- Identify the resources that must be replaced immediately.
- Estimate how long it will take to bring critical functions back online.
- If it will take longer than the previously estimated Maximum Tolerable Downtime (MTD) values to restore operations, then a disaster should be declared and the Business Continuity Planning (BCP) should be put into action.

After this information is collected and assessed, it will indicate what teams need to be called to action and whether the BCP actually needs to be activated. The BCP coordinator and team must develop activation criteria. After the damage assessment, if one or more of the situations outlined in the criteria have taken place, then the team is moved into recovery mode.

☒ **C** is incorrect because a business resumption plan focuses on how to re-create the necessary business processes that need to be reestablished instead of focusing on only IT components (i.e., it is process-oriented instead of procedure-oriented). This plan could be mentioned in the BCP policy, but the policy does not outline the specifics of reestablishing business processes.

☒ **D** is incorrect because a continuity of operations plan (COOP) establishes senior management and a headquarters after a disaster. It provides instructions on how to set up a command center so that all activities and communication take place centrally and in a controlled manner. This type of plan also outlines roles and authorities, orders of succession, and individual role tasks that need to be put into place after a disaster takes place. This plan could be mentioned in the BCP policy, but the policy does not outline the specifics of setting up a command center and its components.

26. The Recovery Time Objective (RTO) and Maximum Tolerable Downtime (MTD) metrics have similar roles, but their values are very different. Which of the following best describes the difference between RTO and MTD metrics?

    A. The RTO is a time period that represents the inability to recover, and the MTD represents an allowable amount of downtime.

    B. The RTO is an allowable amount of downtime, and the MTD represents a time period that represents the inability to recover.

    C. The RTO is a metric used in disruptions, and the MTD is a metric used in disasters.

    D. The RTO is a metric pertaining to loss of access to data, and the MTD is a metric pertaining to loss of access to hardware and processing capabilities.

    ☑ B. The RTO value is smaller than the MTD value, because the MTD value represents the time after which an inability to recover significant operations will mean severe and perhaps irreparable damage to the organization's reputation or bottom line. The RTO assumes that there is a period of acceptable downtime. This means that a company can be out of production for a certain period of time (RTO) and still get back on its feet. But if the company cannot get production up and running within the MTD window, the company is sinking too fast to properly recover.

    ☒ A is incorrect because the MTD is a time period that represents the inability to recover, and the RTO represents an allowable amount of downtime.

    ☒ C is incorrect because the Recovery Time Objective (RTO) is the earliest time period and a service level within which a business process must be restored after a disaster to avoid unacceptable consequences associated with a break in business continuity. The RTO value is smaller than the MTD value, because the MTD value represents the time after which an inability to recover significant operations will mean severe and perhaps irreparable damage to the organization's reputation or bottom line.

    ☒ D is incorrect because the Recovery Time Objective (RTO) is the earliest time period and a service level within which a business process must be restored after a disaster to avoid unacceptable consequences associated with a break in business continuity. The RTO value is smaller than the MTD value, because the MTD value represents the time after which an inability to recover significant operations will mean severe and perhaps irreparable damage to the organization's reputation or bottom line. RTO is not a metric pertaining to loss of access to data, and the MTD is not a metric pertaining to loss of access to hardware and processing capabilities.

27. High availability (HA) is a combination of technologies and processes that work together to ensure that specific critical functions are always up and running at the necessary level. To provide this level of high availability, a

company has to have a long list of technologies and processes that provide redundancy, fault tolerance, and failover capabilities. Which of the following best describes these characteristics?

A. Redundancy is the duplication of noncritical components or functions of a system with the intention of decreasing reliability of the system. Fault tolerance is the capability of a technology to discontinue to operate as expected even if something unexpected takes place. If a technology has a failover capability, this means that if there is a failure that cannot be handled through normal means, then processing is "switched over" to a working system.

B. Redundancy is the duplication of critical components or functions of a system with the intention of increasing reliability of the system. Fault tolerance is the capability of a technology to continue to operate as expected even if something unexpected takes place. If a technology has a failover capability, this means that if there is a failure that cannot be handled through normal means, then processing is "switched over" to a working system.

C. Redundancy is the duplication of critical components or functions of a system with the intention of increasing reliability of the system. Fault tolerance is the capability of a technology to continue to operate as expected even if something unexpected takes place. If a technology has a failover capability, this means that if there is a failure that cannot be handled through normal means, then processing is "switched over" to a nonworking system.

D. Redundancy is the duplication of critical components or functions of a system with the intention of increasing reliability of the system. Fault tolerance is the capability of a technology to continue to operate as expected even if something unexpected takes place. If a technology has a failover capability, this means that if there is a failure that cannot be handled through normal means, then processing is "switched over" to a working system.

☑ **D.** High availability (HA) is a combination of technologies and processes that work together to ensure that specific critical functions are always up and running. The specific thing can be a database, a network, an application, a power supply, etc. To provide this level of high availability, the company has to have a long list of technologies and processes that provide redundancy, fault tolerance, and failover capabilities. Redundancy, fault tolerance, and failover capabilities increase the reliability of a system or network. High reliability allows for high availability.

☒ **A** is incorrect because redundancy within this type of technology encompasses the duplication of critical components or functions of a system with the intention of increasing reliability of the system. Redundancy is commonly built into the network at a routing protocol level. The routing protocols are configured so if one link goes down or gets congested, then traffic is routed over a different network link. Redundant hardware can also be available so if a primary device goes down the backup component can be swapped out and activated.

☒ **B** is incorrect because fault tolerance is the capability of a technology to continue to operate as expected even if something unexpected takes place (a fault). If a database experiences an unexpected glitch, it can roll back to a known good state and continue functioning as though nothing bad happened. If a packet gets lost or corrupted during a TCP session, the TCP protocol will resend the packet so that system-to-system communication is not affected. If a disk within a RAID system gets corrupted, the system uses its parity data to rebuild the corrupted data so that operations are not affected.

☒ **C** is incorrect because if a technology has a failover capability, this means that if there is a failure that cannot be handled through normal means, then processing is "switched over" to a working system.

The following scenario will be used to answer questions 28 and 29.

Sean has been hired as business continuity coordinator. He has been told by his management that he needed to ensure that the company is in compliance with the ISO/IEC standard that pertained to technology readiness for business continuity. He has also been instructed to find a way to transfer the risk of being unable to carry out critical business functions for a period of time because of a disaster.

28. Which of the following is most likely the standard that Sean has been asked to comply with?

   A. ISO/IEC 27031

   B. ISO/IEC 27005

   C. ISO/IEC BS7799

   D. ISO/IEC 2899

   ☑ **A** is correct. ISO/IEC 27031:2011 is a set of guidelines for information and communications technology readiness for business continuity. It is a component of the overall ISO/IEC 27000 series.

   ☒ **B** is incorrect because the purpose of ISO/IEC 27005 is to provide guidelines for information security risk management. It supports the general concepts specified in ISO/IEC 27001 and is designed to assist the satisfactory implementation of information security based on a risk management approach.

This standard deals with developing a formal risk management approach and not necessarily continuity issues.

☒ **C** is incorrect because this is a distracter answer. There is no official standard called ISO/IEC BS7799.

☒ **D** is incorrect because this is a distracter answer. There is no official standard called ISO/IEC 2899.

29. Which of the following would be best for Sean to implement as it pertains to his company's needs?

    A. Infrastructure cloud computing

    B. Co-location at a multiprocessing center

    C. Business interruption insurance

    D. Shared partner extranet with integrated redundancy

    ☑ **C.** A company could choose to purchase a business interruption insurance policy. With this type of policy, if the company is out of business for a certain length of time, the insurance company will pay for specified expenses and lost earnings. Another policy that can be bought insures accounts receivable. If a company cannot collect on its accounts receivable for one reason or another, this type of coverage covers part or all of the losses and costs.

    ☒ **A** is incorrect because infrastructure cloud computing does not have anything to do with transferring risk. It is just a model that allows a company to outsource its infrastructure needs to a service provider.

    ☒ **B** is incorrect because a co-location at a multiprocessing center has nothing to do with transferring risk. If a company carries out multiprocessing at a co-location, that provides redundancy and failover services if a disaster is experienced.

    ☒ **D** is incorrect because a shared partner extranet with integrated redundancy does not address transferring risk to another entity. An extranet is just a shared network segment, and integrated redundancy just means that if a failure takes place the company's functionalities should not be affected.

The following scenario will be used to answer questions 30, 31, and 32.

Jeff is leading the business continuity group in his company. They have completed a business impact analysis and have determined that if the company's credit card processing functionality was unavailable for 48 hours the company would most likely experience such a large financial hit that it would have to go out of business. The team has calculated that this functionality needs to be up and running within 28 hours after experiencing a disaster for the company to stay in business. The team has also determined that the restoration steps must be able to restore data that are one hour old or less.

30. In this scenario, which of the following is the recovery time objective value?

    A. 48 hours

    B. 28 hours

    C. 20 hours

    D. 1 hour

    ☑ B. The Recovery Time Objective (RTO) is the earliest time period and a service level within which a business process must be restored after a disaster to avoid unacceptable consequences associated with a break in business continuity. The RTO value is smaller than the Maximum Tolerable Downtime (MTD) value, because the MTD value represents the time after which an inability to recover significant operations will mean severe and perhaps irreparable damage to the organization's reputation or bottom line. In this scenario 28 hours is the RTO and 48 hours is the MTD.

    ☒ A is incorrect because the RTO value is 28 hours. The RTO assumes that there is a period of acceptable downtime. This means that a company can be out of production for a certain period of time (RTO) and still get back on its feet. But if the company cannot get production up and running within the MTD window, the company is sinking too fast to properly recover.

    ☒ C is incorrect because this value does not represent either the RTO or MTD value.

    ☒ D is incorrect because this value does not represent either the RTO or MTD value.

31. In this scenario, which of the following is the Work Recovery Time value?

    A. 48 hours

    B. 28 hours

    C. 20 hours

    D. 1 hour

    ☑ C. The Work Recovery Time (WRT) is the remainder of the overall MTD value after RTO. RTO usually deals with getting the infrastructure and systems back up and running, and WRT deals with restoring data, testing processes, and then making everything "live" for production purposes.

    ☒ A is incorrect because in this scenario 48 hours is the MTD value.

    ☒ B is incorrect because in this scenario 28 hours is the RTO value.

    ☒ D is incorrect because this value does not represent the Work Recovery Time.

32. In this scenario, what would the 1-hour time period be referred to as?

    A. Recovery Time Period

    B. Maximum Tolerable Downtime

    C. Recovery Point Objective

    D. Recovery Point Time Period

    ☑ **C.** The Recovery Point Objective (RPO) is the acceptable amount of data loss measured in time. This value represents the earliest point in time in which data must be recovered. The higher the business value of data, the more funds or other resources that can be put into place to ensure a smaller amount of data is lost in the event of a disaster.

    ☒ **A** is incorrect because this is a distracter answer. There is no official term Recovery Time Period.

    ☒ **B** is incorrect because the Maximum Tolerable Downtime (MTD) value represents the time after which an inability to recover significant operations will mean severe and perhaps irreparable damage to the organization's reputation or bottom line.

    ☒ **D** is incorrect because this is a distracter answer. There is no official term Recovery Point Time Period.

Legal, Regulations, Investigations, and Compliance

This domain includes questions from the following topics:

- Computer crimes types
- Motives and profiles of attackers
- Various types of evidence
- Laws and acts put into effect to fight computer crime
- Computer crime investigation process and evidence collection
- Incident-handling procedures
- Ethics pertaining to information security and best practices

As society's dependence on technology has grown, criminals have found new opportunities to commit fraud, theft, and embezzlement. Organizations must not only protect themselves from outsiders and the rank-and-file but also demonstrate compliance with federal regulations and industry mandates to prove that executives and employees are acting lawfully and protecting their customers' best interests. Thus, security professionals must understand how to respond to computer crime, the laws their company are subject to, as well as how to uphold ethical practices.

1. Cyberlaw categorizes computer-related crime into three categories. Which of the following is an example of a crime in which the use of a computer would be categorized as incidental?

    A. Carrying out a buffer overflow to take control of a system

    B. The electronic distribution of child pornography

    C. Attacking financial systems to steal funds

    D. Capturing passwords as they are sent to the authentication server

2. Which organization has been developed to deal with economic, social, and governance issues, and with how sensitive data is transported over borders?

    A. European Union

    B. Council of Europe

    C. Safe Harbor

    D. Organisation for Economic Co-operation and Development

3. Different countries have different legal systems. Which of the following correctly describes customary law?

    A. Not many countries work under this law purely; most instead use a mixed system where this law, which deals mainly with personal conduct and patterns of behavior, is an integrated component.

    B. It covers all aspects of human life, but is commonly divided into responsibilities and obligations to others, and religious duties.

    C. It is a rule-based law focused on codified law.

    D. Based on previous interpretations of laws, this system reflects the community's morals and expectations.

4. Widgets Inc. wishes to protect its logo from unauthorized use. Which of the following will protect the logo and ensure that others cannot copy and use it?

    A. Patent

    B. Copyright

    C. Trademark

    D. Trade secret

5. There are four categories of software licensing. Which of the following refers to software sold at a reduced cost?

    A. Shareware

    B. Academic software

C. Freeware

D. Commercial software

6. There are different types of approaches to regulations. Which of the following is an example of self-regulation?

   A. The Health Insurance Portability and Accountability Act

   B. The Sarbanes-Oxley Act

   C. The Computer Fraud and Abuse Act

   D. PCI Data Security Standard

7. Which of the following means that a company did all it could have reasonably done to prevent a security breach?

   A. Downstream liability

   B. Responsibility

   C. Due diligence

   D. Due care

8. There are three different types of incident response teams. Which of the following correctly describes a virtual team?

   A. It consists of experts who have other duties within the organization.

   B. It can be cost prohibitive to smaller organizations.

   C. It is a hybrid model.

   D. Core members are permanently assigned to the team.

9. A suspected crime has been reported within your organization. Which of the following steps should the incident response team take first?

   A. Establish a procedure for responding to the incident.

   B. Call in forensics experts.

   C. Determine that a crime has been committed.

   D. Notify senior management.

10. During an incident response, what stage involves mitigating the damage caused by an incident?

   A. Investigation

   B. Containment

   C. Triage

   D. Analysis

11. Which of the following is a correct statement regarding computer forensics?

    A. It is the study of computer technology.

    B. It is a set of hardware-specific processes that must be followed in order for evidence to be admissible in a court of law.

    C. It encompasses network and code analysis, and may be referred to as electronic data discovery.

    D. Computer forensics responsibilities should be assigned to a network administrator before an incident occurs.

12. Which of the following dictates that all evidence be labeled with information indicating who secured and validated it?

    A. Chain of custody

    B. Due care

    C. Investigation

    D. Motive, Opportunity, and Means

13. There are several categories of evidence. How is a witness's oral testimony categorized?

    A. Best evidence

    B. Secondary evidence

    C. Circumstantial evidence

    D. Conclusive evidence

14. For evidence to be legally admissible, it must be authentic, complete, sufficient, and reliable. Which characteristic refers to the evidence having a reasonable and sensible relationship to the findings?

    A. Complete

    B. Reliable

    C. Authentic

    D. Sufficient

15. Which of the following best describes exigent circumstances?

    A. The methods used to capture a suspect's actions are neither legal nor ethical.

    B. Enticement is used to capture a suspect's actions.

    C. Hacking does not actually hurt anyone.

    D. The seizure of evidence by law enforcement because there is concern that a suspect will attempt to destroy it.

16. What role does the Internet Architecture Board play regarding technology and ethics?

    A. It creates criminal sentencing guidelines.

    B. It issues ethics-related statements concerning the use of the Internet.

    C. It edits Request for Comments.

    D. It maintains ten commandments for ethical behavior.

17. Which of the following statements is not true of dumpster diving?

    A. It is legal.

    B. It is unethical.

    C. It is illegal.

    D. It is a nontechnical attack.

18. Which of the following is a legal form of eavesdropping when performed with prior consent or a warrant?

    A. Denial of Service

    B. Dumpster diving

    C. Wiretapping

    D. Data diddling

19. What type of common law deals with violations committed by individuals against government laws, which are created to protect the public?

    A. Criminal law

    B. Civil law

    C. Tort law

    D. Regulatory law

20. During what stage of incident response is it determined if the source of the incident was internal or external, and how the offender penetrated and gained access to the asset?

    A. Analysis

    B. Containment

    C. Tracking

    D. Follow-up

21. Which of the following is not true of a forensics investigation?

    A. The crime scene should be modified as necessary.

    B. A file copy tool may not recover all data areas of the device that are necessary for investigation.

    C. Contamination of the crime scene may not negate derived evidence, but it should still be documented.

    D. Only individuals with knowledge of basic crime scene analysis should have access to the crime scene.

22. Great care must be taken to capture clues from a computer or device during a forensics exercise. Which of the following does not correctly describe the efforts that should be taken to protect an image?

    A. The original image should be hashed with MD5 and/or SHA-256.

    B. Two time-stamped images should be created.

    C. New media should be properly purged before images are created on them.

    D. Some systems must be imaged while they are running.

23. Which of the following attacks can be best prevented by limiting the amount of electrical signals emitted from a computer system?

    A. Salami attack

    B. Emanations capturing

    C. Password sniffing

    D. IP spoofing

24. As a CISSP candidate, you must sign a Code of Ethics. Which of the following is from the (ISC)² Code of Ethics for the CISSP?

    A. Information should be shared freely and openly; thus, sharing confidential information should be ethical.

    B. Think about the social consequences of the program you are writing or the system you are designing.

    C. Discourage unnecessary fear or doubt.

    D. Do not participate in Internet-wide experiments in a negligent manner.

25. What concept states that a criminal leaves something behind and takes something with them?

    A. Modus Operandi

    B. Profiling

    C. Locard's Principle of Exchange

    D. Motive, Opportunity, and Means

26. Which of the following was the first international treaty seeking to address computer crimes by coordinating national laws and improving investigative techniques and international cooperation?

    A. Council of Global Convention on Cybercrime

    B. Council of Europe Convention on Cybercrime

    C. Organisation for Economic Co-operation and Development

    D. Organisation for Cybercrime Co-operation and Development

27. Lee is a new security manager who is in charge of ensuring that his company complies with the European Union Principles on Privacy when his company is interacting with their European partners. The set of principles that deals with transmitting data considered private is encompassed within which of the following laws or regulations?

    A. Data Protection Directive

    B. Organisation for Economic Co-operation and Development

    C. Federal Private Bill

    D. Privacy Protection Law

28. The common law system is broken down into which of the following categories?

    A. Common, civil, criminal

    B. Legislation, bills, regulatory

    C. Civil, criminal, regulatory

    D. Legislation, bills, civil

29. Privacy is becoming more threatened as the world relies more and more on technology. There are several approaches to addressing privacy, including the generic approach and regulation by industry. Which of the following best describes these two approaches?

    A. The generic approach is vertical enactment. Regulation by industry is horizontal enactment.

    B. The generic approach is horizontal enactment. Regulation by industry is vertical enactment.

    C. The generic approach is government enforced. Regulation by industry is self-enforced.

    D. The generic approach is self-enforced. Regulation by industry is government enforced.

The following scenario will be used for questions 30 and 31.

Stephanie has been put in charge of developing incident response and forensics procedures her company needs to carry out if an incident occurs. She needs to ensure that their procedures map to the international principles for gathering and protecting digital evidence. She also needs to ensure that if and when internal forensics teams are deployed, they have labels, tags, evidence bags, cable ties, imaging software, and other associated tools.

30. Which of the following best describes the organization that developed the best practices that Stephanie needs to ensure her company's procedures map to?

    A. Internet Activities Board

    B. International Organization on Computer Evidence

    C. Department of Defense Forensics Committee

    D. International Forensics Standards Board

31. Which of the following best describes what Stephanie needs to build for the deployment teams?

    A. Local and remote imaging system

    B. Forensics field kit

    C. Chain of custody procedures and tools

    D. Digital evidence collection software

1. B	12. A	23. B
2. D	13. B	24. C
3. A	14. C	25. C
4. C	15. D	26. B
5. B	16. B	27. A
6. D	17. C	28. C
7. D	18. C	29. B
8. A	19. A	30. B
9. C	20. C	31. B
10. B	21. A	
11. C	22. D	

1. Cyberlaw categorizes computer-related crime into three categories. Which of the following is an example of a crime in which the use of a computer would be categorized as incidental?

    A. Carrying out a buffer overflow to take control of a system

    B. The electronic distribution of child pornography

    C. Attacking financial systems to steal funds

    D. Capturing passwords as they are sent to the authentication server

    ☑ **B.** Laws have been created to combat three categories of crime: computer-assisted, computer-targeted, and computer is incidental. If a crime falls into the "computer is incidental" category, this means a computer just happened to be involved in some secondary manner, but its involvement is insignificant. The digital distribution of child pornography is an example of "computer is incidental." The actual crime is obtaining and sharing child pornography pictures or graphics. The pictures could be stored on a file server, or they could be kept in a physical file in someone's desk. So if a crime falls within this category, the computer is not attacking another computer, and a computer is not being attacked, but the computer is still used in some manner. Thus, the computer is a source of additional evidence related to the crime.

    ☒ **A** is incorrect because carrying out a buffer overflow to take control of a system is an example of a computer-targeted crime. A computer-targeted crime concerns incidents where a computer was the victim of an attack crafted to harm it (and its owners) specifically. Other examples of computer-targeted crimes include distributed denial-of-service attacks, installing malware with the intent to cause destruction, and installing rootkits and sniffers for malicious purposes.

    ☒ **C** is incorrect because attacking financial systems to steal funds is an example of a computer-assisted crime. A computer-assisted crime is where a computer was used as a tool to help carry out a crime. Other examples of computer-assisted crimes include obtaining military and intelligence material by attacking military systems, and carrying out information warfare activities by attacking critical national infrastructure systems.

    ☒ **D** is incorrect because capturing passwords as they are sent to the authentication server is an example of a computer-targeted crime. Some confusion typically exists between the two categories, "computer-assisted crimes" and "computer-targeted crimes," because intuitively it would seem any attack would fall into both of these categories. One way to look at it is that a computer-targeted crime could not take place without a computer, while a computer-assisted crime could. Thus, a computer-targeted crime is one that did not, and could not, exist before computers became of common use. In other words, in the good old days, you could not carry out a buffer overflow on your neighbor, or install malware on your enemy's system. These crimes require that computers be involved.

2. Which organization has been developed to deal with economic, social, and governance issues, and with how sensitive data is transported over borders?

   A. European Union

   B. Council of Europe

   C. Safe Harbor

   D. Organisation for Economic Co-operation and Development

   ☑ **D.** Global organizations that move data across other country boundaries must be aware of and follow the Organisation for Economic Co-operation and Development (OECD) Guidelines. Since most countries have a different set of laws pertaining to the definition of private data and how it should be protected, international trade and business gets more convoluted and can negatively affect the economy of nations. The OECD is an international organization that helps different governments come together and tackle the economic, social, and governance challenges of a globalized economy. Because of this, the OECD came up with guidelines for the various countries to follow so that data is properly protected and everyone follows the same type of rules. One of these rules is that subjects should be able to find out whether an organization has their personal information and, if so, what that information is, to correct erroneous data and to challenge denied requests to do so.

   ☒ **A** is incorrect because the European Union is not an organization that deals with economic, social, and governance issues, but does address the protection of sensitive data. The European Union Principles on Privacy are: The reason for the gathering of data must be specified at the time of collection; Data cannot be used for other purposes; Unnecessary data should not be collected; Data should only be kept for as long as it is needed to accomplish the stated task; Only the necessary individuals who are required to accomplish the stated task should be allowed access to the data; Whoever is responsible for securely storing the data should not allow unintentional "leaking" of data.

   ☒ **B** is incorrect because the Council of Europe is responsible for the creation of the Convention on Cybercrime. The Council of Europe Convention on Cybercrime is one example of an attempt to create a standard international response to cybercrime. In fact, it is the first international treaty seeking to address computer crimes by coordinating national laws, and improving investigative techniques and international cooperation. The Convention's objectives include the creation of a framework for establishing jurisdiction and extradition of the accused. For example, extradition is only available by treaty and when the event is a crime in both jurisdictions.

☒ **C** is incorrect because Safe Harbor is not an organization but a set of requirements for organizations that wish to exchange data with European entities. Europe has always had tighter control over protecting privacy information than the U.S. and other parts of the world. So in the past when U.S. and European companies needed to exchange data, confusion erupted and business was interrupted because the lawyers had to get involved to figure out how to work within the structures of the differing laws. To clear up this mess, a "safe harbor" framework was created, which outlines how any entity that is going to move privacy data to and from Europe must go about protecting it. U.S. companies that deal with European entities can become certified against this rule base so data transfer can happen more quickly and easily.

3. Different countries have different legal systems. Which of the following correctly describes customary law?

   A. Not many countries work under this law purely; most instead use a mixed system where this law, which deals mainly with personal conduct and patterns of behavior, is an integrated component.

   B. It covers all aspects of human life, but is commonly divided into responsibilities and obligations to others, and religious duties.

   C. It is a rule-based law focused on codified law.

   D. Based on previous interpretations of laws, this system reflects the community's morals and expectations.

   ☑ **A.** Customary law deals primarily with personal conduct and patterns of behavior. It is based on the traditions and customs of the region. It came about as communities emerged and the cooperation of individuals became necessary. Not many countries work under a purely customary law system; most instead use a mixed system where customary law is an integrated component. (Codified civil law systems emerged from customary law.) Customary law is mainly used in regions of the world that have mixed legal systems; for example, China and India. Restitution in a customary law system is commonly in the form of a monetary fine or service.

   ☒ **B** is incorrect because it describes religious law systems. Where customary law deals mainly with personal conduct and patterns of behavior, religious law systems are commonly divided into responsibilities and obligations to others, and religious duties. Religious law systems are based on the religious beliefs of a region. In Islamic countries, for example, the law is based on the rules of the Koran. The law, however, is different in every Islamic country.

☒ **C** is incorrect because civil (code) law is rule-based and, for the most part, is focused on codified law, i.e., laws that are written down. Civil law is the most widespread legal system in the world and the most common legal system in Europe. It is established by states or nations for self-regulation; thus, civil law can be divided into subdivisions such as French civil law, German civil law, etc.

☒ **D** is incorrect because common law is based on previous interpretations of laws. In the past, judges would walk throughout the country enforcing laws and settling disputes. They did not have a written set of laws, so they based their laws on custom and precedent. This system reflects the community's morals and expectations.

4. Widgets Inc. wishes to protect its logo from unauthorized use. Which of the following will protect the logo and ensure that others cannot copy and use it?

   A. Patent

   B. Copyright

   C. Trademark

   D. Trade secret

   ☑ **C.** Intellectual property can be protected by several different laws, depending upon the type of resource it is. A trademark is used to protect a word, name, symbol, sound, shape, color, or combination of these—such as a logo. The reason a company would trademark one of these, or a combination, is that it represents their company (brand identity) to a group of people or to the world. Companies have marketing departments that work very hard in coming up with something new that will cause the company to be noticed and stand out in a crowd of competitors, and trademarking the result of this work with a government registrar is a way of properly protecting it and ensuring others cannot copy and use it.

   ☒ **A** is incorrect because a patent covers an invention, whereas a trademark protects a word, name, symbol, sound, shape, color, or combination thereof. Patents are given to individuals or companies to grant them legal ownership of, and enable them to exclude others from using or copying, the invention covered by the patent. The invention must be novel, useful, and not obvious. A patent is the strongest form of intellectual property protection.

   ☒ **B** is incorrect because in the United States, copyright law protects the right of an author to control the public distribution, reproduction, display, and adaptation of his original work. The law covers many categories of work: pictorial, graphic, musical, dramatic, literary, pantomimes, motion picture, sculptural, sound recording, and architectural. Copyright law does not cover the specific resource. It protects the expression of the idea of the resource instead of the resource itself. A copyright law is usually used to protect an author's writings, an artist's drawings, a programmer's source code, or specific rhythms and structures of a musician's creation.

☒ **D** is incorrect because trade secret law protects certain types of information or resources from unauthorized use or disclosure. For a company to have its resource qualify as a trade secret, the resource must provide the company with some type of competitive value or advantage. A trade secret can be protected by law if developing it requires special skill, ingenuity, and/or expenditure of money and effort.

5. There are four categories of software licensing. Which of the following refers to software sold at a reduced cost?

A. Shareware

B. Academic software

C. Freeware

D. Commercial software

☑ **B.** When a vendor develops an application, it usually licenses the program rather than selling it outright. The license agreement contains provisions relating to the use and security of the software and the corresponding manuals. If an individual or company fails to observe and abide by those requirements, the license may be terminated, and depending on the actions, criminal charges may be leveled. The risk to the vendor that develops and licenses the software is the loss of profits it would have earned. The four categories of software licensing are shareware, freeware, commercial, and academic. Academic software is software that is provided for academic purposes at a reduced cost.

☒ **A** is incorrect because shareware, or trialware, is a licensing model in which vendors give away a free, trial version of their software. Once the user tries the program, the user is asked to purchase a copy of it. This model is used by vendors to market their software.

☒ **C** is incorrect because freeware is software that is publicly available free of charge and can be used, copied, studied, modified, and redistributed without restriction.

☒ **D** is incorrect because commercial software is software that is sold at full price and typically used for commercial purposes. Most companies use commercial software with bulk licenses. Bulk licenses enable several users to use the product simultaneously. These master agreements define proper use of the software along with restrictions, such as whether corporate software can also be used by employees on their home machines.

6. There are different types of approaches to regulations. Which of the following is an example of self-regulation?

   A. The Health Insurance Portability and Accountability Act

   B. The Sarbanes-Oxley Act

   C. The Computer Fraud and Abuse Act

   D. PCI Data Security Standard

   ☑ **D.** Privacy is becoming more threatened as the world relies more and more on technology. There are several approaches to addressing privacy, including regulations created and enforced by the government and self-regulatory regulations. The Payment Card Industry Data Security Standard (PCI DSS) is an example of a self-regulatory approach. It is mandated by the credit card companies and applies to any entity that processes, transmits, stores, or accepts credit card data. Varying levels of compliance and penalties exist and depend on the size of the customer and the volume of transactions. However, credit cards are used by millions and accepted almost anywhere, which means just about every business in the world must comply with the PCI DSS. PCI DSS is not a government-created and enforced regulation. While the CISSP exam does not require you to know specific regulations, you must understand the different approaches to regulations.

   ☒ **A** is incorrect because the Health Insurance Portability and Accountability Act (HIPAA) is a U.S. federal regulation that applies to any organization that is in possession of personal medical information and healthcare data. This regulation provides a framework and guidelines to ensure security, integrity, and privacy when handling confidential medical information. HIPAA outlines how security should be managed for any facility that creates, accesses, shares, or destroys medical information.

   ☒ **B** is incorrect because the Sarbanes-Oxley Act (SOX) was created by the U.S. government in the wake of corporate scandals and fraud which cost investors billions of dollars and threatened to undermine the economy. The regulation applies to any company that is publicly traded on U.S. markets. Much of the law governs accounting practices and the methods used by companies to report on their financial status. However, some parts, Section 404 in particular, apply directly to information technology.

   ☒ **C** is incorrect because the Computer Fraud and Abuse Act is the primary U.S. federal antihacking statute. It prohibits seven forms of computer activity and makes them federal crimes. These acts range from felonies to misdemeanors with corresponding small to large fines and jail sentences. One example is the knowing access of a protected computer without authorization or in excess of authorization with the intent to defraud. While the CISSP exam does not require you to know specific laws and regulations, you do need to understand why various laws and regulations are put into place and why they are used.

7. Which of the following means that a company did all it could have reasonably done to prevent a security breach?

    A. Downstream liability

    B. Responsibility

    C. Due diligence

    D. Due care

    ☑ **D.** Due care means that a company did all it could have reasonably done, under the circumstances, to prevent security breaches, and also took reasonable steps to ensure that if a security breach did take place, proper controls or countermeasures were in place to mitigate the damages. In short, due care means that a company practiced common sense and prudent management and acted responsibly. If a company has a facility that burns to the ground, the arsonist is only one small piece of this tragedy. The company is responsible for providing fire detection and suppression systems, fire-resistant construction material in certain areas, alarms, exits, fire extinguishers, and backups of all the important information that could be affected by a fire. If a fire burns a company's building to the ground and consumes all the records (customer data, inventory records, and similar information that is necessary to rebuild the business), then the company did not exercise due care to ensure it was protected from such loss (by backing up to an offsite location, for example). In this case, the employees, shareholders, customers, and everyone affected could potentially successfully sue the company. However, if the company did everything expected of it in the previously listed respects, it is harder to successfully sue for failure to practice due care.

    ☒ **A** is incorrect because downstream liability means that one company's activities—or lack of them—can negatively affect another company. If one of the companies does not provide the necessary level of protection and its negligence affects a partner it is working with, the affected company can sue the upstream company. For example, let's say company A and company B have constructed an extranet. Company A does not put in controls to detect and deal with viruses. Company A gets infected with a destructive virus, which is spread to company B through the extranet. The virus corrupts critical data and causes a massive disruption to company B's production. Therefore, company B can sue company A for being negligent. This is an example of downstream liability.

☒ **B** is incorrect because responsibility generally refers to the obligations and expected actions and behaviors of a particular party. An obligation may have a defined set of specific actions that are required, or a more general and open approach, which enables the party to decide how it will fulfill the particular obligation. Due diligence is a better answer to this question. Responsibility is not considered a legal term as the other answers are.

☒ **C** is incorrect because due diligence means that the company properly investigated all of its possible weaknesses and vulnerabilities. Before you can figure out how to properly protect yourself, you need to find out what it is you are protecting yourself against. This is what due diligence is all about—researching and assessing the current level of vulnerabilities so that the true risk level is understood. Only after these steps and assessments take place can effective controls and safeguards be identified and implemented. Due diligence is identifying all of the potential risks and due care is actually doing something to mitigate those risks.

8. There are three different types of incident response teams. Which of the following correctly describes a virtual team?

   A. It consists of experts who have other duties within the organization.

   B. It can be cost prohibitive to smaller organizations.

   C. It is a hybrid model.

   D. Core members are permanently assigned to the team.

   ☑ **A.** All organizations should develop an incident response team, as mandated by the incident response policy, to respond to the large array of possible security incidents. The purpose of having an incident response team is to ensure that there is a group of people who are properly skilled, who follow a standard set of procedures, and who are singled out and called upon when this type of event takes place. There are three different types of incident response teams. A virtual team is made up of experts who have other duties and assignments within the organization or are outside consultants. A virtual team is commonly developed and used when a company cannot afford to dedicate specific individuals to only deal with incidents. The team can be made up of employees who have other jobs within the company and/or outside consultants that would be called in when an incident takes place.

   ☒ **B** is incorrect because a permanent team of dedicated employees who are dedicated strictly to incident response can be cost prohibitive to smaller organizations. A virtual team is made up of individuals who are called upon when needed but have other responsibilities other than just incident management. A virtual team is commonly a more affordable approach.

⊠ C is incorrect because a hybrid model has aspects of both a virtual model and permanent model. It is similar to a virtual model in that some team members are called as needed and have other responsibilities. It is similar to a permanent model in that certain core members are permanently assigned to the team and incident management is their full-time job and responsibility. In a hybrid situation both permanent and virtual people are used when an incident takes place.

⊠ D is incorrect because a virtual team is created specifically when an organization cannot afford to have employees who are dedicated to incident management only. In larger organizations that have high threat levels, there can be dedicated staff members whose only job is incident management, but most organizations cannot afford this and instead use virtual teams.

9. A suspected crime has been reported within your organization. Which of the following steps should the incident response team take first?

A. Establish a procedure for responding to the incident.

B. Call in forensics experts.

C. Determine that a crime has been committed.

D. Notify senior management.

☑ C. When a suspected crime is reported, the incident response team should follow a set of predetermined steps to ensure uniformity in their approach and make sure no steps are skipped. First, the incident response team should investigate the report and determine that an actual crime has been committed. If the team determines that a crime has been carried out, senior management should be informed immediately. At this point, the company must decide if it wants to conduct its own forensics investigation or call in external experts.

⊠ A is incorrect because a procedure for responding to an incident should be established before an incident takes place. Incident handling is commonly a recovery plan that responds to malicious technical threats. While the primary goal of incident handling is to contain and mitigate any damage caused by an incident and to prevent any further damage, other objectives include detecting a problem, determining its cause, resolving the problem, and documenting the entire process.

⊠ B is incorrect because calling in a forensics team does not occur until the incident response team has investigated the report and verified that a crime has occurred. Then the company can decide if it wants to conduct its own forensics investigation or call in external experts. If experts are going to be called in, the system that was attacked should be left alone in order to try and preserve as much evidence of the attack as possible.

☒ **D** is incorrect because the incident response team must first determine that a crime has indeed been carried out before it can notify senior management. There is no need to alarm senior management if the report is false.

10. During an incident response, what stage involves mitigating the damage caused by an incident?

    A. Investigation

    B. Containment

    C. Triage

    D. Analysis

    ☑ **B.** A proper containment strategy buys the incident response team time to properly investigate and determine the incident's root cause. The containment strategy should be based on the category of the attack (i.e., whether it was internal or external), the assets affected by the incident, and the criticality of those assets. Containment strategies can be proactive or reactive. Which is best depends on the environment and the category of the attack. In some cases, the best action might be to disconnect the affected system from the network. Disconnecting the affected system from the network is a reactive strategy, not a proactive strategy. The system is taken offline after it is attacked. If it was taken offline before it was attacked (you'd need some indication that the system was going to be attacked), then the strategy would be proactive.

    ☒ **A** is incorrect because the investigation stage involves the proper collection of relevant data and includes analysis, interpretation, reaction, and recovery. The goals of this stage are to reduce the impact of the incident, identify the cause of the incident, resume operations as soon as possible, and apply what was learned to prevent the incident from recurring. It is also at this stage where computer forensics comes into play. Management must decide if law enforcement should be brought in to carry out the investigation, if evidence should be collected for the purposes of prosecution, or if the hole should just be patched.

    ☒ **C** is incorrect because triage involves taking information about the incident, investigating the incident's severity, and setting priorities on how to deal with it. This begins with an initial screening of the reported event to determine whether it is indeed an incident and whether the incident handling process should be initiated. If the event is determined to be a real incident, it is identified and classified. Incidents should be categorized according to their level of potential risk, which is influenced by the type of incident, the source, its rate of growth, and the ability to contain the damage. This, in turn, determines what notifications are required during the escalation process, and sets the scope and procedures for the investigation.

☒ **D** is incorrect because the analysis stage involves gathering data such as audit logs, video captures, human accounts of activities, etc., to try and figure out the root cause of the incident. The goals are to figure out who did this, how they did it, when they did it, and why. Management must be continually kept abreast of these activities because they will be the ones making the big decisions on how the incident is to be handled.

11. Which of the following is a correct statement regarding computer forensics?

    A. It is the study of computer technology.

    B. It is a set of hardware-specific processes that must be followed in order for evidence to be admissible in a court of law.

    C. It encompasses network and code analysis, and may be referred to as electronic data discovery.

    D. Computer forensics responsibilities should be assigned to a network administrator before an incident occurs.

☑ **C.** Forensics is a science and an art that requires specialized techniques for the recovery, authentication, and analysis of electronic data that could have been affected by a criminal act. It is the coming together of computer science, information technology, and engineering with the legal system. When discussing computer forensics with others, you might hear the terms digital forensics, network forensics, electronic data discovery, cyber forensics, and forensic computing. (ISC)² uses computer forensics as a synonym for all of these other terms, so that's what you will most likely see on the CISSP exam. Computer forensics encompasses all domains in which evidence is in a digital or electronic form, either in storage or on the wire.

☒ **A** is incorrect because computer forensics involves more than just the study of information technology. It encompasses the study of information technology but stretches into evidence gathering and protecting and working within specific legal systems.

☒ **B** is incorrect because computer forensics does not refer to hardware or software. It is a set of specific processes relating to reconstruction of computer usage, examination of residual data, authentication of data by technical analysis or explanation of technical features of data, and computer usage that must be followed in order for evidence to be admissible in a court of law.

☒ **D** is incorrect because computer forensics should be conducted by people with the proper training and skill set, which could or could not be the network administrator. Digital evidence can be fragile and must be worked with appropriately. If someone reboots the attacked system or inspects various files, it could corrupt viable evidence, change timestamps on key files, and erase footprints the criminal may have left.

12. Which of the following dictates that all evidence be labeled with information indicating who secured and validated it?

    A. Chain of custody

    B. Due care

    C. Investigation

    D. Motive, Opportunity, and Means

    ☑ **A.** A crucial piece in the digital forensics process is keeping a proper chain of custody of the evidence. Because evidence from these types of crimes can be very volatile and easily dismissed from court due to improper handling, it is important to follow very strict and organized procedures when collecting and tagging evidence in every single case. Furthermore, the chain of custody should follow evidence through its entire life cycle, beginning with identification and ending with its destruction, permanent archiving, or return to owner. When copies of data need to be made, this process must meet certain standards to ensure quality and reliability. Specialized software for this purpose can be used. The copies must be able to be independently verified and must be tamperproof. Each piece of evidence should be marked in some way with the date, time, initials of the collector, and a case number if one has been assigned. The piece of evidence should then be sealed in a container, which should be marked with the same information. The container should be sealed with evidence tape, and if possible, the writing should be on the tape so that a broken seal can be detected.

    ☒ **B** is incorrect because due care means to carry out activities that a reasonable person would be expected to carry out in the same situation. In short, due care means that a company practiced common sense and prudent management, and acted responsibly. If a company does not practice due care in its efforts to protect itself from computer crime, it can be found negligent and legally liable for damages. A chain of custody, on the other hand, is a history that shows how evidence was collected, analyzed, transported, and preserved in order to be presented in court. Because electronic evidence can be easily modified, a clearly defined chain of custody demonstrates that the evidence is trustworthy.

    ☒ **C** is incorrect because investigation involves the proper collection of relevant data during the incident response process and includes analysis, interpretation, reaction, and recovery. The goals of this stage are to reduce the impact of the incident, identify the cause of the incident, resume operations as soon as possible, and apply what was learned to prevent the incident from recurring. It is also at this stage where it is determined whether a forensics investigation will take place. The chain of custody dictates how this material should be properly collected and protected during its life cycle of being evidence.

☒ **D** is incorrect because Motive, Opportunity, and Means is a strategy used to understand why a crime was carried out and by whom. This is the same strategy used to determine the suspects in a traditional, noncomputer crime. Motive is the "who" and "why" of a crime. Understanding the motive for a crime is an important piece in figuring out who would engage in such an activity. For example, many hackers attack big-name sites because when the sites go down, it is splashed all over the news. However, once these activities are no longer so highly publicized, the individuals will eventually stop initiating these types of attacks because their motive will have been diminished. Opportunity is the "where" and "when" of a crime. Opportunities usually arise when certain vulnerabilities or weaknesses are present. If a company does not have a firewall, hackers and attackers have all types of opportunities within that network. Once a crime fighter finds out why a person would want to commit a crime (motive), she will look at what could allow the criminal to be successful (opportunity). Means pertains to the capabilities a criminal would need to be successful. Suppose a crime fighter was asked to investigate a complex embezzlement that took place within a financial institution. If the suspects were three people who knew how to use a mouse, a keyboard, and a word processing application, but only one of them was a programmer and system analyst, the crime fighter would realize that this person may have the means to commit this crime much more successfully than the other two individuals.

13. There are several categories of evidence. How is a witness's oral testimony categorized?

A. Best evidence

B. Secondary evidence

C. Circumstantial evidence

D. Conclusive evidence

☑ **B.** Several types of evidence can be used in a trial, such as written, oral, computer-generated, and visual or audio. Oral evidence is testimony of a witness. Visual or audio is usually a captured event during the crime or right after it. Not all evidence is equal in the eyes of the law and some types of evidence have more clout, or weight, than others. Secondary evidence is not viewed as reliable and strong in proving innocence or guilt (or liability in civil cases) when compared to best evidence. Oral evidence, such as a witness's testimony, and copies of original documents are placed in the secondary evidence category.

☒ **A is incorrect** because there is no firsthand reliable proof that supports oral evidence's validity. Best evidence is the primary evidence used in a trial because it provides the most reliability. An example of something that would be categorized as best evidence is an original signed contract.

☒ **C is incorrect** because circumstantial evidence can prove an intermediate fact that can then be used to deduce or assume the existence of another fact. This type of fact is used so the judge or jury will logically assume the existence of a primary fact. For example, if a suspect told a friend he was going to bring down eBay's Web site, a case could not rest on that piece of evidence alone because it is circumstantial. However, this evidence can cause the jury to assume that because the suspect said he was going to do it, and hours later it happened, maybe he was the one who did the crime.

☒ **D is incorrect** because conclusive evidence is irrefutable and cannot be contradicted. A witness's testimony can be refuted. Conclusive evidence is very strong all by itself and does not require corroboration.

14. For evidence to be legally admissible, it must be authentic, complete, sufficient, and reliable. Which characteristic refers to the evidence having a reasonable and sensible relationship to the findings?

    A. Complete

    B. Reliable

    C. Authentic

    D. Sufficient

☑ **C. It is important** that evidence be admissible, authentic, complete, sufficient, and reliable to the case at hand. These characteristics of evidence provide a foundation for a case and help ensure that the evidence is legally permissible. For evidence to be authentic, or relevant, it must have a reasonable and sensible relationship to the findings. If a judge rules that a person's past traffic tickets cannot be brought up in a murder trial, this means the judge has ruled that the traffic tickets are not relevant to the case at hand. Thus, the prosecuting lawyer cannot even mention them in court. In addition, authentic evidence must be original; that is, it cannot be a copy or a summary of the original.

☒ **A is incorrect** because evidence that is complete presents the whole truth. All evidence, even exculpatory evidence, must be handed over. This means that a prosecutor cannot present just part of the evidence that is favorable to his side of the case.

☒ **B** is incorrect because evidence that is reliable must be consistent with the facts. Evidence cannot be reliable if it is based on someone's opinion or copies of an original document, because there is too much room for error. Reliable evidence means it is factual and not circumstantial. Examples of unreliable evidence include computer-generated documentation and an investigator's notes because they can be modified without any indication.

☒ **D** is incorrect because evidence that is sufficient, or believable, is persuasive enough to convince a reasonable person of its validity. This means the evidence cannot be subject to personal interpretation. Sufficient evidence also means it cannot be easily doubted.

15. Which of the following best describes exigent circumstances?

    A. The methods used to capture a suspect's actions are neither legal nor ethical.

    B. Enticement is used to capture a suspect's actions.

    C. Hacking does not actually hurt anyone.

    D. The seizure of evidence by law enforcement because there is concern that a suspect will attempt to destroy it.

    ☑ **D.** Search and seizure activities can get tricky, depending on what is being searched for and where. In some circumstances, a law enforcement agent may seize evidence that is not included in the warrant, such as if the suspect tries to destroy the evidence. In other words, if there is an impending possibility that evidence might be destroyed, law enforcement may quickly seize the evidence to prevent its destruction. This is referred to as exigent circumstances, and a judge will later decide whether the seizure was proper and legal before allowing the evidence to be admitted. For example, if a police officer had a search warrant that allowed him to search a suspect's living room but no other rooms, and then he saw the suspect dumping cocaine down the toilet, the police officer could seize the cocaine even though it was in a room not covered under his search warrant.

    ☒ **A** is incorrect because entrapment is used to describe illegal and/or unethical methods that are used to capture a suspect's actions. For example, suppose a Web page has a link that indicates that if an individual clicks it, she could then download thousands of MP3 files for free. However, when she clicks that link, she is taken to the honeypot system instead, and the company records all of her actions and attempts to prosecute. Entrapment does not prove that the suspect had the intent to commit a crime; it only proves she was successfully tricked.

    ☒ **B** is incorrect because enticement means that legal and ethical means were used to capture a suspect's actions, as opposed to illegal and unethical methods, which are referred to as entrapment. A honeypot serves as a good example of enticement. Companies put systems in their screened subnets that either emulate services that attackers usually like to take advantage of or actually have the services enabled. The hope is that if an attacker breaks into the company's network, she will go right to the honeypot instead of the systems that are actual production machines. The attacker will be enticed to go to the honeypot system because it has many open ports and services running and exhibits vulnerabilities that the attacker would want to exploit. The company can log the attacker's actions and later attempt to prosecute.

☒ C is incorrect because the idea that hacking does not actually hurt anyone is a common ethical fallacy. It is used by some in the computing world to justify unethical acts, such as capturing passwords and using them to gain unauthorized access to network resources. The phrase does not define exigent circumstances.

16. What role does the Internet Architecture Board play regarding technology and ethics?

    A. It creates criminal sentencing guidelines.

    B. It issues ethics-related statements concerning the use of the Internet.

    C. It edits Request for Comments.

    D. It maintains ten commandments for ethical behavior.

☑ D. The Internet Architecture Board (IAB) is the coordinating committee for Internet design, engineering, and management. It is responsible for the architectural oversight of the Internet Engineering Task Force (IETF) activities, Internet Standards Process oversight and appeal, and editor of Request for Comments (RFCs). The IAB issues ethics-related statements concerning the use of the Internet. It considers the Internet to be a resource that depends upon availability and accessibility to be useful to a wide range of people. It is mainly concerned with irresponsible acts on the Internet that could threaten its existence or negatively affect others. It sees the Internet as a great gift and works hard to protect it for all who depend upon it. The IAB sees the use of the Internet as a privilege, which should be treated as such and used with respect.

☒ A is incorrect because the Federal Sentencing Guidelines are rules used by judges when determining the proper punitive sentences for specific felonies or misdemeanors that individuals or corporations commit. The guidelines work as a uniform sentencing policy for entities that carry out felonies and/ or serious misdemeanors in the U.S. federal court system. The IAB does not have anything to do with these topics.

☒ **C** is incorrect because, while the Internet Architecture Board is responsible for editing Request for Comments (RFCs), this task is not related to ethics. This answer is a distracter.

☒ **D** is incorrect because the Computer Ethics Institute is a nonprofit organization that works to help advance technology by ethical means. The Computer Ethics Institute has developed its own Ten Commandments of Computer Ethics:

1. Thou shalt not use a computer to harm other people.

2. Thou shalt not interfere with other people's computer work.

3. Thou shalt not snoop around in other people's computer files.

4. Thou shalt not use a computer to steal.

5. Thou shalt not use a computer to bear false witness.

6. Thou shalt not copy or use proprietary software for which you have not paid.

7. Thou shalt not use other people's computer resources without authorization or proper compensation.

8. Thou shalt not appropriate other people's intellectual output.

9. Thou shalt think about the social consequences of the program you are writing or the system you are designing.

10. Thou shalt always use a computer in ways that ensure consideration and respect for your fellow humans.

17. Which of the following statements is not true of dumpster diving?

A. It is legal.

B. It is unethical.

C. It is illegal.

D. It is a nontechnical attack.

☑ **C.** Dumpster diving refers to the concept of rummaging through a company's or individual's garbage for discarded documents, information, and other precious items that could then be used in an attack against that person or company. Dumpster diving is legal. Trespassing is illegal, however, and may be done in the process of dumpster diving. Industrial spies can raid corporate dumpsters to find proprietary and confidential information. Credit card thieves can go through dumpsters to retrieve credit card information from discarded receipts. Phreakers have been known to dumpster-dive at telephone companies, hoping to find manuals on how the internals of the telephone systems work.

☒ **A** is incorrect because dumpster diving is considered legal. Trespassing, on the other hand, is illegal. While the area where garbage is kept is usually not highly guarded, physical access to the premises is required and dumpsters are often located on private property. Trespassing laws concerning dumpster diving vary in different states, as well as how rigorously they are upheld.

☒ **B** is incorrect because dumpster diving is perceived as unethical if used for malicious purposes. Just because something is legal, like dumpster diving, does not make it right. An interesting relationship exists between law and ethics. Most often, laws are based on ethics and are put in place to ensure that others act in an ethical way. However, laws do not apply to everything— that is when ethics should apply. Some things may not be illegal, but that does not necessarily mean they are ethical.

☒ **D** is incorrect because it is true that dumpster diving is a nontechnical attack. Dumpster diving is the act of going through someone's trash with the hope of uncovering useful information.

18. Which of the following is a legal form of eavesdropping when performed with prior consent or a warrant?

    A. Denial of Service

    B. Dumpster diving

    C. Wiretapping

    D. Data diddling

☑ **C.** Most communications signals are vulnerable to some type of wiretapping or eavesdropping. It can usually be done undetected and is referred to as a passive attack. Tools used to intercept communications include cellular scanners, radio receivers, microphone receivers, tape recorders, network sniffers, and telephone-tapping devices. It is illegal to intentionally eavesdrop on another person's conversation under many countries' existing wiretap laws. In many cases, this action is only acceptable if the person consents or there is a court order allowing law enforcement to perform these types of activities. Under the latter circumstances, the law enforcement officers must show probable cause to support their allegation that criminal activity is taking place and can only listen to relevant conversations. These requirements are in place to protect an individual's privacy rights.

☒ **A** is incorrect because Denial of Service (DoS) is an attack, not a form of eavesdropping. A DoS has the intent of overwhelming a victim system so that it can no longer carry out its intended functionality.

☒ **B** is incorrect because dumpster diving is legal unless it involves trespassing. Dumpster diving refers to going through someone's trash to find confidential or useful information. This is not considered a type of eavesdropping.

☒ **D** is incorrect because data diddling is the act of willfully modifying information, programs, or documentation in an effort to commit fraud or disrupt production. Many times, this modification happens before the data is entered into an application or as soon as it completes processing and is outputted from an application. For instance, if a loan processor is entering information for a customer's loan of $100,000, but instead enters $150,000 and then moves the extra approved money somewhere else, this would be a case of data diddling.

19. What type of common law deals with violations committed by individuals against government laws, which are created to protect the public?

   A. Criminal law

   B. Civil law

   C. Tort law

   D. Regulatory law

☑ **A.** Criminal law is used when an individual's conduct violates the government's laws, which have been developed to protect the public. Jail sentences are commonly the punishment for criminal law cases, whereas in civil law cases the punishment is usually an amount of money that the liable individual must pay the victim. For example, in the O.J. Simpson case, he was first tried and found not guilty in the criminal law case, but then was found liable in the civil law case. This seeming contradiction can happen because the burden of proof is lower in civil cases than in criminal cases.

☒ **B** is incorrect because civil law deals with wrongs against individuals or companies that result in damages or loss. This is referred to as tort law. Examples include trespassing, betray, negligence, and products liability. A civil lawsuit would result in financial restitution and/or community service instead of jail sentences. When someone sues another person in civil court, the jury decides upon liability instead of innocence or guilt. If the jury determines the defendant is liable for the act, then the jury decides upon the punitive damages of the case.

☒ **C** is incorrect because tort law is another name for civil law, which deals with wrongs committed against individuals or companies that result in injury or damages. Civil law does not use prison time as a punishment, but usually requires financial restitution.

☒ **D** is incorrect because regulatory law deals with regulatory standards that regulate performance and conduct. Government agencies create these standards, which are applied to companies and organizations within those specific industries. Some examples of regulatory laws could be that every building used for business must have a fire detection and suppression system, must have easily seen exit signs, and cannot have blocked doors, in case of a fire. Companies that produce and package food and drug products are regulated by many standards so the public is protected and aware of their actions.

20. During what stage of incident response is it determined if the source of the incident was internal or external, and how the offender penetrated and gained access to the asset?

   A. Analysis

   B. Containment

   C. Tracking

   D. Follow-up

☑ **C.** Incident response begins with triage. During triage, the scope and severity of the incident is assessed. If it is determined that an incident has indeed occurred, then the incident response team moves to the investigation stage. This stage involves the collection of data, as well as analysis, interpretation, reaction, and recovery. The next stage is containment. The team isolates the systems involved in the incident to buy time to conduct a full investigation. During analysis, more data is collected and analyzed to determine the root cause of the incident. Once we have as much information as we can get in the analysis stage and answered as many questions as we can, we then move to the tracking stage. We determine if the source of the incident was internal or external and how the offender penetrated and gained access to the asset.

☒ **A** is incorrect because during analysis data is gathered (audit logs, video captures, human accounts of activities, system activities) to try to figure out the root cause of the incident.

☒ **B** is incorrect because the purpose of containment is to isolate the incident to prevent further damage and buy the incident response team time to conduct their investigation.

☒ **D** is incorrect because the follow-up or recovery stage occurs after the incident is understood. It involves implementing the necessary fix to ensure this type of incident cannot happen again. This may require blocking certain ports, deactivating vulnerable services or functionalities, switching over to another processing facility, or applying a patch. This is properly called "following recovery procedures," because just arbitrarily making a change to the environment may introduce more problems. The recovery procedures may state that a new image needs to be installed, backup data need to be restored, the system needs to be tested, and all configurations are properly set.

21. Which of the following is not true of a forensics investigation?

    A. The crime scene should be modified as necessary.

    B. A file copy tool may not recover all data areas of the device that are necessary for investigation.

    C. Contamination of the crime scene may not negate derived evidence, but it should still be documented.

    D. Only individuals with knowledge of basic crime scene analysis should have access to the crime scene.

    ☑ A. The principles of criminalistics are included in the forensic investigation process. They are identification of the crime scene, protection of the environment against contamination and loss of evidence, identification of evidence and potential sources of evidence, and collection of evidence. In regard to minimizing the degree of contamination, it is important to understand that it is impossible not to change a crime scene—be it physical or digital. The key is to minimize changes and document what you did and why, and how the crime scene was affected.

    ☒ B is incorrect because it is true that a file copy tool may not recover all data areas of the device necessary for investigation. During the examination and analysis process of a forensics investigation, it is critical that the investigator works from an image that contains all of the data from the original disk. It must be a bit-level copy, sector by sector, to capture deleted files, slack spaces, and unallocated clusters. These types of images can be created through the use of specialized tools such as FTK Imager, DD, EnCase, and Safeback, or the -dd Unix utility.

    ☒ C is incorrect because it is true that if a crime scene becomes contaminated, that should be documented. While it may not negate the derived evidence, it will make investigating the crime and providing useful evidence for court more challenging. Whether the crime scene is physical or digital, it is important to control who comes in contact with the evidence of the crime to ensure its integrity.

    ☒ D is incorrect because the statement is true. Only authorized individuals should be allowed to access the crime scene, and these individuals should have knowledge of basic crime scene analysis. Other measures to protect the crime scene include documenting who is at the crime scene and the last individuals to interact with the system. In court, the integrity of the evidence may be in question if there are too many people milling around.

22. Great care must be taken to capture clues from a computer or device during a forensics exercise. Which of the following does not correctly describe the efforts that should be taken to protect an image?

A. The original image should be hashed with MD5 or SHA-256.

B. Two time-stamps should be created.

C. New media should be properly purged before images are created on them.

D. Some systems must be imaged while they are running.

☑ **D.** Acquiring evidence on live systems and those using network storage complicates matters because you cannot turn off the system in order to make a copy of the hard drive. Business-critical systems commonly cannot suffer downtime. So these systems and others, such as those using on-the-fly encryption, must be imaged while they are running. Thus, the answer, "Some systems must be imaged while they are running," is correct in and of itself. However, this measure is not one that is taken to protect an image, as the question specifies. It is taken to avoid interrupting business operations.

☒ **A** is incorrect because hashing the original image with MD5 or SHA-256 is a measure that is taken to protect the original image during the investigative process. To ensure that the original image is not modified, it is important to create message digests for files and directories before and after the analysis to prove the integrity of the original image. MD5 and SHA-256 are just two of the hashing algorithms that can be used to ensure the integrity of image data.

☒ **B** is incorrect because two time-stamps should be created to ensure the integrity of the data during the investigative process. The original media should have two copies created: a primary image (a control copy that is stored in a library) and a working image (used for analysis and evidence collection). These should be time-stamped to show when the evidence was collected. The investigator works from the duplicate image because it preserves the original evidence, prevents inadvertent alteration of original evidence during examination, and allows re-creation of the duplicate image if necessary.

☒ **C** is incorrect because when newly created images need to be saved to a new medium, the medium has to be "clean" of any residual data. Purging a new medium before an image is created and saved to it is a necessary measure to ensure that any old data does not contaminate the images. The investigator must make sure the new medium has been properly purged, meaning it does not contain any residual data. Some incidents have occurred where drives that were new and right out of the box (shrink-wrapped) contained old data not purged by the vendor.

23. Which of the following attacks can be best prevented by limiting the amount of electrical signals emitted from a computer system?

    A. Salami attack

    B. Emanations capturing

    C. Password sniffing

    D. IP spoofing

    ☑ B. Every electrical device emits electrical radiation into the surrounding environment. These waves contain information, comparable to how wireless technologies work. This radiation can be carried over a distance, depending on the strength of the signals and the material and objects in the surrounding area. Attackers have used devices to capture this radiation and port them to their own computer systems so that they can access information not intended for them. Companies that have information of such sensitive nature that attackers would go through this much trouble usually have special computer systems with shielding that permit only a small amount of electrical signals to be emitted. The companies can also use material within the walls of the building to stop these types of electrical waves from passing through them.

    ☒ A is incorrect because a salami attack is one in which the attacker commits several small crimes with the hope that the overall larger crime will go unnoticed. It has nothing necessarily to do with electrical signals. Salami attacks usually take place in the accounting departments of companies, and the most common example of a salami attack involves subtracting a small amount of funds from many accounts with the hope that such an insignificant amount would be overlooked. For example, a bank employee may alter a banking software program to subtract 5 cents from each of the bank's customers' accounts once a month and move this amount to the employee's bank account. If this happened to all of the bank's 50,000 customer accounts, the intruder could make up to $30,000 a year.

    ☒ C is incorrect because password sniffing involves sniffing network traffic with the hope of capturing passwords being sent between computers or devices. It has nothing necessarily to do with capturing electrical signals. Capturing a password is tricky, because it is a piece of data that is usually only used when a user wants to authenticate into a domain or access a resource. Some systems and applications do send passwords over the network in cleartext, but a majority of them do not anymore. Instead, the user's workstation performs a one-way hashing function on the password and sends only the resulting value to the authenticating system or service. The authenticating system has a file containing all users' password hash values, not the passwords themselves, and when the authenticating system is asked to verify a user's password, it compares the hashing value sent to what it has in its file.

☒ **D** is incorrect because IP spoofing does not involve the capturing of electrical signals. IP spoofing involves either manually changing the IP address within a packet to show a different address or, more commonly, using a tool that is programmed to provide this functionality for the attacker. Several attacks that take place use spoofed IP addresses, which give the victim little hope of finding the real system and individual who initiated the attack.

24. As a CISSP candidate, you must sign a Code of Ethics. Which of the following is from the (ISC)^2 Code of Ethics for the CISSP?

   A. Information should be shared freely and openly; thus, sharing confidential information should be ethical.

   B. Think about the social consequences of the program you are writing or the system you are designing.

   C. Discourage unnecessary fear or doubt.

   D. Do not participate in Internet-wide experiments in a negligent manner.

☑ **C.** (ISC)^2 requires all certified system security professionals to commit to fully supporting its Code of Ethics. If a CISSP intentionally or knowingly violates this Code of Ethics, he or she may be subject to a peer review panel, which will decide whether the certification should be relinquished. The following list is an overview, but each CISSP candidate should read the full version and understand the Code of Ethics before attempting this exam:

   - Act honorably, honestly, justly, responsibly, and legally, and protect society.

   - Work diligently, provide competent services, and advance the security profession.

   - Encourage the growth of research—teach, mentor, and value the certification.

   - Discourage unnecessary fear or doubt, and do not consent to bad practices.

   - Discourage unsafe practices, and preserve and strengthen the integrity of public infrastructures.

- Observe and abide by all contracts, expressed or implied, and give prudent advice.

- Avoid any conflict of interest, respect the trust that others put in you, and take on only those jobs you are fully qualified to perform.

- Stay current on skills, and do not become involved with activities that could injure the reputation of other security professionals.

☒ **A** is incorrect because it is not an ethics statement within the (ISC)^2 canons. It is an ethical fallacy used by many in the computing world to justify unethical acts. Some people in the industry feel as though all information should be available to all people; thus, they might release sensitive information to the world that was not theirs to release because they feel as though they are doing something right.

☒ **B** is incorrect because the statement is from the Computer Ethics Institute's Ten Commandments of Computer Ethics, not the (ISC)^2 canons. The Computer Ethics Institute is a nonprofit organization that works to help advance technology by ethical means.

☒ **D** is incorrect because it is an ethics statement issued by the Internet Architecture Board (IAB). The IAB issues ethics-related statements concerning the use of the Internet. It considers the Internet to be a resource that depends upon availability and accessibility to be useful to a wide range of people. It is mainly concerned with irresponsible acts on the Internet that could threaten its existence or negatively affect others. It sees the Internet as a great gift and works hard to protect it for all who depend upon it.

25. What concept states that a criminal leaves something behind and takes something with them?

    A. Modus Operandi

    B. Profiling

    C. Locard's Principle of Exchange

    D. Motive, Opportunity, and Means

    ☑ **C.** Locard's Principle of Exchange provides information that is useful for profiling. The principle states that a criminal leaves something behind and takes something with him. This principle is the foundation of criminalistics. Even in an entirely digital crime scene, Locard's Principle of Exchange can shed light on who the perpetrator(s) may be.

    ☒ **A** is incorrect because Modus Operandi (MO) refers to a distinct method criminals use to carry out their crime that can be used to help identify them. For example, an MO for computer criminals may include the use of specific hacking tools, or targeting specific systems or networks. The method usually involves repetitive signature behaviors, such as sending e-mail messages or programming syntax. Knowledge of the criminal's MO and signature behaviors can be useful throughout the investigative process. Law enforcement can use the information to identify other offenses by the same criminal, for example.

☒ **B** is incorrect because profiling (or psychological crime scene analysis) is an investigative technique that involves developing behavioral or characteristic patterns of an attacker who has not been caught. By creating an outline of an attacker's characteristics, the investigative team may gain insight into the attacker's thought processes that can then be used to identify him or, at the very least, the tool he used to conduct the crime. Locard's Principle of Exchange, which states that a criminal leaves something behind and takes something with him, provides information that is useful for profiling.

☒ **D** is incorrect because Motive, Opportunity, and Means is a strategy used to determine the suspects of a crime. Motive refers to the "who" and "why" of a crime. Determining the motive for a crime can help investigators identify who would carry out the activity. Opportunity refers to the "where" and "when" of a crime. This is usually a vulnerability or weakness in the environment that allowed the criminal to be successful. Means refers to the capabilities required for the criminal's activities to be successful. Does the criminal have the skills required to hack into a system, for example?

26. Which of the following was the first international treaty seeking to address computer crimes by coordinating national laws and improving investigative techniques and international cooperation?

   A. Council of Global Convention on Cybercrime

   B. Council of Europe Convention on Cybercrime

   C. Organisation for Economic Co-operation and Development

   D. Organisation for Cybercrime Co-operation and Development

   ☑ **B.** The Council of Europe (CoE) Convention on Cybercrime is one example of an attempt to create a standard international response to cybercrime. It is the first international treaty seeking to address computer crimes by coordinating national laws and improving investigative techniques and international cooperation. The convention's objectives include the creation of a framework for establishing jurisdiction and extradition of the accused. For example, extradition can only take place when the event is a crime in both jurisdictions.

   ☒ **A** is incorrect because it is a distracter answer. The official name for the treaty is Council of Europe Convention on Cybercrime. It serves as a guideline for any country developing comprehensive national legislation against cybercrime and as a framework for international cooperation between state parties to this treaty.

☒ C is incorrect because the Organisation for Economic Co-operation and Development (OECD) is an international organization that helps different governments come together and tackle the economic, social, and governance challenges of a globalized economy. Because of this, the OECD came up with guidelines for the various countries to follow so that data are properly protected and everyone follows the same type of rules.

☒ D is incorrect because this is a distracter answer. There is no official entity with this name.

27. Lee is a new security manager who is in charge of ensuring that his company complies with the European Union Principles on Privacy when his company is interacting with their European partners. The set of principles that deals with transmitting data considered private is encompassed within which of the following laws or regulations?

A. Data Protection Directive

B. Organisation for Economic Co-operation and Development

C. Federal Private Bill

D. Privacy Protection Law

☑ A. The European Union (EU) in many cases takes individual privacy much more seriously than most other countries in the world, so they have strict laws pertaining to data that are considered private, which are based on the European Union Principles on Privacy. This set of principles addresses using and transmitting information considered private in nature. The principles and how they are to be followed are encompassed within the EU's Data Protection Directive. All states in Europe must abide by these principles to be in compliance, and any company wanting to do business with an EU company, which will include exchanging privacy type of data, must comply with this directive.

☒ B is incorrect because the Organisation for Economic Co-operation and Development (OECD) is an international organization that helps different governments come together and tackle the economic, social, and governance challenges of a globalized economy. Because of this, the OECD came up with guidelines for the various countries to follow so that data are properly protected and everyone follows the same type of rules.

☒ C is incorrect because this is a distracter answer. There is no official bill with this name.

☒ D is incorrect because this is a distracter answer. There is no official law with this name.

28. The common law system is broken down into which of the following categories?

A. Common, civil, criminal

B. Legislation, bills, regulatory

C. Civil, criminal, regulatory

D. Legislation, bills, civil

☑ C. The common law system is broken down into the following:

- Criminal

  - Based on common law, statutory law, or a combination of both.

  - Addresses behavior that is considered harmful to society.

  - Punishment usually involves a loss of freedom, such as incarceration, or monetary fines.

- Civil/tort

  - Offshoot of criminal law.

  - Under civil law, the defendant owes a legal duty to the victim. In other words, the defendant is obligated to conform to a particular standard of conduct, usually set by what a "reasonable man of ordinary prudence" would do to prevent foreseeable injury to the victim.

- Administrative (regulatory)

  - Laws and legal principles created by administrative agencies to address a number of areas, including international trade, manufacturing, environment, and immigration.

☒ A is incorrect because it only lists two categories of a common law system and incorrectly lists the third category as "common." The correct third category is regulatory.

☒ B is incorrect because this answer does not list categories of a legal system. Legislation (or "statutory law") is law that has been enacted by a legislature or other governing body. A bill is a proposed law under consideration by a legislature. Regulatory relates to administrative regulation laws that are enforced by a governing body. These are components that make up a legal system, but do not represent the specific categories of a common law system.

☒ D is incorrect because this answer does not list categories of a legal system. Legislation (or "statutory law") is law that has been enacted by a legislature or other governing body. A bill is a proposed law under consideration by a legislature. The answer does list civil, which is one category of the common law system.

29. Privacy is becoming more threatened as the world relies more and more on technology. There are several approaches to addressing privacy, including the generic approach and regulation by industry. Which of the following best describes these two approaches?

    A. The generic approach is vertical enactment. Regulation by industry is horizontal enactment.

    B. The generic approach is horizontal enactment. Regulation by industry is vertical enactment.

    C. The generic approach is government enforced. Regulation by industry is self-enforced.

    D. The generic approach is self-enforced. Regulation by industry is government enforced.

    ☑ **B.** The generic approach is horizontal enactment—rules that stretch across all industry boundaries. It affects all industries, including government. Regulation by industry is vertical enactment. It defines requirements for specific verticals, such as the financial sector and health care.

    ☒ **A** is incorrect because the generic approach is horizontal enactment. Regulation by industry is vertical enactment. This answer has the two definitions switched.

    ☒ **C** is incorrect because generic and vertical approaches to regulatory enforcement can be government or industry. Generic just means that privacy protection is enforced across various industries. Vertical means that privacy protection is specific to one industry.

    ☒ **D** is incorrect because generic and vertical approaches can be enforced by the government or carried out through self-enforcement. The terms "generic" and "vertical" have nothing to do with who enforces the privacy protection rules; they just specify if a specific industry is targeted or if the rules apply to several industries in the same manner.

The following scenario will be used for questions 30 and 31.

Stephanie has been put in charge of developing incident response and forensics procedures her company needs to carry out if an incident occurs. She needs to ensure that their procedures map to the international principles for gathering and protecting digital evidence. She also needs to ensure that if and when internal forensics teams are deployed, they have labels, tags, evidence bags, cable ties, imaging software, and other associated tools.

30. Which of the following best describes the organization that developed the best practices that Stephanie needs to ensure her company's procedures map to?

    A. Internet Activities Board

    B. International Organization on Computer Evidence

    C. Department of Defense Forensics Committee

    D. International Forensics Standards Board

    ☑ **B.** The International Organization on Computer Evidence (IOCE) was appointed to draw up international principles for the procedures relating to digital evidence, to ensure the harmonization of methods and practices among nations, and to guarantee the ability to use digital evidence collected by one national state in the courts of another state. The principles developed by IOCE for the standardized recovery of computer-based evidence are governed by the following attributes:

    - Consistency with all legal systems

    - Allowance for the use of a common language

    - Durability

    - Ability to cross international and state boundaries

    - Ability to instill confidence in the integrity of evidence

    - Applicability to all forensic evidence

    - Applicability at every level, including that of individual, agency, and country

    ☒ **A** is incorrect because the Internet Architecture Board (IAB) is the coordinating committee for Internet design, engineering, and management. It is responsible for the architectural oversight of the Internet Engineering Task Force (IETF) activities, Internet Standards Process oversight and appeal, and editor of Request for Comments (RFCs). This organization used to be called the Internet Activities Board but now goes under the new name of Internet Architecture Board.

    ☒ **C** is incorrect because this is a distracter answer. There is no official group with this name.

    ☒ **D** is incorrect because this is a distracter answer. There is no official group with this name.

31. Which of the following best describes what Stephanie needs to build for the deployment teams?

    A. Local and remote imaging system

    B. Forensics field kit

C. Chain of custody procedures and tools

D. Digital evidence collection software

☑ **B.** When forensics teams are deployed to investigate a potential crime, they should be properly equipped with all of the tools and supplies needed. The following are some of the common items in the forensics field kits:

- Documentation tools—Tags, labels, and timelined forms
- Disassembly and removal tools—Antistatic bands, pliers, tweezers, screwdrivers, wire cutters, and so on
- Package and transport supplies—Antistatic bags, evidence bags and tape, cable ties, and others

☒ **A** is incorrect because imaging software and tools only make up some of the tools that a forensics team needs. These types of tools do not include the items identified in the question, which are labels, tags, evidence bags, cable ties, imaging software, and other associated tools. These items should be organized and be in a field kit.

☒ **C** is incorrect because chain of custody procedures and tools only make up some of the components that a forensics team needs. These types of tools do not include the items identified in the question, which are labels, tags, evidence bags, cable ties, imaging software, and other associated tools. These items should be organized and be in a field kit. A chain of custody is a history that shows how evidence was collected, analyzed, transported, and preserved in order to be presented in court. Because electronic evidence can be easily modified, a clearly defined chain of custody demonstrates that the evidence is trustworthy.

☒ **D** is incorrect because digital evidence collection tools only make up some of the components that a forensics team needs. These types of tools do not include the items identified in the question, which are labels, tags, evidence bags, cable ties, imaging software, and other associated tools. These items should be organized and be in a field kit. There are specialized software suites that allow forensics personnel to properly collect, analyze, and manage digital evidence through its life cycle. They are important, but only one component of an overall forensics kit.

Software Development Security

This domain includes questions from the following topics:

- Common software development issues
- Software development life cycles
- Secure software development approaches
- Change control and configuration management
- Programming language types
- Database concepts and security issues
- Expert systems and artificial intelligence
- Malware types and attacks

Security is often—mistakenly—an afterthought when it comes to software development. Patches and hot fixes are created after vulnerabilities put assets at risk, and are band-aid solutions to deeper problems. Adding security after an application or computer system is developed is not only less effective at protecting the product against threats but also more costly. Incorporating security throughout the software development life cycle and integrating security measures within the code itself ensures a functional and protected product. As a CISSP, you must understand application security controls and the vulnerabilities that occur in their absence.

1. Data marts, databases, and data warehouses have distinct characteristics. Which of the following does not correctly describe a data warehouse?

   A. It could increase the risk of privacy violations.

   B. It is developed to carry out analysis.

   C. It contains data from several different sources.

   D. It is created and used for project-based tactical reasons.

2. Database software should meet the requirements of what is known as the ACID test. Why should database software carry out atomic transactions, which is one requirement of the ACID test, when OLTP is used?

   A. So that the rules for database integrity can be established

   B. So that the database performs transactions as a single unit without interruption

   C. To ensure that rollbacks cannot take place

   D. To prevent concurrent processes from interacting with each other

3. Lisa has learned that most databases implement concurrency controls. What is concurrency, and why must it be controlled?

   A. Processes running at different levels, which can negatively affect the integrity of the database if not properly controlled.

   B. The ability to deduce new information from reviewing accessible data, which can allow an inference attack to take place.

   C. Processes running simultaneously, which can negatively affect the integrity of the database if not properly controlled.

   D. Storing data in more than one place within a database, which can negatively affect the integrity of the database if not properly controlled.

4. Robert has been asked to increase the overall efficiency of the sales database by implementing a procedure that structures data to minimize duplication and inconsistencies. What procedure is this?

   A. Polymorphism

   B. Normalization

   C. Implementation of database views

   D. Constructing schema

5. Which of the following correctly best describes an object-oriented database?

   A. When an application queries for data, it receives both the data and the procedure.

   B. It is structured similarly to a mesh network for redundancy and fast data retrieval.

C. Subject must have knowledge of the well-defined access path in order to access data.

D. The relationships between data entities provide the framework for organizing data.

6. Fred has been told he needs to test a component of the new content management application under development to validate its data structure, logic, and boundary conditions. What type of testing should he carry out?

A. Acceptance testing

B. Regression testing

C. Integration testing

D. Unit testing

7. Which of the following is the best description of a component-based system development method?

A. Components periodically revisit previous stages to update and verify design requirements

B. Minimizes the use of arbitrary transfer control statements between components

C. Uses independent and standardized modules that are assembled into serviceable programs

D. Implemented in module-based scenarios requiring rapid adaptations to changing client requirements

8. There are many types of viruses that hackers can use to damage systems. Which of the following is not a correct description of a polymorphic virus?

A. Intercepts antivirus's call to the operating system for file and system information

B. Varies the sequence of its instructions using noise, a mutation engine, or random-number generator

C. Can use different encryption schemes requiring different decryption routines

D. Produces multiple, varied copies of itself

9. Which of the following best describes the role of the Java Virtual Machine in the execution of Java applets?

A. Converts the source code into bytecode and blocks the sandbox

B. Converts the bytecode into machine-level code

C. Operates only on specific processors within specific operating systems

D. Develops the applets, which run in a user's browser

10. What type of database software integrity service guarantees that tuples are uniquely identified by primary key values?

    A. Concurrent integrity

    B. Referential integrity

    C. Entity integrity

    D. Semantic integrity

11. In computer programming, cohesion and coupling are used to describe modules of code. Which of the following is a favorable combination of cohesion and coupling?

    A. Low cohesion, low coupling

    B. High cohesion, high coupling

    C. Low cohesion, high coupling

    D. High cohesion, low coupling

12. When an organization is unsure of the final nature of the product, what type of system development method is most appropriate for them?

    A. Cleanroom

    B. Exploratory Model

    C. Modified Prototype Method

    D. Iterative Development

13. Which of the following statements does not correctly describe SOAP and Remote Procedure Calls?

    A. SOAP was designed to overcome the compatibility and security issues associated with Remote Procedure Calls.

    B. Both SOAP and Remote Procedure Calls were created to enable application-layer communication.

    C. SOAP enables the use of Remote Procedure Calls for information exchange between applications over the Internet.

    D. HTTP was not designed to work with Remote Procedure Calls, but SOAP was designed to work with HTTP.

14. Computer programs that are based on human logic by using "if/then" statements and inference engines are called _____.

    A. Expert systems

    B. Artificial neural networks

    C. Distributed Computing Environment

    D. Enterprise JavaBeans

15. Which of the following is a correct description of the pros and cons associated with third-generation programming languages?

    A. The use of heuristics reduced programming effort, but the amount of manual coding for a specific task is usually more than the preceding generation.

    B. The use of syntax similar to human language reduced development time, but the language is resource intensive.

    C. The use of binary was extremely time consuming but resulted in fewer errors.

    D. The use of symbols reduced programming time, but the language required knowledge of machine architecture.

16. Which of the following is considered the second generation of programming languages?

    A. Machine

    B. Very high-level

    C. High-level

    D. Assembly

17. Mary is creating malicious code that will steal a user's cookies by modifying the original client-side Java script. What type of cross-site scripting vulnerability is she exploiting?

    A. Second order

    B. DOM-based

    C. Persistent

    D. Nonpersistent

18. Of the following steps that describe the development of a botnet, which best describes the step that comes first?

    A. Infected server sends attack commands to the botnet.

    B. Spammer pays a hacker for use of a botnet.

    C. Controller server instructs infected systems to send spam to mail servers.

    D. Malicious code is sent out that has bot software as its payload.

19. Which of the following antivirus detection methods is the most recent to the industry and monitors suspicious code as it executes within the operating system?

    A. Behavior blocking

    B. Fingerprint detection

    C. Signature-based detection

    D. Heuristic detection

20. Which of the following describes object-oriented programming deferred commitment?

   A. Autonomous objects, which cooperate through exchanges of messages

   B. The internal components of an object can be refined without changing other parts of the system

   C. Object-oriented analysis, design, and modeling maps to business needs and solutions

   D. Other programs using same objects

21. What object-oriented programming term, or concept, is illustrated in the graphic that follows?

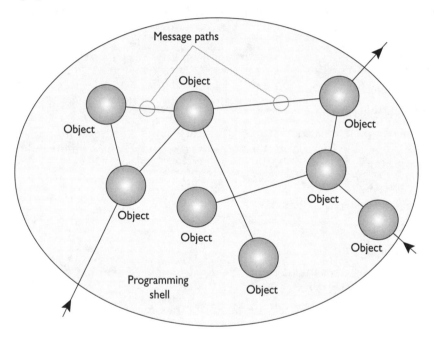

   A. Methods

   B. Messages

   C. Abstraction

   D. Data hiding

22. Protection methods can be integrated into software programs. What type of protection method is illustrated in the graphic that follows?

   A. Polymorphism

   B. Polyinstantiation

C. Cohesiveness

D. Object classes

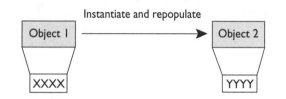

Level	Ship	Cargo	Origin	Destination
Top secret	Oklahoma	Weapons	Delaware	Ukraine
Unclassified	Oklahoma	Food	Delaware	Africa

23. There are several types of attacks that programmers need to be aware of. What attack does the graphic that follows illustrate?

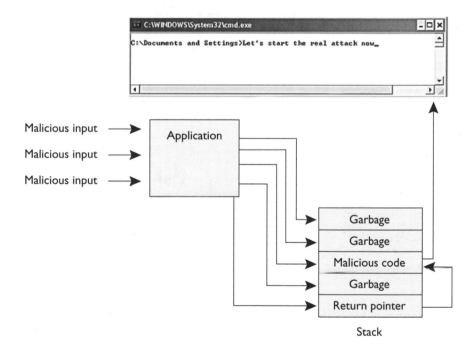

A. Traffic analysis

B. Race condition

C. Covert storage

D. Buffer overflow

24. Databases and applications commonly carry out the function that is illustrated in the graphic that follows. Which of the following best describes the concept that this graphic is showing?

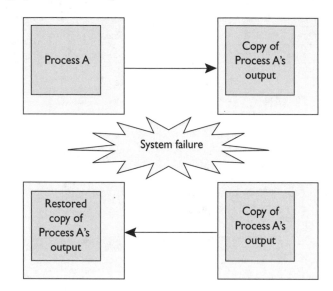

A. Checkpoint

B. Commit

C. Two-phase commit

D. Data dictionary

25. There are several different types of databases. Which type does the graphic that follows illustrate?

A. Relational

B. Hierarchical

C. Network

D. Object-oriented

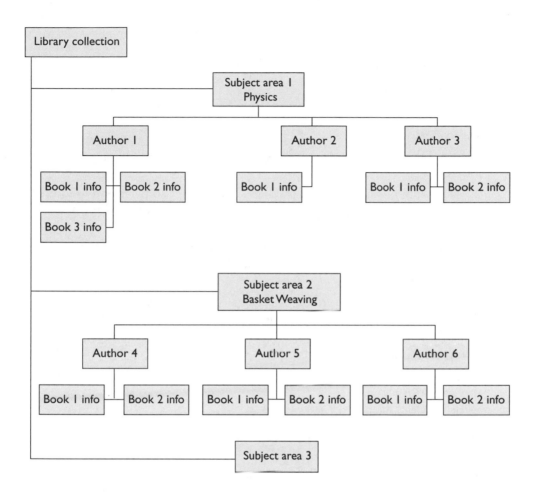

The following scenario will be used for questions 26, 27, and 28.

Trent is the new manager of his company's internal software development department. He has been told by his management that the group needs to be compliant with the international standard that provides guidance to organizations in integrating security into the processes used for managing their applications. His new boss told him that he should join and get familiar with the Web Application Security Consortium, and Trent just received an e-mail stating that one of the company's currently deployed applications has a zero day vulnerability.

26. Which of the following is most likely the standard Trent's company wants to comply with?

    A. ISO/IEC 27005

    B. ISO/IEC 27001

    C. ISO/IEC 27034

    D. BS 7799

27. Which of the following best describes the consortium Trent's boss wants him to join?

    A. Nonprofit organization that produces open-source software and follows widely agreed upon best-practice security standards for the World Wide Web.

    B. U.S. DHS group that provides best practices, tools, guidelines, rules, principles, and other resources for software developers, architects, and security practitioners to use.

    C. Group of experts who create proprietary software tools used to help improve the security of software worldwide.

    D. Group of experts and organizations who certify products based on an agreed-upon security criteria.

28. Which of the following best describes the type of vulnerability mentioned in this scenario?

    A. Dynamic vulnerability that is polymorphic

    B. Static vulnerability that is exploited by server-side injection parameters

    C. Vulnerability that does not currently have an associated solution

    D. Database vulnerability that directly affects concurrency

29. _____ provides a machine-readable description of the specific operations provided by a specific Web service. _____ provides a method for Web services to be registered by service providers and located by service consumers.

    A. Web Services Description Language, Universal Description, Discovery and Integration

    B. Universal Description, Discovery and Integration, Web Services Description Language

    C. Web Services Description Language, Simple Object Access Protocol

    D. Simple Object Access Protocol, Universal Description, Discovery and Integration

30. Sally has found out that software programmers in her company are making changes to software components and uploading them to the main software repository without following version control or documenting their changes. This is causing a lot of confusion and has caused several teams to use the older versions. Which of the following would be the best solution for this situation?

    A. Software change control management

    B. Software escrow

    C. Software configuration management

    D. Software configuration management escrow

1. D	11. D	21. B
2. B	12. C	22. B
3. C	13. C	23. D
4. B	14. A	24. A
5. A	15. B	25. B
6. D	16. D	26. C
7. C	17. B	27. A
8. A	18. D	28. C
9. B	19. A	29. A
10. C	20. B	30. C

1. Data marts, databases, and data warehouses have distinct characteristics. Which of the following does not correctly describe a data warehouse?

    A. It could increase the risk of privacy violations.

    B. It is developed to carry out analysis.

    C. It contains data from several different sources.

    D. It is created and used for project-based tactical reasons.

    ☑ **D.** A data warehouse is not commonly created and used for project-based tactical reasons. That description is characteristic of a data mart, which is a portion of a database that is used for a short period of time mainly for projects to determine tactical approaches to a problem. A data warehouse, on the other hand, is created for the purpose of conducting data mining and analysis for strategic reasons.

    ☒ A is incorrect because data warehouses could increase the risk of privacy violations considering that data is collected from several different sources and is held in one central location (the warehouse). Although this provides easier access and control, because the data warehouse is in one place, it also requires more stringent security. If an intruder got into the data warehouse, she could access all of the company's information at once.

    ☒ B is incorrect because the statement is true; data warehouses are commonly created for the purpose of analysis. The analysis allows for strategic decisions to be made; for example, those related to business trends, fraudulent activities, or marketing effectiveness. The analysis work is commonly carried out through data mining activities.

    ☒ C is incorrect because a data warehouse does contain data from several different sources. Data is extracted from different databases and other data locations, transferred to a central data storage place called a warehouse, and normalized. This enables users to query a single entity rather than accessing and querying different data sources, and allows for more efficient information retrieval and data analysis.

2. Database software should meet the requirements of what is known as the ACID test. Why should database software carry out atomic transactions, which is one requirement of the ACID test, when OLTP is used?

    A. So that the rules for database integrity can be established

    B. So that the database performs transactions as a single unit without interruption

    C. To ensure that rollbacks cannot take place

    D. To prevent concurrent processes from interacting with each other

☑ **B.** Online transaction processing (OLTP) is used when databases are clustered to provide high fault tolerance and performance. It provides mechanisms to watch for and deal with problems when they occur. For example, if a process stops functioning, the monitor mechanisms within OLTP can detect this and attempt to restart the process. If the process cannot be restarted, then the transaction taking place will be rolled back to ensure no data is corrupted or that only part of a transaction happens. OLTP records transactions as they occur (in real time), which usually updates more than one database in a distributed environment. This type of complexity can introduce many integrity threats, so the database software should implement the characteristics of what's known as the ACID test:

- **Atomicity** Divides transactions into units of work and ensures that all modifications take effect or none takes effect. Either the changes are committed or the database is rolled back.

- **Consistency** A transaction must follow the integrity policy developed for that particular database and ensure all data are consistent in the different databases.

- **Isolation** Transactions execute in isolation until completed, without interacting with other transactions. The results of the modification are not available until the transaction is completed.

- **Durability** Once the transaction is verified as accurate on all systems, it is committed, and the databases cannot be rolled back.

The term "atomic" means that the units of a transaction will occur together or not at all, thereby ensuring that if one operation fails, the others will not be carried out and corrupt the data in the database.

☒ **A** is incorrect because OLTP and ACID enforce, but do not establish, the integrity rules that are outlined in the database security policy. Representing the letter C in ACID, consistency relates to the enforcement and enforceability of integrity rules. Database software that demonstrates consistency conducts transactions that follow a specific integrity policy and ensure all data are the same in the different databases.

☒ **C** is incorrect because atomicity divides transactions into units of work and ensures that all modifications take effect or none takes effect. Either the changes are committed or the database is rolled back. This means if something does not happen correctly, the database is reverted (rolled back) to its original state. After the transaction happens properly, a rollback cannot take place, which is the durability component of the ACID test. This question is specifically asking about the atomic transaction approach, not durability.

☒ **D** is incorrect because atomic transactions do not address the isolation of processes that are carrying out database transactions; this is the "isolation" component of the ACID test. It is important that a process that is carrying out a transaction cannot be interrupted or modified by another process. This is to ensure the integrity, accuracy, and confidentiality of the data that is being processed during the transaction.

3. Lisa has learned that most databases implement concurrency controls. What is concurrency and why must it be controlled?

   A. Processes running at different levels, which can negatively affect the integrity of the database if not properly controlled.

   B. The ability to deduce new information from reviewing accessible data, which can allow an inference attack to take place.

   C. Processes running simultaneously, which can negatively affect the integrity of the database if not properly controlled.

   D. Storing data in more than one place within a database, which can negatively affect the integrity of the database if not properly controlled.

   ☑ **C.** Databases are commonly used by many different applications simultaneously and many users interacting with them at one time. Concurrency means that different processes (applications and users) are accessing the database at the same time. If this is not controlled properly, the processes can overwrite each other's data or cause deadlock situations. The negative result of concurrency problems is the reduction of the integrity of the data held within the database. Database integrity is provided by concurrency protection mechanisms. One concurrency control is locking, which prevents users from accessing and modifying data being used by someone else.

   ☒ **A** is incorrect because concurrency refers to processes running simultaneously, not at different levels. Concurrency issues come up when the database can be accessed at the same time by different users and/or applications. If controls are not in place, two users can access and modify the same data at the same time, which can be detrimental to a dynamic environment.

   ☒ **B** is incorrect because the ability to deduce new information from reviewing accessible data occurs when a subject at a lower security level indirectly guesses or infers data at a higher level. This can lead to an inference attack. It is not related to concurrency. Concurrency has to do with integrity, while inference is related to confidentiality.

   ☒ **D** is incorrect because storing data in more than one place is not a problem with concurrency. Concurrency becomes a problem when two subjects or applications are trying to modify the same data at the same time.

4. Robert has been asked to increase the overall efficiency of the sales database by implementing a procedure that structures data to minimize duplication and inconsistencies. What procedure is this?

A. Polymorphism

B. Normalization

C. Implementation of database views

D. Constructing schema

☑ **B.** Normalization is a process that eliminates redundancy, organizes data efficiently, reduces the potential for anomalies during data operations, and improves data consistency within databases. It is a systematic way of ensuring that a database structure is designed properly to be free of certain undesirable characteristics—insertion, update, and deletion anomalies—that could lead to a loss of data integrity.

☒ **A** is incorrect because polymorphism is when different objects are given the same input and react differently. As a simplistic example of polymorphism, suppose three different objects receive the input "Bob." Object A would process this input and produce the output "43-year-old white male." Object B would receive the input "Bob" and produce the output "Husband of Sally." Object C would produce the output "Member of User group." Each object received the same input but responded with a different output.

☒ **C** is incorrect because database views are logical access controls and are implemented to permit one group, or a specific user, to see certain information while restricting another group from viewing it altogether. For example, database views can be implemented to allow middle management to see their departments' profits and expenses without viewing the whole company's profits. Database views do not minimize duplicate data; rather, they manipulate how data is viewed by specific users/groups.

☒ **D** is incorrect because schema of a database system is its structure described in a formal language. In a relational database, the schema defines the tables, the fields, relationships, views, indexes, procedures, queues, database links, directories, and so on. The schema describes the database and its structure, but not the data that will live within that database itself. This is similar to a blueprint of a house. The blueprint can state that there will be four rooms, six doors, 12 windows, and so on without describing the people who will live in the house.

5. Which of the following correctly best describes an object-oriented database?

   A. When an application queries for data, it receives both the data and the procedure.

   B. It is structured similarly to a mesh network for redundancy and fast data retrieval.

   C. Subject must have knowledge of the well-defined access path in order to access data.

   D. The relationships between data entities provide the framework for organizing data.

   ☑ A. In an object-oriented database, objects are instantiated when needed, and the data and procedure (called method) go with the object when it is requested. This differs from a relational database, in which the application uses its own procedures to obtain and process data when retrieved from the database.

   ☒ B is incorrect because a mesh network is a physical topology and has nothing to do with databases. A mesh topology is a network of interconnected routers and switches that provides multiple paths to all the nodes on the network. In a full mesh topology, every node is directly connected to every other node, which provides a great degree of redundancy. In a partial mesh topology, every node is not directly connected. The Internet is an example of a partial mesh topology.

   ☒ C is incorrect because subjects accessing a hierarchical database—not an object-oriented database—must have knowledge of the access path in order to access data. In the hierarchical database model, records and fields are related in a logical tree structure. Parents can have one child, many children, or no children. The tree structure contains branches, and each branch has a number of data fields. To access data, the application must know which branch to start with and which route to take through each layer until the data is reached.

   ☒ D is incorrect because the relationships between data entities provide the framework for organizing data in a relational database. A relational database is composed of two-dimensional tables, and each table contains unique rows, columns, and cells. Each cell contains one data value that represents a specific attribute within a given row. These data entities are linked by relationships, which provide the framework for organizing the data.

6. Fred has been told he needs to test a component of the new content management application under development to validate its data structure, logic, and boundary conditions. What type of testing should he carry out?

A. Acceptance testing

B. Regression testing

C. Integration testing

D. Unit testing

☑ D. Unit testing involves testing an individual component in a controlled environment to validate data structure, logic, and boundary conditions. After a programmer develops a component, it is tested with several different input values and in many different situations. Unit testing can start early in development and usually continues throughout the development phase. One of the benefits of unit testing is finding problems early in the development cycle, when it is easier and less expensive to make changes to individual units.

☒ A is incorrect because acceptance testing is carried out to ensure that the code meets customer requirements. This testing is for part or all of the application, but not commonly one individual component.

☒ B is incorrect because regression testing refers to the retesting of a system after a change has taken place to ensure its functionality, performance, and protection. Essentially, regression testing is done to identify bugs that have caused functionality to stop working as intended as a result of program changes. It is not unusual for developers to fix one problem, only to inadvertently create a new problem, or for the new fix to break a fix to an old problem. Regression testing may include checking previously fixed bugs to make sure they have not re-emerged and rerunning previous tests.

☒ C is incorrect because integration testing involves verifying that components work together as outlined in design specifications. After unit testing, the individual components or units are combined and tested together to verify that they meet functional, performance, and reliability requirements.

7. Which of the following is the best description of a component-based system development method?

   A. Components periodically revisit previous stages to update and verify design requirements

   B. Minimizes the use of arbitrary transfer control statements between components

   C. Uses independent and standardized modules that are assembled into serviceable programs

   D. Implemented in module-based scenarios requiring rapid adaptations to changing client requirements

   ☑ C. Component-based development involves the use of independent and standardized modules. Each standard module consists of a functional algorithm or instruction set and is provided with interfaces to communicate with each other. Component-based development adds reusability and pluggable functionality into programs, and is widely used in modern programming to augment program coherence and substantially reduce software maintenance costs. A common example of these modules is "objects" that are frequently used in object-oriented programming.

   ☒ A is incorrect because the spiral method of system development periodically revisits previous stages to update and verify design requirements. The spiral method builds upon the waterfall method. It uses discrete phases of development with an emphasis on risk analysis, prototypes, and simulations. The spiral method does not specify the development and testing of components.

   ☒ B is incorrect because structured programming development involves the use of logical blocks to achieve system design using procedural programming. A structured program layout minimizes the use of arbitrary transfer control statements like GOTO and emphasizes on single points of entry and exit. This hierarchical approach makes it easier for the program to be understood and modified later on.

   ☒ D is incorrect because extreme programming is a methodology that is generally implemented in scenarios requiring rapid adaptations to changing client requirements. Extreme programming emphasizes client feedback to evaluate project outcomes and to analyze project domains that may require further attention. The coding principle of extreme programming throws out the traditional long-term planning carried out for code reuse and instead focuses on creating simple code optimized for the contemporary assignment.

8. There are many types of viruses that hackers can use to damage systems. Which of the following is not a correct description of a polymorphic virus?

   A. Intercepts antivirus's call to the operating system for file and system information

   B. Varies the sequence of its instructions using noise, a mutation engine, or random-number generator

   C. Can use different encryption schemes requiring different decryption routines

   D. Produces multiple, varied copies of itself

   ☑ A. A tunneling virus—not a polymorphic virus—attempts to install itself under an antivirus program. When the antivirus conducts its health check on critical files, file sizes, modification dates, etc., it makes a request to the operating system to gather this information. If the virus can put itself between the antivirus and the operating system, then when the antivirus sends out a system call for this type of information, the tunneling virus can intercept the call and respond with information that indicates the system is free of virus infections. The polymorphic virus also attempts to fool anti-virus scanners, but it does so by producing varied but operational copies of itself. Even if antivirus software finds and disables one or two copies, other copies may still remain active within the system.

   ☒ B is incorrect because a polymorphic virus can vary the sequence of its instructions by including noise, or bogus instructions, with other useful instructions. It can also use a mutation engine and a random-number generator to change the sequence of its instructions in the hopes of not being detected. The original functionality stays the same, but the code changes, making it close to impossible to identify all versions of the virus using a fixed signature.

   ☒ C is incorrect because a polymorphic virus can use different encryption schemes requiring different decryption routines. This requires an antivirus scan for several scan strings, one for each possible decryption method, in order to identify all copies of this type of virus. Polymorphic virus writers most commonly hide a virus's payload with encryption and add a decryption method to the code. Once it is encrypted, the code is meaningless. However, a virus that is encrypted is not necessarily a polymorphic virus. To be polymorphic, the virus's encryption and decryption algorithms must mutate with each new version of itself.

   ☒ D is incorrect because a polymorphic virus produces multiple, varied copies of itself in an effort to avoid detection by antivirus software. A polymorphic virus has the capability to change its own code, enabling the virus to have hundreds or thousands of variants. These activities can cause the virus scanner to not properly recognize the virus and to leave it to do its damage.

9. Which of the following best describes the role of the Java Virtual Machine in the execution of Java applets?

   A. Converts the source code into bytecode and blocks the sandbox

   B. Converts the bytecode into machine-level code

   C. Operates only on specific processors within specific operating systems

   D. Develops the applets, which run in a user's browser

   ☑ B. Java is an object-oriented, platform-independent programming language. It is employed as a full-fledged programming language and is used to write complete programs and short programs, called applets, which run in a user's browser. Java is platform independent because it creates intermediate code, bytecode, which is not processor-specific. The Java Virtual Machine (JVM) then converts the bytecode into machine-level code that the processor on the particular system can understand.

   ☒ A is incorrect because the Java Virtual Machine converts the bytecode into machine-level code. It does not convert the source code into bytecode—a Java compiler does that. The JVM also creates a virtual machine within an environment called a sandbox. This virtual machine is an enclosed environment in which the applet carries out its activities. Applets are commonly sent over HTTP within a requested Web page, which means the applet executes as soon as it arrives. It can carry out malicious activity on purpose or accidentally if the developer of the applet did not do his part correctly. So the sandbox strictly limits the applet's access to any system resources. The JVM mediates access to system resources to ensure the applet code behaves and stays within its own sandbox.

   ☒ C is incorrect because Java is an object-oriented, platform-independent programming language. Other languages are compiled to object code for a specific operating system and processor. This is why a particular application may run on Windows but not on Macintosh. An Intel processor does not necessarily understand machine code compiled for an Alpha processor, and vice versa. Java is platform-independent because it creates intermediate code—bytecode—which is not processor-specific.

   ☒ D is incorrect because the Java Virtual Machine does not write applets. Java is employed as a full-fledged programming language and is used to write complete programs and short programs, called applets, which run in a user's browser. A programmer creates a Java applet and runs it through a compiler. The Java compiler converts the source code into bytecode. The user then downloads the Java applet. The bytecode is converted into machine-level code by the JVM. Finally, the applet runs when called upon.

10. What type of database software integrity service guarantees that tuples are uniquely identified by primary key values?

   A. Concurrent integrity

   B. Referential integrity

   C. Entity integrity

   D. Semantic integrity

   ☑ **C.** Entity integrity guarantees that the tuples are uniquely identified by primary key values. A tuple is a row in a two-dimensional database. A primary key is a value in the corresponding column that makes each row unique. For the sake of entity integrity, every tuple must contain one primary key. If a tuple does not have a primary key, it cannot be referenced by the database.

   ☒ **A** is incorrect because concurrent integrity is not a database software formal term. This is a distracter answer. There are three main types of integrity services: semantic, referential, and entity. Concurrency refers to a piece of software being accessed by multiple users and/or applications at the same time. If controls are not in place, two users can access and modify the same data simultaneously.

   ☒ **B** is incorrect because referential integrity refers to all foreign keys referencing existing primary keys. There should be a mechanism in place that ensures that no foreign key contains a reference to a primary key of a nonexisting record or a null value. This type of integrity control ensures that the relationships between the different tables are working and can properly communicate to each other.

   ☒ **D** is incorrect because a semantic integrity mechanism ensures that structural and semantic rules of a database are enforced. These rules pertain to data types, logical values, uniqueness constraints, and operations that could adversely affect the structure of the database.

11. In computer programming, cohesion and coupling are used to describe modules of code. Which of the following is a favorable combination of cohesion and coupling?

   A. Low cohesion, low coupling

   B. High cohesion, high coupling

   C. Low cohesion, high coupling

   D. High cohesion, low coupling

   ☑ **D.** When a module is described as having high cohesion and low coupling, that is a good thing. Cohesion reflects how many different types of tasks a module can carry out. High cohesion means that the module carries out one basic task (such as subtraction of values) or several tasks that are very similar (such as subtraction, addition, multiplication). The higher the cohesion, the easier it is to update or modify and not affect the other modules that interact with it. This also means the module is easier to reuse and maintain because it is more straightforward when compared to a module with low cohesion. Coupling is a measurement that indicates how much interaction one module requires to carry out its tasks. If a module has low or loose coupling, this means the module does not need to communicate with many other modules to carry out its job. These modules are easier to understand and easier to reuse than those that depend upon many other modules to carry out their tasks. It is also easier to make changes to these modules without affecting many modules around them.

☒ **A** is incorrect because a module with low cohesion is not desirable. A module with low cohesion carries out multiple different tasks and increases the complexity of the module, which makes it harder to maintain and reuse. The higher a module's cohesion, the fewer tasks it carries out and the easier it is to update or modify that module without affecting others that interact with it.

☒ **B** is incorrect because a module with high coupling is not desirable. High coupling means a module depends upon many other modules to carry out its tasks. This makes it difficult to understand, reuse, and make changes because of the interdependencies with other modules. As an analogy, a company would want its employees to be able to carry out their individual jobs with the least amount of dependencies on other workers. If Joe had to talk with five other people just to get one task done, too much complexity exists, it's too time-consuming, and more places are created where errors can take place.

☒ **C** is incorrect because it states the exact opposite of what is desirable. A module that has low cohesion and high coupling is complex in that it carries out multiple different types of tasks and depends upon many other modules to carry them out. These characteristics make the module harder to maintain and reuse, largely because of the greater possibility of affecting other modules that interact with it.

12. When an organization is unsure of the final nature of the product, what type of system development method is most appropriate for them?

    A. Cleanroom

    B. Exploratory Model

    C. Modified Prototype Method

    D. Iterative Development

    ☑ **C.** Modified Prototype Method is a method specifically designed to confront challenges in Web application development and allows developers to swiftly translate client requirements into a displayable product or prototype.

Modified prototypes are generally used when both the developer and the client are unsure of the final nature of the product. Using modifiable prototypes allows the final product to be carved out as the system specifications become less hazy.

☒ **A** is incorrect because the Cleanroom is an approach that attempts to prevent errors or mistakes by following structured and formal methods of developing and testing. This approach is used for high-quality and critical applications that will be put through a strict certification process. The specifications and clear understanding of the end product must be fully understood before development begins.

☒ **B** is incorrect because the Exploratory Model is a method that is used in instances where clearly defined project objectives have not been presented. Instead of focusing on explicit tasks, the Exploratory Model relies on covering a set of specifications that are likely to encase the final product's working. Testing is an important part of exploratory development, as it ascertains that the current phase of the project is compliant with likely implementation scenarios.

☒ **D** is incorrect because the Iterative Development approach takes a cyclic approach to software development. It focuses on mapping out project milestones through continually assessing the current state of the project with the initial objectives on the basis of resources, time frames, and execution plan. Iterative Development provides a dynamic method of evaluating a project's overall status and allows corrective amendments to improve project effectiveness.

13. Which of the following statements does not correctly describe SOAP and Remote Procedure Calls?

    A. SOAP was designed to overcome the compatibility and security issues associated with Remote Procedure Calls.

    B. Both SOAP and Remote Procedure Calls were created to enable application-layer communication.

    C. SOAP enables the use of Remote Procedure Calls for information exchange between applications over the Internet.

    D. HTTP was not designed to work with Remote Procedure Calls, but SOAP was designed to work with HTTP.

    ☑ **C.** The Simple Object Access Protocol (SOAP) was created to use instead of Remote Procedure Calls (RPCs) to allow applications to exchange information over the Internet. SOAP is an XML-based protocol that encodes messages in a Web service setup. It allows programs running on different operating systems to communicate over Web-based communication methods.

☒ **A** is incorrect because SOAP was created to overcome the compatibility and security issues that RPCs introduced when trying to enable communication between objects of different applications over the Internet. SOAP is designed to work across multiple operating system platforms, browsers, and servers.

☒ **B** is incorrect because it is true that both SOAP and RPCs were created to enable application-layer communication. SOAP is an XML-based protocol that encodes messages in a Web service setup. So if you have a Windows 2000 computer, for instance, and you need to access a Windows 2008 computer that offers a specific Web service, the programs on both systems can communicate using SOAP without running into interoperability issues. This communication most commonly takes place over HTTP, since it is readily available in basically all computers today.

☒ **D** is incorrect because the statement is correct: HTTP was not designed to specifically work with RPCs, but SOAP was designed to work with HTTP. SOAP actually defines an XML schema or a structure of how communication is going to take place. The SOAP XML schema defines how objects communicate directly. One advantage of SOAP is that the program calls will most likely get through firewalls since HTTP communication is commonly allowed. This helps ensure that the client/server model is not broken by getting denied by a firewall in between the communicating entities.

14. Computer programs that are based on human logic by using "if/then" statements and inference engines are called _____.

   A. Expert systems

   B. Artificial neural networks

   C. Distributed Computing Environment

   D. Enterprise JavaBeans

   ☑ **A.** Expert systems emulate human logic to solve problems that would usually require human intelligence and intuition. These systems represent expert knowledge as data or rules within the software. Expert systems collect data of human know-how and hold it in some type of database. These fragments of data are used to reason through a problem. Rule-based programming is a common way of developing expert systems. The rules are based on if-then logic units and specify a set of actions to be performed for a given situation. This is one way expert systems are used to find patterns, which is called pattern matching. A mechanism, called the inference engine, automatically matches facts against patterns and determines which rules are applicable. The actions of the corresponding rules are executed when the inference engine is instructed to begin execution.

   ☒ **B** is incorrect because an artificial neural network (ANN) is a mathematical or computational model based on the neural structure of the brain.

Computers perform activities like calculating large numbers, keeping large ledgers, and performing complex mathematical functions, but they cannot recognize patterns or learn from experience as the brain can. ANNs contain many units that stimulate neurons, each with a small amount of memory. The units work on data that are input through their many connections. Via training rules, the systems are able to learn from examples and have the capability to generalize.

☒ C is incorrect because Distributed Computing Environment (DCE) is a standard developed by the Open Software Foundation (OSF), also called Open Group. It is basically middleware that is available to many vendors to use within their products. DCE has nothing to do with the emulation of human logic. DCE is a set of management services with a communications layer based on RPC. It is a layer of software that sits on the top of the network layer and provides services to the applications above it.

☒ D is incorrect because Enterprise JavaBeans (EJB) is a structural design for the development and implementation of distributed applications written in Java. EJB provides interfaces and methods to allow different applications to be able to communicate across a networked environment. EJB has nothing to do with the emulation of human logic.

15. Which of the following is a correct description of the pros and cons associated with third-generation programming languages?

    A. The use of heuristics reduced programming effort, but the amount of manual coding for a specific task is usually more than the preceding generation.

    B. The use of syntax similar to human language reduced development time, but the language is resource intensive.

    C. The use of binary was extremely time consuming but resulted in fewer errors.

    D. The use of symbols reduced programming time, but the language required knowledge of machine architecture.

    ☑ B. Third-generation programming languages are easier to work with compared to earlier languages because their syntax is similar to human languages. This reduces program development time and allows for simplified and swift debugging. However, these languages can be very resource intensive when compared to the second-generation programming languages.

    ☒ A is incorrect because it attempts to describe the pros and cons of fourth-generation programming. It is true that the use of heuristics in fourth-generation programming languages drastically reduced the programming effort and the possibility of errors in code. However, it is not true that the amount of manual coding was usually more than that required of third-generation languages. On the contrary, the most remarkable aspect of fourth-generation languages is that the amount of manual coding required to perform a specific task may be ten times less than for the same task on a third-generation language.

☒ **C** is incorrect because the statement alludes to the pros and cons of machine language, the first-generation programming language. The first portion of the statement is true: Programming in binary was time consuming. The second half, however, is incorrect. Programming in binary was very prone to errors.

☒ **D** is incorrect because it describes second-generation programming languages. By introducing symbols to represent complicated binary codes, second-generation programming languages reduced programming and debugging times. Unfortunately, these languages required extensive knowledge of machine architecture, and the programs that were written in it were hardware specific.

16. Which of the following is considered the second generation of programming languages?

   A. Machine

   B. Very high-level

   C. High-level

   D. Assembly

☑ **D.** The second generation of programming languages generally starts with the introduction of assembly language in the mid-1950s. Assembly languages introduced symbols (called mnemonics) to represent complicated binary codes. Programmers using assembly languages could use commands like ADD, PUSH, POP, etc., instead of binary codes (1001011010, etc.). Assembly languages used programs called assemblers that would automatically convert these pseudocodes into machine-compatible binary language.

☒ **A** is incorrect because the most primitive form of programming language is machine language, which is considered to be the first generation of programming languages. Machine languages were used as the sole mode of programming in the early 1950s. Early computers used binary instructions as compilers, and interpreters were nonexistent at the time. Programmers had to manually calculate, allot memory addresses, and feed instructions sequentially, as there was no concept of abstraction.

☒ **B** is incorrect because fourth-generation languages (very high-level) are designed to further enhance the natural language approach initiated within third-generation language. Fourth-generation languages are meant to take natural-language-based statements one step ahead. The most common example of fourth-generation language is the SQL database language.

☒ **C** is incorrect because the third generation of programming languages started to emerge in the early 1960s. Third-generation programming languages are known as high-level languages due to their refined programming structures. High-level languages used abstract statements. Abstraction naturalized multiple assembly language instructions into a single high-level statement, e.g., IF–THEN–ELSE. This allowed programmers to leave low-level (system architecture) intricacies to the programming language, and focus on their programming objectives..

17. Mary is creating malicious code that will steal a user's cookies by modifying the original client-side Java script. What type of cross-site scripting vulnerability is she exploiting?

   A. Second order

   B. DOM-based

   C. Persistent

   D. Nonpersistent

   ☑ **B.** Mary is exploiting a document object model (DOM)–based cross-site scripting (XSS) vulnerability, which is also referred to as local cross-site scripting. DOM is the standard structure layout to represent HTML and XML documents in the browser. In such attacks the document components such as form fields and cookies can be referenced through JavaScript. The attacker uses the DOM environment to modify the original client side JavaScript. This causes the victim's browser to execute the resulting abusive JavaScript code. The most effective way to prevent these attacks is to disable scripting support in the browser.

   ☒ **A** is incorrect because a second-order vulnerability, or persistent XSS vulnerability, is targeted at Web sites that allow users to input data that is stored in a database or other location, such as a forum or message board. Second-order vulnerabilities allow the most dominant type of attacks.

   ☒ **C** is incorrect because a persistent XSS vulnerability is simply another name for a second-order vulnerability. As previously stated, these vulnerabilities allow users to input data that is stored in a database or other location such as an online forum or message board. These types of platforms are among the most commonly plagued by XSS vulnerabilities. The best way to overcome these vulnerabilities is through secure programming practices. Each and every user input should be filtered, and only a limited set of known and secure characters should be allowed for user input.

   ☒ **D** is incorrect because nonpersistent XSS vulnerabilities, also referred to as reflected vulnerabilities, occur when an attacker tricks the victim into opening a URL programmed with a rogue script to steal the victim's sensitive information (such as a cookie). The principle behind this attack lies in exploiting lack of proper input or output validation on dynamic Web sites.

18. Of the following steps that describe the development of a botnet, which best describes the step that comes first?

A. Infected server sends attack commands to the botnet.

B. Spammer pays a hacker for use of a botnet.

C. Controller server instructs infected systems to send spam to mail servers.

D. Malicious code is sent out that has bot software as its payload.

☑ **D.** The creation of a botnet begins with the hacker sending systems malicious code that has the bot software as its payload. A bot is a piece of dormant code that carries out functionality for its master. Also known as a zombie, the code can be used to forward items sent to it as in spam or attack commands. The zombie code sends a message to the attacker indicating that a specific system has been compromised and can be used by the attacker. When an attacker has a collection of these compromised systems, it is referred to as a botnet.

☒ **A** is incorrect because before a server can act as a controlling server of the botnet, there must be compromised systems to control. These systems are created by sending malicious code to the individual system that has bot software as its payload. Then, once installed, the bot logs in to an internet relay chat (IRC) server that it is coded to contact. This IRC server then is used to control the botnet. (IRC is just one type of communication channel that can be used.)

☒ **B** is incorrect because the development of a botnet begins with the attacker sending out malicious code that has the bot software as its payload. While a spammer could commission an attacker to develop a botnet, that is not the first step in its actual development. In addition to renting out the botnet to spammers, hackers can use the infected systems to carry out powerful distributed denial-of-service attacks.

☒ **C** is incorrect because the last step in the use of a botnet to send spam is the controller server instructing the infected systems to send out spam messages to mail servers. Spammers use this method so that their messages have a higher likelihood of getting through mail server spam filters since the sending IP addresses are those of the victim's system. Thus, the source IP addresses change constantly. This also helps ensure that the original sender is not located or identified.

19. Which of the following antivirus detection methods is the most recent to the industry and monitors suspicious code as it executes within the operating system?

A. Behavior blocking

B. Fingerprint detection

C. Signature-based detection

D. Heuristic detection

☑ **A.** Of the methods listed, behavior blocking is the most recent evolution in antivirus detection. Behavior blocking allows suspicious code to execute within the operating system and watches its interactions looking for suspicious activities. These activities include writing to startup files or the Run keys in the Registry; opening, deleting, or modifying files; scripting e-mail messages to send executable code; and creating or modifying macros and scripts. If the antivirus program detects some of these potentially malicious activities, it can terminate the software and provide a message to the user. A drawback to behavior blockers is that the malicious code must actually execute in real time. This type of constant monitoring also requires a high level of system resources.

☒ **B** is incorrect because fingerprint detection (also referred to as signature-based detection) does not monitor suspicious code as it is executing. Instead, antivirus software scans incoming data and compares files, e-mail messages, etc., for signatures that match those in the antivirus's database. A signature is a sequence of code that was extracted from the virus itself, or the steps it carries out in its attack. If a match is identified, then the antivirus software takes whatever protective action(s) it is configured to carry out. It may quarantine the file, attempt to clean the file by removing the virus, provide a warning message dialog box to the user, and/or log the event.

☒ **C** is incorrect because signature-based detection uses signatures (virus code patterns) to identify malicious software or activity patterns before they are executed in the operating system. Signature-based detection is an effective way to detect malicious software, but there is a delayed response time to new threats. Once a virus is detected, the antivirus vendor must study it, develop and test a new signature, release the signature, and all customers must download it.

☒ **D** is incorrect because heuristic detection analyzes the overall structure of executable code, evaluates the coded instructions and logic functions, and evaluates the likelihood of it being malicious. Antivirus software that uses heuristic detection has a type of "suspiciousness counter," which is incremented as the program finds more potentially malicious attributes. Once a predefined threshold is met, the code is officially considered dangerous and the antivirus software protects the system.

20. Which of the following describes object-oriented programming deferred commitment?

A. Autonomous objects, which cooperate through exchanges of messages

B. The internal components of an object can be refined without changing other parts of the system

C. Object-oriented analysis, design, and modeling maps to business needs and solutions

D. Other programs using same objects

☑ **B.** Deferred commitment means that the internal components of an object can be refined without changing other parts of the system. Non-object-oriented programming applications are written as monolithic entities. This means an application is just one big pile of code. If you need to change something in this pile, you would need to go through the whole program's logic functions to figure out what your one change is going to break. If you choose to write your program in an object-oriented language, you don't have one monolithic application, but an application that is made up of smaller components (objects). If you need to make changes or updates to some functionality in your application, you can just change the code within the class that creates the object carrying out that functionality and not worry about everything else the program actually carries out.

☒ **A** is incorrect because autonomous objects, which cooperate through exchanges of messages, refer to object-oriented programming's modularity. An object is preassembled code that is a self-contained module. Objects need to be able to communicate with each other, and this happens by using messages that are sent to the receiving object's application programming interface. If object A needs to tell object B that a user's checking account must be reduced by $40, it sends object B a message. The message is made up of the destination, the method that needs to be performed, and the corresponding arguments.

☒ **C** is incorrect because the description, "Object-oriented analysis, design, and modeling maps to business needs and solutions," refers to naturalness. An object's method should naturally map to business objectives. A method is the functionality or procedure an object can carry out. An object may be constructed to accept data from a user and reformat the request so that a back-end server can understand and process it. Another object may perform a method that extracts data from a database and populates a Web page with this information. Or an object may carry out a withdrawal procedure to allow the user of an ATM to extract money from her account. These are business needs.

☒ **D** is incorrect because reusability refers to different programs being able to use the same objects. Most applications have some type of functionality in common. Instead of developing the same code to carry out the same functionality for ten different applications, using OOP allows you to just create the object once and let it be reused in other applications. This reduces development time and saves money. The objects can be catalogued in a library, which provides an economical way for more than one application to call upon the objects. The library provides an index and pointers to where objects actually live within the system or on another system.

21. What object-oriented programming term, or concept, is illustrated in the graphic that follows?

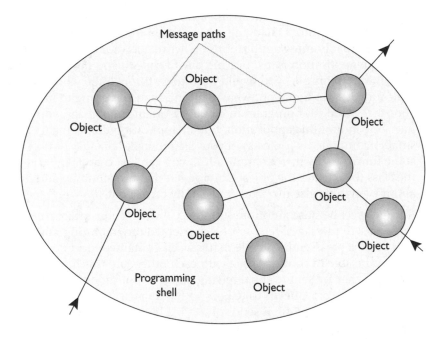

A. Methods

B. Messages

C. Abstraction

D. Data hiding

☑ **B.** In object-oriented programming objects need to be able to communicate with each other and this happens by using messages that are sent to the receiving object's application program interface (API). For example, if object A needs to tell object B that a user's checking account must be reduced by $40, it sends object B a message. The message is made up of the destination, the method that needs to be performed, and the corresponding arguments. This graphic illustrates object communication through the use of their messaging functionality.

☒ **A** is incorrect because a method is the functionality or procedure an object can carry out, not the way objects communicate with each other. An object, for example, may be constructed to accept data from a user and to reformat the request so that a back-end server can understand and process it. These functions are the methods that can be carried out by the specific objects—basically what the object can do. Another object may perform a method that extracts data from a database and populates a Web page with the necessary information. These are just some examples of the various methods objects may carry out.

☒ **C** is incorrect because abstraction is the capability to suppress unnecessary details so the important, inherent properties can be examined and reviewed. Abstraction enables the separation of conceptual aspects of a system. For example, if a software architect needs to understand how data flows through the program, she would want to understand the big pieces of the program and trace the steps the data takes from first being input into the program all the way until it exits the program as output. Abstraction can be provided by OOP, but this is not what is being shown in the graphic.

☒ **D** is incorrect because data hiding refers to the concept that data and operations internal to objects are hidden from other objects. Each object encapsulates its data and processes. Data hiding protects an object's private data from outside access. No object should be allowed to, or have the need to, access another object's internal data or processes. Data hiding is basically keeping what is supposed to be secret, secret.

22. Protection methods can be integrated into software programs. What type of protection method is illustrated in the graphic that follows?

Level	Ship	Cargo	Origin	Destination
Top secret	Oklahoma	Weapons	Delaware	Ukraine
Unclassified	Oklahoma	Food	Delaware	Africa

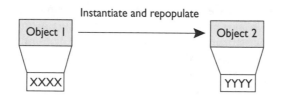

A. Polymorphism

B. Polyinstantiation

C. Cohesiveness

D. Object classes

☑ **B.** Polyinstantiation is the simultaneous existence of multiple information objects, which refer to the same real-world concept but differ by their classification level and/or their contents. The multiple instances are commonly distinguished by their security levels. Polyinstantiation is when more than one copy of an object is made, and the other copy is modified to have different attributes. This can be done for several reasons. A way to use polyinstantiation is for security purposes, to ensure that a lower-level subject could not access an object at a higher level. If a lower subject does not have the clearance of top secret, then it should not be able to access data at this classification level.

☒ **A** is incorrect because polymorphism is the capability of different objects to respond differently to the same message. This is possible because objects can belong to different classes, meaning they will exhibit different behaviors. Polymorphism can take place in the following example: Object A and Object B are created from the same parent class, but Object B is also under a subclass. Object B would have some different characteristics from Object A because of this inheritance from the parent class and the subclass. When Object A and Object B receive the same input, they would result in different outputs because only one of them inherited characteristics from the subclass. An analogy of polymorphism is if someone gave you and me the same message and I responded with X and you responded with Y—so the same input and different outputs.

☒ **C** is incorrect because cohesiveness means that one module is carrying out only one task. If a module is highly cohesive, this means that all elements in the module directly deal with the one basic task the module carries out, or a group of similar tasks. A module should have well-defined responsibilities, which means that it has high cohesiveness. If you were a highly cohesive module, you would carry out your one specific task you were built to do, for example taking out the trash.

☒ **D** is incorrect because an object class is a blueprint or prototype that defines the variables (data) and methods (procedures) common to all objects within it. A class provides a type of empty template of variables that will be populated when the object is instantiated. Objects are members, or instances, of classes. A real-world object, such as a table, is a member (or an instance) of a larger class of objects called "furniture." The furniture class will have a set of attributes associated with it, and when an object is generated, it inherits these attributes. The attributes may be color, dimensions, weight, style, and cost. These attributes apply if a chair, table, or loveseat object is generated or instantiated. Because the table is a member of the class furniture, the table inherits all attributes defined for the class.

23. There are several types of attacks that programmers need to be aware of. What attack does the graphic that follows illustrate?

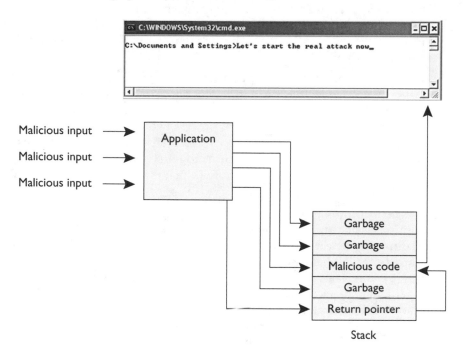

A. Traffic analysis

B. Race condition

C. Covert storage

D. Buffer overflow

☑ **D.** A buffer is an area reserved by an application to store something in it, like some user input. After the application receives the input, an instruction pointer points the application to do something with the input that's been put in the buffer. A buffer overflow occurs when an application erroneously allows an invalid amount of input to be written into the buffer area, overwriting the instruction pointer in the code that told the program what to do with the input. Once the instruction pointer is overwritten, whatever code has been placed in the buffer can then be executed, all under the security context of the application.

☒ **A** is incorrect because traffic analysis is a method of uncovering information by watching traffic patterns on a network. For example, heavy traffic between the HR department and headquarters could indicate an upcoming layoff. Another example is if there is a lot of traffic between two military units, this may indicate that a military attack is being planned. Traffic padding can be used to counter this kind of attack, in which decoy traffic is sent out over the network to disguise patterns and make it more difficult to uncover them.

☒ **B** is incorrect because when two different processes need to carry out their tasks on a resource, they need to follow the correct sequence. Process one needs to carry out its work before process two accesses the same resource and carries out its tasks. If process two goes before process one, the outcome could be very different. If an attacker could manipulate the processes so that process two did its thing first, she is controlling the outcome of the processing procedure, which is referred to as a race condition attack.

☒ **C** is incorrect because in a covert storage channel, processes are able to communicate through some type of storage space on the system. For example, System A is infected with a Trojan horse that has installed software that will be able to communicate to another process in a nefarious way. System A has a very sensitive file (File 2) that is of great interest to a particular attacker. The software the Trojan horse installed is able to read this file and it needs to send the contents of the file to the attacker, which can only happen one bit at a time. The intrusive software is going to communicate to the attacker by locking a specific file (File 3). When the attacker attempts to access File 3 and finds it has a software lock enabled on it, the attacker interprets this to mean the first bit in the sensitive file is a 1. The second time the attacker attempts to access File 3, it is not locked. The attacker interprets this value to be zero. This continues until all of the data in the sensitive file are sent to the attacker.

24. Databases and applications commonly carry out the function that is illustrated in the graphic that follows. Which of the following best describes the concept that this graphic is showing?

   A. Checkpoint

   B. Commit

   C. Two-phase commit

   D. Data dictionary

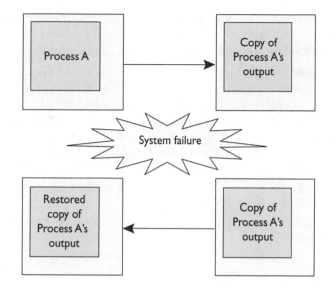

☑ **A.** A checkpoint is used to recover data if there is a system failure or problem during a transaction. It is used to periodically save the state of the application and the user's information. It is used so that if the application endures a glitch, it has the necessary tools to bring the user back to his working environment without losing any data. You can experience this with a word processor when it asks you if you want to review the recovered version of a file you were working on. The word processor has saved your document as you have worked on it and is able to bring it back in case the system runs into trouble.

☒ **B** is incorrect because a commit operation completes a transaction and executes all changes just made by the user. As its name indicates, once the commit command is executed, the changes are committed and reflected in the database. These changes can be made to data or schema information. When these changes are committed, they are then available to all other applications and users. If a user attempts to commit a change and it cannot complete correctly, a rollback is performed. This ensures that partial changes do not take place and that data is not corrupted.

☒ **C** is incorrect because a two-phase commit mechanism is a control that is used in databases to ensure the integrity of the data held within the database. Databases commonly carry out transaction processes, which means the user and the database interact at the same time. The databases need to make sure each database is properly modified, or no modification takes place at all. When a database change is submitted by the user, the different databases initially store these changes temporarily. A transaction monitor will then send out a "precommit" command to each database. If all the right databases respond with an acknowledgment, then the monitor sends out a "commit" command to each database. This ensures that all of the necessary information is stored in all the right places at the right time.

☒ **D** is incorrect because a data dictionary is a central collection of data element definitions, schema objects, and reference keys for a database. The schema objects can contain tables, views, indexes, procedures, functions, and triggers. A data dictionary can also contain the default values for columns, integrity information, the names of users, the privileges and roles for users, and auditing information. It is a tool used to centrally manage parts of a database by controlling data about the data (referred to as metadata) within the database. It provides a cross-reference between groups of data elements and the databases.

25. There are several different types of databases. Which type does the graphic that follows illustrate?

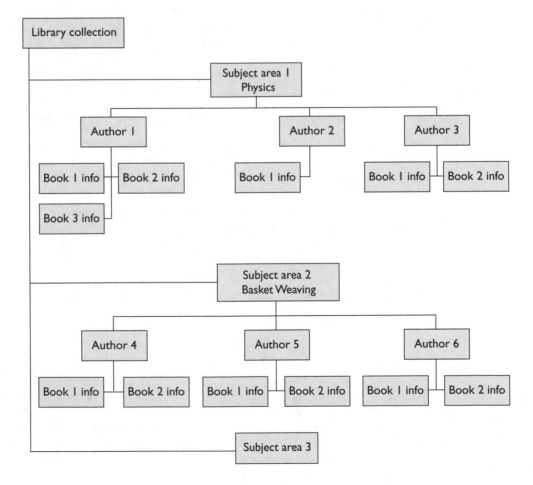

A. Relational

B. Hierarchical

C. Network

D. Object-oriented

☑ **B.** A hierarchical database uses a tree-like structure to define relationships between data elements, using a parent/child relationship. The structure and relationship between the data elements are different from those in a relational database. The tree structure contains branches, and each branch has a number of leaves, or data fields. These databases have well-defined, prespecified access paths, but they are not as flexible in creating relationships between data elements as a relational database. Hierarchical databases are useful for mapping one-to-many relationships.

☒ **A** is incorrect because a relational database model uses attributes (columns) and tuples (rows) to contain and organize information. It presents information in the form of tables. A relational database is composed of two-dimensional tables, and each table contains unique rows, columns, and cells (the intersection of a row and a column). Each cell contains only one data value that represents a specific attribute value within a given tuple. These data entities are linked by relationships. The relationships between the data entities provide the framework for organizing data.

☒ **C** is incorrect because a network database model is built upon the hierarchical data model, but instead of being constrained by having to "know" how to go from one branch to another and then from one parent to a child to find a data element, the network database model allows each data element to have multiple parent and child records. This forms a redundant network-like structure instead of a strict tree structure. (The name does not indicate it is on or distributed throughout a network, it just describes the data element relationships.)

☒ **D** is incorrect because an object-oriented database is designed to handle a variety of data (images, audio, documents, video). An object-oriented database management system (ODBMS) is more dynamic in nature than a hierarchical database, because objects can be created when needed and the data and procedure (called method) go with the object when it is requested. In a hierarchical database, the application has to use its own procedures to obtain data from the database and then process the data for its needs. The hierarchical database does not actually provide procedures, as object-oriented databases do. The object-oriented database has classes to define the attributes and procedures of its objects.

The following scenario will be used for questions 26, 27, and 28.

Trent is the new manager of his company's internal software development department. He has been told by his management that the group needs to be compliant with the international standard that provides guidance to organizations in integrating security into the processes used for managing their applications. His new boss told him that he should join and get familiar with the Web Application Security Consortium, and Trent just received an e-mail stating that one of the company's currently deployed applications has a zero day vulnerability.

26. Which of the following is most likely the standard Trent's company wants to comply with?

   A. ISO/IEC 27005

   B. ISO/IEC 27001

   C. ISO/IEC 27034

   D. BS 7799

   ☑ C. ISO/IEC 27034 is the international standard that provides guidance to organizations in integrating security to the processes used for managing their applications. It is applicable to in-house developed applications, applications acquired from third parties, and where the development or the operation of the application is outsourced.

   ☒ A is incorrect because ISO/IEC 27005:2011 provides guidelines for information security risk management. It supports ISO/IEC 27001 and is designed to assist in the proper implementation of information security based on a risk management approach.

   ☒ B is incorrect because ISO/IEC 27001:2005 specifies the requirements for establishing, implementing, operating, monitoring, reviewing, maintaining, and improving a documented information security management system within the context of the organization's overall business risks. It specifies requirements for the implementation of security controls customized to the needs of individual organizations or parts thereof.

   ☒ D is incorrect because BS 7799 was written by the UK government's Department of Trade and Industry and outlines how an information security management system (ISMS) (aka security program) should be built and maintained. The goal was to provide guidance to organizations on how to design, implement, and maintain policies, processes, and technologies to manage risks to its sensitive information assets.

27. Which of the following best describes the consortium Trent's boss wants him to join?

   A. Nonprofit organization that produces open-source software and follows widely agreed upon best-practice security standards for the World Wide Web.

B. U.S. DHS group that provides best practices, tools, guidelines, rules, principles, and other resources for software developers, architects, and security practitioners to use.

C. Group of experts who create proprietary software tools used to help improve the security of software worldwide.

D. Group of experts and organizations who certify products based upon an agreed-upon security criteria.

☑ **A.** The Web Application Security Consortium (WASC) is a nonprofit organization made up of an international group of experts, industry practitioners, and organizational representatives who produce open-source and widely agreed upon best-practice security standards for the World Wide Web.

☒ **B** is incorrect because the U.S. Department of Homeland Security (DHS) provides best practices, tools, guidelines, rules, principles, and other resources that software developers, architects, and security practitioners can use to build security into software in every phase of its development. This DHS initiative is called Build Security In (BSI), and it is a collaborative effort that allows many entities across the industry to participate and provide useful material.

☒ **C** is incorrect because this is a distracter answer. There is no official organization that provides proprietary tools for the listed purpose.

☒ **D** is incorrect because the Web Application Security Consortium does not certify products. Instead it provides guidance and open-source best practices on how to integrate security into software.

28. Which of the following best describes the type of vulnerability mentioned in this scenario?

A. Dynamic vulnerability that is polymorphic

B. Static vulnerability that is exploited by server-side injection parameters

C. Vulnerability that does not currently have an associated solution

D. Database vulnerability that directly affects concurrency

☑ **C.** Zero day vulnerabilities are vulnerabilities that do not currently have a resolution. If a vulnerability is identified and there is not a pre-established fix (patch, configuration, update), it is considered a zero day. A zero day attack is an attack that exploits a previously unknown vulnerability in a system, meaning that the attack occurs between the time it is identified and the solution is prepared—that is, on "day zero" of the awareness of the vulnerability. This leaves zero days for the victim to react and apply a patch to the vulnerability.

☒ **A** is incorrect because a zero day vulnerability can be any type of vulnerability that does not have a current resolution that victims and potential victims can implement. A zero day vulnerability is not specific in nature, as in a dynamic polymorphic vulnerability; it is just a general category that can include this type of vulnerability and many more. A polymorphic attack just means that it changes itself, with the goal of being undetected.

⊠ **B** is incorrect because a zero day vulnerability can be any type of vulnerability that does not have a current resolution that victims and potential victims can implement. A zero day vulnerability is not specific in nature, as in server-side injection; it is just a general category that can include this type of vulnerability and many more. Server-side includes (SSI) injection attacks allow the exploitation of a Web application by injecting scripts in HTML pages or executing arbitrary codes remotely.

⊠ **D** is incorrect because concurrency within databases specifically pertains to correctly executing several transactions simultaneously. If there is a vulnerability that directly affects the successful execution of database transactions, then there is a risk of negatively affecting the integrity of the data held within and processed by database software. This does not have anything to do directly with a zero day vulnerability.

29. _____ provides a machine-readable description of the specific operations provided by a specific Web service. _____ provides a method for Web services to be registered by service providers and located by service consumers.

   A. Web Services Description Language, Universal Description, Discovery and Integration

   B. Universal Description, Discovery and Integration, Web Services Description Language

   C. Web Services Description Language, Simple Object Access Protocol

   D. Simple Object Access Protocol, Universal Description, Discovery and Integration

☑ **A.** Services within a service-oriented architecture (SOA) are usually provided through Web services. A Web service allows for Web-based communication to happen seamlessly using Web-based standards as in Simple Object Access Protocol (SOAP), HTTP, Web Services Description Language (WSDL), Universal Description, Discovery and Integration (UDDI), and XML. WSDL provides a machine-readable description of the specific operations provided by the service. UDDI is an XML-based registry that lists available services. UDDI provides a method for services to be registered by service providers and located by service consumers.

⊠ **B** is incorrect because the terms are not in the correct order and do not map to the definitions provided within the question. WSDL provides a machine-readable description of the specific operations provided by the service.

UDDI is an XML-based registry that lists available services. UDDI provides a method for services to be registered by service providers and located by service consumers.

☒ **C** is incorrect because Simple Object Access Protocol (SOAP) is an XML-based protocol that encodes messages in a Web service environment. SOAP actually defines an XML schema of how communication is going to take place. The SOAP XML schema defines how objects communicate directly. SOAP is not an item identified in this question.

☒ **D** is incorrect because Simple Object Access Protocol (SOAP) is an XML-based protocol that encodes messages in a Web service environment. SOAP actually defines an XML schema of how communication is going to take place. The SOAP XML schema defines how objects communicate directly. This is not what the question is addressing.

30. Sally has found out that software programmers in her company are making changes to software components and uploading them to the main software repository without following version control or documenting their changes. This has caused a lot of confusion and has caused several teams to use the older versions. Which of the following would be the best solution for this situation?

    A. Software change control management

    B. Software escrow

    C. Software configuration management

    D. Software configuration management escrow

    ☑ **C.** When changes take place to a software product during its development life cycle, a configuration management system can be put into place that allows for change control processes to take place through automation. A product that provides software configuration management (SCM) identifies the attributes of software at various points in time and performs a methodical control of changes for the purpose of maintaining software integrity and traceability throughout the software development life cycle. It defines the need to track changes and provides the ability to verify that the final delivered software has all of the approved changes that are supposed to be included in the release. During a software development project the centralized code repositories are often kept in systems that can carry out SCM functionality, which manages and tracks revisions made by multiple people against a single master set.

    ☒ **A** is incorrect because this is not the official term for this type of functionality. Software change control management is only a part of software configuration management. A software configuration management system also provides concurrency management, versioning, and synchronization.

☒ **B** is incorrect because in a software escrow framework, a third party keeps a copy of the source code, and possibly other materials, which it will release to the customer only if specific circumstances arise, mainly if the vendor who developed the code goes out of business or for some reason is not meeting its obligations and responsibilities. This procedure protects the customer, because the customer pays the vendor to develop software code for them, and if the vendor goes out of business, the customer otherwise would no longer have access to the actual code.

☒ **D** is incorrect because this is a distracter answer. This is not an official term.

Security Operations

This domain includes questions from the following topics:

- Administrative management responsibilities
- Operations department responsibilities
- Configuration management
- Trusted recovery states
- Redundancy and fault-tolerant systems
- E-mail security
- Threats to operations security

Operations security consists of the routine tasks involved with maintaining a network and its systems after they are developed and implemented. It includes ensuring that entities have the proper access privileges, that oversight is implemented, that network and systems run correctly and securely, and that applications are running in a secure and protected manner. It is also a very important topic, because as networks and computing environments continually evolve, individuals responsible for security operations must respond accordingly.

1. Which of the following is not a common component of configuration management change control steps?

   A. Tested and presented

   B. Service-level agreement approval

   C. Report change to management

   D. Approval of the change

2. A change management process should include a number of procedures. Which of the following incorrectly describes a characteristic or component of a change control policy?

   A. Changes that are unanimously approved by the change control committee must be tested to uncover any unforeseen results.

   B. Changes approved by the change control committee should be entered into a change log.

   C. A schedule that outlines the projected phases of the change should be developed.

   D. An individual or group should be responsible for approving proposed changes.

3. The requirement of erasure is the end of the media life cycle if it contains sensitive information. Which of the following best describes purging?

   A. Changing the polarization of the atoms on the media.

   B. It is uacceptable when media are to be reused in the same physical environment for the same purposes.

   C. Data formerly on the media is made unrecoverable by overwriting it with a pattern.

   D. Information is made unrecoverable, even with extraordinary effort.

4. Device backup and other availability solutions are chosen to balance the value of having information available against the cost of keeping that information available. Which of the following best describes fault-tolerant technologies?

   A. They are among the most expensive solutions and are usually only for the most mission-critical information.

   B. They help service providers identify appropriate availability services for the specific customer.

C. They are required to maintain integrity, regardless of the other technologies in place.

D. They allow a failed component to be replaced while the system continues to run.

5. Which of the following refers to the amount of time it will be expected to take to get a device fixed and back into production?

A. SLA

B. MTTR

C. Hot-swap

D. MTBF

6. Which of the following correctly describes Direct Access and Sequential Access storage devices?

A. Any point on a Direct Access Storage Device may be promptly reached, whereas every point in between the current position and the desired position of a Sequential Access Storage Device must be traversed in order to reach the desired position.

B. RAIT is an example of a Direct Access Storage Device, while RAID is an example of a Sequential Access Storage Device.

C. MAID is a Direct Access Storage Device, while RAID is an example of a Sequential Access Storage Device.

D. As an example of Sequential Access Storage, tape drives are faster than Direct Access Storage Devices.

7. There are classifications for operating system failures. Which of the following refers to what takes place when an unexpected kernel or media failure happens and the regular recovery procedure cannot recover the system to a more consistent state, requiring an administrator to intervene?

A. Emergency system restart

B. Trusted recovery

C. System cold start

D. System reboot

8. Various levels of RAID dictate the type of activity that will take place within the RAID system. Which level is associated with byte-level parity?

A. RAID Level 0

B. RAID Level 3

C. RAID Level 5

D. RAID Level 10

9. Which of the following incorrectly describes IP spoofing and session hijacking?

   A. Address spoofing helps an attacker to hijack sessions between two users without being noticed.

   B. IP spoofing makes it harder to track down an attacker.

   C. Session hijacking can be prevented with mutual authentication.

   D. IP spoofing is used to hijack SSL and IPSec secure communications.

10. RAID systems use a number of techniques to provide redundancy and performance. Which of the following activities divides and writes data over several drives?

   A. Parity

   B. Mirroring

   C. Striping

   D. Hot-swapping

11. What is the difference between hierarchical storage management and storage area network technologies?

   A. HSM uses optical or tape jukeboxes, and SAN is a standard of how to develop and implement this technology.

   B. HSM and SAN are one and the same. The difference is in the implementation.

   C. HSM uses optical or tape jukeboxes, and SAN is a network of connected storage.

   D. SAN uses optical or tape jukeboxes, and HSM is a network of connected storage systems.

12. John and his team are conducting a penetration test of a client's network. The team will conduct its testing armed only with knowledge it acquired from the Web. The network staff is aware that the testing will take place, but the penetration testing team will only work with publicly available data and some information from the client. What is the degree of the team's knowledge and what type of test is the team carrying out?

   A. Full knowledge; blind test

   B. Partial knowledge; blind test

   C. Partial knowledge; double-blind test

   D. Zero knowledge; targeted test

13. What type of exploited vulnerability allows more input than the program has allocated space to store it?

A. Symbolic links

B. File descriptors

C. Kernel flaws

D. Buffer overflows

14. There are often scenarios where the IT staff must react to emergencies and quickly apply fixes or change configurations. When dealing with such emergencies, which of the following is the best approach to making changes?

A. Review the changes within 48 hours of making them.

B. Review and document the emergency changes after the incident is over.

C. Activity should not take place in this manner.

D. Formally submit the change to a change control committee and follow the complete change control process.

15. Organizations should keep system documentation on hand to ensure that the system is properly cared for, that changes are controlled, and that the organization knows what's on the system. What does not need to be in this type of documentation?

A. Functionality

B. Changes

C. Volume of transactions

D. Identity of system owner

16. Fred is a new security officer who wants to implement a control for detecting and preventing users who attempt to exceed their authority by misusing the access rights that have been assigned to them. Which of the following best fits this need?

A. Management review

B. Two-factor identification and authentication

C. Capturing this data in audit logs

D. Implementation of a strong security policy

17. Which of the following is the best way to reduce brute-force attacks that allow intruders to uncover users' passwords?

A. Increase the clipping level.

B. Lock out an account for a certain amount of time after the clipping level is reached.

C. After a threshold of failed login attempts is met, the administrator must physically lock out the account.

D. Choose a weaker algorithm that encrypts the password file.

18. Brandy could not figure out how Sam gained unauthorized access to her system, since he has little computer experience. Which of the following is most likely the attack Sam used?

    A. Dictionary attack

    B. Shoulder surfing attack

    C. Covert channel attack

    D. Timing attack

19. The relay agent on a mail server plays a role in spam prevention. Which of the following incorrectly describes mail relays?

    A. Antispam features on mail servers are actually antirelaying features.

    B. Relays should be configured "wide open" to receive any e-mail message.

    C. Relay agents are used to send messages from one mail server to another.

    D. If a relay is configured "wide open," the mail server can be used to send spam.

20. John is responsible for providing a weekly report to his manager outlining the week's security incidents and mitigation steps. What steps should he take if a report has no information?

    A. Send his manager an e-mail telling her so.

    B. Deliver last week's report and make sure it's clearly dated.

    C. Deliver a report that states "No output."

    D. Don't do anything.

21. Brian, a security administrator, is responding to a virus infection. The antivirus application reports that a file has been infected with a dangerous virus and disinfecting it could damage the file. What course of action should Brian take?

    A. Replace the file with the file saved from the day before.

    B. Disinfect the file and contact the vendor.

    C. Restore an uninfected version of the patched file from backup media.

    D. Back up the data and disinfect the file.

22. Guidelines should be followed to allow secure remote administration. Which of the following is not one of those guidelines?

    A. A small number of administrators should be allowed to carry out remote functionality.

    B. Critical systems should be administered locally instead of remotely.

    C. Strong authentication should be in place.

    D. Telnet should be used to send commands and data.

23. In a redundant array of inexpensive disks (RAID) systems, data and parity information are striped over several different disks. What is parity information used for?

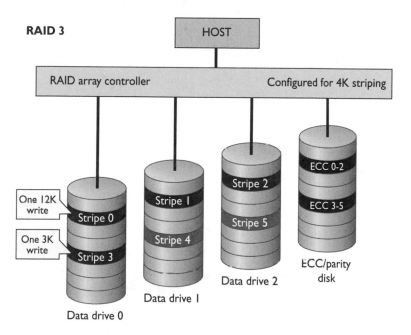

    A. Information used to create new data

    B. Information used to erase data

    C. Information used to rebuild data

    D. Information used to build data

24. Mirroring of drives is when data is written to two drives at once for redundancy purposes. What similar type of technology is shown in the graphic that follows?

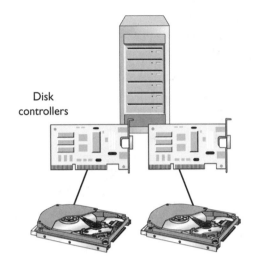

Disk controllers

A. Direct access storage

B. Disk duplexing

C. Striping

D. Massive array of inactive disks

25. There are several different types of important architectures within backup technologies. Which architecture does the graphic that follows represent?

A. Clustering

B. Grid computing

C. Backup tier security

D. Hierarchical Storage Management

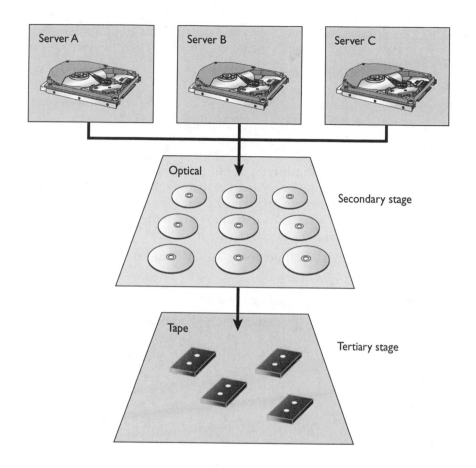

26. Which of the following is not considered a countermeasure to port scanning
    and operating system fingerprinting?

    A. Allow access at the perimeter network to all internal ports

    B. Remove as many banners as possible within operating systems and
       applications

    C. Use TCP wrappers on vulnerable services that have to be available

    D. Disable unnecessary ports and services

27. _____ provides for availability and scalability. It groups physically different systems and combines them logically, which helps to provide immunity to faults and improves performance.

    A. Disc duping

    B. Clustering

    C. RAID

    D. Virtualization

28. Bob is a new security administrator at a financial institution. The organization has experienced some suspicious activity on one of the critical servers that contain customer data. When reviewing how the systems are administered, he uncovers some concerning issues pertaining to remote administration. Which of the following should not be put into place to reduce these concerns?

    i. Commands and data should not be sent in cleartext.

    ii. SSH should be used, not Telnet.

    iii. Truly critical systems should be administered locally instead of remotely.

    iv. Only a small number of administrators should be able to carry out remote functionality.

    v. Strong authentication should be in place for any administration activities.

    A. i, ii

    B. None of them

    C. ii, iv

    D. All of them

The following scenario will be used for questions 29 and 30.

John is a network administrator and has been told by one of his network staff members that two servers on the network have recently had suspicious traffic traveling to them and then from them in a sporadic manner. The traffic has been mainly ICMP, but the patterns were unusual compared to other servers over the last 30 days. John lists the directories and subdirectories on the systems and finds nothing unusual. He inspects the running processes and again finds nothing suspicious. He sees that the systems' NICs are not in promiscuous mode, so he is assured that sniffers have not been planted.

29. Which of the following describes the most likely situation as described in this scenario?

    A. Servers are not infected, but the traffic illustrates attack attempts.

    B. Servers have been infected with rootkits.

C. Servers are vulnerable and need to be patched.

D. Servers have been infected by spyware.

30. Which of the following best explains why John does not see anything suspicious on the reported systems?

   A. The systems have not yet been infected.

   B. He is not running the correct tools. He needs to carry out a penetration test on the two systems.

   C. Trojaned files have been loaded and executed.

   D. A back door has been installed and the attacker enters the system sporadically.

1. B	11. C	21. C
2. A	12. B	22. D
3. D	13. D	23. C
4. A	14. B	24. B
5. B	15. C	25. D
6. A	16. A	26. A
7. C	17. B	27. B
8. B	18. B	28. B
9. D	19. B	29. B
10. C	20. C	30. C

1. Which of the following is not a common component of configuration management change control steps?

   A. Tested and presented

   B. Service-level agreement approval

   C. Report change to management

   D. Approval of the change

   ☑ **B.** A well-structured change management process should be established to aid staff members through many different types of changes to the environment. This process should be laid out in the change control policy. Although the types of changes vary, a standard list of procedures can help keep the process under control and ensure it is carried out in a predictable manner. A change control policy should include procedures for requesting a change to take place, approving the change, documentation of the change, testing and presentation, implementation, and reporting the change to management. Configuration management change control processes do not commonly have an effect on service-level agreement approvals.

   ☒ **A** is incorrect because testing and presentation should be included in a standard change control policy. All changes must be fully tested to uncover any unforeseen results. Depending on the severity of the change and the company's organization, the change and implementation may need to be presented to a change control committee. This helps show different sides to the purpose and outcome of the change and the possible ramifications.

   ☒ **C** is incorrect because a procedure for reporting a change to management should be included in a standard change control policy. After a change is implemented, a full report summarizing the change should be submitted to management. This report can be submitted on a periodic basis to keep management up to date and ensure continual support.

   ☒ **D** is incorrect because a procedure for obtaining approval for the change should be included in a standard change control policy. The individual requesting the change must justify the reasons and clearly show the benefits and possible pitfalls of the change. Sometimes the requester is asked to conduct more research and provide more information before the change is approved.

2. A change management process should include a number of procedures. Which of the following incorrectly describes a characteristic or component of a change control policy?

   A. Changes that are unanimously approved by the change control committee must be tested to uncover any unforeseen results.

   B. Changes approved by the change control committee should be entered into a change log.

   C. A schedule that outlines the projected phases of the change should be developed.

   D. An individual or group should be responsible for approving proposed changes.

   ☑ A. A well-structured change management process should be put into place to aid staff members through many different types of changes to the environment. This process should be laid out in the change control policy. Although the types of changes vary, a standard list of procedures can help keep the process under control and ensure it is carried out in a predictable manner. All changes approved by the change control committee must be fully tested to uncover any unforeseen results. Depending on the severity of the change and the company's organization, the change and implementation may need to be presented to a change control committee. This helps show different sides to the purpose and outcome of the change and the possible ramifications.

   ☒ B is incorrect because it is true that changes approved by the change control committee should be entered into a change log. The log should be updated as the process continues toward completion. It is important to track and document all changes that are approved and implemented.

   ☒ C is incorrect because once a change is fully tested and approved, a schedule should be developed that outlines the projected phases of the change being implemented and the necessary milestones. These steps should be fully documented, and progress should be monitored.

   ☒ D is incorrect because requests should be presented to an individual or group that is responsible for approving changes and overseeing the activities of changes that take place within an environment.

3. The requirement of erasure is the end of the media life cycle if it contains sensitive information. Which of the following best describes purging?

    A. Changing the polarization of the atoms on the media.

    B. It is uacceptable when media are to be reused in the same physical environment for the same purposes.

    C. Data formerly on the media is made unrecoverable by overwriting it with a pattern.

    D. Information is made unrecoverable, even with extraordinary effort.

    ☑ **D.** Purging is the removal of sensitive data from a system, storage device, or peripheral device with storage capacity at the end of a processing period. This action is performed in such a way that there is assurance proportional to the sensitivity of the data that the data cannot be reconstructed. Deleting files on a medium does not actually make the data disappear; it only deletes the pointers to where the data in those files still live on the medium. This is how companies that specialize in restoration can recover the deleted files intact after they have been apparently/accidentally destroyed. Even simply overwriting media with new information may not eliminate the possibility of recovering the previously written information. This is why zeroization and secure overwriting algorithms are required. And, if any part of a medium containing highly sensitive information cannot be cleared or purged, then physical destruction must take place.

    ☒ A is incorrect because it describes degaussing, which is an example of purging. A device that performs degaussing generates a coercive magnetic force that reduces the magnetic flux density of the storage media to zero. This magnetic force is what properly erases data from media. Data is stored on magnetic media by the representation of the polarization of the atoms. Degaussing changes this polarization by using a type of large magnet to bring it back to its original flux (magnetic alignment).

    ☒ B is incorrect because purging is required when media will be repurposed to a different compartment. When media are erased (cleared of their contents), they are said to be sanitized. This means erasing information so that it is not readily retrieved using routine operating system commands or commercially available forensic/data recovery software.

    ☒ C is incorrect because it describes zeroization, which is an example of purging but does not describe purging itself. Media holding sensitive data must be properly purged, which can be accomplished through zeroization, degaussing, or media destruction.

4. Device backup and other availability solutions are chosen to balance the value of having information available against the cost of keeping that information available. Which of the following best describes fault-tolerant technologies?

   A. They are among the most expensive solutions and are usually only for the most mission-critical information.

   B. They help service providers identify appropriate availability services for the specific customer.

   C. They are required to maintain integrity, regardless of the other technologies in place.

   D. They allow a failed component to be replaced while the system continues to run.

   ☑ A. Fault-tolerant technologies keep information available not only against individual storage device faults but even against whole system failures. Fault tolerance is among the most expensive possible solutions for availability and is commonly justified only for the most mission-critical information. All technology will eventually experience a failure of some form. A company that would suffer irreparable harm from any unplanned downtime can justify paying the high cost for fault-tolerant systems.

   ☒ B is incorrect because service-level agreements (SLAs) help service providers, whether they are an internal IT operation or an outsourcer, decide what type of availability technology and service is appropriate. From this determination, the price of a service or the budget of the IT operation can be set. The process of developing an SLA with a business is also beneficial to the business. While some businesses have performed this type of introspection on their own, many have not, and being forced to go through the exercise as part of budgeting for their internal IT operations or external sourcing helps the business understand the real value of its information.

   ☒ C is incorrect because fault-tolerant technologies do not necessarily have anything to do with data or system integrity.

   ☒ D is incorrect because "hot-swappable" hardware does not require shutting down the system and may or may not be considered a fault-tolerant technology. Hot-swapping allows the administrator to replace the failed component while the system continues to run and information remains available; usually degraded performance results, but unplanned downtime is avoided.

5. Which of the following refers to the amount of time it will be expected to take to get a device fixed and back into production?

   A. SLA

   B. MTTR

   C. Hot swap

   D. MTBF

   ☑ **B.** Mean time to repair (MTTR) is the amount of time it will be expected to take to get a device fixed and back into production. For a hard drive in a redundant array, the MTTR is the amount of time between the actual failure and the time when, after noticing the failure, someone has replaced the failed drive and the redundant array has completed rewriting the information on the new drive. This is likely to be measured in hours. For a nonredundant hard drive in a desktop PC, the MTTR is the amount of time between when the drive goes down and the time when the replaced hard drive has been reloaded with the operating system, software, and any backed-up data belonging to the user. This is likely to be measured in days. For an unplanned reboot, the MTTR is the amount of time between the failure of the system and the point in time when it has rebooted its operating system, checked the state of its disks, restarted its applications, allowed its applications to check the consistency of their data, and once again begun processing transactions.

   ☒ **A** is incorrect because a service-level agreement (SLA) addresses the degree of availability that will be provided to a customer, whether that customer be an internal department within the same organization or an external customer. The MTTR is the amount of time it will be expected to get a device fixed and back into production. The MTTR may pertain to fixing a component or the device or replacing the device.

   ☒ **C** is incorrect because hot-swapping refers to the replacement of a failed component while the system continues to run and information remains available. Usually degraded performance results, but unplanned downtime is avoided. Hot-swapping does not refer to the amount of time needed to get a system back up and running.

   ☒ **D** is incorrect because MTBF refers to mean time between failure, which is the estimated lifespan of a piece of equipment. It is calculated by the vendor of the equipment or a third party. The reason for using this value is to know approximately when a particular device will need to be replaced. It is used as a benchmark for reliability by predicting the average time that will pass in the operation of a component or a system until it needs to be replaced.

6. Which of the following correctly describes Direct Access and Sequential Access storage devices?

   A. Any point on a Direct Access Storage Device may be promptly reached, whereas every point in between the current position and the desired position of a Sequential Access Storage Device must be traversed in order to reach the desired position.

   B. RAIT is an example of a Direct Access Storage Device, while RAID is an example of a Sequential Access Storage Device.

   C. MAID is a Direct Access Storage Device, while RAID is an example of a Sequential Access Storage Device.

   D. As an example of Sequential Access Storage, tape drives are faster than Direct Access Storage Devices.

   ☑ **A.** Direct Access Storage Device (DASD) is a general term for magnetic disk storage devices, which historically have been used in mainframe and minicomputer (mid-range computer) environments. A redundant array of independent disks (RAID) is a type of DASD. The key distinction between Direct Access and Sequential Access storage devices is that any point on a Direct Access Storage Device may be promptly reached, whereas every point in between the current position and the desired position of a Sequential Access Storage Device must be traversed in order to reach the desired position. Tape drives are Sequential Access Storage Devices. Tape storage is the lowest-cost option for very large amounts of data but is very slow compared to disk storage.

   ☒ **B** is incorrect because RAIT stands for redundant array of independent tapes. RAIT uses tape drives, which are Sequential Access Storage Devices. In RAIT, data are striped in parallel to multiple tape drives, with or without a redundant parity drive. This provides the high capacity at low cost typical of tape storage, with higher than usual tape data transfer rates, and optional data integrity. RAID, or redundant array of independent disks, is a type of Direct Access Storage Device. RAID combines several physical disks and aggregates them into logical arrays. When data is saved, the information is written across all drives. A RAID appears as a single drive to applications and other devices.

   ☒ **C** is incorrect because both MAID, a massive array of inactive disks, and RAID, a redundant array of independent disks, are examples of Direct Access Storage Devices. Any point on these magnetic disk storage devices can be reached without traversing every point between the current and desired positions. This makes Direct Access Storage Devices faster than Sequential Access Storage Devices.

   ☒ **D** is incorrect because Sequential Access Storage Devices are slower than Direct Access Storage Devices. Tape drives are an example of Sequential Access Storage Device technology.

7. There are classifications for operating system failures. Which of the following refers to what takes place when an unexpected kernel or media failure happens and the regular recovery procedure cannot recover the system to a more consistent state, requiring an administrator to intervene?

A. Emergency system restart

B. Trusted recovery

C. System cold start

D. System reboot

☑ C. An operating system's response to a failure can be classified as either a system reboot, an emergency system restart, or a system cold start. A system cold start takes place when an unexpected kernel or media failure happens and the regular recovery procedure cannot recover the system to a more consistent state. The system, kernel, and user objects may remain in an inconsistent state while the system attempts to recover itself, and intervention is commonly required by the user or administrator to restore the system.

☒ A is incorrect because an emergency system restart takes place after a system failure happens in an uncontrolled manner without the need of a person to be involved. The failure could be a kernel or media failure caused by lower-privileged user processes attempting to access memory segments that are restricted. The system sees this as an insecure activity that it cannot properly recover from without rebooting. The kernel and user objects could be in an inconsistent state, and data could be lost or corrupted. The system thus reboots itself and goes into maintenance mode and recovers from the actions taken. Then it is brought back up in a consistent and stable state.

☒ B is incorrect because trusted recovery is not one of the three classifications for an operating system's response to a type of failure. Trusted recovery is a general term that means that when an operating system or application crashes or freezes, it should not put the system in any type of insecure state. The usual reason for a system crash in the first place is that it encountered something it perceived as insecure or did not understand and decided it was safer to freeze, shut down, or reboot than to perform the current activity.

☒ D is incorrect because a system reboot takes place after the system shuts itself down in a controlled manner in response to a kernel (trusted computing base) failure and does not require a person to be involved. If the system finds inconsistent object data structures, or if there is not enough space in some critical tables, a system reboot may take place. This releases resources and returns the system to a more stable and safer state.

8. Various levels of RAID dictate the type of activity that will take place within the RAID system. Which level is associated with byte-level parity?

    A. RAID Level 0

    B. RAID Level 3

    C. RAID Level 5

    D. RAID Level 10

    ☑ **B.** Redundant array of inexpensive disks (RAID) provides fault tolerance for hard drives and can improve system performance. Redundancy and speed are provided by breaking up the data and writing it across several disks so that different disk heads can work simultaneously to retrieve the requested information. Recovery data is also created—this is called parity—so that if one disk fails, the parity data can be used to reconstruct the corrupted or lost information. Different activities that provide fault tolerance or performance improvements occur at different levels of a RAID system. RAID Level 3 is a scheme employing byte-level striping and a dedicated parity disk. Data is striped over all but the last drive with parity data held on only the last drive. If a drive fails, it can be reconstructed from the parity drive. The most common RAID levels used today are Levels 1, 3, and 5.

    ☒ **A** is incorrect because only striping occurs at Level 0. Data are striped over several drives. No redundancy or parity is involved. If one volume fails, the entire volume can be unusable. Level 0 is used for performance only.

    ☒ **C** is incorrect because RAID 5 employs block-level striping and interleaving parity across all disks. Data are written in disk block units to all drives. Parity is written to all drives also, which ensures there is no single point of failure. RAID Level 5 is the most commonly used mode.

    ☒ **D** is incorrect because Level 10 is associated with striping and mirroring. It is a combination of Levels 1 and 0. Data are simultaneously mirrored and striped across several drives and can support multiple drive failures.

9. Which of the following incorrectly describes IP spoofing and session hijacking?

    A. Address spoofing helps an attacker to hijack sessions between two users without being noticed.

    B. IP spoofing makes it harder to track down an attacker.

    C. Session hijacking can be prevented with mutual authentication.

    D. IP spoofing is used to hijack SSL and IPSec secure communications.

    ☑ **D.** Secure Sockets Layer (SSL) and IPSec can protect the integrity, authenticity, and confidentiality of network traffic. Even if an attacker spoofed an IP address, he would not be able to successfully manipulate or read SSL- or IPSec-encrypted traffic, as he would not have access to the keys and other cryptographic material required.

☒ **A** is incorrect because the statement is true. Address spoofing helps an attacker to hijack sessions between two users without being noticed. If an attacker wanted to take over a session between two computers, she would need to put herself in the middle of their conversation without being detected. Tools like Juggernaut and the HUNT Project enable the attacker to spy on the TCP connection and then hijack it.

☒ **B** is incorrect because the statement is true. Spoofing is the presentation of false information, usually within packets, to trick other systems and hide the origin of the message. This is usually done by hackers so that their identity cannot be successfully uncovered.

☒ **C** is incorrect because the statement is true. If session hijacking is a concern on a network, the administrator can implement a protocol, such as IPSec or Kerberos, that requires mutual authentication between users or systems.

10. RAID systems use a number of techniques to provide redundancy and performance. Which of the following activities divides and writes data over several drives?

   A. Parity

   B. Mirroring

   C. Striping

   D. Hot-swapping

   ☑ **C.** Redundant array of inexpensive disks (RAID) is a technology used for redundancy and/or performance improvement. It combines several physical disks and aggregates them into logical arrays. When data is saved, the information is written across all drives. A RAID appears as a single drive to applications and other devices. When striping is used, data is written across all drives. This activity divides and writes the data over several drives. Both write and read performance are increased dramatically because more than one head is reading or writing data at the same time.

   ☒ **A** is incorrect because parity is used to rebuild lost or corrupted data. Various levels of RAID dictate the type of activity that will take place within the RAID system. Some levels deal only with performance issues, while other levels deal with performance and fault tolerance. If fault tolerance is one of the services a RAID level provides, parity is involved. If a drive fails, the parity is basically instructions that tell the RAID system how to rebuild the lost data on the new hard drive. Parity is used to rebuild a new drive so that all the information is restored.

   ☒ **B** is incorrect because mirroring occurs when data is written to two drives at once. If one drive fails, the other drive has the exact same data available.

Mirroring provides redundancy. Mirroring occurs at Level 1 of RAID systems, and with striping in Level 10.

☒ **D** is incorrect because hot-swappable refers to a type of disk that is in most RAID systems. RAID systems with hot-swapping disks are able to replace drives while the system is running. When a drive is swapped out, or added, the parity data is used to rebuild the data on the new disk that was just added.

11. What is the difference between hierarchical storage management and storage area network technologies?

    A. HSM uses optical or tape jukeboxes, and SAN is a standard of how to develop and implement this technology.

    B. HSM and SAN are one and the same. The difference is in the implementation.

    C. HSM uses optical or tape jukeboxes, and SAN is a network of connected storage.

    D. SAN uses optical or tape jukeboxes, and HSM is a network of connected storage systems.

    ☑ **C.** Hierarchical storage management (HSM) provides continuous online backup functionality. It combines hard disk technology with the cheaper and slower optical or tape jukeboxes. The HSM system dynamically manages the storage and recovery of files, which are copied to storage media devices that vary in speed and cost. The faster media hold the data that is accessed more often, and the seldom-used files are stored on the slower devices, or near-line devices. The storage media could include optical disks, magnetic disks, and tapes. This functionality happens in the background without the knowledge of the user or any need for user intervention. A storage area network, on the other hand, consists of large amounts of storage devices linked together by a high-speed private network and storage-specific switches. When a user makes a request for a file, he does not need to know which server or tape drive to go to—the SAN software finds it and provides it to the user.

    ☒ **A** is incorrect because SAN is not a standard for how to develop and implement HSM. A SAN is a network of connected storage devices. SANs provide redundancy, fault tolerance, reliability, and backups, and they allow the users and administrators to interact with the SAN as one virtual entity. Because the network that carries the data in the SAN is separate from a company's regular data network, all of this performance, reliability, and flexibility come, without impact to the data networking capabilities of the systems on the network.

    ☒ **B** is incorrect because HSM and SAN are not the same. Hierarchical storage management (HSM) uses conventional hard disk backup processes combined with optical/tape jukeboxes. A storage area network (SAN) uses a networked system of storage devices integrated into an established network.

☒ **D** is incorrect because the statement is backward. HSM uses optical or tape jukeboxes, and SAN is a network of connected storage systems. HSM was created to save money and time. It provides an economical and efficient way of storing data by combining higher-speed, higher-cost storage media for frequently accessed data with lower-speed, lower-cost media for infrequently accessed data. SANs, on the other hand, are for companies that have to keep track of terabytes of data and have the funds for this type of technology. They are not commonly used in large or mid-sized companies.

12. John and his team are conducting a penetration test of a client's network. The team will conduct its testing armed only with knowledge it acquired from the Web. The network staff is aware that the testing will take place, but the penetration testing team will only work with publicly available data and some information from the client. What is the degree of the team's knowledge and what type of test is the team carrying out?

A. Full knowledge; blind test

B. Partial knowledge; blind test

C. Partial knowledge; double-blind test

D. Zero knowledge; targeted test

☑ **B.** The penetration testing team can have varying degrees of knowledge about the penetration target before the tests are actually carried out. These degrees of knowledge are zero knowledge, partial knowledge, and full knowledge. John and his team have partial knowledge; the team has some information about the target. Tests may also be blind, double-blind, or targeted. John's team is carrying out a blind test, meaning that the network staff knows that the test will take place.

☒ **A** is incorrect because John and his team do not have full knowledge of the target. Full knowledge means that the team has intimate knowledge of the target and fully understands the network, its software, and configurations. John's team has information it gathered from the Web and partial information from the client. This is partial knowledge. The rest of the answer is correct; the team is conducting a blind test.

☒ **C** is incorrect because John and his team are not conducting a double-blind test. A double-blind test, also called a stealth assessment, is when the assessor carries out a blind test without the security staff's knowledge. This enables the test to evaluate the network's security level and the staff's responses, log monitoring, and escalation processes, and is a more realistic demonstration of the likely success or failure of an attack.

☒ **D** is incorrect because John and his team do not have zero knowledge, nor are they conducting a targeted test. Zero knowledge means that the team does not have any knowledge of the target and must start from ground zero. John's team is starting the project with knowledge it acquired about the target online and with information provided by the client. Targeted tests commonly involve external consultants and internal staff carrying out focused tests on specific areas of interest. For example, before a new application is rolled out, the team might test it for vulnerabilities before installing it into production. John's team is not focusing its testing efforts on any one specific area.

13. What type of exploited vulnerability allows more input than the program has allocated space to store it?

    A. Symbolic links

    B. File descriptors

    C. Kernel flaws

    D. Buffer overflows

    ☑ **D.** Poor programming practices allow more input than the software has allocated space to store it. This overwrites data or program memory after the end of the allocated buffer, and sometimes it allows the attacker to inject program code and then cause the processor to execute it in what is called a buffer overflow. This gives the attacker the same level of access as that held by the software that was successfully attacked. If the program was run as an administrative user or by the system itself, this can mean complete access to the system. Good programming practice, automated source code scanners, enhanced programming libraries, and strongly typed languages that disallow buffer overflows are all ways of reducing this type of vulnerability.

    ☒ **A** is incorrect because a symbolic link is a stub file that redirects access to system files or data to another place. If an attacker can compromise the symbolic link, then the attacker may be able to gain unauthorized access. (Symbolic links are used in Unix and Linux type systems.) This may allow the attacker to damage important data and/or gain privileged access to the system. A historical example of this was to use a symbolic link to cause a program to delete a password database, or replace a line in the password database with characters that, in essence, created an unpassworded root-equivalent account. Programs, and especially scripts, must be written to assure that the full path to the file cannot be circumvented.

    ☒ **B** is incorrect because file descriptors are exploited if a program makes unsafe use of a file descriptor and an attacker is able to cause unexpected input to be provided to the program, or cause output to go to an unexpected place with the privileges of the executing program. File descriptors are numbers many operating systems use to represent open files in a process. Certain file descriptor numbers are universal, meaning the same thing to all programs. Good programming practices, automated source code scanners, and application security testing are all ways of reducing file descriptor attacks.

☒ C is incorrect because kernel flaws are problems that occur below the level of the user interface, deep inside the operating system. Flaws in the kernel that can be reached by an attacker, if exploitable, give the attacker the most powerful level of control over the system. It is important to ensure that security patches to operating systems—after sufficient testing—are promptly deployed in the environment to keep the window of vulnerability as small as possible.

14. There are often scenarios where the IT staff must react to emergencies and quickly apply fixes or change configurations. When dealing with such emergencies, which of the following is the best approach to making changes?

    A. Review the changes within 48 hours of making them.

    B. Review and document the emergency changes after the incident is over.

    C. Activity should not take place in this manner.

    D. Formally submit the change to a change control committee and follow the complete change control process.

    ☑ B. After the incident or emergency is over, the staff should review the changes to ensure that they are correct and do not open security holes or affect interoperability. The changes need to be properly documented and the system owner needs to be informed of changes.

    ☒ A is incorrect because it is not the best answer. The changes should be reviewed after the incident is over, but not necessarily within 48 hours. Many times the changes should be reviewed hours after they are implemented—not days.

    ☒ C is incorrect because, while it would be nice if emergencies didn't happen, they are unavoidable. At one point or another, for example, an IT administrator will have to roll out a patch or change configurations to protect systems against a high-profile vulnerability.

    ☒ D is incorrect because if an emergency is taking place, then there is no time to go through the process of submitting a change to the change control committee and following the complete change control process. These steps usually apply to large changes that take place to a network or environment. These types of changes are typically expensive and can have lasting effects on a company.

15. Organizations should keep system documentation on hand to ensure that the system is properly cared for, that changes are controlled, and that the organization knows what's on the system. What does not need to be in this type of documentation?

A. Functionality

B. Changes

C. Volume of transactions

D. Identity of system owner

☑ C. It is not important to have the amount of work that the system carries out included in the system documentation. The number of transactions usually changes daily and thus is usually captured through some type of automated performance tool if the company needs to keep track of this information.

☒ A is incorrect because system documentation should include a description of the system's functionality. Functionality is the reason we have systems and software. The functionality of a system and how it interacts with other systems should be fully understood and documented.

☒ B is incorrect because changes made to the system should be included in the system documentation. Documentation is very important for data processing and networked environments. If changes are not properly documented, employees will forget what actually took place with each device. If the environment needs to be rebuilt, for example, it may be done incorrectly if the procedure was poorly or improperly documented.

☒ D is incorrect because the system owner's identity should be included in the system documentation. The system owner is responsible for the functionality and availability of the system. If something goes wrong, the system owner needs to be contacted; thus, this information must be documented.

16. Fred is a new security officer who wants to implement a control for detecting and preventing users who attempt to exceed their authority by misusing the access rights that have been assigned to them. Which of the following best fits this need?

A. Management review

B. Two-factor identification and authentication

C. Capturing this data in audit logs

D. Implementation of a strong security policy

☑ A. The goal of this question is for you to realize that management and supervisor involvement is critical to ensure that these types of things do not take place or are properly detected and acted upon if they do take place. If the users know that management will take action if they misbehave, this can be considered preventive in nature. The activities will only be known of after they take place, which means that the security office has to carry out some type of detective activity so that he can then inform management.

☒ **B** is incorrect because identification and authentication is preventive, not detective.

☒ **C** is incorrect because audit logs are detective but not preventive. However, in order to be detective, the audit logs must be reviewed by a security administrator. While some of the strongest security protections come from preventive controls, detective controls such as reviewing audit logs are also required.

☒ **D** is incorrect because a security policy is preventive, not detective. A security policy is developed and implemented to inform users of what is expected of them and the potential ramifications if they do not follow the constructs of the policy.

17. Which of the following is the best way to reduce brute-force attacks that allow intruders to uncover users' passwords?

   A. Increase the clipping level.

   B. Lock out an account for a certain amount of time after the clipping level is reached.

   C. After a threshold of failed login attempts is met, the administrator must physically lock out the account.

   D. Choose a weaker algorithm that encrypts the password file.

   ☑ **B.** A brute-force attack is an attack that continually tries different inputs to achieve a predefined goal, which can then be used to obtain credentials for unauthorized access. A brute-force attack to uncover passwords means that the intruder is attempting all possible sequences of characters to uncover the correct password. If the account would be disabled (or locked out) after this type of attack attempt took place, this would prove to be a good countermeasure.

   ☒ **A** is incorrect because clipping levels should be implemented to establish a baseline of user activity and acceptable errors. An entity attempting to log in to an account should be locked out once the clipping level is met. A higher clipping level gives an attacker more attempts between alerts or lockout. Decreasing the clipping level would be a good countermeasure.

   ☒ **C** is incorrect because it is not practical to have an administrator physically lock out accounts. This type of activity can easily be taken care of through automated software mechanisms. Accounts should be automatically locked out for a certain amount of time after a threshold of failed login attempts has been met.

☒ D is incorrect because using a weaker algorithm that encrypts passwords and/or password files would increase the likelihood of success of a brute-force attack.

18. Brandy could not figure out how Sam gained unauthorized access to her system, since he has little computer experience. Which of the following is most likely the attack Sam used?

A. Dictionary attack

B. Shoulder surfing attack

C. Covert channel attack

D. Timing attack

☑ B. Shoulder surfing is a type of browsing attack in which an attacker looks over another's shoulder to see items on that person's monitor or what is being typed in at the keyboard. Sam probably viewed Brandy's password as she typed it. Of the attacks listed, this is the easiest to execute in that it does not require any real knowledge of computer systems.

☒ A is incorrect because a dictionary attack is an automated attack involving the use of tools like Crack or L0phtcrack. Sam would need to be aware of these tools and know how to find and use them. A dictionary attack requires more knowledge of how computer systems work compared to shoulder surfing.

☒ C is incorrect because a covert channel attack requires computer expertise. A covert channel is a communications path that enables a process to transmit information in a way that violates the system's security policy. Identifying and using a covert channel requires a lot more computer expertise compared to a shoulder surfing attack.

☒ D is incorrect because a timing attack requires intimate knowledge of how software executes its instruction sets so that they can be manipulated. Commonly a person who could successfully carry out this attack requires programming experience.

19. The relay agent on a mail server plays a role in spam prevention. Which of the following incorrectly describes mail relays?

A. Antispam features on mail servers are actually antirelaying features.

B. Relays should be configured "wide open" to receive any e-mail message.

C. Relay agents are used to send messages from one mail server to another.

D. If a relay is configured "wide open," the mail server can be used to send spam.

☑ **B.** Most companies have their public mail servers in their DMZ and may have one or more servers within their LAN. The mail servers in the DMZ are in this protected space because they are directly connected to the Internet. These servers should be tightly locked down and their relaying mechanisms should be correctly configured. If relays are configured "wide open" on a mail server, the mail server can be used to receive any mail message and send it on to the intended recipients, thereby contributing to the distribution of spam. Therefore, mail relays should not be configured "wide open."

☒ **A** is incorrect because it is true that antispam features are actually antire-laying features. It is important that mail servers have the proper antispam features enabled. Many companies also employ antivirus and content-filtering applications on their mail servers to try to stop the spread of malicious code, and not allow unacceptable messages through the e-mail gateway. It is important to filter both incoming and outgoing messages. This helps ensure that inside employees are not spreading viruses or sending out messages that are against company policy.

☒ **C** is incorrect because it is true that mail servers use a relay agent to send a message from one mail server to another. This relay agent needs to be properly configured so that a company's mail server is not used by another for spamming activity. Spamming usually is illegal, so the people doing the spamming do not want the traffic to seem as though it originated from their equipment. They will find mail servers on the Internet or within company DMZs that have loosely configured relaying mechanisms and use these computers to send their spam.

☒ **D** is incorrect because it is true that if a relay is configured "wide open" the mail server can be used to send spam—and any other mail message it receives. This means that the server can be used to distribute advertisements for other companies, spam messages, and pornographic material.

20. John is responsible for providing a weekly report to his manager outlining the week's security incidents and mitigation steps. What steps should he take if a report has no information?

    A. Send his manager an e-mail telling her so.

    B. Deliver last week's report and make sure it's clearly dated.

    C. Deliver a report that states "No output."

    D. Don't do anything.

    ☑ **C.** If a report has no information (nothing to report), it should state, "No output." This ensures that the manager is aware that there is no information to report and that John isn't just slacking in his responsibilities.

☒ **A** is incorrect because John should still deliver his manager a report. It should say "No output." Even though an e-mail achieves the objective of communicating that there's nothing to report, a report should still be delivered for consistency.

☒ **B** is incorrect because delivering last week's report does not provide documentation or communicate to John's manager that there is nothing to report this week. He should give his manager a report that reads, "No output."

☒ **D** is incorrect because if John doesn't do anything when there is nothing to report, his manager must track John down and ask him for the report. For all she knows, John is slacking on his job duties. By providing a report that reads, "No output," John is communicating this information to his manager in an efficient manner that she has come to expect.

21. Brian, a security administrator, is responding to a virus infection. The antivirus application reports that a file has been infected with a dangerous virus and disinfecting it could damage the file. What course of action should Brian take?

    A. Replace the file with the file saved from the day before.

    B. Disinfect the file and contact the vendor.

    C. Restore an uninfected version of the patched file from backup media.

    D. Back up the data and disinfect the file.

    ☑ **C.** The best course of action is to install an uninfected version of a patched file from backup media. Attempts to disinfect the file could corrupt it, and it is important to restore a file that is known to be "clean."

    ☒ **A** is incorrect because the previous day's file could also be infected. It is best to replace the file entirely with a freshly installed and patched version.

    ☒ **B** is incorrect because disinfecting the file could cause damage, as stated in the question. In addition, the vendor of the application will not necessarily be useful in this situation. It is easier to restore a clean version of the file and move on with production.

    ☒ **D** is incorrect because backing up the file will also back up the virus, and as the question stated, disinfecting the file will cause damage and potential data loss.

22. Guidelines should be followed to allow secure remote administration. Which of the following is not one of those guidelines?

    A. A small number of administrators should be allowed to carry out remote functionality.

    B. Critical systems should be administered locally instead of remotely.

C. Strong authentication should be in place.

D. Telnet should be used to send commands and data.

☑ **D.** Telnet should not be allowed for remote administration because it sends all data, including administrator credentials, in cleartext. This type of communication should go over more secure protocols, as in SSH.

☒ **A** is incorrect because it is true that only a small number of administrators should be able to carry out remote functionality. This helps minimize the risk posed to the network.

☒ **B** is incorrect because it is true that critical systems should be administered locally instead of remotely. It is safer to send administrative commands over the internal, private network than it is to do so over a public network.

☒ **C** is incorrect because it is true that strong authentication should be in place for any administration activities. Anything less than strong authentication, such as a password, would be easy for an attacker to crack and thereby gain administrative access.

23. In redundant array of inexpensive disks (RAID) systems, data and parity information are striped over several different disks. What is parity information used for?

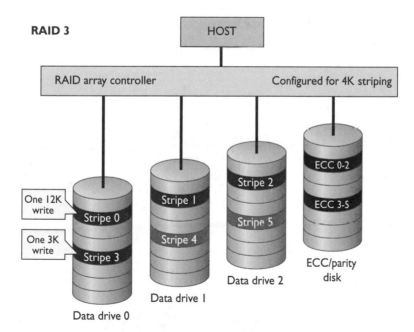

A. Information used to create new data

B. Information used to erase data

C. Information used to rebuild data

D. Information used to build data

☑ **C.** Redundant array of inexpensive disks (RAID) provides fault tolerance for hard drives and the data they hold and can improve system performance. Redundancy and speed are provided by breaking up the data and writing it across several disks so that different disk heads can work simultaneously to retrieve the requested information. Control data is also spread across each disk—this is called parity—so that if one disk fails, the other disks can work together and restore its data. If fault tolerance is one of the services a RAID level provides, parity is involved.

☒ **A** is incorrect because parity information is not used to create new data but is used as instructions on how to re-create data that has been lost or corrupted. If a drive fails, the parity is basically instructions that tell the RAID system how to rebuild the lost data on the new hard drive. Parity is used to rebuild a new drive so that all the information is restored.

☒ **B** is incorrect because parity information is not used to erase data but is used as instructions on how to re-create data that has been lost or corrupted.

☒ **D** is incorrect because parity information is not used to build data but is used as instructions on how to re-create data that has been lost or corrupted.

24. Mirroring of drives is when data is written to two drives at once for redundancy purposes. What similar type of technology is shown in the graphic that follows?

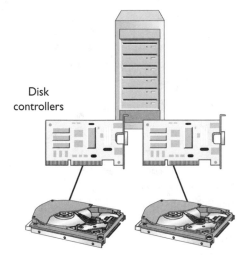

Disk
controllers

A. Direct access storage

B. Disk duplexing

C. Striping

D. Massive array of inactive disks

☑ **B.** Information that is required to always be available should be mirrored or duplexed. In both mirroring (also known as RAID 1) and duplexing, every data write operation occurs simultaneously or nearly simultaneously in more than one physical place. The distinction between mirroring and duplexing is that with mirroring the two (or more) physical places where the data is written may be attached to the same controller, leaving the storage still subject to the single point of failure of the controller itself; in duplexing, two or more controllers are used.

☒ **A** is incorrect because direct access storage is a general term for magnetic disk storage devices, which historically have been used in mainframe and minicomputer (mid-range computer) environments. A redundant array of independent disks (RAID) is a type of Direct Access Storage Device (DASD).

☒ **C** is incorrect because when data is written across all drives, the technique of striping is used. This activity divides and writes the data over several drives. The write performance is not affected, but the read performance is increased dramatically because more than one head is retrieving data at the same time. Parity information is used to rebuild lost or corrupted data. Striping just means data and potentially parity information is written across multiple disks.

☒ **D** is incorrect because in a massive array of inactive disks (MAID), rack-mounted disk arrays have all inactive disks powered down, with only the disk controller alive. When an application asks for data, the controller powers up the appropriate disk drive(s), transfers the data, and then powers the drive(s) down again. By powering down infrequently accessed drives, energy consumption is significantly reduced, and the service life of the disk drives may be increased.

25. There are several different types of important architectures within backup technologies. Which architecture does the graphic that follows represent?

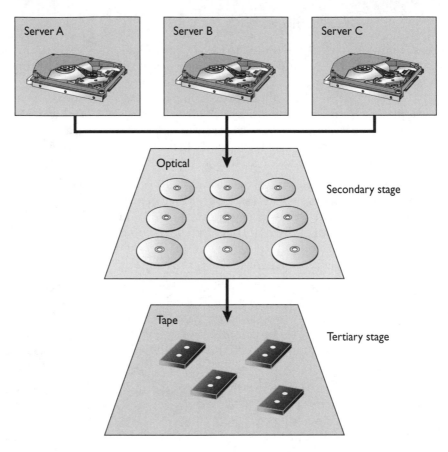

A. Clustering

B. Grid computing

C. Backup tier security

D. Hierarchical Storage Management

☑ D. Hierarchical Storage Management provides continuous online backup functionality. It combines hard disk technology with the cheaper and slower optical or tape jukeboxes. The HSM system dynamically manages the storage and recovery of files, which are copied to storage media devices that vary in speed and cost. The faster media hold the data that are accessed more often, and the seldom-used files are stored on the slower devices, or near-line devices.

☒ **A** is incorrect because clustering is a fault-tolerant server technology that is similar to redundant servers, except each server takes part in processing services that are requested. A server cluster is a group of servers that are viewed logically as one server to users and can be managed as a single logical system. Clustering provides for availability and scalability. It groups physically different systems and combines them logically, which provides immunity to faults and improves performance.

☒ **B** is incorrect because grid computing is load-balanced parallel means of massive computation, similar to clusters, but implemented with loosely coupled systems that may join and leave the grid randomly. Most computers have extra CPU processing power that is not being used many times throughout the day. Just like the power grid provides electricity to entities on an as-needed basis, computers can volunteer to allow their extra processing power to be available to different groups for different projects. The first project to use grid computing was SETI (Search for Extra-Terrestrial Intelligence), where people allowed their systems to participate in scanning the universe looking for aliens who are trying to talk to us.

☒ **C** is incorrect because backup tier security is not a formal technology and is a distracter answer.

26. Which of the following is not considered a countermeasure to port scanning and operating system fingerprinting?

    A. Allow access at the perimeter network to all internal ports

    B. Remove as many banners as possible within operating systems and applications

    C. Use TCP wrappers on vulnerable services that have to be available

    D. Disable unnecessary ports and services

    ☑ **A.** Access to internal ports is not a countermeasure. Several countermeasures should be put in place to reduce this threat:

    - Disable unnecessary ports and services.
    - Block access at the perimeter network using firewalls, routers, and proxy servers.
    - Use an IDS to identify this type of activity.
    - Use TCP wrappers on vulnerable services that have to be available.
    - Remove as many banners as possible within operating systems and applications.
    - Upgrade or update to more secure operating systems, applications, and protocols.

☒ **B** is incorrect because removing banners from operating systems and applications are countermeasures that should be put into place to make it harder for an attacker to fingerprint (identify) the software that is running on a system.

☒ **C** is incorrect because TCP wrappers (software components) monitor incoming network traffic to the host computer and control what can and cannot access the services mapped to specific ports. When a request comes to a computer at a specific port, the target operating system will check to see if this port is enabled. If it is enabled and the operating system sees that the corresponding service is wrapped, it knows to look at an access control list, which spells out who can access this service.

☒ **D** is incorrect because disabling ports and services is a critical countermeasure to reduce potential fingerprinting efforts. Enabled ports and services are clues used by the attacker to learn more about an environment. This knowledge enables the attacker to figure out the most successful ways of attacking.

27. _____ provides for availability and scalability. It groups physically different systems and combines them logically, which helps to provide immunity to faults and improves performance.

A. Disc duping

B. Clustering

C. RAID

D. Virtualization

☑ **B.** Clustering is a fault-tolerant server technology that is similar to redundant servers, except each server takes part in processing services that are requested. A server cluster is a group of servers that are viewed logically as one server to users and can be managed as a single logical system. Clustering provides for availability and scalability. It groups physically different systems and combines them logically, which helps to provide immunity to faults and improves performance. Clusters work as an intelligent unit to balance traffic, and users who access the cluster do not know they may be accessing different systems at different times. To the users, all servers within the cluster are seen as one unit.

☒ **A** is incorrect because this is a distracter answer. There is not an official technology with this name.

☒ **C** is incorrect because redundant array of inexpensive disks (RAID) provides fault tolerance for hard drives and can improve system performance. Redundancy and speed are provided by breaking up the data and writing them across several disks so different disk heads can work simultaneously to retrieve the requested information. RAID does not address scalability and performance.

- ☒ **D** is incorrect because virtualization is the creation of a virtual version of something, such as a hardware platform, operating system, storage device, or network resource. Hardware virtualization or platform virtualization refers to the creation of a virtual machine that acts like a real system with an operating system. Software executed on these virtual machines is separated from the underlying hardware resources by an abstraction layer.

28. Bob is a new security administrator at a financial institution. The organization has experienced some suspicious activity on one of the critical servers that contain customer data. When reviewing how the systems are administered, he uncovers some concerning issues pertaining to remote administration. Which of the following should not be put into place to reduce these concerns?

    i. Commands and data should not be sent in cleartext.

   ii. Secure Shell (SSH) should be used, not Telnet.

  iii. Truly critical systems should be administered locally instead of remotely.

  iv. Only a small number of administrators should be able to carry out remote functionality.

   v. Strong authentication should be in place for any administration activities.

  A. i, ii

  B. None of them

  C. ii, iv

  D. All of them

- ☑ **B.** All of these countermeasures should be put into place for proper remote administration activities.

- ☒ **A** is incorrect because sensitive commands and data should not be sent in cleartext (that is, they should be encrypted) to critical systems. For example, SSH should be used, not Telnet. SSH is a network protocol for secure data communication. It allows for remote shell services and command execution and other secure network services between two networked systems. It was designed as a replacement for Telnet and other insecure remote shell protocols such as the Berkeley rsh and rexec protocols, which send information, notably passwords, in plaintext, rendering them susceptible to interception and disclosure.

- ☒ **C** is incorrect because sensitive commands and data should not be sent in cleartext (that is, they should be encrypted). For example, SSH should be used, not Telnet. Truly critical systems should be administered locally instead of remotely. Only a small number of administrators should be able to carry out this remote functionality.

☒ **D** is incorrect because all of these countermeasures should be put into place for proper remote administration activities.

The following scenario will be used for questions 29 and 30.

John is a network administrator and has been told by one of his network staff members that two servers on the network have recently had suspicious traffic traveling to them and then from them in a sporadic manner. The traffic has been mainly ICMP, but the patterns were unusual compared to other servers over the last 30 days. John lists the directories and subdirectories on the systems and finds nothing unusual. He inspects the running processes and again finds nothing suspicious. He sees that the systems' NICs are not in promiscuous mode, so he is assured that sniffers have not been planted.

29. Which of the following describes the most likely situation as described in this scenario?

    A. Servers are not infected, but the traffic illustrates attack attempts.

    B. Servers have been infected with rootkits.

    C. Servers are vulnerable and need to be patched.

    D. Servers have been infected by spyware.

    ☑ **B.** Once the level of access is achieved, the attacker can upload a bundle of tools, collectively called a rootkit. A rootkit is software that implements stealth capabilities that are designed to hide the existence of certain processes or programs. Rootkit detection is difficult because a rootkit may be able to subvert the software that is intended to find it.

    ☒ **A** is incorrect because in the situation laid out in the scenario, the system most likely is infected. The ICMP traffic is probably the commands and status data sent between the attacker and the compromised systems.

    ☒ **C** is incorrect because it is not the best answer. The servers may be vulnerable and may need to be patched, but that is not what is being asked in the question. Plus applying a patch will not eradicate an infected system of a rootkit.

    ☒ **D** is incorrect because it is not the best answer. The scenario best describes a situation where rootkits have been installed. Spyware may be a component of the rootkit, but Trojaned files are most likely installed, which can only happen with rootkits, not spyware.

30. Which of the following best explains why John does not see anything suspicious on the reported systems?

    A. The systems have not yet been infected.

    B. He is not running the correct tools. He needs to carry out a penetration test on the two systems.

C. Trojaned files have been loaded and executed.

D. A back door has been installed and the attacker enters the system sporadically.

☑ **C.** The other tools in the rootkit may vary, but they usually comprise utilities that are used to cover the attacker's tracks. For example, every operating system has basic utilities that a root or administrator user can use to detect the presence of the rootkit, an installed sniffer, and the back door. The hacker replaces these default utilities with new utilities, which share the same name. They are referred to as "Trojaned programs" because they carry out the intended functionality but do some devious activity in the background.

☒ **A** is incorrect because it is not the best answer. It is possible that the systems are not infected, but this question asks what is the most likely situation.

☒ **B** is incorrect because most rootkits have Trojaned programs that replace these utilities, because the root user could run ps or top and see there is a back-door service running, and thus detect the presence of an attack. Most rootkits also contain sniffers, so the data can be captured and reviewed by the attacker. For a sniffer to work, the system's NIC must be put into promiscuous mode, which just means it can "hear" all the traffic on the network link. The default ipconfig utility allows the root user to employ a specific parameter to see whether or not the NIC is running in promiscuous mode. So, the rootkit also contains a Trojaned ipconfig program, which hides the fact that the NIC is in promiscuous mode.

☒ **D** is incorrect because there is most likely more than just installed back doors on these servers. Rootkits include back-door programs to allow attackers to remotely control compromised systems, but rootkits contain many other tools also.

About the Free Online Practice Questions and Audio Lectures

As a bonus, with the purchase of this book you also have access to 500 free CISSP practice exam questions and more than 24 hours of audio lectures featuring Shon Harris herself! Shon Harris has written three bestselling CISSP books and has taught CISSP courses around the world for more than 12 years. Now you have access to her full audio training in MP3 format along with the practice exam questions she has used to teach some of the best security professionals in the industry.

Accessing the Online Practice Questions and Audio Lectures

To access the online practice questions and MP3 audio lectures, go to www.mhprofessional.com/CISSPExams. You will be required to complete a free online registration in order to gain access to the content. It's well worth taking the time to answer the practice questions and to listen to the audio lectures. They're free and they will definitely help you prepare for the real CISSP certification exam.

System Requirements
The following system requirements are needed to access and interact with the online content:

- Internet connection
- Flash Player 7 or later is recommended, and one of the following browsers:
  - Windows: Internet Explorer 6 or later, Firefox 1.x or later, Safari 3 or later, Google Chrome, Opera 9.5 or later
  - Macintosh: Firefox 1.x or later, Safari 3 or later
  - Linux: Firefox 1.x or later

- MP3-comptible audio player
  - Windows: Windows Media Player
  - Macintosh: QuickTime Player

Technical Support

For questions regarding the operation of the site, email techsolutions@mhedu.com or visit http://www.mhprofessional.com/techsupport/.

For questions regarding the content of the online practice questions and audio lectures, email customer.service@mcgraw-hill.com. For customers outside the United States, email international_cs@mcgraw-hill.com.

INDEX

Numbers

802.1AE (MACSec), 223
802.1AF, 223
802.1AR secure device provisioning, 222–223
802.1x authentication technology, 214–215

A

AAA (authentication, authorization, and auditing)
    protocols, 77–78
abstract machine, 108
abstract statements, high-level languages, 386
abstraction, object-oriented programming, 391
academic software licensing, 332
acceptance testing, software, 375
access control
    anomaly–based and signature-based IDS, 71
    audit log protection, 68–69
    authorization creep, 25–26
    capability lists, 74
    centralized protocols for, 77–78
    as delaying mechanism, 159, 177–179
    directory services and, 32–33
    evaluating products for, 70
    federated identity and, 64–65
    GML as predecessor to SGML, 62
    identity theft, 73
    masquerading for, 22
    mechanisms embedded in OS, 128–129
    monitoring audit logs for physical, 151–152
    one-time passwords, 84–85
    password attacks, 64
    password management, 59
    phishing vs. pharming, 65–66
    privacy-aware role-based, 61
    race conditions, 86
    reference monitor and, 108
    RFID issues, 87–88
    rule-based IDS, 72
    SAML, SOAP and HTTP for Web services, 86–87
    security event management systems for, 88–89
    separation of duties and job rotation for, 75
    side-channel attacks, 60
    single sign-on protocols and technologies, 82–84
    social engineering attacks, 64
    SPML, 76–77
    threat modeling, 89–90
    transparency, 67–68
    virtual directories, 63–64
    WAM software process, 59
    XACML, 68
access control lists (ACLs), 74, 79
access control matrix, 78–79
access models
    Bell-LaPadula, 107, 117
    Biba, 107
    Brewer-Nash, 107, 116
    Clark-Wilson, 107, 116
    Graham-Denning, 116
    security measures in types of, 126–127
access triple, Clark-Wilson model, 107
account takeover identity theft, 73
ACID test, database software, 371–373
ACLs (access control lists), 74, 79
acoustical detection IDS systems, 165
acrylic glass windows, combustibility of, 153
Active Directory, 59
ad hoc WLANs, 216
adaptive ciphertext, 268–269
address buses, 132
address space layout randomization (ASLR), 135
address spoofing, 422–423
administrators
    accessing audit trail information, 69
    compensating vs. preventive controls, 42
    preventive controls, 41
    remote, 432–433
Advanced Encryption Standard. *See* AES (Advanced
    Encryption Standard)
Advisory policies, 35–36
AES (Advanced Encryption Standard)
    bulk data encryption with, 253
    included with TKIP, 216
    as symmetric block cipher, 250
aggregation, 115
ALE (annualized loss expectancy), 25, 40
analysis, data warehouses for, 371
analysis stage, incident response, 338, 347
ANNs (artificial neural networks), 383–384
Annualized Rate of Occurrence (ARO), 40
annunciator system, CCTVs, 156

anomaly-based IDSs, 71–72
answer key, for this book. *See* quick answer keys, in
    this book
antenna, satellite, 212
antihacking statute, Computer Fraud and Abuse Act,
    333–334
antispam software
    antirelaying used by, 430
    risk mitigation with, 20
antivirus detection
    methods, 388
    risk mitigation with, 20
    tunneling viruses fooling, 378
ANZ 4360 risk methodology, 29
applets, Java, 379
approval of change, change control policy, 415, 416
architecture
    design vs., 133
    security. *See* security architecture and design
ARO (Annualized Rate of Occurrence), 40
artificial neural networks (ANNs), 383–384
ASLR (address space layout randomization),
    preventing buffer overflows, 135
ASs (autonomous systems), Internet routing, 205
assembly language, second-generation
    programming, 385
assessment, physical security, 158, 177–179
asset value
    calculating residual risk, 25
    calculating total risk, 25
    determining, 23–24
assets
    masquerading to gain access to company, 22–23
    risk assessment identifying, 20
    threat modeling identifying, 90
assisted password reset, 59
asymmetric algorithms
    calculating number of keys required in PKI, 249
    elliptic curve cryptosystem, 246
    PKI using hybrid system of, 245
    providing authentication and nonrepudiation, 245
    public key cryptography as, 244
    symmetric systems vs., 242
asynchronous token device, one-time passwords, 85
ATM (Asynchronous Transfer Mode), 216–217
atomic transactions, database software, 372
attributes (columns), relational database, 397
audit logs
    as detective, not preventive, 428
    monitoring for physical access control, 151–152
    protecting with strict access control, 68–69
    scrubbing, 69
    security event management systems for, 88–89

auditing
    AAA protocols for, 77–78
    audit committee responsibilities, 17
    CobiT used for, 27
authentic evidence, 341
authentication
    AAA protocols for, 77–78
    administrative activities requiring strong, 433
    assisted password reset and, 59
    asymmetric systems providing, 245
    data and voice network, 202
    digital signatures for, 252–253, 262–263
    directory services configuring, 58
    e-mail spoofing from inadequate SMTP, 210
authorization
    AAA protocols for, 77–78
    directory services configuring, 58
authorization creep, 25–26
auto-iris lens , CCTVs, 154
autonomous objects, object-oriented programming's
    modularity, 389
autonomous systems (ASs), Internet routing, 205
availability, compensating controls and, 43
awareness, 36

B

backdoors, 86
backup
    determining offsite facility, 296
    disaster recovery plan, 297
    electronic vaulting, 301, 309
    IDSs not coming with power for, 167
    for keys, 248
    online with HSM. *See* HSM (hierarchical storage
        management)
    redundant sites, 309
    remote journaling, 308–309
    restoring and using tapes from warm site, 287
    tape vaulting, 308–309
    types of, 290
banners, preventing fingerprinting, 438
Basic Rate Interface (BRI), ISDN, 219
Basic Service Set (BSS), 216
BCP (business continuity plan)
    assessing via tests, 298
    benefits to organizations of, 293–294
    best practices for, 284
    BIA. *See* BIA (business impact analysis)
    damage assessment, 291
    management support, 294–295
    outdated, 292–293
    ranking threats, 305–306
    reconstitution phase, 299

Committee of Sponsoring Organizations of the Treadway Commission. *See* COSO (Committee of Sponsoring Organizations of the Treadway Commission) framework
common combustible materials, Class A fires, 175
Common Criteria, 103, 112–113
common law
  civil/tort, 346, 355
  criminal, 346, 355
  overview of, 331
  regulatory (administrative), 347, 355
company data, CPO protecting, 27–28
compensating controls, 42–43
complete evidence, 341
compliance. *See* legal, regulations, investigations and compliance
component-based system development, 377
compromised state, state-based IDS, 71
computations, asymmetric vs. symmetric, 242
computer-assisted crimes, 328–329
Computer Ethics Institute, 344, 352
computer forensics, 338–339
Computer Fraud and Abuse Act, 333–334
"computer is incidental" category, computer crime, 328
computer-related crimes, 328–329
computer-targeted crimes, 328–329
concealment cipher, 239, 259
conclusive evidence, 341
concurrency, database, 373, 400
concurrent integrity, 380
confidentiality. *See also* encryption
  AES providing, 253
  Bell-LaPadula model enforcing, 117, 127
  compensating controls and, 43
  encryption algorithms providing, 252
  memory manager role for, 119
  noninterference model enforcing, 114, 127
  one-time pad providing, 259
  overview of, 21
  symmetric algorithms providing, 245
configuration management, change control steps, 415
conflicts of interest, Chinese Wall model, 126
connection-oriented protocol, TCP, 197
connectionless protocol, UDP, 197
consistency transactions, database software, 372
constant-voltage transformers, brownouts, 180
constrained user interfaces, user access, 79
construction materials
  bank external walls, 154–155
  bank windows in area with fire risk, 152–153
  walls, 174–175
  windows prohibited by fire code, 150–151

containment stage, incident response, 337–338, 347
contamination, forensics investigations, 348
continuity of operations plan (COOP), 292, 311
control gap, 25
Control Objectives for Information and related Technology. *See* CobiT (Control Objectives for Information and related Technology)
controls
  auditing or evaluating, 29
  compensating, 42–43
  data custodians implementing, 29
  for different user groups with different privileges, 24
  types of, 41
convergence, in VoIP, 211
COOP (continuity of operations plan), 292, 311
cooperative multitasking mode, OS, 105
coordinator, business continuity, 303–304, 314–315
copyright law, 331–332
COSO (Committee of Sponsoring Organizations of the Treadway Commission) framework
  CobiT derived from, 14
  corporate governance model, 14, 16
  purpose of, 26–27
cost
  of compensating controls, 42–43
  determining asset value, 23
  expense of IDSs, 167
  virtual incident response team, 335–336
cost-effectiveness
  of data classification levels, 19
  of risk assessments, 20
  of VoIP, 211
Council of Europe Convention on Cybercrime, 353
Counter (CTR) Mode, block ciphers, 264
counter synchronous token device, one-time passwords, 85
coupling and cohesion, 380–381
covert channel attacks, 430
covert storage channels, 114, 394
CPO (Chief Privacy Officer) role, 27–28
CPTED (Crime Prevention Through Environmental Design)
  components of, 172–173
  overview of, 170
  physical and environmental security, 162–163
CPUs, 105, 109
cracking attacks, 104
credentials, Web access control, 59
crime rate, physical security and, 162–163, 165
crime scene protection, forensics investigation, 348–349
criminal law, 346, 355

E

e-mail
    countermeasures against spam, 195
    pharming attacks not using, 66
    spoofing, 210
EALs (evaluation assurance levels), Common Criteria, 112, 124–125
EAP (Extensible Authentication Protocol), 214
eavesdropping
    with prior consent or warrant, 345–346
    threat to VoIP networks, 202, 211
ECB (Electronic Code Book) Mode, block ciphers, 263–264
ECC (elliptic curve cryptosystem), 246
EDI (electronic data interchange) infrastructure, VAN, 204
EEPROM (electrically erasable programmable read-only memory), 120
efficiency of resource use, ECCs, 246
EGP (Exterior Gateway Protocol), 205, 206
EJB (Enterprise JavaBeans), 384
electric power
    implementing voltage regulators, 169–170, 181
    in-rush currents and, 180
    smart grid concerns, 176
electrical combustion, Class C fires, 175
electrical signals from computer, emanations capturing, 350
electrically erasable programmable read-only memory (EEPROM), 120
electromagnetic analysis attacks, 60
electromagnetic interference (EMI), 180
electromechanical systems, volumetric IDSs vs., 161–162
Electronic Code Book (ECB) Mode, block ciphers, 263–264
electronic data interchange (EDI) infrastructure, VAN, 204
electronic monitoring (sniffing), 64
electronic vaulting, 301, 309
elliptic curve cryptosystem (ECC), 246
emanations capturing, 350–351
embedded operating system, 138
embedded wires, windows, 153
emergency
    approaches to making changes in, 427
    response procedures for disaster recovery plan, 297
emergency system restart, OS failures, 420
EMI (electromagnetic interference), 180
employee data, CPO protecting, 27–28
encapsulation of objects, process isolation, 117

encryption
    advances in processing power causing attacks on, 104
    algorithms, 252
    end-to-end, 244, 256
    link, 256
    one-time pad. *See* one-time pad
    of polymorphic viruses, 378
    PPTP, 243–244
    RFID security issues, 88
    steganography vs., 239
    using AES for bulk data, 253
    using SSL. *See* SSL (Secure Sockets Layer)
    voice data, 202
    VPNs, 199
end-to-end encryption, 244, 256
Enterprise JavaBeans (EJB), 384
enticement, capturing suspect's actions, 342–343
entity integrity, software development, 380
entrapment, capturing suspect's actions, 342
environmental security. *See* physical security
EPL (Evaluated Products List), 125
EPROM (erasable and programmable read-only memory), 120
escrow, key, 248
ethics
    Code of Ethics for CISSP, 351–352
    Computer Ethics Institute, 344
    dumpster diving and, 345
    Internet Architecture Board, 343, 352
    relationship between law and, 345
European Union Principles on Privacy, 15, 329, 354
European Union, Safe Harbor between U.S. and, 15
Evaluated Products List (EPL), 125
evaluation assurance level section, protection profile, 112
evaluation assurance levels (EALs), Common Criteria, 112, 124–125
evaluation criteria, IDS, 103–104
evidence. *See also* forensics investigation
    building forensics field kit, 357–358
    categories of, 340–341
    chain of custody for, 339–340, 358
    "computer is incidental" category of crime, 328
    crime scene protection, 348–349
    exigent circumstances, 342
    incident response stages, 347–348
    legal admissibility of, 341–342
    Locard's Principle of Exchange, 352
    protecting images from computer/device, 349
exclusive-OR (XOR), one-time pad, 250
execution domain switching, 109
executive succession planning, 301

exigent circumstances, seizure of evidence and, 342–343
expert systems, 72, 383
Exploratory Model, software development, 382
Extensible Authentication Protocol (EAP), 214
Extensible Markup Language (XML), 68, 76
Exterior Gateway Protocol (EGP), 205, 206
external entities, controlling access with WAM, 59
extraction of data, 19, 21
extranet, with integrated redundancy, 315
extreme programming, 375

F

fail-safe protection, doors, 150
fail-secure protection, doors, 150
fail-soft protection, doors, 150
failover capability, high availability, 313–314
fault and error containment, virtual machines, 115
fault, as momentary power outage, 169
fault tolerance, 313–314, 418
FDDI (Fiber Distributed Data Interface), 221
Federal Sentencing Guidelines, 343
federated identity, 64–65, 80–81
fences, physical security, 158, 170–171, 177–178
FHSS (frequency hopping spread spectrum), 215
Fiber Distributed Data Interface (FDDI), 221
field of view, CCTVs, 154, 158
file copy tool, forensic investigations, 348
file descriptor exploit, 426–427
filtering spam, 195
financial information, accuracy of, 28
fingerprint detection, 388, 437–438
fire
  classes of, 175
  construction materials complying with codes for, 154
  detectors, 171–172
  installing windows for bank in area at risk for, 152–153
  sprinkler system design, 156–157
  windows prohibited by codes for, 150–151
fire extinguishers, classes of fire, 175–176
fire station, choosing site location, 164
firewalls, 213, 224–225
fixed focal length lenses, CCTVs, 153–154
fixed-temperature sensors, heat-activated smoke and fire detectors, 171
flash memory, 120
flexibility, VoIP, 211
fluorescent lights, shielded cabling, 169
focal length, CCTV lenses, 160
follow-up stage, incident response, 347–348
footprint, satellite communications, 212

forensics investigation. *See also* evidence
  computer, 338–339
  forensic field kits, 357–358
  incident response team determining need for, 336
  IOCE guidelines for, 357
  overview of, 348–350
fourth-generation languages, 385
fraudulent financial activities, and COSO framework, 27
freeware, 332
frequency, and power line monitors, 169
frequency, calculating residual risk, 25
frequency-division multiplexing, 217
frequency hopping spread spectrum (FHSS), 215
full backups, 290
full-interruption tests, 286
full knowledge, penetration testing, 425–426
functionality, documenting system's, 428

G

garbage collectors, 119
gas, suppressing electrical fires (Class C), 175
gates, classification levels for, 170
gateway, filtering spam at, 195
glass-clad polycarbonate windows, 151, 153
GML (Generalized Markup Language), 62, 68
Graham-Denning model, 116
granularity of permissions, 24
grid computing, 436–437
grouping classified information, hierarchical and restrictive security, 19

H

HA (high availability), 312–314
hardened operating systems, 138
hash values, digital signatures, 251–252
hashing algorithms
  birthday attacks on, 263
  collisions, 263
  creating digital signatures, 262–263
  one-time pad, 258–259
  providing integrity, 245, 253
hashing images, computer forensics, 349
headers, link vs. end-to-end encryption, 256
headquarters, continuity of operations plan for, 291–292
Health Insurance Portability and Accountability Act (HIPPA), 15, 333
heat-activated smoke and fire detectors, 171
heat waves, passive infrared IDS, 163
heavy timber construction material, office buildings, 155, 175

help-desk call volume, password synchronization and, 59
heuristic detection, 388
heuristics, third-generation programming languages, 384–385
hierarchical database
directories following format of, 81
hierarchical database
directory services managing, 57–58
logical tree structure of, 375
object-oriented database vs., 397
overview of, 397
hierarchical storage management (HSM), 424–425, 436
high availability (HA), 312–314
high impact, high probability risks, 32–33
high impact, low probability risks, 32–33
high-level languages, 386
HIPPA (Health Insurance Portability and Accountability Act), 15, 333
honeypots, 343
horizontal enactment, privacy, 356
host environment, virtual machines, 113
host file manipulation, 201
host names, hiding from Internet, 209–210
hot sites, 288, 306–307
hot-swapping, 418–419, 424
HSM (hierarchical storage management), 424–425, 436
HTML (Hypertext Markup Language), 62, 76–77
HTTP (HyperText Transfer Protocol), Web services, 86–87
human intervention, IDSs requiring, 167
HUNT Project, 423
hybrid incident response team, 336
hybrid microkernel architecture, 138
Hypertext Markup Language (HTML), 62, 76–77
HyperText Transfer Protocol (HTTP), Web services, 86–87
hypervisor integration, 224–225

I

I/O (input/output) operations
address bus hardwired to devices for, 132
methods of software, 120–121
overview of, 109
IaaS (Infrastructure as a Service) cloud service model, 223–224
IAB (Internet Architecture Board)
design, engineering and management, 357
ethics statements, 352
role in technology and ethics, 343–344

ICSs (industrial control systems), SCADA for, 176
identity management
with directory services, 58
federated identity, 64–65, 80–81
with virtual directories, 63–64
identity stores, 63
identity theft, true name vs. account takeover, 73
IDSs (intrusion detection systems)
anomaly–based and signature-based, 71
as detection tool, 177–178
as detective control, 41–42
electromechanical or volumetric systems for, 161–162
evaluation criteria, 103
features of, 167
rule-based, 72
SEM and SIEM vs., 89
IEC (International Electrotechnical Commission), ISO/IEC 27000, 38–39
IEEE standards
802.1AE (MACSec), 223
802.1AF, 223
802.1AR (secure device provisioning), 222–223
OSI Layer 2 sublayers, 194
IETF (Internet Engineering Task Force), IAB overseeing, 343
IGP (Internet Routing Protocol), 205
IGRP (Interior Gateway Routing Protocol), 205
illumination requirements, CCTVs, 158, 161
IM (instant messaging), 212–213
images, computer forensics investigation, 349–350
imaging software and tools, computer forensics, 358
impact, risk management scorecard, 32–33
in-rush currents, 169, 180
incident handling, incident response team, 336
incident response
stages of, 337–338
team, 335–336
team, after suspected crime, 336–337
tracking stage, 347–348
triage stage, 347
incremental backups, 290
independent modules, component-based development, 375
industrial control systems (ICSs), SCADA for, 176
inference attacks, 114–115, 373
inference engine, expert system, 71
inference engine, expert systems, 383
information gathering, BIA first step, 286, 289
information owner role, 17–18
information security governance
Chief Privacy Officer role, 27–28
data classification levels, 18–19

ISC Code of Ethics for CISSP, 351–352
ISDN (Integrated Services Digital Network)
  communications protocol, 219
ISMS (information security management systems),
  38–39
ISO/IEC 27000 standard, 38–39
ISO/IEC 27001 standard, 398
ISO/IEC 27002 standard, 38–39
ISO/IEC 27003 standard, 39
ISO/IEC 27004 standard, 39
ISO/IEC 27005 standard, 38, 314–315, 398
ISO/IEC 27031 standard, 314
ISO/IEC 27034 standard, 398
ISO/IEC 42010 standard, 111, 133
ISO (International Organization for Standardization),
  16, 38–39
isolation transactions, database software, 372–373
IT contingency plan, 292
Iterative Development approach, software, 382
ITIL (Information Technology Infrastructure Library)
  defined, 14
    IT service management best practices, 40
    relationship between CobIT and, 14
    sets of instructional books, 122–123
ITSEC (Information Technology Security Evaluation
  Criteria), 103
IVs (initialization vectors), cryptography, 267–268

J

Java applets, JVM executing, 379
job rotation, separation of duties vs., 75
Juggernaut, 423
JVM (Java Virtual Machine), executing Java
  applets, 379

K

KDF (Key Derivation Functions), cryptography,
  245–246
Kerberos, 82–83
kernel flaws, 427
key clustering, 265
keys
  AES, 253
  capability list, 74
  generating using PKI algorithm, 249–250
  management principles, 248
keyword filtering, for spam, 210
knowledge base, expert systems, 72
knowledge, in penetration testing, 425–426

L

L2TP, 199, 220–221
laminated glass windows, 151
LaTEX markup language, 62–63
Layer 2 sublayers, OSI model, 194
layered defense model, 162
layered operating system architecture, 136, 138
LDAP (Lightweight Directory Access Protocol), 57, 81
learning objectives, 36–37
least critical functions, restoring in original facility
  after disaster, 294
least privilege, authorization creep violating, 26
least significant bit (LSB), steganography, 241
legacy applications, virtual machines allowing,
  113–114
legal admissibility of evidence, 341–342
legal issues
  choosing access control product, 70
  cybersquatting, 210
  domain litigation, 201–202
  protecting audit logs for admissibility in court, 69
legal, regulations, investigations and compliance
  addressing privacy threats, 356
  approaches to, 333–334
  categories of computer-related crime, 328–329
  categories of evidence, 340–341
  chain of custody of evidence, 339–340
  Code of Ethics for CISSP, 351–352
  common law categories, 355–356
  computer forensics, 338–339
  containment strategy, incident response, 337–338
  Council of Europe Convention on Cybercrime,
    353–354
  criminal law, 346–347
  describing customary law, 330–331
  downstream liability, 334
  due care, 334
  due diligence, 335
  dumpster diving, 344–345
  eavesdropping legally, 345–346
  emanations capturing, 350–351
  European Union Principles on Privacy
    compliance, 354
  exigent circumstances, 342–343
  forensic field kits, 357–358
  forensic investigations, 348–350
  incident response teams, 335–337
  intellectual property laws, 331–332
  International Organization on Computer
    Evidence, 357
  Internet Architecture Board role, 343–344
  Locard's Principle of Exchange, 352–353

P

PaaS (Platform as a Service) cloud service, 223–224
packets
    sockets and, 198–199
    TCP vs. UDP transport layer protocols, 197–198
PACs (Privileged Attribute Certificates), SESAME, 82
page frames, 106
panic bars, server room doors, 166
parallel tests, 286
parent/child relationships
    hierarchical database. *See* hierarchical database
    network database, 397
parity, RAID, 422–423, 433–434
partial backups, 290
partial knowledge, penetration testing, 425–426
partner data, CPO protecting, 28
PAS (Privileged Attribute Server), SESAME, 83
passive infrared (PIR) IDS systems, 163
password sniffing, 350–351
passwords
    advances in processing power causing attacks
        on, 104
    approaches to managing, 59
    attacks on, 64
    brute-force attacks on. *See* brute-force attacks
    creating one-time, 84–85
    vulnerabilities of synchronized, 59
patents, protecting inventions, 331
pattern matching, expert systems, 383
payload, steganography, 239
Payment Card Industry Data Security (PCI DSS)
    Standard, 333
PCCIP (President's Commission on Critical
    Infrastructure Protection), 171
PCI DSS (Payment Card Industry Data Security)
    Standard, 333
penetration tests, 90, 425–426
performance
    affect of security components on, 67
    microkernel architecture issues, 136–137
    security governance program analyzing, 31
    sharing files over IM and, 213
perimeter fences, physical security, 177
Perimeter Intrusion Detection and Assessment
    System (PIDAS) fencing, 170–171, 177–178
perimeter, security, 128–129
permissions, and authorization creep, 26
persistent XSS vulnerability, 203, 386
personnel, restoring in facility after disaster, 294
perspectives, Zachman Framework, 110
pharming
    identity theft in, 73
    phishing attacks vs., 65–66

phishing
    identity theft vs., 73
    as masquerading, 22
    pharming attacks vs., 65–66
photoelectric (or optical) smoke and fire
    detectors, 171
photoelectric (or photometric) IDS system, 164–165
physical layer technologies. *See* SSL (Secure Sockets
    Layer)
physical phone lines, IP telephony vs., 208
physical preventive controls, 41–42
physical security
    auditing physical access, 151–152
    CCD light-sensitive chips in CCTV cameras,
        155–156
    classes of fire, 175
    construction materials for walls, 174–175
    construction materials for walls of bank, 154–155
    Crime Prevention Through Environmental
        Design, 162–163, 172–173
    door types, 150
    electric power protection, 169–170
    electric power via smart grids, 176
    electromechanical systems for IDSs, 161–162
    fence detection, 170–171
    field of view in CCTV lenses, 158
    IDSs, 167
    irises in CCTV lens, 160–161
    lenses in CCTV, 153–154
    line conditioners, 181
    locks and access controls, 159
    locks for server room doors, 166
    locks, fortifying on exterior doors, 178
    mantraps, 179–180
    overview of, 139
    perimeter fences and warning signs, 177
    proximity detectors, or capacitance detectors, 165
    quick answer key, 149
    risk analysis as first step in program for, 167–168
    in-rush current situation, 180
    security guards, 178–179
    site location, 164–165
    smoke and fire detectors, 171–172
    sprinkler system design, 156–157
    volumetric IDSs, 163–164
    windows, 150–153
PID (process identification) values, naming
    distinctions, 118
PIDAS (Perimeter Intrusion Detection and
    Assessment System) fencing, 170–171,
    177–178
PIR (passive infrared) IDS systems, 163
PKI (public key infrastructure)

CA signing certificate in, 243
calculating number of keys for, 249–250
cross-certification architecture, 260–261
public key cryptography vs., 244–245
plaintext attacks, 269
plan testing and drills, disaster recovery/contingency
    planning, 296
Platform as a Service (PaaS) cloud service, 223–224
platform, virtualization, 115
PoE (Power over Ethernet), 176
point-to-point (PPP) connections, EAP for, 214
Point-to-Point Tunneling Protocol (PPTP), 199,
    243–244
police station, choosing site location, 164
policies. *See* security policies
policy statement, continuity plans, 284
polycarbonate acrylic windows, 150–151, 153
polyinstantiation, 391–392
polymorphic viruses, 378
polymorphism, 374, 392
pop-up forms, phishing vs. pharming attacks, 66
port blocking, 213
port scanning countermeasures, 437–438
portable identity, federated identity as, 65
ports, reducing fingerprinting, 438
power line interference, 180
power line monitors, 169
Power over Ethernet (PoE), 176
PPP (point-to-point) connections, EAP for, 214
PPTP (Point-to-Point Tunneling Protocol), 199,
    243–244
preaction fire sprinkler systems, 157
predetermined steps, executive succession
    planning, 302
preemptive multitasking mode, OS, 105
premapped I/O, 121
presentation layer, three-tiered architecture, 196
President's Commission on Critical Infrastructure
    Protection (PCCIP), 171
preventive controls, continuity plans, 284
PRI (Primary Rate Interface), ISDN, 219
primary keys, entity integrity, 380
Primary Rate Interface (PRI), ISDN, 219
primary server room door, 166
PRINCE2 (PRojects IN Controlled Environments), 40
privacy
    data warehouses increasing risk of violations
        to, 371
    European Union Principles on Privacy, 354
    global governance for sensitive data, 329–330
    governance bodies for data, 15
    handling increase in threats on, 356
    horizontal enactment addressing, 356

privacy-aware role-based access control, 61
private keys
    creating digital signatures, 251–252, 262–263
    SSL connection setup process, 254
    zero-knowledge proof and, 265
Privileged Attribute Certificates (PACs), SESAME, 82
Privileged Attribute Server (PAS), SESAME, 83
privileges
    adding on "need-to-know" basis, 26
    controls for different user groups with different, 24
    elevating to gain access, 22
    enforcing least privilege on user accounts, 26
probability, risk management scorecard, 32–33
procedures, administrative preventive controls, 41
procedures (methods), object-oriented
    programming, 375, 391
process
    deactivation, 109
    isolation, 117–118
    as program in memory, 131–132
    tables, 132–133
process identification (PID) values, naming
    distinctions, 118
process improvement program, CMMI, 39
processing power, attacks caused by increased, 104
production operations, and asset value, 23–24
profile, behavioral-based IDS products, 71
profiling criminals, 352–353
programmable I/O, 121
programmable read-only memory (PROM), 120
programming languages
    fourth-generation, 385
    object-oriented. *See* object-oriented programming
    second-generation, 385–386
    third-generation, 384–385
project initiation phase, BCP, 299
PRojects IN Controlled Environments (PRINCE2), 40
PROM (programmable read-only memory), 120
properly configured mail relay servers, 195
proprietary interior protocols, IGRP, 206
proprietary protocol, SSL, 239
protecting lives, BCP, 294
protection, memory manager role, 119
protection profiles, Common Criteria
    access models, 107
    attacks cause by increased processing power, 104
    CMMI process improvement approach, 123
    execution domain switching initiated by TCB, 109
    Graham-Denning access model, 116
    IDS evaluation criteria, 103–104
    interrupt-driven I/O, 121
    ITIL sets of instructional books, 122–123
    memory manager responsibilities, 118–119

regression testing, software, 375

regulations. *See also* legal, regulations, investigations and compliance

    access control products and, 70

    approaches to, 333–334

regulatory (administrative) law, 347, 355

regulatory policies, 35

relational databases, 375, 397

relationships, relational database, 397

reliable evidence, 342

religious law systems, 330

relocation, as memory manager responsibility, 119

remote administration, 432–433, 439–440

Remote Authentication Dial-In User Service (RADIUS) protocol, 78

remote journaling, 308–309

Remote Procedure Calls (RPCs), and SOAP, 382–383

Repeatable level (CMMI Level 2), 123

replay attacks, unauthorized access via, 64

report changes to management, change control policy, 415

Request for Comments (RFCs), 343

residual risk, calculating, 25

resource records, 224

resources needing immediate replacement, damage assessment, 291

response

    IDSs requiring human intervention and, 167

    physical security design for, 158

restitution, customary law, 330

restoration team, BCP, 300

reusability, component-based development, 375

RFCs (Request for Comments), 343

RFI (radio frequency interference), 180

RFID (radio-frequency identification), 87–88

RIP (Routing Information Protocol), 205–206

risk acceptance, 20–21

risk analysis

    in business impact analysis, 294

    as first step in security program, 167–168

    qualitative, 37–38

risk assessment

    activities in, 19–20

    methodologies, 29–30

risk assignment, 32

risk avoidance, 19, 21

risk exposure, executive succession planning, 302

risk management

    calculating residual risk, 25

    committee, 16–17

    risk transference in, 31–32

    scorecard, 32–33

risk mitigation, 20–21, 31–32

risk rejection, 32

risk transference, 21, 31

rogue devices, on IP telephony/data networks, 202

role-based access control (RBAC), 61, 79–80

rollbacks, 372, 395

ROM, PROM vs. EEPROM, 119–120

rootkits, 440–441

routing, 204–207

Routing Information Protocol (RIP), 205–206

rows (tuples), relational database, 380, 397

RPCs (Remote Procedure Calls), and SOAP, 382–383

RPO (Recovery Time Period), 316

RSA, 250

RTO (Recovery Time Objective), 312, 316

rule-based IDS, 72

rule-based programming, expert systems, 383

rules

    Bell-LaPadula and Biba models, 107

    Graham-Denning model, 116

running key ciphers, 259

S

SA (security association) values, IPSec, 257–258

SaaS (Software as a Service) cloud service, 223–224

SABSA (Sherwood Applied Business Security Architecture), 39–40

Safe Harbor, 14, 330

safety, business continuity plan and, 294

sag, momentary low voltage, 169

salami attacks, 350

salvage team role, BCP, 300

SAML (Security Assertion Markup Language), Web services, 86–87

sandbox, Java Virtual Machine, 379

Sarbanes-Oxley Act (SOX), accounting practices, 333

SASD (Sequential Access Storage Device), 415

satellite communications, 212

SCADA (supervisory control and data acquisition), ICSs, 176

schedule of change, change control policy, 416

schema, 374

SCM (software configuration management), 401–402

scoped addresses, IPv6, 222

scorecard, risk management, 32–33

screened host (one-tiered) architecture, 196

SCRIPT/VS. GML markup, 62

scrubbing audit logs, 69

sealing hard disk drives, TPMs, 266

search and seizure activities, as exigent circumstances, 342

SEC (Security Exchange Commission), 27

second-generation programming languages, 385–386